Related Titles from Morgan K~~auf~~

Structured Parallel Programming

Structured Parallel Programming
Patterns for Efficient Computation

Michael McCool

Arch D. Robison

James Reinders

AMSTERDAM • BOSTON • HEIDELBERG • LONDON
NEW YORK • OXFORD • PARIS • SAN DIEGO
SAN FRANCISCO • SINGAPORE • SYDNEY • TOKYO

Morgan Kaufmann Publishers is an imprint of Elsevier

ELSEVIER

Acquiring Editor: Todd Green
Development Editor: Robyn Day
Project Manager: Paul Gottehrer
Designer: Joanne Blank

Morgan Kaufmann is an imprint of Elsevier
225 Wyman Street, Waltham, MA 02451, USA

Library of Congress Cataloging-in-Publication Data
Application submitted.

British Library Cataloguing-in-Publication Data
A catalogue record for this book is available from the British Library.

ISBN: 978-0-12-415993-8

For information on all MK publications
visit our website at *http://store.elsevier.com*

Printed and bound by CPI Group (UK) Ltd, Croydon, CR0 4YY

Transferred to digital print 2012

Working together to grow
libraries in developing countries

www.elsevier.com | www.bookaid.org | www.sabre.org

ELSEVIER   BOOK AID International   Sabre Foundation

Contents

PART I   PATTERNS

PART II   EXAMPLES

APPENDICES

Listings

Preface

All computers are now parallel computers, so we assert that all programmers are, or should be, parallel programmers. With parallel programming now mainstream, it simply needs to be included in the definition of "programming" and be part of the skill set of *all* software developers. Unfortunately, many existing texts on parallel programming are overspecialized, with too much emphasis given to particular programming models or particular computer architectures. At the other extreme, several existing texts approach parallel computing as an abstract field of study and provide the reader with insufficient information to actually write real applications. We saw a need for a text on parallel programming treating the topic in a mainstream, pragmatic fashion, so that readers can immediately use it to write real applications, but at a level of abstraction that still spans multiple computer architectures and programming models.

We feel that teaching parallel programming as an advanced topic, with serial programming as the default basis, is not the best approach. Parallel programming should be taught from the beginning to avoid over-learning of serial assumptions and thought patterns. Unfortunately, at present the default teaching style is based on the serial code and algorithms. Serialization has become excessively woven into our teaching, our programs, and even the tools of our trade: our programming languages. As a result, for many programmers parallel programming seems more difficult than it should be. Many programs are serial not because it was natural to solve the problem serially, but because the programming tools demanded it and the programmer was trained to think that way.

Despite the fact that computer hardware is naturally parallel, computer architects chose 40 years ago to present a serial programming abstraction to programmers. Decades of work in computer architecture have focused on maintaining the illusion of serial execution. Extensive efforts are made inside modern processors to translate serial programs into a parallel form so they can execute efficiently using the fine-grained parallel hardware inside the processor. Unfortunately, driven by the exponential increase in the number of transistors provided by Moore's Law, the need for parallelism is now so great that it is no longer possible to maintain the serial illusion while continuing to scale performance. It is now necessary for programmers to *explicitly* specify parallel algorithms if they want their performance to scale. Parallelism is everywhere, and it is the path to performance on modern computer architectures. Parallelism, even within a single desktop (or laptop!) computer, is available in many ways, including vector (SIMD) instructions, multicore processors, GPUs, co-processors, and many-core processors. Programming today needs to address all these forms of hardware parallelism in a manner that is abstract enough to avoid limiting the implementation to a particular style of hardware.

We also saw a need for a structured approach to parallel programming. In this book, we explain and illustrate essential strategies needed for writing efficient, scalable programs using a set of *patterns*. We have found that patterns are highly effective both for learning this subject and for designing efficient, structured, and maintainable programs. Using standard names for patterns is also a tremendous aid to communication. Because vocabulary is important, we have assembled an extensive glossary. This should help limit the need to read the book sequentially. The glossary also points to key discussions or explanations of a term within a section of the book when appropriate.

To ensure that the book is useful in practice, we combine patterns with a set of examples showing their use. Since there are many parallel programming models, the question arose: Which programming model(s) should we use for examples? We wanted to show enough examples to allow the reader to write sophisticated applications without having to depend heavily on external references. That constraint argued for sticking to one programming model or a small number of them. On the other hand, we wanted to demonstrate that the patterns we are presenting are universal and span a large number of programming models.

As a compromise, we decided to show a large number of examples focused on a couple of primary models and a small number in other "secondary" models. For the primary models, we chose Intel Threading Building Blocks (Intel TBB) and Intel Cilk Plus. These two models are efficient and well-supported. Both are readily available, with both open source licenses and commercial support. TBB is a C++ template library that works with many different ISO C++ compilers, while Cilk Plus is a C/C++ language extension, so they provide contrasting syntactic approaches. Together they are capable of expressing all the patterns discussed in this book. Complete working code for all the examples in the primary programming models, as well as a variety of other material, can be found online at

http://parallelbook.com

We feel a sufficient number of examples have been provided that, along with the standard documentation, this book can be used for learning how to program in both TBB and Cilk Plus.

However, the patterns we discuss apply to almost any parallel programming model; therefore, to provide a broader perspective, we look at three secondary programming models: Intel Array Building Blocks (ArBB), OpenCL, and OpenMP. ArBB uses a parallel virtual machine provided as a library. The ArBB virtual machine (VM) supports explicit, programmer-directed runtime code generation and is designed to be usable from multiple languages. In this book, we use the C++ front-end to the ArBB VM, which embeds a parallel language syntax into C++ using normal C++ mechanisms such as macros and operator overloading. We also show some examples in OpenCL and OpenMP. Both OpenCL and OpenMP are standards, with OpenCL primarily designed to target GPU-like architectures, and OpenMP targeting shared-memory multicore CPU architectures. OpenCL is based on a separately compiled kernel language which is provided as a string to an library interface. Like ArBB, OpenCL supports dynamic compilation. In contrast, OpenMP is based on annotations in an existing language and is designed to be statically compiled. These five programming models take different syntactic approaches to the expression of parallelism, but as we will see, the patterns apply to all of them. This reinforces the fact that patterns are universal, and that a study of patterns is useful not only for today's programming models but also for what may come in the future.

This book is neither a theory book nor a cookbook. It is a pragmatic strategic guide, with case studies, that will allow you to understand how to implement efficient parallel applications. However, this book is not aimed at supercomputing programmers, although it might be interesting to them. This is a book for mainstream C and C++ programmers who may have no prior knowledge of parallel programming and who are interested in improving the performance of their applications. To this end, we also discuss performance models. In particular, we present the work-span model of parallel complexity, which goes beyond the simplistic assumptions of Amdahl's Law and allows better prediction of an algorithm's speedup potential, since it gives both upper and lower bounds on speedup and provides a tighter upper bound.

We hope to provide you with the capacity to design and implement efficient, reliable, and maintainable parallel programs for modern computers. This book purposely approaches parallel programming from a programmer's point of view without relying on an overly detailed examination or prior knowledge of parallel computer architecture. We have avoided the temptation to make this a computer architecture book. However, we have still taken care to discuss important architecture constraints and how to deal with them. The goal is to give you, as a programmer, precisely the understanding of the computer architecture that you need to make informed decisions about how to structure your applications for the best performance and scalability.

Our vision is that effective parallel programming can be learned by studying appropriate patterns and examples. We present such a set of patterns, give them concrete names, and ground them in reality with numerous examples. You should find that this approach directly enables you to produce effective and efficient parallel programs and also allows you to communicate your designs to others. Indirectly, it may spark interest in parallel computer architecture, parallel language design, and other related topics. No book could possibly include information on all the topics of interest related to parallel programming, so we have had to be selective. For those so inclined, we have included suggestions for further reading in an appendix. Our web site at http://parallelbook.com also includes material that goes beyond the basics presented here.

We hope you find this book to be effective at extending your definition of "programming" to include "parallel programming."

James Reinders
Portland, Oregon, USA

Arch Robison
Champaign, Illinois, USA

Michael McCool
Waterloo, Ontario, Canada
Tokyo, Japan

Comments on the Second Printing

In the short time since this book was first published, the use of parallelism to improve computing performance has continued to evolve rapidly. New parallel processors have become available and parallel programming models have been extended. With these recent developments the topics covered by this book are becoming increasingly relevant. In particular, the need for parallel programming and the patterns and programming techniques introduced in this book are becoming even more important.

In November 2012, the Intel Xeon Phi coprocessors using the MIC architecture referred to in this book were introduced by Intel, and have already been deployed in several supercomputers. The Intel Xeon Phi coprocessors have proven to be so efficient that supercomputers built using them have placed highly on the Green 500 list of energy-efficient supercomputers, including the Beacon supercomputer which occupies the #1 spot for power efficiency. Supercomputers with these coprocessors have also been used in 7 out of 10 computers on the Top 500 as of November 2012. The Intel Xeon Phi co-processor has up to 61 cores each supporting 512-bit-wide vector instructions, and is capable of over a trillion double-precision floating-point operations a second. Using the Xeon Phi coprocessor effectively requires a significant of parallelism. Its full potential can only be achieved with scalable parallel programs that are also highly vectorized. Writing such programs is, of course, the focus of this book. Fortunately, exactly the same programming models (and parallel patterns) that are useful for ordinary multicore processors can be used with the Xeon Phi coprocessor.

Parallelism is not just about supercomputers. The processors used in laptops and desktops continue to advance, with more cores and larger and more powerful integrated graphics engines. Most importantly, these new graphics engines feature close integration with the CPUs that they share die area and memory systems with. Discrete graphics processors have evolved as well, with the latest models incorporating more and more CPU-like features. In general, parallel programming models appear to be converging. For example, since this book was first released, an explicitly vectorizing loop construct was voted into the next OpenMP specification. This vectorizing construct is close to the "pragma simd" construct that we introduce in this book under Cilk Plus, and so brings OpenMP and Cilk Plus into closer alignment. Cilk Plus tasking constructs have also been proposed for C++ standardization, although that proposal is still under discussion.

These changes have taken place in a mere eight months since the English version of this book was finalized. The computer industry is maintaining its rapid pace of innovation. Fortunately, this book was written based on patterns. Parallel patterns span multiple programming models and computer architectures, and the content has only grown in relevance. The only way to make effective use of a massively parallel architecture like the Intel Xeon Phi coprocessor is to use techniques like those described in this book. Moore's Law shows no sign of abating, and so we can expect to see such techniques become essential parts of programming. As all processors become massively parallel, programmers need to make parallel programming part of their ordinary practice in order to see continued increases in performance with each new generation.

We hope that this book will help you realize the potential of these processors even as they continue to evolve. We also hope that this book will help establish definitions and terminology for parallel patterns so that software developers can more clearly define, articulate, and implement high-performance parallel architectures for their applications.

Preliminaries

ASSUMED KNOWLEDGE

This book assumes a working knowledge of C and/or C++, and many examples are presented in these languages (primarily C++). To get the most out of the book these examples should be studied carefully. No knowledge of assembly language or systems programming is needed. No prior course on algorithms is required. In particular, the basics of asymptotic complexity analysis, needed for parallel performance analysis, are presented in this book in a self-contained way. Prior experience with these concepts would be useful but is not necessary. Detailed knowledge of a specific operating system is not required, although an operating systems course would be useful. We purposefully avoid programming to operating-system-specific threading models and avoid locks in our examples, so prior experience with these concepts is not necessary. Windows, Linux, and Mac OS X are all well supported by the primary programming models used, TBB and Cilk Plus, which allow for a wide selection of operating system choices for practical application of the material in this book. No prior experience with TBB and Cilk Plus is required and we provide enough background in appendices to make the book self-contained. However, for practical application development it is recommended that this text be supplemented with a reading of additional tutorial material and documentation on TBB and Cilk Plus. The section on "Parallel Programming Models" in Appendix A makes specific recommendations for such further reading. The secondary programming models, OpenMP, OpenCL, and ArBB, are not presented in depth; however, these models support many operating systems as well.

FOR INSTRUCTORS

This book supports teaching parallel programming in any programming class using C or C++, or as a focused topic in a semester-long class. If added to an existing course, and only one assignment for parallel programming is to be used, we recommend teaching the map pattern, as that illustrates both parallelism and the concept of patterns quite well. The remaining patterns are generally ordered from simplest to most challenging, so following the chapter order is recommended. We have included a summary chapter for all the patterns but it can be skipped on a first reading if necessary. We have found that a pattern-based approach is an effective way to teach and learn parallel programming in a structured manner.

Teaching material related to the book is available online, and may be used freely for courses taught in conjunction with this book. This material includes slides and example code. This material can be downloaded from

```
http://parallelbook.com/download
```

An explanation of the available teaching material, as well as additional information on using them in courses, can be found at

```
http://parallelbook.com/instructor
```

In particular, this material includes suggested reading roadmaps for use of this text in courses of different lengths and at different levels.

We invite you to share your own teaching insights when using our book and the online materials. Suggestions for additional material, such as new patterns or examples, would also be welcome. This book establishes a framework for "structured parallel programming," but it is only the beginning of what can be done in this area. In particular, it does not exhaust the space of examples. There are also some useful patterns that are not included in this book or are mentioned only briefly, so we intend to use online material to expand our discussion of both. Please contact us via our web site or email us at authors@parallelbook.com.

FOR STUDENTS

You are encouraged to download supplemental material from our web site at

> http://parallelbook.com/student

This material includes code for the examples used in this book and possibly additional material to be used in conjunction with a course. Patterns are everywhere, but given the limited space in the book we could only print a tiny representative set of examples. We hope to be able to add more examples online over time, perhaps contributed by students like yourself.

We hope this book helps make "Thinking Parallel" an intuitive part of programming for you. Parallelism is now essential for all computing, but due to its complexity it requires a structured, disciplined approach.

We have chosen to organize this book around patterns to provide that structure. Patterns are the best way to share good programming strategies. The patterns we discuss have, in practice, been shown to lead to scalable, high-performance code while being implementable, understandable, and debuggable. These patterns are not a provably perfect set of what you need to know. Rather, patterns represent the best starting points that exist today. Opportunities to refine these patterns, and find more, are certainly there. We're sure that once you understand the concept of patterns, you will begin to see them everywhere and they will become an essential part of your vocabulary as a programmer.

FOR PROFESSIONAL PROGRAMMERS

Regardless of whether you have done some or no parallel programming, this book will help make "Thinking Parallel" an intuitive part of programming for you. We also hope that you will gain an appreciation for patterns as a way to structure your programs. Good patterns will also help you write good programs, since they encapsulate best known methods for achieving scalable and efficient results.

Patterns are effective structures of computation and data access; however, patterns by themselves are insufficient, since they are too abstact. Therefore, we also supply real example code to study. Part I of this book covers the patterns and also has many examples, while Part II has several additional examples.

We do not limit ourselves by using teaching languages in this book. We use proven programming models that are already in serious industrial use by professional programmers around the world. Intel Threading Building Blocks (TBB) and OpenMP are the two most popular models in use today, and are heavily used in this book. Additionally, Intel Cilk Plus and OpenCL have gained sufficient recognition and usage to be worth exploring as well. You should also look at our web site—we hope to add additional examples there that would not fit in the book, and you can also download the source code for all examples in the book from that site.

A deep knowledge of computer architecture is not needed to understand this book and use the patterns we present. We have purposefully left out any in-depth discussion of parallel computer architecture, except for a short summary of some key points. Instead of teaching computer architecture and then parallel programming, we use patterns to lead to programming styles that map well onto real parallel hardware. Performance matters, so we make sure that our patterns and our discussion of them include the information needed to get excellent results. We do not discourage learning computer architecture, but we feel that it should not be a requirement to learn programming.

We know that vocabulary is important, so we have assembled a lengthy glossary that can be very helpful to review in order to more quickly be able to decipher parallel programming jargon.

USING CODE EXAMPLES

While the book itself is copyrighted, all example programming code found in this book is provided without any restrictions on reuse. You may use this code freely in your own projects, commercial or otherwise. However, we do not provide any promise or warrantee of any kind. The examples can all be downloaded at

```
http://parallelbook.com/download
```

where additional information on our code reuse policy can also be found.

We appreciate, but do not require, attribution. This is true of our teaching materials as well, which are are also available on the same web site. An attribution usually includes the title, author, publisher, and ISBN. For example:

Structured Parallel Programming by Michael McCool, Arch Robison, and James Reinders, copyright 2012, published by Morgan Kaufmann, ISBN 978-0-124-15993-8.

If you have any questions, feel free to contact us at

```
permissions@parallelbook.com
```

HOW TO CONTACT US

We invite you to share your own insights when using our book. We can be reached via our web site or via email at

```
http://parallelbook.com
authors@parallelbook.com
```

This web site provides supplemental material including a list of errata, the ability to download all examples, and additional teaching materials. It is also our intention to distribute additional examples at this site, since limited space in this book did not permit us to include as many examples as we would have liked.

To comment or ask technical questions about this book, send email to:

bookquestions@parallelbook.com

For more information from the publisher Morgan Kaufmann, please visit their web site at

http://mkp.com

ACKNOWLEDGMENTS

This book would not have been possible without the dedicated people at Intel who have tirelessly worked to produce great technology and products. Their passion to help others also helped us produce the best book we could.

Much of the discussion for best practices for OpenMP in the desktop environment was derived from an analysis by Jay Hoeflinger and Brian Bliss of Intel.

The Bzip2 example code is derived from Julian Seward's Bzip2 implementation, available at

http://bzip.org

The TBB code for Bzip2 descends from a port done by Hyojin Sung while she was an intern at Intel. The cache-oblivious stencil code (Section 10.5) was adapted from code by Matteo Frigo and Yuxiong He.

An early draft of this book was reviewed by Jim Cownie, Mark Davis, Michèle Delsol, Stefanus Du Toit, Kathy A. Farrel, Balaji Iyer, Anton Malakhov, Tim Mattson, Priya Natarajan, John Pieper, Krishna Ramkumar, Elizabeth Reinders, Jim Sukha, Peter Tang, Barry Tannenbaum, Michael Voss, Bob Weems, Barry Wilkinson, and Terry Wilmarth. Their feedback was incredibly helpful and vastly improved the book. We would like to especially thank Tim Mattson who provided some additional OpenCL and OpenMP examples.

We all wish to thank our families and friends who put up with the wrinkles, early mornings, and late nights, sometimes simultaneous, that book writing brought into our lives.

Introduction

All computers are now parallel. Specifically, all modern computers support parallelism in hardware through at least one parallel feature, including vector instructions, multithreaded cores, **multicore processors**, multiple processors, graphics engines, and parallel co-processors. This statement does not apply only to supercomputers. Even the smallest modern computers, such as phones, support many of these features. It is also necessary to use explicit parallel programming to get the most out of such computers. Automatic approaches that attempt to parallelize serial code simply cannot deal with the fundamental shifts in algorithm structure required for effective parallelization.

Since parallel programming is no longer a special topic applicable to only select computers, this book is written with a simple premise: Parallel programming *is* programming. The evolution of computers has made parallel programming mainstream. Recent advances in the implementation of efficient parallel programs need to be applied to mainstream applications.

We explain how to design and implement efficient, reliable, and maintainable programs, in C and C++, that scale performance for all computers. We build on skills you already have, but without assuming prior knowledge of parallelism. Computer architecture issues are introduced where their impact must be understood in order to design an efficient program. However, we remain consistently focused on programming and the programmer's perspective, not on the hardware. This book is for programmers, not computer architects.

We approach the problem of practical parallel programming through a combination of patterns and examples. **Patterns** are, for our purposes in this book, valuable algorithmic structures that are commonly seen in efficient parallel programs. The kinds of patterns we are interested in are also called "algorithm skeletons" since they are often used as fundamental organizational principles for algorithms. The patterns we will discuss are expressions of the "best known solutions" used in effective and efficient parallel applications. We will discuss patterns both "from the outside," as abstractions, and "from the inside," when we discuss efficient implementation strategies. Patterns also provide a vocabulary to design new efficient parallel algorithms and to communicate these designs to others. We also include many examples, since examples show how these patterns are used in practice. For each example, we provide working code that solves a specific, practical problem.

Higher level programming models are used for examples rather than raw threading interfaces and vector intrinsics. The task of programming (formerly known as "parallel programming") is presented in a manner that focuses on capturing algorithmic intent. In particular, we show examples that are *appropriately* freed of unnecessary distortions to map algorithms to particular hardware. By focusing on the most important factors for performance and expressing those using models with low-overhead implementations, this book's approach to programming can achieve efficiency and scalability on a range of hardware.

The goal of a programmer in a modern computing environment is not just to take advantage of processors with two or four cores. Instead, it must be to write **scalable** applications that can take advantage of any amount of parallel hardware: all four cores on a quad-core processor, all eight cores on octo-core processors, thirty-two cores in a multiprocessor machine, more than fifty cores on new many-core processors, and beyond. As we will see, the quest for scaling requires attention to many factors, including the minimization of data movement, serial bottlenecks (including locking), and other forms of overhead. Patterns can help with this, but ultimately it is up to the diligence and intelligence of the software developer to produce a good algorithm design.

The rest of this chapter first discusses why it is necessary to "Think Parallel" and presents recent hardware trends that have led to the need for explicit parallel programming. The chapter then discusses the structured, pattern-based approach to programming used throughout the book. An introduction to the programming models used for examples and some discussion of the conventions and organization of this book conclude the chapter.

1.1 THINK PARALLEL

Parallelism is an intuitive and common human experience. Everyone reading this book would expect parallel checkout lanes in a grocery store when the number of customers wishing to buy groceries is sufficiently large. Few of us would attempt construction of a major building alone. Programmers naturally accept the concept of parallel work via a group of workers, often with specializations.

Serialization is the act of putting some set of operations into a specific order. Decades ago, computer architects started designing computers using serial machine languages to simplify the programming interface. **Serial semantics** were used even though the hardware was naturally parallel, leading to something we will call the **serial illusion**: a mental model of the computer as a machine that executes operations sequentially. This illusion has been successfully maintained over decades by computer architects, even though processors have become more and more parallel internally. The problem with the serial illusion, though, is that programmers came to depend on it too much.

Current programming practice, theory, languages, tools, data structures, and even most algorithms focus almost exclusively on serial programs and assume that operations are serialized. Serialization has been woven into the very fabric of the tools, models, and even concepts all programmers use. However, frequently serialization is actually unnecessary, and in fact is a poor match to intrinsically parallel computer hardware. Serialization is a learned skill that has been over-learned.

Up until the recent past, serialization was not a substantial problem. Mainstream computer architectures even in 2002 did not significantly penalize programmers for overconstraining algorithms with serialization. But now—they do. Unparallelized applications leave significant performance on the table for current processors. Furthermore, such serial applications will not improve in performance over time. Efficiently parallelized applications, in contrast, will make good use of current processors and should be able to scale automatically to even better performance on future processors. Over time, this will lead to large and decisive differences in performance.

Serialization has its benefits. It is simple to reason about. You can read a piece of serial code from top to bottom and understand the temporal order of operations from the structure of the source code. It helps that modern programming languages have evolved to use structured control flow to emphasize this aspect of serial semantics. Unless you intentionally inject randomness, serial programs also always do the same operations in the same order, so they are naturally **deterministic**. This means they give the same answer every time you run them with the same inputs. Determinism is useful for debugging, verification, and testing. However, deterministic behavior is not a natural characteristic of parallel programs. Generally speaking, the timing of task execution in parallel programs, in particular the relative timing, is often non-deterministic. To the extent that timing affects the computation, parallel programs can easily become non-deterministic.

Given that parallelism is necessary for performance, it would be useful to find an effective approach to parallel programming that retains as many of the benefits of serialization as possible, yet is also similar to existing practice.

In this book, we propose the use of structured patterns of parallelism. These are akin to the patterns of structured control flow used in serial programming. Just as structured control flow replaced the use of goto in most programs, these patterns have the potential to replace low-level and architecture-specific parallel mechanisms such as threads and vector intrinsics. An introduction to the pattern concept and a summary of the parallel patterns presented in this book are provided in Section 1.4. Patterns provide structure but have an additional benefit: Many of these patterns avoid non-determinism, with a few easily visible exceptions where it is unavoidable or necessary for performance. We carefully discuss when and where non-determinism can occur and how to avoid it when necessary.

Even though we want to eliminate unnecessary serialization leading to poor performance, current programming tools still have many **serial traps** built into them. Serial traps are constructs that make, often unnecessary, serial assumptions. Serial traps can also exist in the design of algorithms and in the abstractions used to estimate complexity and performance. As we proceed through this book, starting in Section 1.3.3, we will describe several of these serial traps and how to avoid them. However, serial semantics are still useful and should not be discarded in a rush to eliminate serial traps. As you will see, several of the programming models to be discussed are designed around generalizations of the semantics of serial programming models in useful directions. In particular, parallel programming models often try to provide equivalent behavior to a particular serial ordering in their parallel constructs, and many of the patterns we will discuss have serial equivalents. Using these models and patterns makes it easier to reason about and debug parallel programs, since then at least some of the nice properties of serial semantics can be retained.

Still, effective programming of modern computers demands that we regain the ability to "Think Parallel." Efficient programming will not come when parallelism is an afterthought. Fortunately, we can get most of "Think Parallel" by doing two things: (1) learning to recognize serial traps, some of which we examine throughout the remainder of this section, and (2) programming in terms of parallel patterns that capture best practices and using efficient implementations of these patterns.

Perhaps the most difficult part of learning to program in parallel is recognizing and avoiding serial traps—assumptions of serial ordering. These assumptions are so commonplace that often their existence goes unnoticed. Common programming idioms unnecessarily overconstrain execution order, making parallel execution difficult. Because serialization had little effect in a serial world, serial assumptions went unexamined for decades and many were even designed into our programming languages and tools.

We can motivate the **map** pattern (see Chapter 4) and illustrate the shift in thinking from serialized coding styles to parallel by a simple but real example.

For example, searching content on the World Wide Web for a specific phrase could be looked at as a serial problem or a parallel problem. A simplisitic approach would be to code such a search as follows:

```
for (i = 0; i < number_web_sites; ++i) {
    search(searchphrase, website[i]);
}
```

This uses a loop construct, which is used in serial programming as an idiom to "do something with a number of objects." However, what it actually means is "do something with a number of objects *one after the other*."

Searching the web as a parallel problem requires thinking more like

```
parallel_for (i = 0; i < number_web_sites; ++i) {
    search(searchphrase, website[i]);
}
```

Here the intent is the same—"do something with a number of objects"—but the constraint that these operations are done one after the other has been removed. Instead, they may be done simultaneously.

However, the serial semantics of the original `for` loop allows one search to leave information for the next search to use if the programmer so chooses. Such temptation and opportunity are absent in the `parallel_for` which requires each invocation of the search algorithm to be independent of other searches. That fundamental shift in thinking, to using parallel patterns when appropriate, is critical to harness the power of modern computers. Here, the `parallel_for` implements the map pattern (described in Chapter 4). In fact, different uses of iteration (looping) with different kinds of dependencies between iterations correspond to different parallel patterns. To parallelize serial programs written using iteration constructs you need to recognize these idioms and convert them to the appropriate parallel structure. Even better would be to design programs using the parallel structures in the first place.

In summary, if you do not already approach every computer problem with parallelism in your thoughts, we hope this book will be the start of a new way of thinking. Consider ways in which you may be unnecessarily serializing computations. Start thinking about how to organize work to expose parallelism and eliminate unnecessary ordering constraints, and begin to "Think Parallel."

1.2 PERFORMANCE

Perhaps the most insidious serial trap is our affection for discussing algorithm performance with all attention focused on the minimization of the total amount of computational work. There are two problems with this. First of all, computation may not be the bottleneck. Frequently, access to memory or (equivalently) *communication* may constrain performance. Second, the potential for scaling performance on a parallel computer is constrained by the algorithm's **span**. The span is the time it takes to perform the longest chain of tasks that must be performed sequentially. Such a chain is known as a critical path, and, because it is inherently sequential, it cannot be sped up with parallelism, no matter how many parallel processors you have. The span is a crucial concept which will be used throughout the book. Frequently, getting improved performance requires finding an alternative way to solve a problem that shortens the span.

This book focuses on the **shared memory** machine model, in which all parts of application have access to the same shared memory address space. This machine model makes communication implicit: It happens automatically when one worker writes a value and another one reads it. Shared memory is convenient but can hide communication and can also lead to unintended communication. Unfortunately, communication is not free, nor is its cost uniform. The cost in time and energy of communication varies depending upon the location of the worker. The cost is minimal for lanes of a vector unit (a few instructions), relatively low for hardware threads on the same core, more for those sharing an on-chip cache memory, and yet higher for those in different sockets.

Fortunately, there is a relatively simple abstraction, called **locality**, that captures most of these cost differences. The locality model asserts that memory accesses close together in time and space (and communication between processing units that are close to each other in space) are cheaper than those that are far apart. This is not completely true—there are exceptions, and cost is non-linear with respect to locality—but it is better than assuming that all memory accesses are uniform in cost. Several of the data access patterns in this book are used to improve locality. We also describe several pitfalls in memory usage that can hurt performance, especially in a parallel context.

The concept of span was previously mentioned. The span is the critical path or, equivalently, the longest chain of operations. To achieve scaling, minimizing an algorithm's span becomes critical. Unsurprisingly, parallel programming is simplest when the tasks to be done are completely independent. In such cases, the span is just the longest task and communication is usually negligible (not zero, because we still have to check that all tasks are done). Parallel programming is much more challenging when tasks are not independent, because that requires communication between tasks, and the span becomes less obvious.

Span determines a limit on how fast a parallel algorithm can run even given an infinite number of cores and infinitely fast communication. As a simple example, if you make pizza from scratch, having several cooks can speed up the process. Instead of preparing dough, sauce, and topping one at a time (serially), multiple cooks can help by mixing the dough and preparing the toppings in parallel. But the crust for any given pizza takes a certain amount of time to bake. That time contributes to the span of making a single pizza. An infinite number of cooks cannot reduce the cooking time, even if they can prepare the pizza faster and faster before baking. If you have heard of **Amdahl's Law** giving an upper bound on scalability, this may sound familiar. However, the concept of span is more precise, and gives tighter bounds on achievable scaling. We will actually show that Amdahl was both an optimist and a pessimist. Amdahl's Law is a relatively loose upper bound on scaling. The use of the **work-span** model provides a tighter bound and so is more realistic, showing that Amdahl was an optimist. On the other hand, the scaling situation is usually much less pessimistic if the size of the problem is allowed to grow with the number of cores.

When designing a parallel algorithm, it is actually important to pay attention to three things:

- The total amount of computational work.
- The span (the critical path).
- The total amount of communication (including that implicit in sharing memory).

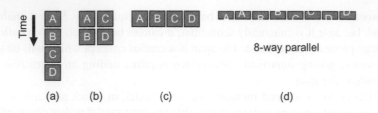

(a)   (b)   (c)   (d)

FIGURE 1.1

Independent software tasks can be run in parallel on multiple workers. In theory, this can give a linear speedup. In reality, this is a gross oversimplification. It may not be possible to uniformly subdivide an application into independent tasks, and there may be additional overhead and communication resulting from the subdivision.

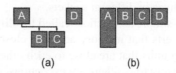

(a)   (b)

FIGURE 1.2

Tasks running in parallel: some more complex situations. (a) Tasks can be arranged to run in parallel as long as dependencies are honored. (b) Tasks may take different amounts of time to execute. Both of these issues can increase the span and reduce scalability.

In order for a program to scale, span and communication limitations are as important to understand and minimize as the total computational work.

A few examples are probably helpful at this point. In Figure 1.1a, a serial program with no parallelism simply performs tasks A, B, C, and D in sequence. As a convention, the passage of time will be shown in our diagrams as going from top to bottom. We highlight this here with an arrow showing the progress of time, but will generally just assume this convention elsewhere in the book.

A system with two parallel workers might divide up work so one worker performs tasks A and B and the other performs tasks C and D, as shown in Figure 1.1b. Likewise, a four-way system might perform tasks A, B, C, and D, each using separate resources as shown in Figure 1.1c. Maybe you could even contemplate subdividing the tasks further as shown in Figure 1.1d for eight workers. However, this simple model hides many challenges. What if the tasks depend on each other? What if some tasks take longer to execute than others? What if subdividing the tasks into subtasks requires extra work? What if some tasks cannot be subdivided? What about the costs for communicating between tasks?

If the tasks were not independent we might have to draw something like Figure 1.2a. This illustration shows that tasks A and D are independent of each other, but that tasks B and C have a dependency on A completing first. Arrows such as these will be used to show dependencies in this book, whether they are data or control dependencies. If the individual tasks cannot be subdivided further, then the running time of the program will be at least the sum of the running time of tasks A and B, the sum of the running time of tasks A and C, or the running time of D, whichever is longer. This is the span of this parallel algorithm. Adding more workers cannot make the program go faster than the time it takes to execute the span.

In most of this book, the illustrations usually show tasks as having equal size. We do not mean to imply this is true; we do it only for ease of illustration. Considering again the example in Figure 1.1c, even if the tasks are completely independent, suppose task A takes longer to run than the others. Then the illustration might look like Figure 1.2b. Task A alone now determines the span.

We have not yet considered limitations due to communication. Suppose the tasks in a parallel program all compute a partial result and they need to be combined to produce a final result. Suppose that this combination is simple, such as a summation. In general, even such a simple form of communication, which is called a **reduction**, will have a span that is logarithmic in the number of workers involved.

Effectively addressing the challenges of decomposing computation and managing communications are essential to efficient parallel programming. Everything that is unique to parallel programming will be related to one of these two concepts. Effective parallel programming requires effective management of the distribution of work and control of the communication required. Patterns make it easier to reason about both of these. Efficient programming models that support these patterns, that allow their efficient implementation, are also essential.

For example, one such implementation issue is **load balancing**, the problem of ensuring that all processors are doing their fair share of the work. A load imbalance can result in many processors idling while others are working, which is obviously an inefficient use of resources. The primary programming models used in this book, Cilk Plus and TBB, both include efficient work-stealing schedulers to efficiently and automatically balance the load. Basically, when workers run out of things to do, they actively find new work, without relying on a central manager. This decentralized approach is much more scalable than the use of a centralized work-list. These programming models also provide mechanisms to subdivide work to an appropriate **granularity** on demand, so that tasks can be decomposed when more workers are available.

1.3 MOTIVATION: PERVASIVE PARALLELISM

Parallel computers have been around for a long time, but several recent trends have led to increased parallelism at the level of individual, mainstream personal computers. This section discusses these trends. This section also discusses why taking advantage of parallel hardware now generally requires explicit parallel programming.

1.3.1 Hardware Trends Encouraging Parallelism

In 1965, Gordon Moore observed that the number of transistors that could be integrated on silicon chips were doubling about every 2 years, an observation that has become known as **Moore's Law**. Consider Figure 1.3, which shows a plot of transistor counts for Intel microprocessors. Two rough data points at the extremes of this chart are on the order of 1000 (10^3) transistors in 1971 and about 1000 million (10^9) transistors in 2011. This gives an average slope of 6 orders of magnitude over 40 years, a rate of 0.15 orders of magnitude every year. This is actually about $1.41\times$ per year, or $1.995\times$ every 2 years. The data shows that Moore's prediction of $2\times$ every two years has been amazingly accurate. While we only give data for Intel processors, processors from other vendors have shown similar trends.

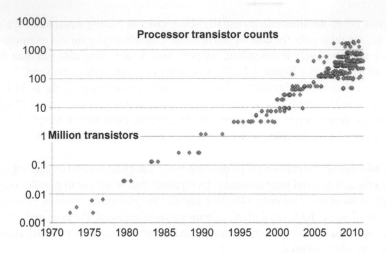

FIGURE 1.3

Moore's Law, which states roughly that the number of transistors that can be integrated on a chip will double about every 2 years, continues to this day (log scale). The straight line on this graph, which is on a logarithmic scale, demonstrates exponential growth in the total number of transistors in a processor from 1970 to the present. In more recent times, with the advent of multicore processors, different versions of processors with different cache sizes and core counts have led to a greater diversity in processor sizes in terms of transistor counts.

This exponential growth has created opportunities for more and more complex designs for microprocessors. Until 2004, there was also a rise in the switching speed of transistors, which translated into an increase in the performance of microprocessors through a steady rise in the rate at which their circuits could be clocked. Actually, this rise in clock rate was also partially due to architectural changes such as instruction pipelining, which is one way to automatically take advantage of instruction-level parallelism. An increase in clock rate, if the instruction set remains the same (as has mostly been the case for the Intel architecture), translates roughly into an increase in the rate at which instructions are completed and therefore an increase in computational performance. This increase is shown in Figure 1.4. Actually, many of the increases in processor complexity have also been to increase performance, even on single-core processors, so the actual increase in performance has been greater than this.

From 1973 to 2003, clock rates increased by three orders of magnitude (1000×), from about 1 MHz in 1973 to 1 GHz in 2003. However, as is clear from this graph clock rates have now ceased to grow and are now generally in the 3 GHz range. In 2005, three factors converged to limit the growth in performance of single cores and shift new processor designs to the use of multiple cores. These are known as the "three walls":

Power wall: Unacceptable growth in power usage with clock rate.
Instruction-level parallelism (ILP) wall: Limits to available low-level parallelism.
Memory wall: A growing discrepancy of processor speeds relative to memory speeds.

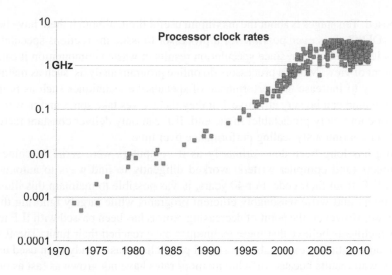

FIGURE 1.4

Growth of processor clock rates over time (log scale). This graph shows a dramatic halt by 2005 due to the power wall, although current processors are available over a diverse range of clock frequencies.

The power wall results because power consumption (and heat generation) increases non-linearly as the clock rate increases. Increasing clock rates any further will exceed the power density that can be dealt with by air cooling, and also results in power-inefficient computation.

The second wall is the instruction-level parallelism (ILP) wall. Many programmers would like parallelization to somehow be done automatically. The fact is that automatic parallelization *is already* being done at the instruction level, and has been done for decades, but has reached its limits. Hardware is naturally parallel, and modern processors typically include a large amount of circuitry to extract available parallelism from serial instruction streams. For example, if two nearby instructions do not depend on each other, modern processors can often start them both at the same time, a technique called **superscalar instruction issue**. Some processors can issue up to six instructions at the same time (an example being the POWER2 architecture), but this is about the useful limit for most programs on real processors. Analysis of large code bases show that on average there is not much more available superscalar parallelism at the instruction level than this [BYP+91, JW89, RDN93, TEL95]. More specifically, more parallelism may be available, but it is bursty or otherwise hard to use in a sustained way by real processors with finite resources. A related technique is **Very Large Instruction Word** (VLIW) processing, in which the analysis of which instructions to execute in parallel is done in advance by the compiler. However, even with the help of offline program analysis, it is difficult to find significant sustained parallelism in most programs [HF99] without diminishing returns on hardware investments. Modern processors also use **pipelining**, in which many operations are broken into a sequence of stages so that many instructions can be processed at once in an assembly-line fashion, which can greatly increase the overall instruction processing throughput of a processor. However, pipelining is accomplished by reducing the amount of logic per stage to reduce the time between clocked circuits, and there is a practical limit to the number of stages into which instruction processing can be decomposed. Ten stages is about the maximum useful limit, although there have been processors with 31 stages [DF90]. It is even possible for a processor to issue instructions speculatively, in order to increase parallelism. However, since speculation results in wasted computation it can be expensive from a power point of view. Modern processors do online program analysis, such as maintaining branch history tables to try to increase the performance of speculative techniques such as branch prediction and prefetching, which can be very effective, but they themselves take space and power, and programs are by nature not completely predictable. In the end, ILP can only deliver constant factors of speedup and cannot deliver continuously scaling performance over time.

Programming has long been done primarily as if computers were serial machines. Meanwhile, computer architects (and compiler writers) worked diligently to find ways to automatically extract parallelism, via ILP, from their code. For 40 years, it was possible to maintain this illusion of a serial programming model and write reasonably efficient programs while largely ignoring the true parallel nature of hardware. However, the point of decreasing returns has been passed with ILP techniques, and most computer architects believe that these techniques have reached their limit. The ILP wall reflects the fact that the automatically extractable low-level parallelism has already been used up.

The memory wall results because off-chip memory rates have not grown as fast as on-chip computation rates. This is due to several factors, including power and the number of pins that can be easily incorporated into an integrated package. Despite recent advances, such as double-data-rate (DDR) signaling, off-chip *communication* is still relatively slow and power-hungry. Many of the transistors used in today's processors are for cache, a form of on-chip memory that can help with this problem. However, the performance of many applications is fundamentally bounded by memory performance, not compute performance. Many programmers have been able to ignore this due to the effectiveness of large caches for serial processors. However, for parallel processors, interprocessor communication is also bounded by the memory wall, and this can severely limit scalability. Actually, there are two problems with memory (and communication): **latency** and **bandwidth**. Bandwidth (overall data rate) can still be scaled in several ways, such as optical interconnections, but latency (the time between when a request is submitted and when it is satisfied) is subject to fundamental limits, such as the speed of light. Fortunately, as discussed later in Section 2.5.9, latency can be hidden—given sufficient additional parallelism, above and beyond that required to satisfy multiple computational units. So the memory wall has two effects: Algorithms need to be structured to avoid memory access and communication as much as possible, and fundamental limits on latency create even more requirements for parallelism.

In summary, in order to achieve increasing performance over time for each new processor generation, you cannot depend on rising clock rates, due to the power wall. You also cannot depend on automatic mechanisms to find (more) parallelism in naïve serial code, due to the ILP wall. To achieve higher performance, you now *have* to write explicitly parallel programs. And finally, when you write these parallel programs, the memory wall means that you also have to seriously consider communication and memory access costs and may even have to use additional parallelism to hide latency.

Instead of using the growing number of transistors predicted by Moore's Law for ways to maintain the ''serial processor illusion,'' architects of modern processor designs now provide multiple mechanisms for explicit parallelism. However, you must use them, and use them well, in order to achieve performance that will continue to scale over time.

The resulting trend in hardware is clear: More and more parallelism at a hardware level will become available for any application that is written to utilize it. However, unlike rising clock rates, non-parallelized application performance will not change without active changes in programming. The "free lunch" [Sut05] of automatically faster serial applications through faster microprocessors has ended. The new "free lunch" requires scalable parallel programming. The good news is that once you design a program for scalable parallelism, it will continue to scale as processors with more parallelism become available.

1.3.2 Observed Historical Trends in Parallelism

Parallelism in hardware has been present since the earliest computers and reached a great deal of sophistication in mainframe and vector supercomputers by the late 1980s. However, for mainstream computation, miniaturization using integrated circuits started with designs that were largely devoid of hardware parallelism in the 1970s. Microprocessors emerged first using simple single-threaded designs that fit into an initially very limited transistor budget. In 1971, the Intel 4004 4-bit microprocessor was introduced, designed to be used in an electronic calculator. It used only 2,300 transistors in its design. The most recent Intel processors have enough transistors for well over a million Intel 4004 microprocessors. The Intel Xeon E7-8870 processor uses 2.6×10^9 transistors, and the upcoming Intel MIC architecture co-processor, known as Knights Corner, is expected to roughly double that. While a processor with a few million cores is unlikely in the near future, this gives you an idea of the potential.

Hardware is naturally parallel, since each transistor can switch independently. As transistor counts have been growing in accordance with Moore's Law, as shown in Figure 1.3, hardware parallelism, both implicit and explicit, gradually also appeared in microprocessors in many forms. Growth in word sizes, superscalar capabilities, vector (SIMD) instructions, out-of-order execution, multithreading (both on individual cores and on multiple cores), deep pipelines, parallel integer and floating point arithmetic units, virtual memory controllers, memory prefetching, page table walking, caches, memory access controllers, and graphics processing units are all examples of using additional transistors for parallel capabilities.

Some variability in the number of transistors used for a processor can be seen in Figure 1.3, especially in recent years. Before multicore processors, different cache sizes were by far the driving factor in this variability. Today, cache size, number of cores, and optional core features (such as vector units) allow processors with a range of capabilities to be produced. This is an additional factor that we must take into account when writing a program: Even at a single point in time, a program may need to run on processors with different numbers of cores, different vector instruction sets and vector widths, different cache sizes, and possibly different instruction latencies.

The extent to which software needed to change for each kind of additional hardware mechanism using parallelism has varied a great deal. Automatic mechanisms requiring the least software change, such as instruction-level parallelism (ILP), were generally introduced first. This worked well until several issues converged to force a shift to explicit rather than implicit mechanisms in the multicore era. The most significant of these issues was power. Figure 1.5 shows a graph of total power consumption over time. After decades of steady increase in power consumption, the so-called *power wall* was hit about 2004. Above around 130W, air cooling is no longer practical. Arresting power growth required that clock rates stop climbing. From this chart we can see that modern processors now span a large range of power consumption, with the availability of lower power parts driven by the growth of mobile and embedded computing.

The resulting trend toward explicit parallelism mechanisms is obvious looking at Figure 1.6, which plots the sudden rise in the number of hardware threads[1] after 2004. This date aligns with the halt in the

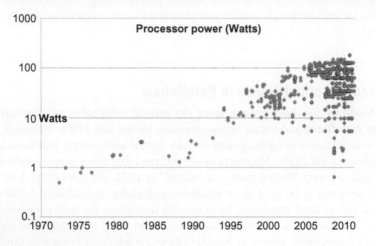

FIGURE 1.5

Graph of processor total power consumption (log scale). The maximum power consumption of processors saw steady growth for nearly two decades before the multicore era. The inability to dissipate heat with air cooling not only brought this growth to a halt but increased interest in reduced power consumption, greater efficiencies, and mobile operation created more options at lower power as well.

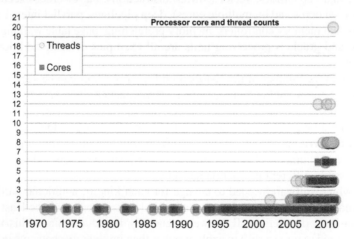

FIGURE 1.6

The number of cores and hardware threads per processor was one until around 2004, when growth in hardware threads emerged as the trend instead of growth in clock rate.

---

[1] It is common to refer to hardware parallelism as processor cores and to stress multicore. But it is more precise to speak of hardware threads, since some cores can execute more than one thread at a time. We show both in the graph.

growth in clock rate. The power problem was arrested by adding more cores and more threads in each core rather than increasing the clock rate. This ushered in the multicore era, but using multiple hardware threads requires more software changes than prior changes. During this time vector instructions were added as well, and these provide an additional, multiplicative form of explicit parallelism. **Vector parallelism** can be seen as an extension of data width parallelism, since both are related to the width of hardware registers and the amount of data that can be processed with a single instruction. A measure of the growth of data width parallelism is shown in Figure 1.7. While data width parallelism growth predates the halt in the growth of clock rates, the forces driving multicore parallelism growth are also adding motivation to increase data width. While some automatic **parallelization** (including **vectorization**) is possible, it has not been universally successful. Explicit parallel programming is generally needed to fully exploit these two forms of hardware parallelism capabilities.

Additional hardware parallelism will continue to be motivated by Moore's Law coupled with power constraints. This will lead to processor designs that are increasingly complex and diverse. Proper abstraction of parallel programming methods is necessary to be able to deal with this diversity and to deal with the fact that Moore's Law continues unabated, so the maximum number of cores (and the diversity of processors) will continue to increase.

Counts of the number of hardware threads, vector widths, and clock rates are only indirect measures of performance. To get a more accurate picture of how performance has increased over time, looking at

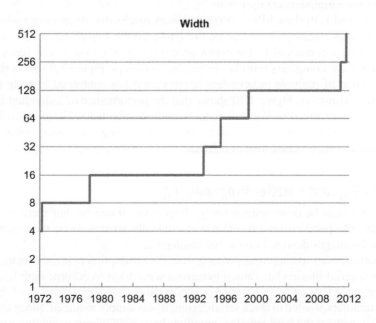

FIGURE 1.7

Growth in data processing widths (log scale), measured as the number of bits in registers over time. At first the width of scalar elements grew, but now the number of elements in a register is growing with the addition of vector (SIMD) instructions that can specify the processing of multiple scalar elements at once.

benchmarks can be helpful. Unfortunately, long-term trend analysis using benchmarks is difficult due to changes in the benchmarks themselves over time.

We chose the industry standard CPU2006 SPEC benchmarks. Unfortunately, these are exclusively from the multicore era as they only provide data from 2006 [Sub06]. In preparing the graphs in this section of our book, we also choose to show only data related to Intel processors. Considering only one vendor avoids a certain blurring effect that occurs when data from multiple vendors is included. Similar trends are observable for processors from other vendors, but the trends are clearer when looking at data from a single vendor.

Some discussion of the nature of the CPU2006 benchmarks is important so the results can be properly understood. First, these benchmarks are not explicitly parallelized, although autoparallelization is allowed. Autoparallelization must be reported, however, and may include the use of already-parallelized libraries. It is however not permitted to change the source code of these benchmarks, which prohibits the use of new parallel programming models. In fact, even standardized OpenMP directives, which would allow explicit parallelization, must be explicitly disabled by the SPEC run rules. There are SPEC benchmarks that primarily stress floating point performance and other benchmarks that primarily stress integer and control flow performance. The FP and INT designations indicate the floating-point and integer subsets. INT benchmarks usually also include more complex control flow. The "rate" designations indicate the use of multiple copies of the benchmarks on computers with multiple hardware threads in order to measure throughput. These "rate" (or throughput) results give some idea of the potential for speedup from parallelism, but because the benchmark instances are completely independent these measurements are optimistic.

Figures 1.8, 1.9, and 1.10 show SPEC2006 benchmark results that demonstrate what has happened to processor performance during the multicore era (since 2006). Figure 1.8 shows that performance per Watt has improved considerably for entire processors as the core count has grown. Furthermore, on multiprocessor computers with larger numbers of cores, Figure 1.9 shows that **throughput** (the total performance of multiple independent applications) has continued to scale to considerably higher performance. However, Figure 1.10 shows that the performance of individual benchmarks has remained nearly flat, even though autoparallelization is allowed by the SPEC process. The inescapable conclusion is that, while overall system performance is increasing, increased performance of single applications requires *explicit* parallelism in software.

1.3.3 **Need for Explicit Parallel Programming**

Why can't parallelization be done automatically? Sometimes it can be, but there are many difficulties with automatically parallelizing code that was originally written under the assumption of serial execution, and in languages designed under that assumption.

We will call unnecessary assumptions deriving from the assumption of serial execution **serial traps**. The long-sustained serial illusion has caused numerous serial traps to become built into both our tools and ways of thinking. Many of these force serialization due to over-specification of the computation. It's not that programmers wanted to force serialization; it was simply assumed. Since it was convenient and there was no penalty at the time, serial assumptions have been incorporated into nearly everything. We will give several examples in this section. We call these assumptions "traps" because they cause modern systems to be unable to use parallelism even though the algorithm writer did not explicitly intend to forbid it.

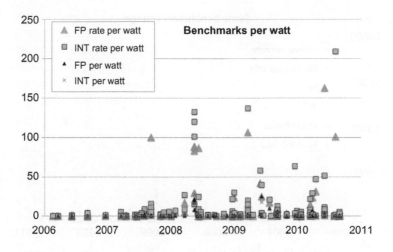

FIGURE 1.8

Performance per Watt using data derived from SPEC2006 benchmarks and processor (not system) power ratings from Intel corporation. The FP per Watt and INT per Watt give single benchmark performance. Autoparallelization is allowed but for the most part these benchmarks are not parallelized. The FP rate and INT rate per Watt results are based on running multiple copies of the benchmark on a single processor and are meant to measure throughput. The FP and INT results have not increased substantially over this time period, but the FP rate and INT rate results have. This highlights the fact that performance gains in the multicore era are dominated by throughput across cores, not from increased performance of a core.

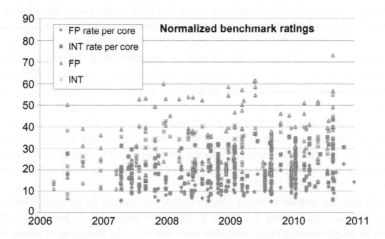

FIGURE 1.9

Performance in the multicore era, on a per hardware thread basis, does not show a strong and obvious trend as it did in the single-core megahertz era. Data derived from SPEC2006 benchmarks and processor (not system) power ratings, but with rate results divided by the number of parallel benchmark instances (hardware threads) used.

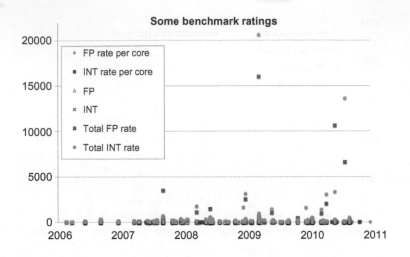

FIGURE 1.10

SPEC2006 performance on multiprocessor computers in the multicore era. Large machines can yield overall systems performance that dwarfs the per core performance numbers (note the two orders of magnitude shift in Y-axis scale vs. Figure 1.9). Data derived from SPEC benchmark archives.

Accidents of language design can make it difficult for compilers to discover parallelism or prove that it is safe to parallelize a region of code. Compilers *are* good at "packaging" parallelism they see even if it takes many detailed steps to do so. Compilers *are not* reliable at discovering parallelism opportunities. Frequently, the compiler cannot disprove some minor detail that (rarely) *might* be true that would make parallelism impossible. Then, to be safe, in such a situation it cannot parallelize.

Take, for example, the use of pointers. In C and C++, pointers allow the modification of any region of memory, at any time. This is very convenient and maps directly onto the underlying machine language mechanism (itself an abstraction of the hardware...) for memory access. With serial semantics, even with this freedom it is still clear what the state of memory will be at any time. With parallel hardware, this freedom becomes a nightmare. While great strides have been made in automatic pointer analysis, it is still difficult for a compiler in many situations to determine that the data needed for parallel execution will not be modified by some other part of the application at an inconvenient time, or that data references do not overlap in a way that would cause different orders of execution to produce different results.

Parallelism can also be hidden because serial control constructs, in particular loops, over-specify ordering. Listing 1.1 through Listing 1.7 show a few other examples of hiding parallelism that are common practice in programming languages that were not initially designed to allow explicit parallel programming. Parallel programming models often provide constructs that avoid some of these constraints. For concreteness, in this section we will show several solutions in Cilk Plus that remove these serial constraints and allow parallelism.

The straightforward C code in Listing 1.1 cannot be parallelized by a compiler in general because the arrays a, b, and c might partially overlap, as in Listing 1.2. The possibility of overlap adds a serial

```
1  void
2  addme(int n, double a[n], double b[n], double c[n]) {
3    int i;
4    for (i = 0; i < n; ++i)
5      a[i] = b[i] + c[i];
6  }
```

LISTING 1.1

Add two vectors in C, with implied serial ordering.

```
1  double a[10];
2  a[0] = 1;
3  addme(9, a+1, a, a); // pointer arithmetic causing aliasing
```

LISTING 1.2

Overlapping (aliased) arguments in C. By calling the *serial* addme with overlapping arguments, this code fills a with powers of two. Such devious but legal usage is probably unintended by the author of addme, but the compiler does not know that.

```
1  void
2  addme(int n, double a[n], double b[n], double c[n]) {
3    a[:] = b[:] + c[:];
4  }
```

LISTING 1.3

Add two vectors using Cilk Plus array notation.

constraint, even if the programmer never intended to exploit it. Parallelization requires reordering, but usually you want all the different possible orders to produce the same result.

A syntax that treats arrays as a whole, as shown in Listing 1.3, makes the parallelism accessible to the compiler by being explicit. This Cilk Plus array notation used here actually allows for simpler code than the loop shown in Listing 1.1, as well. However, use of this syntax also *requires* that the arrays not be partially overlapping (see Section B.8.5), unlike the code in Listing 1.1. This additional piece of information allows the compiler to parallelize the code.

Loops can specify different kinds of computations that must be parallelized in different ways. Consider Listing 1.4. This is a common way to sum the elements of an array in C.

Each loop iteration depends on the prior iteration, and thus the iterations cannot be done in parallel. However, if reordering floating-point addition is acceptable here, this loop *can* be both parallelized and vectorized, as explained in Section 5.1. But the compiler alone cannot tell whether the serial dependency was deliberate or just convenient. Listing 1.5 shows a way to convey parallel intent, both to the compiler and a human maintainer. It specifies a parallel loop and declares mysum in a way that

```
1  double summe(int n, double a[n]) {
2      double mysum = 0;
3      int i;
4      for (i = 0; i < n; ++i)
5          mysum += a[i];
6      return mysum;
7  }
```

LISTING 1.4

An ordered sum creates a dependency in C.

```
1  double summe(int n, double a[n]) {
2      sum_reducer<double> mysum (0);
3      cilk_for (int i = 0; i < n; ++i)
4          mysum += a[i];
5      return mysum.get_value();
6  }
```

LISTING 1.5

A parallel sum, expressed as a reduction operation in Cilk Plus.

```
1  void callme() {
2      foo();
3      bar();
4  }
```

LISTING 1.6

Function calls with step-by-step ordering specified in C.

says that reordering the individual operations making up the sum is okay. This additional freedom allows the system to choose an order that gives the best performance.

As a final example, consider Listing 1.6, which executes foo and bar in exactly that order. Suppose that foo and bar are separately compiled library functions, and the compiler does not have access to their source code. Since foo *might* modify some global variable that bar might depend on, and the compiler cannot prove this is not the case, the compiler *has* to execute them in the order specified in the source code.

However, suppose you modify the code to explicitly state that foo and bar can be executed in parallel, as shown in Listing 1.7. Now the programmer has given the compiler permission to execute these functions in parallel. It does not mean the system *will* execute them in parallel, but it now has the option, if it would improve performance.

```
1  void callme() {
2     cilk_spawn foo();
3     bar();
4  }
```

LISTING 1.7

Function calls with no required ordering in Cilk Plus.

Later on we will discuss the difference between **mandatory parallelism** and **optional parallelism**. Mandatory parallelism forces the system to execute operations in parallel but may lead to poor performance—for example, in the case of a recursive program generating an exponential number of threads. Mandatory parallelism also does not allow for hierarchical composition of parallel software components, which has a similar problem as recursion. Instead, the Cilk Plus `cilk_spawn` notation simply identifies tasks that are *opportunities* for parallelism. It is up to the system to decide when, where, and whether to use that parallelism. Conversely, when you use this notation you should not assume that the two tasks are necessarily active simultaneously. Writing portable parallel code means writing code that can deal with any order of execution—including serial ordering.

Explicit parallel programming constructs allow algorithms to be expressed without specifying unintended and unnecessary serial constraints. Avoiding specifying ordering and other constraints when they are not required is fundamental. Explicit parallel constructs also provide additional information, such as declarations of independence of data and operations, so that the system implementing the programming model knows that it can safely execute the specified operations in parallel. However, the programmer now has to ensure that these additional constraints are met.

1.4 STRUCTURED PATTERN-BASED PROGRAMMING

History does not repeat itself, but it rhymes.

(attributed to Mark Twain)

In this book, we are taking a structured approach to parallel programming, based on patterns.

Patterns can be loosely defined as commonly recurring strategies for dealing with particular problems. Patterns have been used in architecture [Ale77], natural language learning [Kam05], object-oriented programming [GHJV95], and software architecture [BMR+96, SSRB00]. Others have also applied patterns specifically to parallel software design [MAB+02, MSM04, MMS05], as we do here. One notable effort is the OUR pattern language, an ongoing project to collaboratively define a set of parallel patterns [Par11].

We approach patterns as tools, and we emphasize patterns that have proven useful as tools. As such, the patterns we present codify practices and distill experience in a way that is reusable. In this book, we discuss several prerequisites for achieving parallel scalability, including good data locality and avoidance of overhead. Fortunately, many good strategies have been developed for achieving these objectives.

We will focus on **algorithm strategy patterns**, as opposed to the more general **design patterns** or system-specific **implementation patterns**. Design patterns emphasize high-level design processes.

These are important but rather abstract. Conversely, implementation patterns address low-level details that are often specific to a particular machine architecture, although occasionally we will discuss important low-level issues if they seriously impact performance. Algorithm strategy patterns lie in between these two extremes. They affect how your algorithms are organized, and so are also known as **algorithmic skeletons** [Col89, AD07].

Algorithm strategy patterns have two parts: semantics and implementation. The semantics describe how the pattern is used as a building block of an algorithm, and consists of a certain arrangement of tasks and data dependencies. The semantic view is an abstraction that intentionally hides some details, such as whether the tasks making up the pattern will actually run in parallel in a particular implementation. The semantic view of a pattern is used when an algorithm is designed. However, patterns also need to be implemented well on real machines. We will discuss several issues related to the implementation of patterns, including (for example) granularity control and good use of cache. The key point is that different implementation choices may lead to different performances, but *not* to different semantics. This separation makes it possible to reason about the high-level algorithm design and the low-level (and often machine-specific) details separately. This separation is not perfect; sometimes you will want to choose one pattern over another based on knowledge of differences in implementation. That's all right. Abstractions exist to simplify and structure programming, not to obscure important information.

Algorithm strategy patterns tend to map onto programming model features as well, and so are useful in understanding programming models. However, algorithm strategy patterns transcend particular languages or programming models. They do not have to map directly onto a programming language feature to be usable. Just as it is possible to use structured control flow in FORTRAN 66 by following conventions for disciplined use of `goto`, it is possible to employ the parallel patterns described in this book even in systems that do not directly support them. The patterns we present, summarized in Figure 1.11, will occur (or be usable) in almost any sufficiently powerful parallel programming model, and if used well should lead to well-organized and efficient programs with good scaling properties. Numerous examples in this book show these patterns in practice. Like the case with structured control flow in serial programming, structured parallel patterns simplify code and make it more understandable, leading to greater maintainability.

Three patterns deserve special mention: **nesting**, **map**, and **fork–join**. Nesting means that patterns can be hierarchically composed. This is important for modular programming. Nesting is extensively used in serial programming for **composability** and information hiding, but is a challenge to carry over into parallel programming. The key to implementing nested parallelism is to specify optional, not mandatory, parallelism. The map pattern divides a problem into a number of uniform parts and represents a regular parallelization. This is also known as **embarrassing parallelism**. The map pattern is worth using whenever possible since it allows for both efficient parallelization and efficient vectorization. The fork–join pattern recursively subdivides a problem into subparts and can be used for both regular and irregular parallelization. It is useful for implementing a **divide-and-conquer** strategy. These three patterns also emphasize that in order to achieve scalable parallelization we should focus on **data parallelism**: the subdivision of the problem into subproblems, with the number of subproblems able to grow with the overall problem size.

In summary, patterns provide a common vocabulary for discussing approaches to problem solving and allow reuse of best practices. Patterns transcend languages, programming models, and even computer architectures, and you can use patterns whether or not the programming system you are using explicitly supports a given pattern with a specific feature.

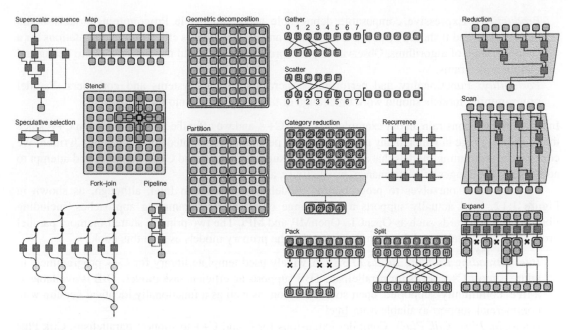

FIGURE 1.11

Overview of parallel patterns.

1.5 PARALLEL PROGRAMMING MODELS

We will discuss parallel programming models that can support a wide range of parallel programming needs. This section gives some basic background on the programming models used in this book. It will also discuss what makes a good programming model. Appendices B and C provide more information on the primary programming models used for examples in this book, TBB and Cilk Plus, as well as links to online resources.

1.5.1 Desired Properties

Unfortunately, none of the most popular programming languages in use today was designed for parallel programming. However, since a large amount of code has already been written in existing serial languages, practically speaking it is necessary to find an evolutionary path that extends existing programming practices and tools to support parallelism. Broadly speaking, while enabling dependable results, parallel programming models should have the following properties:

Performance: Achievable, scalable, predictable, and tunable. It should be possible to predictably achieve good performance and to scale that performance to larger systems.

Productivity: Expressive, composable, debuggable, and maintainable. Programming models should be complete and it should be possible to directly and clearly express efficient implementations for a suitable range of algorithms. Observability and predictability should make it possible to debug and maintain programs.

Portability: Functionality and performance, across operating systems and compilers. Parallel programming models should work on a range of targets, now and into the future.

In this book, we constrain all our examples to C and C++, and we offer the most examples in C++, since that is the language in which many new mainstream performance-oriented applications are written. We consider programming models that add parallelism support to the C and C++ languages and attempt to address the challenges of performance, productivity, and portability.

We also limit ourselves to programming models available from Intel, although, as shown in Figure 1.12, Intel actually supports a wide range of parallel programming approaches, including libraries and standards such as OpenCL, OpenMP, and MPI. The two primary shared-memory parallel programming models available from Intel are also the primary models used in this book:

Intel Threading Building Blocks (TBB): A widely used template library for C++ programmers to address most C++ needs for parallelism. TBB supports an efficient task model. TBB is available as a free, community-supported, open source version, as well as a functionally identical version with commercial support available from Intel.

Intel Cilk Plus (Cilk Plus): Compiler extensions for C and C++ to support parallelism. Cilk Plus has an efficient task model and also supports the explicit specification of vector parallelism through a set of array notations and elemental functions. Cilk Plus has both open source and commercially supported product options.

In the following, we will first discuss some desirable properties of parallel programming models, then introduce the programming models used in this book.

Intel Cilk Plus	Intel Threading Building Blocks	Domain-Specific Libraries	Established Standards	Research and Development
C/C++ language extensions to simplify parallelism	Widely used C++ template library for parallelism	Intel Integrated Performance Primitives (IPP)	Message Passing Interface (MPI)	Intel Concurrent Collections (CnC)
			OpenMP	Offload Extensions
		Intel Math Kernel Library (MKL)	Coarray Fortan	River Trail: Parallel Javascript
			OpenCL	Intel Array Building Blocks (ArBB)
Open sourced. Also an Intel product.	Open sourced. Also an Intel product.			Intel SPMD Program Compiler (ISPC)

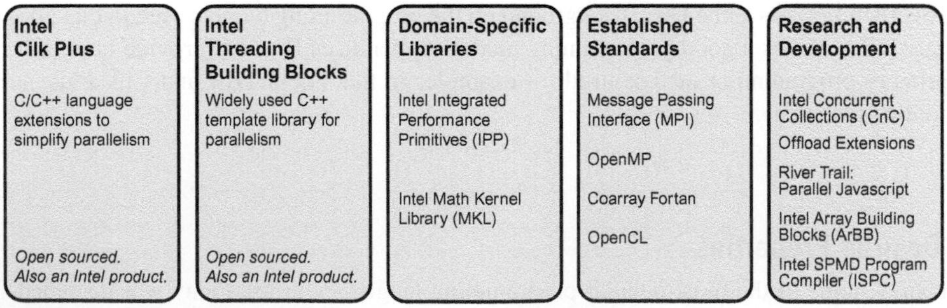

FIGURE 1.12

Parallel programming models supported by Intel. A choice of approaches is available, including pre-optimized parallel libraries; standards such as MPI, Coarray Fortran, OpenMP, and OpenCL; dynamic data-parallel virtual machines such as ArBB; domain-specific languages targeting SPMD vector parallelism such as ISPC; coordination languages such as CnC; and the primary programming models used in this book: Cilk Plus and TBB.

1.5.2 **Abstractions Instead of Mechanisms**

To achieve portable parallel programming you should avoid directly using hardware mechanisms. Instead, you should use abstractions that map onto those mechanisms. In particular, you should avoid **vector intrinsics** that map directly onto vector instructions and instead use array operations. You should also avoid using threads directly and program in terms of a **task** abstraction. Tasks identify only opportunities for parallelism, not the actual parallel execution mechanism. Programming should focus on the decomposition of the problem and the design of the algorithm rather than the specific mechanisms by which it will be parallelized.

There are three big reasons to avoid programming directly to specific parallel hardware mechanisms:

1. Portability is impaired severely when programming "close to the hardware."
2. Nested parallelism is important and nearly impossible to manage well using the mandatory parallelism implied by specific mechanisms such as threads.
3. Other mechanisms for parallelism, such as vectorization, exist and need to be considered. In fact, some implementations of a parallel algorithm might use threads on one machine and vectors on another, or some combination of different mechanisms.

Using abstractions for specifying vectorization rather than vector intrinsics avoids dependencies on the peculiarities of a particular vector instruction set, such as the number of elements in a vector. Even within Intel's processor product line, there are now different vector instruction set extensions with 4, 8, and 16 single-precision floating point elements per SIMD register. Fortunately there are good abstractions available to deal with these differences. For example, in both Cilk Plus and ArBB it is also possible to use either **array operations** or **elemental functions** to specify vector parallelism in a machine-independent way. OpenCL primarily depends on elemental functions. In these three cases, easily vectorized code is specified using portable abstractions.

The reasons for avoiding direct threading are more subtle, but basically a task model has less overhead, supports better composability, and gives the system more freedom to allocate resources. In particular, tasks support the specification of optional parallelism. Optional (as opposed to mandatory) parallelism supports nesting and efficient distributed **load balancing**, and can better manage converting potential to actual parallelism as needed. Nested parallelism is important for developing parallel libraries that can be used inside other parallel programs without exposing the internals of the implementation of those libraries. Such composability is fundamental to software engineering. If you want to understand more about the reasons for this shift to programming using tasks, an excellent detailed explanation of the perils of direct threading is "The Problem with Threads" [Lee06].

Tasks were the basis of an MIT research project that resulted in Cilk, the basis of Cilk Plus. This research led to the efficient work-stealing schedulers and tasking models that are now considered the best available solutions to scalable and low-overhead load balancing. TBB likewise offers an extensive set of algorithms for managing tasks using efficient, scalable mechanisms.

Cilk Plus and TBB each offer both parallel loops and parallel function invocation. The data parallel focus of ArBB generates task parallelism by allowing programmers to specify many independent operations to be run in parallel. However, ArBB does not explicitly manage tasks, leaving that to the mechanisms supplied by Cilk Plus and TBB. This also means that ArBB is composable with these models.

OpenCL is a standard based on a elemental function abstraction, and implementations vary. However, the most important pattern used by OpenCL is the map pattern (the replicated execution of a single function), and we will discuss how this can be implemented efficiently.

OpenMP has several features that make it difficult to implement a built-in load balancer. It is based on loop parallelism, but unfortunately it directly exposes certain underlying aspects of its implementation. We will present some OpenMP examples in order to demonstrate that the patterns also apply to the OpenMP standard, but we recommend that new software use one of Cilk Plus or TBB to benefit from their superior composability and other advantages.

1.5.3 Expression of Regular Data Parallelism

Data parallelism is the key to achieving scalability. Merely dividing up the source code into tasks using functional decomposition will not give more than a constant factor speedup. To continue to scale to ever larger numbers of cores, it is crucial to generate more parallelism as the problem grows larger. Data parallelism achieves this, and all programming models used for examples in this book support data parallelism.

Data parallelism is a general term that actually applies to any form of parallelism in which the amount of work grows with the size of the problem. Almost all of the patterns discussed in this book, as well as the task models supported by TBB and Cilk Plus, can be used for data parallelism. However, there is a subcategory of data parallelism, **regular data parallelism**, which can be mapped efficiently onto vector instructions in the hardware, as well as to hardware threads. Use of vector instruction mechanisms can give a significant additional boost to performance. However, since vector instructions differ from processor to processor, portability requires abstractions to express such forms of data parallelism.

Abstractions built into Cilk Plus, ArBB, and OpenCL make it natural to express regular data parallelism explicitly without having to rely on the compiler inferring it. By expressing regular data parallelism explicitly, the ability of the programming model to exploit the inherent parallelism in an algorithm is enhanced.

As previously discussed, reducing everything to a serially executed procedure is a learned skill. However, such serial processing can in fact be quite unnatural for regular data-parallel problems. You are probably so used to serial programming constructs such as loops that you may not notice anymore how unnatural they can be, but the big problem for parallel programming systems is that a serial ordering of operations is in fact unnecessary in many cases. By forcing ordering of operations in a serial fashion, existing serial languages are actually removing opportunities for parallelism unnecessarily.

Consider again the simple loop shown in Listing 1.8 to add two vectors. The writer of the code probably really just meant to say "add all of the corresponding elements in b and c and put the result in

```
1  for (i = 0; i < 10000; ++i) {
2      a[i] = b[i] + c[i];
3  }
```

LISTING 1.8

Serial vector addition coded as a loop in C.

```
1   a[0:10000] = b[0:10000] + c[0:10000];
```

LISTING 1.9

Parallel vector addition using Cilk Plus.

```
1   a = b + c;
```

LISTING 1.10

Parallel vector addition using ArBB.

the corresponding element of a." But this code implies more: It implies that the additions are done in a certain *order* as well. It might be possible for the compiler to infer that these operations can be done in parallel and do so, but it is not clear from the literal semantics of the code given that this is what is meant. Also, languages such as C and C++ make it possible to use pointers for these arrays, so in theory the data storage for a, b, and c could overlap or be misaligned, making it hard for the compiler to automatically use the underlying vector mechanisms effectively. For example, see Listing 1.2, which shows that unfortunately, the order does matter if the memory for the arrays in the above code could overlap.

Cilk Plus has the ability to specify data parallel operations explicitly with new array notation extensions for C and C++. The array notations make it clear to the compiler that regular data parallelism is being specified and avoids, by specification, the above difficulties. Using array notation, we can rewrite the above loop as shown in Listing 1.9.

ArBB is even simpler, as long as the data is already stored in ArBB containers: If a, b, and c are all ArBB containers, the vector addition simplifies to the code shown in Listing 1.10. ArBB containers have the additional advantage that the actual data may be stored in a remote location, such as the local memory of a co-processor.

You can use these notations when you just want to operate on the elements of arrays, and you do not care in what order the individual operations are done. This is exactly what the parallel constructs of Cilk Plus and ArBB add to C and C++. Explicit array operations such as this are not only shorter but they also get rid of the unnecessary assumption of serial ordering of operations, allowing for a more efficient implementation.

Cilk Plus, ArBB, and OpenCL also allow the specification of regular data parallelism through **elemental functions**. Elemental functions can be called in regular data parallel contexts—for example, by being applied to all the elements of an array at once. Elemental functions allow for **vectorization** by replication of the computation specified across vector lanes. In Cilk Plus, the internals of these functions are given using normal C/C++ syntax, but marked with a **pragma** and called from inside a vectorized context, such as a vectorized loop or an array slice. In ArBB, elemental functions are defined over ArBB types and called from a map operation—but the concept is the same. In OpenCL, elemental functions are specified in a separate C-like language. These "kernels" are then bound to data and invoked using an **application programming interface (API)**. Elemental functions are consistent with leaving the semantics of existing serial code largely intact while adding the ability to take advantage of vector mechanisms in the hardware. Both array expressions and elemental functions can also simultaneously map computations over hardware thread parallelism mechanisms.

Consider the code in Listing 1.11. Suppose the function my_simple_add is compiled separately, or perhaps accessed by a function pointer or virtual function call. Perhaps this function is passed in by a user to a library, and it is the library that is doing the parallel execution. Normally it would be hard for this case to be vectorized. However, by declaring my_simple_add as an elemental function, then it is possible to vectorize it in many of these cases. Using ArBB, it is even possible to vectorize this code in the case of function pointers or virtual function calls, since ArBB can dynamically inline code.

Getting at the parallelism in existing applications has traditionally required non-trivial rewriting, sometimes referred to as **refactoring**. Compiler technology can provide a better solution.

For example, with Cilk Plus, Listing 1.12 shows two small additions (the __declspec(vector) and the pragma) to Listing 1.11 that result in a program that can use either SSE or AVX instructions to yield significant speedups from vector parallelism. This will be the case even if my_simple_add is compiled separately and made available as a binary library. The compiler will create vectorized versions of elemental functions and call them whenever it detects an opportunity, which in this case is provided by the pragma to specify vectorization of the given loop. In the example shown, the number of calls to the function can be reduced by a factor of 8 for AVX or a factor of 4 for SSE. This can result in significant performance increases.

Another change that may be needed in order to support vectorization is conversion of data layouts from **array-of-structures** to **structure-of-arrays** (see Section 6.7). This transformation can be auto-

```
1  float my_simple_add(float x1, float x2) {
2     return x1 + x2;
3  }
4  ...
5  for (int j = 0; j < N; ++j) {
6     outputx[j] = my_simple_add(inputa[j], inputb[j]);
7  }
```

LISTING 1.11

Scalar function for addition in C.

```
1  __declspec(vector)
2  float my_simple_add(float x1, float x2) {
3     return x1 + x2;
4  }
5  ...
6  #pragma simd
7  for (int j = 0; j < N; ++j) {
8     outputx[j] = my_simple_add(inputa[j], inputb[j]);
9  }
```

LISTING 1.12

Vectorized function for addition in Cilk Plus.

mated by ArBB. So, while ArBB requires changes to the types used for scalar types, it can automate larger scale code transformations once this low-level rewriting has been done.

These two mechanisms, array expressions and elemental functions, are actually alternative ways to express one of the most basic parallel patterns: map. However, other regular data-parallel patterns, such as the **scan** pattern and the **reduce** pattern (discussed in Chapter 5) are also important and can also be expressed directly using the programming models discussed in this book. Some of these patterns are harder for compilers to infer automatically and so are even more important to be explicitly expressible.

1.5.4 Composability

Composability is the ability to use a feature without regard to other features being used elsewhere in your program. Ideally, every feature in a programming language is composable with every other.

Imagine if this was not true and use of an if statement meant you could not use a for statement anywhere else in an application. In such a case, linking in a library where any if statement was used would mean for statements would be disallowed throughout the rest of the application. Sounds ridiculous? Unfortunately, similar situations exist in some parallel programming models or combinations of programming models. Alternatively, the composition may be allowed but might lead to such poor performance that it is effectively useless.

There are two principal issues: incompatibility and inability to support hierarchical composition. Incompatibility means that using two parallel programming models simultaneously may lead to failures or possible failures. This can arise for many more-or-less subtle reasons, such as inconsistent use of thread-local memory. Such incompatibility can lead to failure even if the parallel regions do not directly invoke each other.

Even if two models are compatible, it may not be possible to use them in a nested or hierarchical fashion. A common case of this is when a library function is called from a region parallelized by one model, and the library itself is parallelized with a different model. Ideally a software developer should not need to know that the library was parallelized, let alone with what programming model. Having to know such details violates information hiding and separation of concerns, fundamental principles of software engineering, and leads to many practical problems. For example, suppose the library was originally serial but a new version of the library comes out that is parallelized. With models that are not composable, upgrading to the new version of this library, even if the binary interface is the same, might break the code with which it is combined.

A common failure mode in the case of nested parallelism is **oversubscription**, where each use of parallelism creates a new set of threads. When parallel routines that do this are composed hierarchically a very large number of threads can easily be created, causing inefficiencies and possibly exceeding the number of threads that the system can handle. Such soft failures can be harder to deal with than hard failures. The code might work when the system is quiet and not using a large number of threads, but fail under heavy load or when other applications are running.

Cilk Plus and TBB, the two primary programming models discussed in this book, are fully compatible and composable. This means they can be combined with each other in a variety of situations without causing failures or oversubscription. In particular, nested use of Cilk Plus with TBB is fine, as is nested use of TBB with itself or Cilk Plus with itself. ArBB can also be used from inside TBB or Cilk Plus since its implementation is based in turn on these models. In all these cases only a fixed number of threads will be created and will be managed efficiently.

These three programming models are also, in practice, compatible with OpenMP, but generally OpenMP routines should be used in a peer fashion, rather than in a nested fashion, in order to avoid over-subscription, since OpenMP creates threads as part of its execution model.

Because composability is ultimately so important, it is reasonable to hope that non-composable models will completely give way to composable models.

1.5.5 Portability of Functionality

Being able to run code on a wide variety of platforms, regardless of operating systems and processors, is desirable. The most widely used programming languages such as C, C++, and Java are portable.

All the programming models used in this book are portable. In some cases, this is because a single portable implementation is available; in other cases, it is because the programming model is a standard with multiple implementations.

TBB has been ported to a wide variety of platforms, is implemented using standard C++, and is available under an open source license. Cilk Plus is growing in adoption in compilers and is available on the most popular platforms. The Cilk Plus extensions are available in both the Intel compiler and are also being integrated into the GNU gcc compiler. Both TBB and Cilk Plus are available under open source licenses. ArBB, like TBB, is a portable C++ library and has been tested with a variety of C++ compilers. TBB and Cilk Plus are architecturally flexible and can work on a variety of modern shared-memory systems.

OpenCL and OpenMP are standards rather than specific portable implementations. However, OpenCL and OpenMP implementations are available for a variety of processors and compilers. OpenCL provides the ability to write parallel programs for CPUs as well as GPUs and co-processors.

1.5.6 Performance Portability

Portability of performance is a serious concern. You want to know that the code you write today will continue to perform well on new machines and on machines you may not have tested it on. Ideally, an application that is tuned to run within 80% of the peak performance of a machine should not suddenly run at 30% of the peak performance on another machine. However, performance portability is generally only possible with more abstract programming models. Abstract models are removed enough from the hardware design to allow programs to map to a wide variety of hardware without requiring code changes, while delivering reasonable performance relative to the machine's capability.

Of course, there are acceptable exceptions when hardware is considered exotic. However, in general, the more flexible and abstract models can span a wider variety of hardware.

Cilk Plus, TBB, OpenMP, and ArBB are designed to offer strong performance portability. OpenCL code tends to be fairly low level and as such is more closely tied to the hardware. Tuning OpenCL code tends to strongly favor one hardware device over another. The code is (usually) still functionally portable but may not perform well on devices for which it was not tuned.

1.5.7 Safety, Determinism, and Maintainability

Parallel computation introduces several complications to programming, and one of those complications is non-determinism. **Determinism** means that every time the program runs, the answer is the same. In serial computation, the order of operations is fixed and the result is naturally deterministic. However, parallel programs are not naturally deterministic. The order of operation of different threads may be interleaved in an arbitrary order. If those threads are modifying shared data, it is possible that different runs of a program may produce different results even with the same input. This is known, logically enough, as **non-determinism**. In practice, the randomness in non-deterministic parallel programs arises from the randomness of thread scheduling, which in turn arises from a number of factors outside the control of the application.

Non-determinism is not necessarily bad. It is possible, in some situations, for non-deterministic algorithms to outperform deterministic algorithms. However, many approaches to application testing assume determinism. For example, for non-deterministic programs testing tools cannot simply compare results to one known good solution. Instead, to test a non-deterministic application, it is necessary to prove that the result is correct, since different but correct results may be produced on different runs. This may be as simple as testing against a tolerance for numerical applications, but may be significantly more involved in other cases. Determinism or repeatability may even be an application requirement (for example, for legal reasons), in which case you will want to know how to achieve it.

Non-determinism may also be an error. Among the possible interleavings of threads acting on shared data, some may be incorrect and lead to incorrect results or corrupted data structures. The problem of safety is how to ensure that only correct orderings occur.

One interesting observation is that many of the parallel patterns used in this book are either deterministic by nature or have deterministic variants. Therefore, one way to achieve complete determinism is to use only the subset of these patterns that are deterministic. An algorithm based on a composition of deterministic patterns will be deterministic. In fact, the (unique) result of each deterministic pattern can be made equivalent to some serial ordering, so we can also say that such programs are **serially consistent**—they always produce results equivalent to some serial program. This makes debugging and reasoning about such programs much simpler.

Of the programming models used in this book, ArBB in particular emphasizes determinism. In the other models, determinism can (usually) be achieved with some discipline. Some performance may be lost by insisting on determinism, however. How much performance is lost will depend on the algorithm. Whether a non-deterministic approach is acceptable will necessarily have to be decided on a case-by-case basis.

1.5.8 Overview of Programming Models Used

We now summarize the basic properties of the programming models used in this book.

Cilk Plus

The Cilk Plus programming model provides the following features:

- Fork–join to support irregular parallel programming patterns and nesting
- Parallel loops to support regular parallel programming patterns, such as map
- Support for explicit vectorization via array sections, `pragma simd`, and elemental functions

- **Hyperobjects** to support efficient reduction
- Serial semantics if keywords are ignored (also known as **serial elision**)
- Efficient load balancing via work-stealing

The Cilk Plus programming model is integrated with a C/C++ compiler and extends the language with the addition of keywords and array section notation.

The Cilk (pronounced "silk") project originated in the mid-1990s at M.I.T. under the guidance of Professor Charles E. Leiserson. It has generated numerous papers, inspired a variety of "work stealing" task-based schedulers (including TBB, Cilk Plus, TPL, PPL and GCD), has been used in teaching, and is used in some university-level textbooks.

Cilk Plus evolved from Cilk and provides very simple but powerful ways to specify parallelism in both C and C++. The simplicity and power come, in no small part, from being embedded in the compiler. Being integrated into the compiler allows for a simple syntax that can be added to existing programs. This syntax includes both array sections and a small set of keywords to manage fork–join parallelism.

Cilk started with two keywords and a simple concept: the asynchronous function call. Such a call, marked with the keyword `cilk_spawn`, is like a regular function call except that the caller can keep going in parallel with the callee. The keyword `cilk_sync` causes the current function to wait for all functions that it spawned to return. Every function has an implicit `cilk_sync` when it returns, thus guaranteeing a property similar to plain calls: When a function returns, the entire call tree under it has completed.

Listings 1.13 and 1.14 show how inserting a few of these keywords into serial code can make it parallel. The classic recursive function to compute Fibonacci numbers serves as an illustration. The addition of one `cilk_spawn` and one `cilk_sync` allows parallel execution of the two recursive calls, waiting for them to complete, and then summing the results afterwards. Only the first recursive call is spawned, since the caller can do the second recursive call.

This example highlights the key design principle of Cilk: A parallel Cilk program is a serial program with keyword "annotations" indicating where parallelism is permitted (but not mandatory). Furthermore there is a strong guarantee of serial equivalence: In a well-defined Cilk program, the parallel program computes the same answer as if the keywords are ignored. In fact, the Intel implementation of Cilk Plus ensures that when the program runs on one processor, operations happen in the same order as the equivalent serial program. Better yet, the serial program can be recovered using the preprocessor; just #define `cilk_spawn` and `cilk_sync` to be whitespace. This property enables Cilk code to be compiled by compilers that do not support the keywords.

Since the original design of Cilk, one more keyword was added: `cilk_for`. Transforming a loop into a parallel loop by changing `for` to `cilk_for` is often possible and convenient. Not all serial loops can be converted this way; the iterations must be independent and the loop bounds must not be modified in the loop body. However, within these constraints, many serial loops can still be parallelized. Conversely, `cilk_for` can always be replaced with `for` by the preprocessor when necessary to obtain a serial program.

The implementation of `cilk_for` loops uses a recursive approach (Section 8.3) that spreads overhead over multiple tasks and manages **granularity** appropriately. The alternative of writing a serial `for` loop that spawns each iteration is usually much inferior, because it puts all the work of spawning on a single task and bottlenecks the load balancing mechanism, and a single iteration may be too small to justify spawning it as a separate task.

```
1  int fib (int n) {
2    if (n < 2) {
3      return n;
4    } else {
5      int x, y;
6      x = fib(n − 1);
7      y = fib(n − 2);
8      return x + y;
9    }
10 }
```

LISTING 1.13

Serial Fibonacci computation in C. It uses a terribly inefficient algorithm and is intended only for illustration of syntax and semantics.

```
1  int fib (int n) {
2    if (n < 2) {
3      return n;
4    } else {
5      int x, y;
6      x = cilk_spawn fib(n − 1);
7      y = fib(n − 2);
8      cilk_sync;
9      return x + y;
10   }
11 }
```

LISTING 1.14

Parallel Cilk Plus variant of Listing 1.13.

Threading Building Blocks (TBB)

The Threading Building Blocks (TBB) programming model supports parallelism based on a tasking model. It provides the following features:

- Template library supporting both regular and irregular parallelism
- Direct support for a variety of parallel patterns, including map, fork–join, task graphs, reduction, scan, and pipelines
- Efficient work-stealing load balancing
- A collection of thread-safe data structures
- Efficient low-level primitives for atomic operations and memory allocation

TBB is a library, not a language extension, and thus can be used with with any compiler supporting ISO C++. Because of that, TBB uses C++ features to implement its "syntax." TBB requires the use of function objects (also known as **functors**) to specify blocks of code to run in parallel. These were somewhat tedious to specify in C++98. However, the C++11 addition of **lambda expressions** (see Appendix D) greatly simplifies specifying these blocks of code, so that is the style used in this book.

TBB relies on templates and generic programming. Generic programming means that algorithms are written with the fewest possible assumptions about data structures, which maximizes potential for reuse. The C++ Standard Template Library (STL) is a good example of generic programming in which the interfaces are specified only by requirements on template types and work across a broad range of types that meet those requirements. TBB follows a similar philosophy.

Like Cilk Plus, TBB is based on programming in terms of tasks, not threads. This allows it to reduce overhead and to more efficiently manage resources. As with Cilk Plus, TBB implements a common thread pool shared by all tasks and balances load via work-stealing. Use of this model allows for nested parallelism while avoiding the problem of over-subscription.

The TBB implementation generally avoids global locks in its implementation. In particular, there is no global task queue and the memory allocator is lock free. This allows for much more scalability. As discussed later, global locks effectively serialize programs that could otherwise run in parallel.

Individual components of TBB may also be used with other parallel programming models. It is common to see the TBB parallel memory allocator used with Cilk Plus or OpenMP programs, for example.

OpenMP

The OpenMP programming model provides the following features:

- Creation of teams of threads that jointly execute a block of code
- Conversion of loops with bounded extents to parallel execution by a team of threads with a simple annotation syntax
- A tasking model that supports execution by an explicit team of threads
- Support for atomic operations and locks
- Support for reductions, but only with a predefined set of operations

The OpenMP interface is based on a set of compiler directives or pragmas in Fortran, C and C++ combined with an API for thread management. In theory, if the API is replaced with a stub library and the pragmas are ignored then a serial program will result. With care, this serial program will produce a result that is the "same" as the parallel program, within numerical differences introduced by reordering of floating-point operations. Such reordering, as we will describe later, is often required for parallelization, regardless of the programming model.

OpenMP is a standard organized by an independent body called the OpenMP Architecture Review Board. OpenMP is designed to simplify parallel programming for application programmers working in high-performance computing (HPC), including the parallelization of existing serial codes. Prior to OpenMP (first released in 1997), computer vendors had distinct directive-based systems. OpenMP standardized common practice established by these directive-based systems. OpenMP is supported by most compiler vendors including the GNU compilers and other open source compilers.

The most common usage of OpenMP is to parallelize loops within a program. The pragma syntax allows the reinterpretation of loops as parallel operations, which is convenient since the code inside the loop can still use normal Fortran, C, or C++ syntax and memory access. However, it should be noted that (as with Cilk Plus) only loops that satisfy certain constraints can be annotated and converted into parallel structures. In particular, iteration variable initialization, update, and termination tests must be one of a small set of standard forms, it must be possible to compute the number of iterations in advance, and the loop iterations must not depend on each other. In other words, a "parallel loop" in OpenMP implements the **map** pattern, using the terminology of this book. In practice, the total number of iterations is broken up into blocks and distributed to a team of threads.

OpenMP implementations do not, in general, check that loop iterations are independent or that race conditions do not exist. As with Cilk Plus, TBB, and OpenCL, avoiding incorrect parallelizations is the responsibility of the programmer.

The main problem with OpenMP for mainstream users is that OpenMP exposes the threads used in a computation. Teams of threads are explicit and must be understood to understand the detailed meaning of a program. This constrains the optimizations available from the OpenMP runtime system and makes the tasking model within OpenMP both more complex to understand and more challenging to implement.

The fact that threads are exposed encourages a programmer to think of the parallel computation in terms of threads and how they map onto cores. This can be an advantage for algorithms explicitly designed around a particular hardware platform's memory hierarchy, which is common in HPC. However, in more mainstream applications, where a single application is used on a wide range of hardware platforms, this can be counterproductive. Furthermore, by expressing the programming model in terms of explicit threads, OpenMP encourages (but does not require) algorithm strategies based on explicit control over the number of threads. On a dedicated HPC machine, having the computation depend upon or control the number of threads may be desirable, but in a mainstream application it is better to let the system decide how many threads are appropriate.

The most serious problem caused by the explicit threading model behind OpenMP is the fact that it limits the ability of OpenMP to compose with itself. In particular, if an OpenMP parallel region creates a team of threads and inside that region a library is called that also uses OpenMP to create a team of threads, it is possible that n^2 threads will be created. If repeated (for example, if recursion is used) this can result in exponential oversubscription. The resulting explosion in the number of threads created can easily exhaust the resources of the operating system and cause the program to fail. However, this only happens if a particular OpenMP option is set: OMP_NESTED=TRUE. Fortunately the default is OMP_NESTED=FALSE, and it should generally be left that way for mainstream applications. When OpenMP and a model like TBB or Cilk Plus are nested and the default setting OMP_NESTED=FALSE is used, at worst $2p$ workers will be created, where p is the number of cores. This can be easily managed by the operating system.

It is also recommended to use OMP_WAIT_POLICY=ACTIVE and OMP_DYNAMIC=TRUE to enable dynamic scheduling. Using static scheduling in OpenMP (OMP_DYNAMIC=FALSE) is not recommended in a mainstream computing environment, since it assumes that a fixed number of threads will be used from one parallel region to the next. This constrains optimizations the runtime system may carry out.

HPC programmers often use OpenMP to explicitly manage a team of threads using the thread ID available through the OpenMP API and the number of threads to control how work is mapped to threads. This also limits what the runtime system can do to optimize execution of the threads. In particular, it limits the ability of the system to perform load balancing by moving work between threads. TBB and Cilk Plus intentionally do not include these features.

In OpenMP, point-to-point synchronization is provided through low-level (and error-prone) locks. Another common synchronization construct in OpenMP is the **barrier**. A classical barrier synchronizes a large number of threads at once by having all threads wait on a lock until all other threads arrive at the same point. In Cilk Plus and TBB, where similar constructs exist (for example, implicitly at the end of a `cilk_for`), they are implemented as pairwise joins, which are more scalable.

Array Building Blocks (ArBB)

The Array Building Blocks (ArBB) programming model supports parallelization by the specification of sequences of data-parallel operations. It provides the following features:

- High-level data parallel programming with both elemental functions and vector operations
- Efficient **collective operations**
- Automatic fusion of multiple operations into more intensive kernels
- Dynamic code generation under programmer control
- Offload to **attached co-processors** without change to source code
- Deterministic by default, safe by design

ArBB is compiler independent and, like TBB, in conjunction with its embedded C++ front-end can in theory be used with any ISO C++ compiler. The vectorized code generation supported by its virtual machine library is independent of the compiler it is used with.

Array Building Blocks is the most high level of the models used in this book. It does not explicitly depend on tasks in its interface, although it does use them in its implementation. Instead of tasks, parallel computations are expressed using a set of operations that can act over collections of data. Computations can be expressed by using a sequence of parallel operations, by replicating elemental **functions** over the elements of a collection, or by using a combination of both.

Listing 1.15 shows how a computation in ArBB can be expressed using a sequence of parallel operations, while Listing 1.16 shows how the same operation can be expressed by replicating a function over a collection using the `map` operation. In addition to per-element vector operations, ArBB also supports a set of collective and data-reorganization operations, many of which map directly onto patterns discussed in later chapters.

```
1   void arbb_vector (
2       dense<f32>& A,
3       dense<f32> B,
4       dense<f32> C,
5       dense<f32> D
6   ) {
7       A += B - C/D;
8   }
9
10  dense<f32> A, B, C, D;
11  // fill A, B, C, D with data ...
12
13  // invoke function over entire collections
14  call(arbb_vector)(A,B,C,D);
```

LISTING 1.15

Vector computation in ArBB.

```
1   void arbb_map (
2       f32& a,  // input and output
3       f32 b,   // input
4       f32 c,   // input
5       f32 d    // input
6   ) {
7       a += b - c/d;
8   }
9
10  void arbb_call (
11      dense<f32>& A,  // input and output
12      dense<f32> B,   // input
13      dense<f32> C,   // input
14      f32 d           // input (uniform; will be replicated)
15  ) {
16      map(arbb_map)(A,B,C,d);
17  }
```

LISTING 1.16

Elemental function computation in ArBB.

ArBB manages data as well as code. This has two benefits: Data can be laid out in memory for better vectorization and data locality, and data and computation can be offloaded to attached co-processors with no changes to the code. It has the disadvantage that extra code is required to move data in and out of the data space managed by ArBB, and extra data movement may be required.

OpenCL

The OpenCL programming model provides the following features:

- Ability to offload computation and data to an attached co-processor with a separate memory space
- Invocation of a regular grid of parallel operations using a common kernel function
- Support of a task queue for managing asynchronous kernel invocations

The OpenCL programming model includes both a kernel language for specifying kernels and an API for managing data transfer and execution of kernels from the host. The kernel language is both a superset and a subset of C99, in that it omits certain features, such as `goto`, but includes certain other features, such as a "swizzle" notation for reordering the elements of short vectors.

OpenCL is a standard organized by Khronos and supported by implementations from multiple vendors. It was primarily designed to allow offload of computation to GPU-like devices, and its memory and task grouping model in particular reflects this. In particular, there are explicit mechanisms for allocating local on-chip memory and for sharing that memory between threads in a workgroup. However, this sharing and grouping are not arranged in an arbitrary hierarchy, but are only one level deep, reflecting the hardware architecture of GPUs. However, OpenCL can also in theory be used for other co-processors as well as CPUs.

The kernel functions in OpenCL corresponds closely to what we call "elemental functions," and kernel invocation corresponds to the map pattern described in this book.

OpenCL is a relatively low-level interface and is meant for performance programming, where the developer must specify computations in detail. OpenCL may also be used by higher level tools as a target language. The patterns discussed in this book can be used with OpenCL but few of these patterns are reflected directly in OpenCL features. Instead, the patterns must be reflected in algorithm structure and conventions.

As a low-level language, OpenCL provides direct control over the host and the compute devices attached to the host. This is required to support the extreme range of devices addressed by OpenCL: from CPUs and GPUs to embedded processors and field-programmable gate arrays (FPGAs). However, OpenCL places the burden for performance portability on the programmer's shoulders. Performance portability is possible in OpenCL, but it requires considerable work by the programmer, often to the point of writing a different version of a single kernel for each class of device.

Also, OpenCL supports only a simple two-level memory model, and for this and other reasons (for example, lack of support for nested parallelism) it lacks composability.

In placing OpenCL in context with the other programming models we have discussed, it is important to appreciate the goals for the language. OpenCL was created to provide a low-level "hardware abstraction layer" to support programmers needing full control over a heterogeneous platform. The low-level nature of OpenCL was a strategic decision made by the group developing OpenCL. To best support the emergence of high-level programming models for heterogeneous platforms, first a portable hardware abstraction layer was needed.

OpenCL is not intended for mainstream programmers the way TBB, Cilk Plus, or OpenMP are. Lacking high-level programming models for heterogeneous platforms, application programmers often turn to OpenCL. However, over time, higher level models will likely emerge to support mainstream application programmers and OpenCL will be restricted to specialists writing the runtimes for these higher level models or for detailed performance-oriented libraries.

However, we have included it in this book since it provides an interesting point of comparison.

1.5.9 When to Use Which Model?

When multiple programming models are available, the question arises: When should which model be used? As we will see, TBB and Cilk Plus overlap significantly in functionality, but do differ in deployment model, support for vectorization, and other factors. OpenCL, OpenMP, and ArBB are each appropriate in certain situations.

Cilk Plus can be used whenever a compiler supporting the Cilk Plus extensions, such as the Intel C++ compiler or gcc, can be used. It targets both hardware thread and vector mechanisms in the processor and is a good all-around solution. It currently supports both C and C++.

Threading Building Blocks (TBB) can be used whenever a compiler-portable solution is needed. However, TBB does not, itself, do vectorization. Generation of vectorized code must be done by the compiler TBB is used with. TBB does, however, support **tiling** ("blocking") and other constructs so that opportunities for vectorization are exposed to the underlying compiler.

TBB and Cilk Plus are good all-around models for C++. They differ mainly in whether a compiler with the Cilk Plus extensions can be used. We also discuss several other models in this book, each of which may be more appropriate in certain specific circumstances.

OpenMP is nearly universally available in Fortran, C, and C++ compilers. It has proven both popular and effective with scientific code, where any shortcomings in composability tend to be unimportant because of the dominance of intense computational loops as opposed to complex nested parallelism. Also, the numerous options offered for OpenMP are highly regarded for the detailed control they afford for the difficult task of tuning supercomputer code.

Array Building Blocks can be used whenever a high-level solution based on operations on collections of data is desired. It supports dynamic code generation, so it is compiler independent like TBB but supports generation of vectorized code like Cilk Plus.

Because of its code generation capabilities, ArBB can also be used for the implementation of custom parallel languages, a topic not discussed at length in this book. If you are interested in this use of ArBB, please see the online documentation for the ArBB Virtual Machine, which provides a more suitable interface for this particular application of ArBB than the high-level C++ interface used in this book. ArBB can also be used to offload computation to co-processors.

OpenCL provides a standard solution for offloading computation to GPUs, CPUs, and accelerators. It is rather low level and does not directly support many of the patterns discussed in this book, but many of them can still be implemented. OpenCL tends to use minimal abstraction on top of the physical mechanisms.

OpenMP is also a standard and is available in many compilers. It can be used when a solution is needed that spans compilers from multiple vendors. However, OpenMP is not as composable as Cilk Plus or TBB. If nested parallelism is needed, Cilk Plus or TBB would be a better choice.

1.6 ORGANIZATION OF THIS BOOK

This chapter has provided an introduction to some key concepts and described the motivation for studying this book. It has also provided a basic introduction to the programming models that we will use for examples.

Chapter 2 includes some additional background material on computer architecture and performance analysis and introduces the terminology and conventions to be used throughout this book.

Chapters 3 to 9 address the most important and common parallel patterns. Gaining an intuitive understanding of these is fundamental to effective parallel programming. Chapter 3 provides a general overview of all the patterns and discusses serial patterns and the relationship of patterns to structured programming. Chapter 4 explains map, the simplest and most scalable parallel pattern and one of the first that should be considered. Chapter 5 discusses collective patterns such as reduce and scan. Collectives address the need to combine results from map operations while maintaining the benefits of parallelism. Chapter 6 discusses data reorganization. Effective data management is often the key to efficient parallel algorithms. This chapter also discusses some memory-related optimizations, such as conversion of array-of-structures to structures-of-arrays. Chapter 8 explains the fork–join pattern and its relationship to tasks. This pattern provides a method to subdivide a problem recursively while distributing overhead in an efficient fashion. This chapter includes many detailed examples, including discussions of how to implement other patterns in terms of fork–join. Chapter 9 discusses the pipeline pattern, where availability of data drives execution rather than control flow.

The remainder of the chapters in the book consist of examples to illustrate and extend the fundamentals from earlier chapters.

The appendices include a list of further reading and self-contained introductions to the primary programming models used in this book.

1.7 SUMMARY

In this chapter, we have described recent trends in computer architecture that are driving a need for explicit parallel programming. These trends include a continuation of Moore's Law, which is leading to an exponentially growing number of transistors on integrated devices. Three other factors are limiting the potential for non-parallelized applications to take advantage of these transistors: the power wall, the ILP (instruction-level-parallelism) wall, and the memory wall. The power wall means that clock rates cannot continue to scale without exceeding the air-cooling limit. The ILP wall means that, in fact, we are *already* taking advantage of most low-level parallelism in scalar code and do not expect any major improvements in this area. We conclude that explicit parallel programming is likely necessary due to the significant changes in approach needed to achieve scalability. Finally, the memory wall limits performance since the bandwidth and latency of communication are improving more slowly than the capability to do computation. The memory wall affects scalar performance but is also a major factor in the scalability of parallel computation, since communication between processors can introduce overhead and latency. Because of this, it is useful to consider the memory and communication structure of an algorithm even before the computational structure.

In this book, we take a structured approach to parallel computation. Specifically, we describe a set of patterns from which parallel applications can be composed. Patterns provide a vocabulary and a set of best practices for describing parallel applications. The patterns embody design principles that will help you design efficient and scalable applications.

Throughout this book, we give many examples of parallel applications. We have chosen to use multiple parallel programming models for these examples, but with an emphasis on TBB and Cilk Plus. These models are portable and also provide high performance and portability. However, by using multiple programming models, we seek to demonstrate that the patterns we describe can be used in a variety of programming systems.

When designing an algorithm, it is useful as you consider various approaches to have some idea of how each possible approach would perform. In the next chapter, we provide additional background especially relevant for predicting performance and scalability. First, we describe modern computer architectures at a level of detail sufficient for this book, with a focus on the key concepts needed for predicting performance. Then, we describe some classic performance models, including Amdahl's Law and Gustafson-Barsis' Law. These laws are quite limited in predictive power, so we introduce another model, the work-span model, that is much more accurate at predicting scalability.

Background

Good parallel programming requires attention to both the theory and the reality of parallel computers. This chapter covers background material applicable to most forms of parallel programming, including a (short) review of relevant computer architecture and performance analysis topics. Section 2.1 introduces basic vocabulary and the graphical notation used in this book for patterns and algorithms. Section 2.2 defines and names some general strategies for designing parallel algorithms. Section 2.3 describes some general mechanisms used in modern processors for executing parallel computations. Section 2.4 discusses basic machine architecture with a focus on mechanisms for parallel computation and communication. The impact of these on parallel software design is emphasized. Section 2.5 explains performance issues from a theoretical perspective, in order to provide guidance on the design of parallel algorithms. Section 2.6 discusses some common pitfalls of parallel programming and how to avoid them. By the end of this chapter, you should have obtained a basic understanding of how modern processors execute parallel programs and understand some rules of thumb for scaling performance of parallel applications.

2.1 VOCABULARY AND NOTATION

The two fundamental components of algorithms are **tasks** and **data**. A task operates on data, either modifying it in place or creating new data. In a parallel computation multiple tasks need to be managed and coordinated. In particular, **dependencies** between tasks need to be respected. Dependencies result in a requirement that particular pairs of tasks be ordered. Dependencies are often but not always associated with the transfer of data between tasks. In particular, a **data dependency** results when one task cannot execute before some data it requires is generated by another task. Another kind of dependency, usually called a **control dependency**, results when certain events or side effects, such as those due to I/O operations, need to be ordered. We will not distinguish between these two kinds of dependency, since in either case the fundamental requirement is that tasks be ordered in time.

For task management the **fork–join** pattern is often used in this book. In the fork–join pattern, new serial control flows are created by splitting an existing serial control flow at a **fork point**. Conversely, two separate serial control flows are synchronized by merging them together at a **join point**. Within a single serial control flow, tasks are ordered according to the usual serial semantics. Due to the implicit serial control flow before and after these points, control dependencies are also needed between fork and join points and tasks that precede and follow them. In general, we will document all dependencies, even those generated by serial control flows.

FIGURE 2.1

Our graphical notation for the fundamental components of algorithms: tasks and data. We use two additional symbols to represent the splitting and merging of serial control flows via fork and join and arrows to represent dependencies.

We use the graphical notation shown in Figure 2.1 to represent these fundamental concepts throughout this book. These symbols represent tasks, data, fork and join points, and dependencies. They are used in graphs representing each of the patterns we will present, and also to describe parallel algorithms. This notation may be augmented from time to time with polygons representing subgraphs or common serial control flow constructs from flow-charts, such as diamonds for selection.

2.2 STRATEGIES

The best overall strategy for **scalable parallelism** is **data parallelism** [HSJ86, Vis10]. Definitions of data parallelism vary. Some narrow definitions permit only collection-oriented operations, such as applying the same function to all elements of an array, or computing the sum of an array. We take a wide view and define data parallelism as any kind of parallelism that grows as the data set grows or, more generally, as the problem size grows. Typically the data is split into chunks and each chunk processed with a separate task. Sometimes the splitting is flat; other times it is recursive. What matters is that bigger data sets generate more tasks.

Whether similar or different operations are applied to the chunks is irrelevant to our definition. Data parallelism can be applied whether or not a problem is regular or irregular. For example, the symmetric rank update in Section 15.4 does different operations in parallel: two symmetric rank reductions and one matrix multiplication. This is an example of an irregular computation, but the scalable data parallelism comes from recursively applying this three-way decomposition.

In practice applying more than few different operations in parallel, at least at a given conceptual level, can make a program hard to understand. However, whether operations are considered "different" can depend on the level of detail. For example, consider a collection of source files to be compiled. At a high level, this is matter of applying the same "compile a file" operation across all source files. But each compilation may involve radically different control flow, because each source file may contain radically different content. When considering these low-level details, the operations look different. Still, since the amount of work grows with the number of input files, this is still data parallelism.

The opposite of data parallelism is **functional decomposition**, an approach that runs different program functions in parallel. At best, functional decomposition improves performance by a constant factor. For example, if a program has functions f, g, and h, running them in parallel at best triples performance, but only if all three functions take exactly the same amount of time to execute and do not depend on each other, and there is no overhead. Otherwise, the improvement will be less.

Sometimes functional decomposition can deliver an additional bit of parallelism required to meet a performance target, but it should not be your primary strategy, because it does not scale. For example, consider an interactive oil prospecting visualization application that simulates seismic wave propagation, reservoir behavior, and seismogram generation [RJ10]. A functional decomposition that runs these three simulations in parallel might yield enough **speedup** to reach a frame rate target otherwise unobtainable on the target machine. However, for the application to scale, say for high-resolution displays, it needs to employ data parallelism, such as partitioning the simulation region into chunks and simulating each chunk with a separate task.

We deliberately avoid the troublesome term **task parallelism**, because its meaning varies. Some programmers use it to mean (unscalable) functional decomposition, others use it to mean (scalable) recursive fork–join, and some just mean any kind of parallelism where the tasks differ in control flow.

A more useful distinction is the degree of regularity in the dependencies between tasks. We use the following terminology for these:

- **Regular parallelism:** The tasks are similar and have predictable dependencies.
- **Irregular parallelism:** The tasks are dissimilar in a way that creates unpredictable dependencies.

Decomposing a dense matrix multiplication into a set of dot products is an example of a **regular parallelization**. All of the dot products are similar and the data dependencies are predictable. Sparse matrix multiplication may be less regular—any unpredictable zeros eliminate dependencies that were present for the dense case. Even more irregular is a chess program involving parallel recursive search over a decision tree. **Branch and bound** optimizations on this tree may dynamically cull some branches, resulting in unpredictable dependencies between parallel branches of the tree.

Any real application tends to combine different approaches to parallelism and also may combine parallel and serial strategies. For example, an application might use a (serial) sequence of parallelized phases, each with its own parallel strategy. Within a parallel phase, the computations are ultimately carried out by serial code, so efficient implementation of serial code remains important. Section 2.5.6 formalizes this intuition: You cannot neglect the performance of your serial code, hoping to make up the difference with parallelism. You need *both* good serial code and a good parallelization strategy to get good performance overall.

2.3 MECHANISMS

Various hardware mechanisms enable parallel computation. The two most important mechanisms are **thread parallelism** and **vector parallelism**:

- **Thread parallelism:** A mechanism for implementing parallelism in hardware using a separate flow of control for each worker. Thread parallelism supports both regular and irregular parallelism, as well as functional decomposition.
- **Vector parallelism:** A mechanism for implementing parallelism in hardware using the same flow of control on multiple data elements. Vector parallelism naturally supports regular parallelism but also can be applied to irregular parallelism with some limitations.

A **hardware thread** is a hardware entity capable of independently executing a **program** (a flow of instructions with data-dependent control flow) by itself. In particular it has its own "instruction pointer" or "program counter." Depending on the hardware, a core may have one or multiple hardware threads. A **software thread** is a virtual hardware thread. An operating system typically enables many more software threads to exist than there are actual hardware threads by mapping software threads to hardware threads as necessary. A computation that employs multiple threads in parallel is called **thread parallel**.

Vector parallelism refers to single operations replicated over collections of data. In mainstream processors, this is done by **vector instructions** that act on **vector registers**. Each vector register holds a small array of elements. For example, in the Intel Advanced Vector Extensions (Intel AVX) each register can hold eight single-precision (32 bit) floating point values. On supercomputers, the vectors may be much longer, and may involve streaming data to and from memory. We consider both of these to be instances of vector parallelism, but we normally mean the use of vector instructions when we use the term in this book.

The elements of vector units are sometimes called **lanes**. Vector parallelism using N lanes requires less hardware than thread parallelism using N threads because in vector parallelism only the registers and the functional units have to be replicated N times. In contrast, N-way thread parallelism requires replicating the instruction fetch and decode logic and perhaps enlarging the instruction cache. Furthermore, because there is a single flow of control, vector parallelism avoids the need for complex synchronization mechanisms, thus enabling efficient fine-grained parallelism. All these factors can also lead to greater power efficiency. However, when control flow must diverge, thread parallelism is usually more appropriate.

Thread parallelism can easily emulate vector parallelism—just apply one thread per lane. However, this approach can be inefficient since thread synchronization overhead will often dominate. Threads also have different memory behavior than vector operations. In particular, in vector parallelism we often want nearby vector lanes to access nearby memory locations, but if threads running on different cores access nearby memory locations it can have a negative impact on performance (due to **false sharing** in **caches**, which we discuss in Section 2.4). A simple way around both problems is to break large vector operations into chunks and run each chunk on a thread, possibly also vectorizing within each chunk.

Less obviously, vector hardware can emulate a limited form of thread parallelism, specifically elemental functions including control flow. We call such pseudo-threads **fibers**.[1] Two approaches to implementing elemental functions with control flow are **masking** and **packing**. The latter implementation mechanism is also known as stream compaction [BOA09, Wal11, LLM08, HLJH09].

Masking conditionally executes some lanes. The illusion of independent flows of control can be achieved by assigning one fiber per lane and executing *all* control-flow paths that *any* of the fibers take. When executing code for paths not taken by a particular fiber, that fiber's lane is masked to not execute, or at least not update any memory or cause other side effects. For example, consider the following code:

```
if (a&1)
    a = 3*a + 1;
else
    a = a/2;
```

---

[1] Warning: This definition of "fiber" should not be confused with the meaning on Microsoft® Windows, where it means an application-scheduled software thread.

In the masking approach, the vector unit executes both *both* a=3*a+1 and a=a/2. However, each lane is masked off for one of the two statements, depending upon whether a&1 is zero or not. It is as if the code were written:

```
p = (a&1);
t = 3*a + 1;
if (p) a = t;
t = a/2;
if (!p) a = t;
```

where if (...)a = t represents a single instruction that does conditional assignment, not a branch. Emulation of control flow with masking does not have the same performance characteristics as true threads for irregular computation. With masking, a vector unit executes both arms of the original if statement but keeps only one of the results. A thread executes only the arm of interest. However, this approach can be optimized by actually branching around code if all test results in the mask are either true or false [Shi07]. This case, **coherent masks**, is the only case in which this approach actually avoids computation when executing conditionals. This is often combined with using actual multiple threads over vectorized chunks, so that the masks only have to be coherent within a chunk to avoid work. Loops can be also be emulated. They are iterated until all lanes satisfy the exit conditions. Lanes that have already satisfied their exit conditions continue to execute but don't write back their results.

Packing is an alternative implementation approach that rearranges fibers so that those in the same vector have similar control flow. Suppose many fibers execute the previous example. Packing first evaluates the condition in parallel for all fibers. Then, fibers with (a&1)!= 0 are packed into a single contiguous vector, and all elements of this vector execute a = 3*a + 1. All fibers with (a&1)== 0 are packed into another contiguous vector and execute a = a/2. Note that packing can in theory operate in place on a single vector in memory since we can pack the false and true values into opposite ends of a single vector. This is sometimes also known as a **split operation**. Finally, after the divergent computations are performed, the results are interleaved (unpacked) back into a single result vector in their original order. Though packing retains the asymptotic performance characteristics of true threads, it involves extra overhead that can become prohibitive when there are many branches. One option to avoid the overhead is to only use packing for "large" blocks of code where the cost can be amortized, and use masking otherwise.

Section 2.4.3 says more about the emulation of **elemental functions** (functions which act on all elements of a collection at once) with control flow on vector hardware.

The process of compiling code to vector instructions is called **vectorization**. When applied automatically to serial code it is called **auto-vectorization**. Auto-vectorization is fairly limited in applicability so often explicit approaches are necessary to get the best performance.

Vector **intrinsics** are a low-level, direct approach to explicit vectorization. Intrinsics are special data types and functions that map directly onto specific instructions. For example, on x86 processors the intrinsic function _mm_addps(x,y) performs vector addition of vectors x and y. Both arguments must be 4-element vectors declared as intrinsic type _m128. Vector intrinsics are not the same as assembly language since the compiler still handles register allocation and other matters. However, intrinsics are definitely low level. Relatively simple mathematical formula become obscure when expressed with intrinsics, and the resulting code becomes dependent on a particular instruction set and hardware vector length. For example, code written with 4-element intrinsics becomes suboptimal when 8-element vector units become available. This book stresses high-level machine-independent approaches that enable portable, efficient vector code.

We use **task** to refer to a unit of **potentially parallel** work with a separate flow of control. Tasks are executed by scheduling them onto software threads, which in turn the OS schedules onto hardware threads. A single software thread may run many tasks, though it actively runs only one task at a time. Scheduling of software threads onto hardware threads is usually **preemptive**—it can happen at any time. In contrast, scheduling of tasks onto software threads is typically non-preemptive (**cooperative**)—a thread switches tasks only at predictable switch points. Non-preemptive scheduling enables significantly lower overhead and stronger reasoning about space and time requirements than threads. Hence, tasks are preferable to software threads as an abstraction for scalable parallelism.

In summary, threads and vectors are two hardware features for parallel execution. Threads deal with all kinds of parallelism but pay the cost of replicating control-flow hardware whether the replication is needed or not. Vectors are more efficient at regular computations when suitable vector instructions exist but can emulate irregular computations with some limitations and inefficiencies. In the best case, especially for large-scale regular computations, careful design can combine these mechanisms multiplicatively.

2.4 MACHINE MODELS

In order to write efficient programs, it is important to have a clear mental model of the organization of the hardware resources being used. We can do this without a deep dive into computer architecture. To write portable programs, by necessity this model needs to be somewhat abstract. However, there are key mechanisms shared by most modern computers that are likely to be in future computers. These concepts include **cores**, **vector units**, **cache**, and **non-uniform memory** systems. In addition, **heterogeneous computing** introduces the concept of an **attached co-processor**. We describe these key concepts here so that the book is self-contained, and to define the terminology used throughout the rest of the book.

2.4.1 Machine Model

Figure 2.2 is a sketch of a typical **multicore processor**. Inside every **core** there are multiple **functional units**, each such functional unit being able to do a single arithmetic operation. By considering functional units as the basic units of computation rather than cores, we can account for both thread and vector parallelism. A **cache** memory hierarchy is typically used to manage the tradeoff between memory performance and capacity.

Instruction Parallelism

Since cores usually have multiple functional units, multiple arithmetic operations can often be performed in parallel, even in a single core. Parallel use of multiple functional units in a single core can be done either implicitly, by **superscalar** execution of serial instructions, hardware multithreading, or by explicit vector instructions. A single-core design may use all three. A **superscalar processor** analyzes

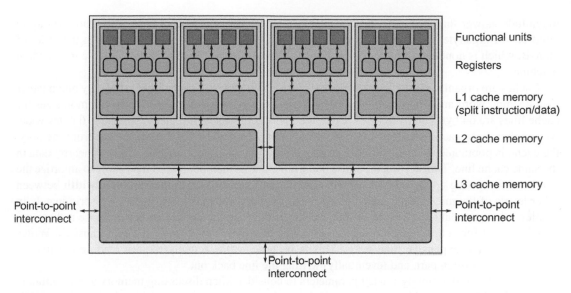

FIGURE 2.2

Multicore processor with hierarchical cache. Each core has multiple functional units and (typically) an instruction cache and a data cache. Larger, slower caches are then shared between increasing numbers of cores in a hierarchy.

an instruction stream and executes multiple instructions in parallel as long as they do not depend on each other. A core with hardware multithreading supports running multiple hardware threads at the same time. There are multiple implementation approaches to this, including **simultaneous multi-threading**, where instructions from multiple streams feed into a superscalar scheduler [TEL95, KM03], and **switch-on-event multithreading**, where the hardware switches rapidly to a different hardware thread when a long-latency operation, such as a memory read, is encountered [ALKK90]. Vector instructions enable explicit use of multiple functional units at once by specifying an operation on a small collection of data elements. For example, on Intel architectures vector instructions in the Streaming SIMD Extension (SSE) allows specification of operations on 128-bit vectors, which can be two 64-bit values, four 32-bit values, eight 16-bit values, or sixteen 8-bit values. The new Advanced Vector Extensions (AVX) extends this feature to 256-bit vectors, and the Many Integrated Cores (MIC) architecture extends it yet again to 512-bit vectors.

Memory Hierarchy

Processors also have a memory hierarchy. Closest to the functional units are small, very fast memories known as **registers**. Functional units operate directly on values stored in registers. Next there are instruction and data **caches**. Instructions are cached separately from data at this level since their usage patterns are different. These caches are slightly slower than registers but have more space. Additional levels of cache follow, each cache level being slower but more capacious than the one above it, typically by an order of magnitude in both respects. Access to main memory is typically two orders of magnitude slower than access to the last level of cache but is much more capacious, currently up to hundreds of gigabytes on large servers. Currently, large on-chip cache memories are on the order of 10 MB, which is nonetheless a tiny sliver of the total physical memory typically available in a modern machine.

Caches are organized into blocks of storage called **cache lines**. A cache line is typically much larger than a single word and often (but not always) bigger than a vector. Some currently common sizes for cache lines are 64 bytes and 128 bytes. Compared with a 128-bit SSE register, which is 16 bytes wide, we see that these cache lines are 4 to 8 SSE vector registers wide. When data is read from memory, the cache is populated with an entire cache line. This allows subsequent rapid access to nearby data in the same cache line. Transferring the entire line from external memory makes it possible to amortize the overhead for setting up the transfer. On-chip, wide buses can be used to increase **bandwidth** between other levels of the memory hierarchy. However, if memory accesses jump around indiscriminately in memory, the extra data read into the cache goes unused. Peak memory access performance is therefore only obtained for coherent memory accesses, since that makes full use of the line transfers. Writes are usually more expensive than reads. This is because writes actually require reading the line in, modifying the written part, and (eventually) writing the line back out.

There are also two timing-related parameters to consider when discussing memory access: **latency** and **bandwidth**. Bandwidth is the amount of data that can be transferred per unit time. **Latency** is the amount of time that it takes to satisfy a transfer request. Latency can often be a crucial factor in performance. Random reads, for example due to "pointer chasing," can leave the processor spending most of its time waiting for data to be returned from off-chip memory. This is a good case where hardware multithreading on a single core be beneficial, since while one thread is waiting for a memory read another can be doing computation.

Caches maintain copies of data stored elsewhere, typically in main memory. Since caches are smaller than main memory, only a subset of the data in the memory (or in the next larger cache) can be stored, and bookkeeping data needs to be maintained to keep track of where the data came from. This is the other reason for using cache lines: to amortize the cost of the bookkeeping. When an address is accessed, the caches need to be searched quickly to determine if that address' data is in cache. A **fully associative cache** allows any address' data to be stored anywhere in the cache. It is the most flexible kind of cache but expensive in hardware because the entire cache must be searched. To do this quickly, a large number of parallel hardware comparators are required.

At the other extreme are **direct-mapped caches**. In a direct-mapped cache, data can be placed in only one location in cache, typically using a modular function of the address. This is very simple. However, if the program happens to access two different main memory locations that map to the same location in the cache, data will get swapped into that same location repeatedly, defeating the cache. This is called a **cache conflict**. In a direct-mapped cache, main memory locations with conflicts are located far apart, so a conflict is theoretically rare. However, these locations are typically located at a power of two separation, so certain operations (like accessing neighboring rows in a large image whose dimensions are a power of two) can be pathological.

A **set-associative cache** is a common compromise between full associativity and direct mapping. Each memory address maps to a set of locations in the cache; hence, searching the cache for an address involves searching only the set it maps to, not the entire cache. Pathological cases where many accesses hit the same set can occur, but they are less frequent than for direct-mapped caches. Interestingly, a k-way set associative cache (one with k elements in each set) can be implemented using k direct-mapped caches plus a small amount of additional external hardware. Usually k is a small number, such as 4 or 8, although it is as large as 16 on some recent Intel processors.

Caches further down in the hierarchy are typically also shared among an increasing number of cores. Special hardware keeps the contents of caches consistent with one another. When cores communicate using "shared memory," they are often really just communicating through the **cache coherence** mechanisms. Another pathological case can occur when two cores access data that happens to lie in the same cache line. Normally, cache coherency protocols assign one core, the one that last modifies a cache line, to be the "owner" of that cache line. If two cores write to the same cache line repeatedly, they fight over ownership. Importantly, note that this can happen even if the cores are not writing to the same part of the cache line. This problem is called **false sharing** and can significantly decrease performance. In particular, as noted in Section 2.3, this leads to a significant difference in the benefit of memory coherence in threads and vector mechanisms for parallelism.

Virtual Memory

Virtual memory lets each processor use its own logical address space, which the hardware maps to the actual physical memory. The mapping is done per **page**, where pages are relatively large blocks of memory, on the order of 4 KB to 16 KB. Virtual memory enables running programs with larger data sets than would fit in physical memory. Parts of the virtual memory space not in active use are kept in a disk file called a **swap file** so the physical memory can be remapped to other local addresses in use. In a sense, the main memory acts as cache for the data stored on disk. However, since disk access latency is literally *millions* of times slower than memory access latency, a **page fault**—an attempt to access a location that is not in physical memory—can take a long time to resolve. If the page fault rate is high, then performance can suffer. Originally, virtual memory was designed for the situation in which many users were time-sharing a computer. In this case, applications would be "swapped out" when a user was not active, and many processes would be available to hide latency. In other situations, virtual memory may not be able to provide the illusion of a large memory space efficiently, but it is still useful for providing isolation between processes and simplifying memory allocation.

Generally speaking, **data locality** is important at the level of virtual memory for two reasons. First, good performance requires that the page fault rate be low. This means that the ordering of accesses to data should be such that the **working set** of the process—the total amount of physical memory that needs to be accessed within a time period that is short relative to the disk access time—should fit in the set of physical memory pages that can be assigned to the process. Second, addresses must be translated rapidly from virtual addresses to physical addresses. This is done by specialized hardware called a **Translation Lookaside Buffer (TLB)**. The TLB is a specialized cache that translates logical addresses to physical addresses for a small set of active pages. Like ordinary caches, it may have hierarchical levels and may be split for instructions versus data. If a memory access is made to a page not currently in the TLB, then a **TLB miss** occurs. A TLB miss requires walking a page table in memory to find the translation. The walk is done by either specialized hardware or a trap to the operating system. Since the TLB is finite, updating the TLB typically requires the eviction of some other translation entry.

The important issue is that the number of page translation entries in the TLB is relatively small, on the order of 8 to 128 entries for the first-level TLB, and TLB misses, while not as expensive as page faults, are not cheap. Therefore, accessing a large number of pages in a short timeframe can cause **TLB thrashing**, a high TLB miss rate that can significantly degrade performance.

A typical case for this issue is a **stencil** on a large 3D array. Suppose a program sweeps through the array in the obvious order—row, column, page—accessing a stencil of neighboring elements for each location. If the number of pages touched by a single row sweep is larger than the size of the TLB, this will tend to cause a high TLB miss rate. This will be true even if the page fault rate is low. Of course, if the 3D array is big enough, then a high page fault rate might also result. Reordering the stencil to improve locality (for example, as in Chapter 10) can lower the TLB miss rate and improve performance. Another way to address this is to use large pages so that a given number of TLB entries can cover a larger amount of physical memory. Some processors partition the TLB into portions for small and large pages, so that large pages can be used where beneficial, and not where they would do more harm than good.

Multiprocessor Systems

Processors may be combined together to form **multiple-processor systems**. In modern systems, this is done by attaching memory directly to each processor and then connecting the processors (or actually, their caches) with fast point-to-point communications channels, as in Figure 2.3. The cache coherency protocol is extended across these systems, and processors can access memory attached to other processors across the communication channels.

However, access to memory attached to a remote processor is slower (has higher latency and also typically reduced bandwidth) than access to a local memory. This results in **non-uniform memory access (NUMA)**. Ideally, threads should be placed on cores close to the data they should process, or vice versa. The effect is not large for machines with a small number of processors but can be pronounced for large-scale machines. Because NUMA also affects cache coherency, other problems, such as false sharing, can be magnified in multiprocessor machines.

One basic theoretical model of parallel computation, the Parallel Random Access Machine (PRAM), assumes uniform memory-access times for simplicity, and there have been attempts to build real machines like this [Vis11]. However, both caching and NUMA invalidate this assumption. Caches make access time depend on previous accesses, and NUMA makes access time depend on the location of data. The constants involved are not small, either. Access to main memory can be hundreds of times slower than access to cache. Designing algorithms to have good cache behavior is important for serial programs, but becomes even more important for parallel programs.

Theoretical models that extend PRAM to quantify overhead of interprocessor communication include the Synchronous Parallel (BSP) [Val90] and the LogP [CKP+96] models.

Attached Devices

Other devices are often attached to the processor. For example, a **PCIe bus** allows devices to be installed by end users. **A Network Interface Controller (NIC)** is a typical PCIe device that provides access to the network. High-performance NICs can require high bandwidth and additionally the overall system performance of a cluster can depend crucially on communication latency. The PCIe bus protocol allows for such devices to perform **direct memory access (DMA)** and read or write data directly to memory, without involving the main processor (except for coordination).

Other devices with high memory requirements may also use DMA. Such devices included attached processing units such as **graphics accelerators** and **many-core processors**.

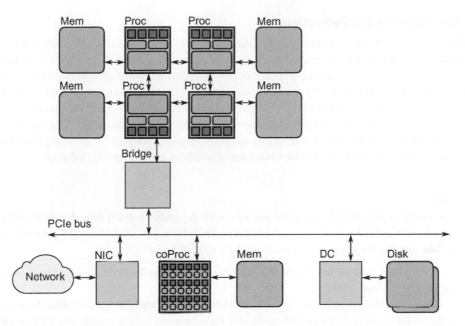

FIGURE 2.3

Multiprocessor system organization. Each processor has its own memory bank(s), and processors are interconnected using point-to-point communication channels. A processor can access its own memory directly and other banks over the communication channels. A bridge chip connects the processors to other devices, often through a bus such as a PCIe bus. Communication devices (Network Interface Controllers, or NICs) and other processors (GPUs or attached co-processors) can be attached to the PCIe bus (actually, the PCIe bus is not an actual shared bus but another set of point-to-point data links).

Such co-processors can be quite sophisticated systems in their own right. The Intel Many Integrated Core (MIC) architecture, for example, is a high-performance processor with a large number of simple cores (over 50) and its own cache and memory system. Each MIC core also has wide vector units, 512 bits, which is twice as wide as AVX. These characteristics make it more suitable for highly parallelizable and vectorizable workloads with regular data parallelism than multicore processors, which are optimized for high scalar performance.

While the main function of graphics accelerators is the generation of images, they can also be used to provide supplemental processing power, since they also have wide vector units and many cores. Graphics accelerators used as computational engines are usually programmed using the **SIMT** model discussed in Section 2.4.3 through a programming model such as OpenCL or (for graphics accelerators from NVIDIA) CUDA.

However, while graphics accelerators must be programmed with a specialized programming model such as OpenCL, the Intel MIC architecture runs a full operating system (Linux) and can be programmed with nearly any parallel programming model available on multicore processors. This includes (but is not limited to) all the programming models discussed in this book.

2.4.2 Key Features for Performance

Given the complexities of computer architecture, and the fact that different computers can vary significantly, how can you optimize code for performance across a range of computer architectures?

The trick is to realize that modern computer architectures are designed around two key assumptions: *data locality* and the *availability of parallel operations*. Get these right and good performance can be achieved on a wide range of machines, although perhaps after some per-machine tuning. However, if you violate these assumptions, you cannot expect good performance no matter how much low-level tuning you do. In this section, we will also discuss some useful strategies for avoiding dependence on particular machine configurations: **cache oblivious** algorithms and parameterized code.

Data Locality

Good use of memory bandwidth and good use of cache depends on good **data locality**, which is the reuse of data from nearby locations in time or space. Therefore, you should design your algorithms to have good data locality by using one or more of the following strategies:

* Break work up into chunks that can fit in cache. If the **working set** for a chunk of work does not fit in cache, it will not run efficiently.
* Organize data structures and memory accesses to reuse data locally when possible. Avoid unnecessary accesses far apart in memory and especially simultaneous access to multiple memory locations located a power of two apart. The last consideration is to avoid **cache conflicts** on caches with low associativity.
* To avoid unnecessary **TLB misses**, avoid accessing too many pages at once.
* Align data with cache line boundaries. Avoid having unrelated data accesses from different cores access the same **cache lines**, to avoid **false sharing**.

Some of these may require changes to data layout, including reordering items and adding padding to achieve (or avoid) alignments with the hardware architecture. Not only is breaking up work into chunks and getting good alignment with the cache good for parallelization but these optimizations can also make a big difference to single-core performance.

However, these guidelines can be hard to follow when writing portable code, since then you have no advance knowledge of the cache line sizes, the cache organization, or the total size of the caches. In this case, use memory allocation routines that can be customized to the machine, and parameterize your code so that the **grain size** (the size of a chunk of work) can be selected dynamically. If code is parameterized in this way, then when porting to a new machine the tuning process will involve only finding optimal values for these parameters rather than re-coding. If the search for optimal parameters is done automatically it is known as **autotuning**, which may also involve searching over algorithm variants as well.

Another approach to tuning grain size is to design algorithms so that they have locality at all scales, using recursive decomposition. This so-called **cache oblivious** approach avoids the need to know the size or organization of the cache to tune the algorithm. Section 8.8 says more about the cache oblivious approach.

Another issue that affects the achievable performance of an algorithm is **arithmetic intensity**. This is the ratio of computation to communication. Given the fact that on-chip compute performance is still rising with the number of transistors, but off-chip bandwidth is not rising as fast, in order to achieve scalability approaches to parallelism should be sought that give high arithmetic intensity. This ideally means that a large number of on-chip compute operations should be performed for every off-chip memory access. Throughout this book we discuss several optimizations that are aimed at increasing arithmetic intensity, including **fusion** and **tiling**.

Sometimes there is conflict between small grain sizes (which give high parallelism) and high arithmetic intensity. For example, in a 2D **recurrence** tiling (discussed in Chapter 7), the amount of work in a tile might grow as $\Theta(n^2)$ while the communication grows as $\Theta(n)$. In this case the arithmetic intensity grows by $\Theta(n) = \Theta(n^2)/\Theta(n)$, which favors larger grain sizes. In practice, the largest grain size that still fits in cache will likely give the best performance with the least overhead. However, a large grain size may also reduce the available parallelism ("**parallel slack**") since it will reduce the total number of work units.

Parallel Slack

Parallel slack is the amount of "extra" parallelism available (Section 2.5.6) above the minimum necessary to use the parallel hardware resources. Specifying a significant amount of **potential parallelism** higher than the **actual parallelism** of the hardware gives the underlying software and hardware schedulers more flexibility to exploit machine resources.

Normally you want to choose the smallest work units possible that reasonably amortize the overhead of scheduling them and give good arithmetic intensity. Breaking down a problem into exactly as many chunks of work as there are cores available on the machine is tempting, but not necessarily optimal, even if you know the number of cores on the machine. If you only have one or a few tasks on each core, then a delay on one core (perhaps due to an operating system interrupt) is likely to delay the entire program.

Having lots of parallel slack works well with the Intel Cilk Plus and Intel TBB task schedulers because they are designed to exploit slack. In contrast when using OS threading interfaces such as POSIX threads, too much actual parallelism can be detrimental. This problem often does not happen on purpose but due to nesting parallelism using direct threading. Suppose on a 16-core system that an algorithm f creates 15 extra threads to assist its calling thread, and each thread calls a library routine g. If the implementer of g applies the same logic, now there are 16×15 threads running concurrently! Because these threads have **mandatory concurrency** semantics (they *must* run in parallel), the OS must time-slice execution among all 240 threads, incurring overhead for context switching and reloading items into cache. Using tasks instead is better here, because tasks have semantics that make actual parallelism optional. This enables the task scheduler to automatically match actual parallelism to the hardware capability, even when parallelism is nested or irregular.

As mentioned earlier, having more potential parallelism than cores can also help performance when the cores support hardware multithreading. For example, if pointer-chasing code using dependent memory reads cannot be avoided, then additional parallelism can enable hardware-multithreading to hide the latency of the memory reads. However, if additional parallelism is used for this purpose, the total working set needs to be considered so that the cache size is not exceeded for all concurrently active threads. If parallelism is increased for this purpose, the grain size might have to be reduced for best performance.

2.4.3 Flynn's Characterization

One way to coarsely characterize the parallelism available in processor types is by how they combine control flow and data management. A classic categorization by Flynn [Fly72] divides parallel processors into categories based on whether they have multiple flows of control, multiple streams of data, or both.

- **Single Instruction, Single Data (SISD):** This is just a standard non-parallel processor. We usually refer to this as a scalar processor. Due to **Amdahl's Law** (discussed in Section 2.5.4), the performance of scalar processing is important; if it is slow it can end up dominating performance.
- **Single Instruction, Multiple Data (SIMD):** A single operation (task) executes simultaneously on multiple elements of data. The number of elements in a SIMD operation can vary from a small number, such as the 4 to 16 elements in short vector instructions, to thousands, as in streaming vector processors. SIMD processors are also known as **array processors**, since they consist of an array of functional units with a shared controller.
- **Multiple Instruction, Multiple Data (MIMD):** Separate instruction streams, each with its own flow of control, operate on separate data. This characterizes the use of multiple cores in a single processor, multiple processors in a single computer, and multiple computers in a **cluster**. When multiple processors using different architectures are present in the same computer system, we say it is a **heterogeneous computer**. An example would be a host processor and a co-processor with different instruction sets.

The last possible combination, MISD, is not particularly useful and is not used.

Another way often used to classify computers is by whether every processor can access a common **shared memory** or if each processor can only access memory local to it. The latter case is called **distributed memory**. Many distributed memory systems have local shared-memory subsystems. In particular, **clusters** are large distributed-memory systems formed by connecting many shared-memory computers ("**nodes**") with a high-speed communication network. Clusters are formed by connecting otherwise independent systems and so are almost always MIMD systems. Often shared-memory computers really do have physically distributed memory systems; it's just that the communication used to create the illusion of shared memory is implicit.

There is another related classification used especially by GPU vendors: **Single Instruction, Multiple Threads (SIMT)**. This corresponds to a **tiled SIMD** architecture consisting of multiple SIMD processors, where each SIMD processor emulates multiple "threads" (**fibers** in our terminology) using masking. SIMT processors may appear to have thousands of threads, but in fact blocks of these share a control processor, and divergent control flow can significantly reduce efficiency within a block. On the other hand, synchronization between fibers is basically free, because when control flow is emulated with masking the fibers are always running synchronously.

Memory access patterns can also affect the performance of a processor using the SIMT model. Typically each SIMD subprocessor in a SIMT machine is designed to use the data from a cache line. If memory access from different fibers access completely different cache lines, then performance drops since often the processor will require multiple memory cycles to resolve the memory access. These are called **divergent memory accesses**. In contrast, if all fibers in a SIMD core access the same cache lines, then the memory accesses can be coalesced and performance improved. It is important to note that this is exactly the opposite of what we want to do if the fibers really were separate threads. If the fibers were running on different cores, then we want to *avoid* having them access the same cache line. Therefore, while code written to use fibers may be implemented using hardware threads on multiple cores, code properly optimized for fibers will actually be suboptimal for threads when it comes to memory access.

2.4.4 **Evolution**

Predictions are very difficult, especially about the future.

(Niels Bohr)

Computers continue to evolve, although the fundamentals of parallelism and data locality will continue to be important. An important recent trend is the development of attached processing such as graphics accelerators and co-processors specialized for highly parallel workloads.

Graphics accelerators are also known as **GPUs**. While originally designed for graphics, GPUs have become general-purpose enough to be used for other computational tasks.

In this book we discuss, relatively briefly, a standard language and **application programming interface (API)** called OpenCL for programming **many-core** devices from multiple vendors, including GPUs. GPUs from NVIDIA can also be programmed with a proprietary language called CUDA. For the most part, OpenCL replicates the functionality of CUDA but provides the additional benefit of portability. OpenCL generalizes the idea of computation on a GPU to computation on multiple types of attached processing. With OpenCL, it is possible to write a parallel program that can run on the main processor, on a co-processor, or on a GPU. However, the semantic limitations of the OpenCL programming model reflect the limitations of GPUs.

Running computations on an accelerator or co-processor is commonly referred to as **offload**. As an alternative to OpenCL or CUDA, several compilers (including the Intel compiler) now support offload **pragmas** to move computations and data to an accelerator or co-processor with minimal code changes. Offload pragmas allow annotating the original source code rather than rewriting the "kernels" in a separate language, as with OpenCL. However, even with an offload pragma syntax, any code being offloaded still has to fit within the semantic limitations of the accelerator or co-processor to which it is being offloaded. Limitations of the target may force multiple versions of code. For example, if the target processor does not support recursion or function pointers, then it will not be possible to offload code that uses these language features to that processor. This is true even if the feature is being used implicitly. For example, the "virtual functions" used to support C++ class inheritance use function pointers in their implementation. Without function pointer support in the target hardware it is therefore not possible to offload general C++ code.

Some tuning of offloaded code is also usually needed, even if there is a semantic match. For example, GPUs are designed to handle large amounts of fine-grained parallelism with relatively small working sets and high coherence. Unlike traditional general-purpose CPUs, they have relatively small on-chip memories and depend on large numbers of active threads to hide latency, so that data can be streamed in from off-chip memory. They also have wide vector units and simulate many fibers (pseudo-threads) at once using masking to emulate control flow.

These architectural choices can be good tradeoffs for certain types of applications, which has given rise to the term **heterogeneous computing**: the idea that different processor designs are suitable for different kinds of workloads, so a computer should include multiple cores of different types. This would allow the most efficient core for a given application, or stage of an application, to be used. This concept can be extended to even more specialized hardware integrated into a processor, such as video decoders, although usually it refers to multiple types of programmable processor.

GPUs are not the only offload device available. It is also possible to use programmable hardware such as field programmable gate arrays (FPGAs) and co-processors made of many-core processors, such as the Intel MIC (Many Integrated Cores) architecture. While the MIC architecture can be programmed with OpenCL, it is also possible to use standard CPU programming models with it. However, the MIC architecture has many more cores than most CPUs (over 50), and each core has wide vector units (16 single-precision floats). This is similar in some ways to GPU architectures and enables high peak floating point performance. The tradeoff is that cache size per core is reduced, so it is even more important to have good data locality in implementations.

However, the main difference between MIC and GPUs is in the variety of programming models supported: The MIC is a general-purpose processor running a standard operating system (Linux) with full compiler support for C, C++, and Fortran. It also appears as a distributed-memory node on the network. The MIC architecture is therefore not limited to OpenCL or CUDA but can use any programming model (including, for instance, MPI) that would run on a mainstream processor. It also means that offload pragma syntax does not have to be limited by semantic differences between the *host processor* and the **target processor**.

Currently, GPUs are primarily available as discrete devices located on the PCIe bus and do not share memory with the host. This is also the current model for the MIC co-processor. However, this model has many inefficiencies, since data must be transferred across the PCIe bus to a memory local to the device before it can be processed.

As another possible model for integrating accelerators or co-processors within a computer system, GPU cores with their wide vector units have been integrated into the same die as the main processor cores by both AMD and Intel. NVIDIA also makes integrated CPU/GPU processors using ARM main cores for the embedded and mobile markets. For these, physical memory is shared by the GPU and CPU processors. Recently, APIs and hardware support have been rapidly evolving to allow data sharing without copying. This approach will allow much finer-grained heterogeneous computing, and processors may in fact evolve so that there are simply multiple cores with various characteristics on single die, not separate CPUs, GPUs, and co-processors.

Regardless of whether a parallel program is executed on a CPU, a GPU, or a many-core co-processor, the basic requirements are the same: Software must be designed for a high level of parallelism and with good data locality. Ultimately, these processor types are not that different; they just represent different points on a design spectrum that vary in the programming models they can support most efficiently.

2.5 PERFORMANCE THEORY

The primary purpose of parallelization, as discussed in this book, is performance. So what is performance? Usually it is about one of the following:

*   Reducing the *total time* it takes to compute a single result (**latency**; Section 2.5.1)
*   Increasing the *rate* at which a series of results can be computed (**throughput**; Section 2.5.1)
*   Reducing the *power consumption* of a computation (Section 2.5.3)

All these valid interpretations of "performance" can be achieved by parallelization.

There is also a distinction between improving performance to reduce costs or to meet a deadline. To reduce costs, you want to get more done within a fixed machine or power budget and usually are not willing to increase the total amount of computational work. Alternatively, to meet a deadline, you might be willing to increase the total amount of work if it means the jobs gets done sooner. For instance, in an interactive application, you might need to complete work fast enough to meet a certain frame rate or response time. In this case, extra work such as redundant or speculative computation might help meet the deadline. Choose such extra work with care, since it may actually decrease performance, as discussed in Section 2.5.6.

Once you have defined a performance target, then generally you should iteratively modify an application to improve its performance until the target is reached. It is important during this optimization process to start from a working implementation and validate the results after every program transformation. Fast computation of wrong answers is pointless, so continuous validation is strongly recommended to avoid wasting time tuning a broken implementation.

Validation should be given careful thought, in light of the original purpose of the program. Obtaining results "bit identical" to the serial program is sometimes unrealistic if the algorithm needs to be modified to support parallelization. Indeed, the parallel program's results, though different, may be as good for the overall purpose as the original serial program, or even better.

During the optimization process you should measure performance to see if you are making progress. Performance can be measured empirically on real hardware or estimated using analytic models based on ideal theoretical machines. Both approaches are valuable. Empirical measures account for real-world effects but often give little insight into root causes and therefore offer little guidance as to how performance could be improved or why it is limited. Analytic measures, particularly the **work-span** model explained in Section 2.5.6, ignore some real-world effects but give insight into the fundamental scaling limitations of a parallel algorithm. Analytic approaches also allow you to compare parallelization strategies at a lower cost than actually doing an implementation. We recommend using analytic measures to guide selection of an algorithm, accompanied by "back of the envelope" estimates of plausibility. After an algorithm is implemented, use empirical measures to understand and deal with effects ignored by the analytic model.

2.5.1 Latency and Throughput

The time it takes to complete a task is called **latency**. It has units of time. The scale can be anywhere from nanoseconds to days. Lower latency is better.

The rate a which a series of tasks can be completed is called **throughput**. This has units of work per unit time. Larger throughput is better. A related term is **bandwidth**, which refers to throughput rates that have a frequency-domain interpretation, particularly when referring to memory or communication transactions.

Some optimizations that improve throughput may increase the latency. For example, processing of a series of tasks can be parallelized by **pipelining**, which overlaps different stages of processing. However, pipelining adds overhead since the stages must now synchronize and communicate, so the time it takes to get one complete task through the whole pipeline may take longer than with a simple serial implementation.

Related to latency is **response time**. This measure is often used in transaction processing systems, such as web servers, where many transactions from different sources need to be processed. To maintain a given quality of service each transaction should be processed in a given amount of time. However, some latency may be sacrificed even in this case in order to improve throughput. In particular, tasks may be queued up, and time spent waiting in the queue increases each task's latency. However, queuing tasks improves the overall utilization of the computing resources and so improves throughput and reduces costs.

"Extra" parallelism can also be used for **latency hiding**. Latency hiding does not actually reduce latency; instead, it improves utilization and throughput by quickly switching to another task whenever one task needs to wait for a high-latency activity. Section 2.5.9 says more about this.

2.5.2 Speedup, Efficiency, and Scalability

Two important metrics related to performance and parallelism are **speedup** and **efficiency**. Speedup compares the latency for solving the identical computational problem on one hardware unit (**"worker"**) versus on P hardware units:

$$\text{speedup} = S_P = \frac{T_1}{T_P} \tag{2.1}$$

where T_1 is the latency of the program with one worker and T_P is the latency on P workers.

Efficiency is speedup divided by the number of workers:

$$\text{efficiency} = \frac{S_P}{P} = \frac{T_1}{PT_P}. \tag{2.2}$$

Efficiency measures return on hardware investment. Ideal efficiency is 1 (often reported as 100%), which corresponds to a linear speedup, but many factors can reduce efficiency below this ideal.

If T_1 is the latency of the parallel program running with a single worker, Equation 2.1 is sometimes called **relative speedup**, because it shows relative improvement from using P workers. This uses a serialization of the parallel algorithm as the baseline. However, sometimes there is a better serial algorithm that does not parallelize well. If so, it is fairer to use that algorithm for T_1, and report **absolute speedup**, as long as both algorithms are solving an identical computational problem. Otherwise, using an unnecessarily poor baseline artificially inflates speedup and efficiency.

In some cases, it is also fair to use algorithms that produce numerically different answers, as long as they solve the same problem according to the problem definition. In particular, reordering floating point computations is sometimes unavoidable. Since floating point operations are not truly associative, reordering can lead to differences in output, sometimes radically different if a floating point comparison leads to a divergence in control flow. Whether the serial or parallel result is actually more accurate depends on the circumstances.

Speedup, not efficiency, is what you see in advertisements for parallel computers, because speedups can be large impressive numbers. Efficiencies, except in unusual circumstances, do not exceed 100% and often sound depressingly low. A speedup of 100 sounds better than an efficiency of 10%, even if both are for the same program and same machine with 1000 cores.

An algorithm that runs P times faster on P processors is said to exhibit **linear speedup**. Linear speedup is rare in practice, since there is extra work involved in distributing work to processors and coordinating them. In addition, an optimal serial algorithm may be able to do less work overall than an optimal parallel algorithm for certain problems, so the achievable speedup may be sublinear in P, even on theoretical ideal machines. Linear speedup is usually considered optimal since we can serialize the parallel algorithm, as noted above, and run it on a serial machine with a linear slowdown as a worst-case baseline.

However, as exceptions that prove the rule, an occasional program will exhibit **superlinear speedup**—an efficiency greater than 100%. Some common causes of superlinear speedup include:

- Restructuring a program for parallel execution can cause it to use cache memory better, even when run on with a single worker! But if T_1 from the old program is still used for the speedup calculation, the speedup can appear to be superlinear. See Section 10.5 for an example of restructuring that often reduces T_1 significantly.
- The program's performance is strongly dependent on having a sufficient amount of cache memory, and no single worker has access to that amount. If multiple workers bring that amount to bear, because they do not all share the same cache, absolute speedup really can be superlinear.
- The parallel algorithm may be *more* efficient than the equivalent serial algorithm, since it may be able to avoid work that its serialization would be forced to do. For example, in search tree problems, searching multiple branches in parallel sometimes permits chopping off branches (by using results computed in sibling branches) sooner than would occur in the serial code.

However, for the most part, sublinear speedup is the norm.

Section 2.5.4 discusses an important limit on speedup: **Amdahl's Law**. It considers speedup as P varies and the problem size remains fixed. This is sometimes called **strong scalability**. Section 2.5.5 discusses an alternative, **Gustafson-Barsis' Law**, which assumes the problem size grows with P. This is sometimes called **weak scalability**. But before discussing speedup further, we discuss another motivation for parallelism: power.

2.5.3 Power

Parallelization can reduce power consumption. CMOS is the dominant circuit technology for current computer hardware. CMOS power consumption is the sum of dynamic power consumption and static power consumption [VF05]. For a circuit supply voltage V and operating frequency f, CMOS dynamic power dissipation is governed by the proportion

$$\mathcal{P}_{dynamic} \propto V^2 f.$$

The frequency dependence is actually more severe than the equation suggests, because the highest frequency at which a CMOS circuit can operate is roughly proportional to the voltage. Thus dynamic power varies as the *cube* of the maximum frequency. Static power consumption is nominally independent of frequency but is dependent on voltage. The relation is more complex than for dynamic power, but, for sake of argument, assume it varies cubically with voltage. Since the necessary voltage is proportional to the maximum frequency, the static power consumption varies as the cube of the maximum frequency, too. Under this assumption we can use a simple overall model where the total power consumption varies by the cube of the frequency.

Suppose that parallelization speeds up an application by 1.5× on two cores. You can use this speedup either to reduce latency or reduce power. If your latency requirement is already met, then reducing the clock rate of the cores by 1.5× will save a significant amount of power. Let $\mathcal{P}_1$ be the power consumed by one core running the serial version of the application. Then the power consumed

Table 2.1 Running Fewer Cores Faster [Cor11c]. The table shows how the maximum core frequency for an Intel core i5-2500T chip depends on the number of active cores. The last column shows the parallel efficiency over all four cores required to match the speed of using only one active core.

Active Cores	Maximum Frequency (GHz)	Breakeven Efficiency
4	2.4	34%
3	2.8	39%
2	3.2	52%
1	3.3	100%

by two cores running the parallel version of the application will be given by:

$$P_2 = 2 \left(\frac{1}{1.5} \right)^3 P_1$$

$$\approx 0.6 P_1,$$

where the factor of 2 arises from having two cores. Using two cores running the parallelized version of the application at the lower clock rate has the same latency but uses (in this case) 40% less power.

Unfortunately, reality is not so simple. Current chips have so many transistors that frequency and voltage are already scaled down to near the lower limit just to avoid overheating, so there is not much leeway for raising the frequency. For example, Intel Turbo Boost Technology enables cores to be put to sleep so that the power can be devoted to the remaining cores while keeping the chip within its thermal design power limits. Table 2.1 shows an example. Still, the table shows that even low parallel efficiencies offer more performance on this chip than serial execution.

Another way to save power is to "race to sleep" [DHKC09]. In this strategy, we try to get the computation done as fast as possible (with the lowest latency) so that *all* the cores can be put in a sleep state that draws very little power. This approach is attractive if a significant fraction of the wakeful power is fixed regardless of how many cores are running.

Especially in mobile devices, parallelism can be used to reduce latency. This reduces the time the device, including its display and other components, is powered up. This not only improves the user experience but also reduces the overall power consumption for performing a user's task: a win-win.

2.5.4 Amdahl's Law

> *... the effort expended on achieving high parallel processing rates is wasted unless it is accompanied by achievements in sequential processing rates of very nearly the same magnitude.*
>
> **(Gene Amdahl [Amd67])**

Amdahl argued that the execution time T_1 of a program falls into two categories:

- Time spent doing non-parallelizable serial work
- Time spent doing parallelizable work

Call these W_{ser} and W_{par}, respectively. Given P workers available to do the parallelizable work, the times for sequential execution and parallel execution are:

$$T_1 = W_{ser} + W_{par},$$
$$T_P \geq W_{ser} + W_{par}/P.$$

The bound on T_P assumes no superlinear speedup, and is an exact equality only if the parallelizable work can be perfectly parallelized. Plugging these relations into the definition of speedup yields **Amdahl's Law**:

$$S_P < \frac{W_{ser} + W_{par}}{W_{ser} + W_{par}/P}. \tag{2.3}$$

Figure 2.4 visualizes this bound.

Amdahl's Law has an important corollary. Let f be the non-parallelizable serial fraction of the total work. Then the following equalities hold:

$$W_{ser} = f T_1,$$
$$W_{par} = (1 - f)T_1.$$

Substitute these into Equation 2.3 and simplify to get:

$$S_P \leq \frac{1}{f + (1 - f)/P}. \tag{2.4}$$

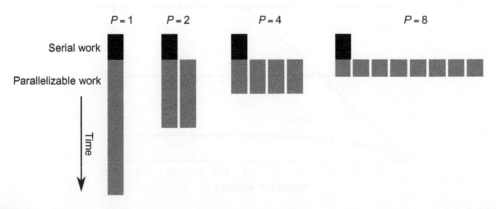

FIGURE 2.4

Amdahl's Law. Speedup is limited by the non-parallelizable serial portion of the work.

Now consider what happens when P tends to infinity:

$$S_\infty \le \frac{1}{f}. \tag{2.5}$$

Speedup is limited by the fraction of the work that is not parallelizable, even using an infinite number of processors. If 10% of the application cannot be parallelized, then the maximum speedup is 10×. If 1% of the application cannot be parallelized, then the maximum speedup is 100×. In practice, an infinite number of processors is not available. With fewer processors, the speedup may be reduced, which gives an upper bound on the speedup. Amdahl's Law is graphed in Figure 2.5, which shows the bound for various values of f and P. For example, observe that even with $f = 0.001$ (that is, only 0.1% of the application is serial) and $P = 2048$, a program's speedup is limited to 672×. This limitation on speedup can also be viewed as inefficient use of parallel hardware resources for large serial fractions, as shown in Figure 2.6.

2.5.5 Gustafson-Barsis' Law

. . . speedup should be measured by scaling the problem to the number of processors, not by fixing the problem size.

(John Gustafson [Gus88])

Amdahl's Law views programs as fixed and the computer as changeable, but experience indicates that as computers get new capabilities, applications change to exploit these features. Most of today's

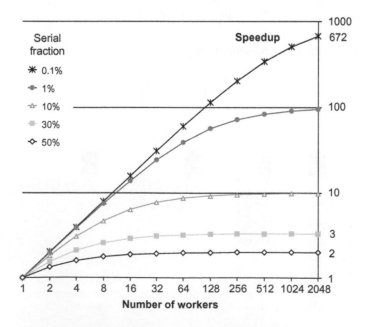

FIGURE 2.5

Amdahl's Law: speedup. The scalability of parallelization is limited by the non-parallelizable (serial) portion of the workload. The serial fraction is the percentage of code that is not parallelized.

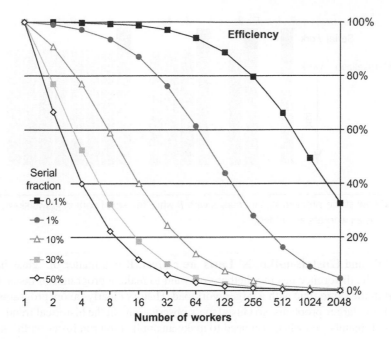

FIGURE 2.6

Amdahl's Law: efficiency. Even when speedups are possible, the *efficiency* can easily become poor. The serial fraction is the percentage of code that is not parallelized.

applications would not run on computers from 10 years ago, and many would run poorly on machines that are just 5 years old. This observation is not limited to obvious applications such as games; it applies also to office applications, web browsers, photography software, DVD production and editing software, and Google Earth.

More than two decades after the appearance of Amdahl's Law, John Gustafson[2] noted that several programs at Sandia National Labs were speeding up by over 1000×. Clearly, Amdahl's Law could be evaded.

Gustafson noted that problem sizes grow as computers become more powerful. As the problem size grows, the work required for the parallel part of the problem frequently grows much faster than the serial part. If this is true for a given application, then as the problem size grows the serial fraction decreases and speedup improves.

Figure 2.7 visualizes this using the assumption that the serial portion is constant while the parallel portion grows linearly with the problem size. On the left is the application running with one worker. As workers are added, the application solves bigger problems in the same time, not the same problem in less time. The serial portion still takes the same amount of time to perform, but diminishes as a fraction of the whole. Once the serial portion becomes insignificant, speedup grows practically at the same rate as the number of processors, thus achieving linear speedup.

---

[2]His paper gives credit to E. Barsis, hence we call it Gustafson-Barsis' Law. It is sometimes called just Gustafson's Law.

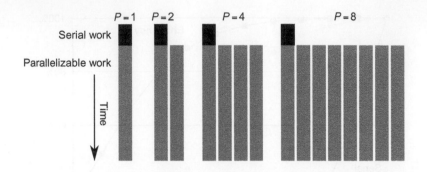

FIGURE 2.7

Gustafson-Barsis' Law. If the problem size increases with *P* while the serial portion grows slowly or remains fixed, speedup grows as workers are added.

Both Amdahl's and **Gustafson-Barsis' Laws** are correct. It is a matter of "glass half empty" or "glass half full." The difference lies in whether you want to make a program run faster with the same workload or run in the same time with a larger workload. History clearly favors programs getting more complex and solving larger problems, so Gustafson's observations fit the historical trend. Nevertheless, Amdahl's Law still haunts you when you need to make an application run faster on the same workload to meet some latency target.

Furthermore, Gustafson-Barsis' observation is not a license for carelessness. In order for it to hold it is critical to ensure that serial work grows much more slowly than parallel work, and that synchronization and other forms of overhead are scalable.

2.5.6 Work-Span Model

This section introduces the **work-span** model for parallel computation. The work-span model is much more useful than Amdahl's law for estimating program running times, because it takes into account imperfect parallelization. Furthermore, it is not just an upper bound as it also provides a lower bound. It lets you estimate T_P from just two numbers: T_1 and $T\infty$.

In the **work-span** model, tasks form a **directed acyclic graph**. A task is ready to run if all of its predecessors in the graph are done. The basic work-span model ignores communication and memory access costs. It also assumes task scheduling is **greedy**, which means the scheduler never lets a hardware worker sit idle while there is a task ready to run.

The extreme times for $P = 1$ and $P = \infty$ are so important that they have names. Time T_1 is called the **work** of an algorithm. It is the time that a serialization of the algorithm would take and is simply the total time it would take to complete all tasks. Time T_∞ is called the **span** of an algorithm. The span is the time a parallel algorithm would take on an ideal machine with an infinite number of processors. Span is equivalent to the length of the **critical path**. The critical path is the longest chain of tasks that must be executed one after each other. Synonyms for span in the literature are **step complexity** or **depth**.

Figure 2.8 shows an example. Each box represents a task taking unit time, with arrows showing dependencies. The work is 18, because there are 18 tasks. The span is 6, because the longest chain of

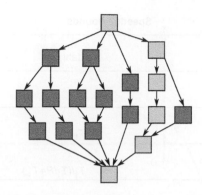

FIGURE 2.8

Work and span. Arrows denote dependencies between tasks. Work is the total amount of computation, while span is given by the critical path. In this example, if each task takes unit time, the work is 18 and the span is 6.

tasks that must be evaluated one after the other contains 6 tasks.

Work and span each put a limit on speedup. Superlinear speedup is impossible in the work-span model:

$$S_P = \frac{T_1}{T_P} \leq \frac{T_1}{T_1/P} = P. \tag{2.6}$$

On an ideal machine with greedy scheduling, adding processors never slows down an algorithm:

$$S_P = \frac{T_1}{T_P} \leq \frac{T_1}{T_\infty}. \tag{2.7}$$

Or more colloquially:

$$\text{speedup} \leq \frac{\text{work}}{\text{span}}.$$

For example, the speedup for Figure 2.8 can never exceed 3, because $T_1/T_\infty = 18/6 = 3$. Real machines introduce synchronization overhead, not only for the synchronization constructs themselves, but also for communication. A span that includes these overheads is called a **burdened span** [HLL10].

The span provides more than just an upper bound on speedup. It can also be used to estimate a *lower* bound on speedup for an ideal machine. An inequality known as **Brent's Lemma** [Bre74] bounds T_P in terms of the work T_1 and the span T_∞:

$$T_P \leq (T_1 - T_\infty)/P + T_\infty. \tag{2.8}$$

Here is the argument behind the lemma. The total work T_1 can be divided into two categories: perfectly parallelizable work and imperfectly parallelizable work. The *imperfectly parallelizable work* takes time T_∞ no matter how many workers there are. The *perfectly parallelizable work* remaining takes time $T_1 - T_\infty$ with a single worker, and since it is perfectly parallelizable it speeds up by P if

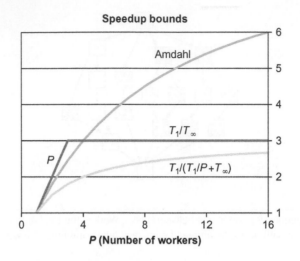

Speedup bounds

FIGURE 2.9

Amdahl was an optimist. Using the work and span of Figure 2.8, this graph illustrates that the upper bound by Amdahl's Law is often much higher than what work-span analysis reveals. Furthermore, work-span analysis provides a *lower* bound for speedup, too, assuming greedy scheduling on an ideal machine.

all P workers are working on it. But if not all P workers are working on it, then at least one worker is working on the T_∞ component. The argument resembles Amdahl's argument, but generalizes the notion of an *inherently serial* portion of work to *imperfectly parallelizable* work.

Though the argument resembles Amdahl's argument, it proves something quite different. Amdahl's argument put a *lower* bound on T_P and is exact only if the parallelizable portion of a program is perfectly parallelizable. Brent's Lemma puts an *upper* bound on T_P. It says what happens if the worst possible assignment of tasks to workers is chosen.

In general, work-span analysis is a far better guide than Amdahl's Law, because it usually provides a tighter upper bound and also provides a lower bound. Figure 2.9 compares the bounds given by Amdahl's Law and work-span analysis for the task graph in Figure 2.8. There are 18 tasks. The first and last tasks constitute serial work; the other tasks constitute parallelizable work. Hence, the fraction of serial work is $2/18 = 1/9$. By Amdahl's Law, the limit on speedup is 9. Work-span analysis says the speedup is limited by the $\min(P, T_1/T_\infty) = \min(P, 18/6)$, which is at most 3, a *third* of what Amdahl's law indicates. The difference is that the work-span analysis accounted for *how parallelizable* the parallel work really is. The bottom curve in the figure is the lower bound provided by Brent's lemma. It says, for example, that with 4 workers a speedup of 2 is guaranteed, no matter how the tasks are assigned to workers.

Brent's Lemma leads to a useful formula for estimating T_P from the work T_1 and span T_∞. To get much speedup, T_1 must be significantly larger than T_∞, In this case, $T_1 - T_\infty \approx T_1$ and the right side of 2.8 also turns out to be a good lower bound estimate on T_P. So the following approximation works well in practice for estimating running time:

$$T_P \approx T_1/P + T_\infty \quad \text{if } T_\infty \ll T_1. \tag{2.9}$$

The approximation says a lot:

- Increasing the total work T_1 hurts parallel execution proportionately.
- The span T_∞ impacts scalability, even when P is finite.

When designing a parallel algorithm, avoid creating significantly more work for the sake of parallelization, and focus on reducing the span, because the span is the fundamental asymptotic limit on scalability. Increase the work only if it enables a drastic decrease in span. An example of this is the scan pattern, where the span can be reduced from linear to logarithmic complexity by doubling the work (Section 8.11).

Brent's Lemma also leads to a formal motivation for **overdecomposition**. From Equation 2.8 the following condition can be derived:

$$S_P = T_1/T_P \approx P \quad \text{if } T_1/T_\infty \gg P. \tag{2.10}$$

It says that **greedy scheduling** achieves linear speedup if a problem is overdecomposed to create much more potential parallelism than the hardware can use. The excess parallelism is called the **parallel slack**, and is defined by:

$$\text{parallel slack} = \frac{S_\infty}{P} = \frac{T_1}{PT_\infty} \tag{2.11}$$

In practice, a parallel slack of at least 8 works well.

If you remember only one thing about time estimates for parallel programs, remember Equation 2.9. From it, you can derive performance estimates just by knowing the work T_1 and span T_∞ of an algorithm. However, this formula assumes the following three important qualifications:

- Memory bandwidth is not a limiting resource.
- There is no speculative work. In other words, the parallel code is doing T_1 total work, period.
- The scheduler is greedy.

The task schedulers in Intel Cilk Plus and Intel TBB are close enough to greedy that you can use the approximation as long as you avoid **locks**. Locks make scheduling non-greedy, because a worker can get stuck waiting to acquire a contended lock while there is other work to do. Making performance predictable by Equation 2.9 is another good reason to avoid locks. Another trait that can make a scheduler non-greedy is requiring that certain tasks run on certain cores. In a greedy scheduler, if a core is free it should immediately be able to start work on any available task.

2.5.7 Asymptotic Complexity

Asymptotic complexity is the key to comparing algorithms. Comparing absolute times is not particularly meaningful, because they are specific to particular hardware. Asymptotic complexity reveals deeper mathematical truths about algorithms that are independent of hardware.

In a serial setting, the **time complexity** of an algorithm summarizes how the execution time of algorithm grows with the input size. The **space complexity** similarly summarizes how the amount of memory an algorithm requires grows with the input size. Both these complexity measures ignore constant factors, because those depend on machine details such as instruction set or clock rate. Complexity measures instead focus on asymptotic growth, which is independent of the particular machine and thus permit comparison of different algorithms without regard to particular hardware. For sufficiently large inputs, asymptotic effects will dominate any constant factor advantage.

Asymptotic time complexity computed from the work-span model is not perfect as a tool for predicting performance. The standard work-span model considers only computation, not communication or memory effects. Still, idealizations can be instructive, such as the ideal massless pulleys and frictionless planes encountered in physics class. Asymptotic complexity is the equivalent idealization for analyzing algorithms; it is a strong indicator of performance on large-enough problem sizes and reveals an algorithm's fundamental limits.

Here is a quick reminder of asymptotic complexity notation [Knu76]:

- The **"big O notation"** denotes a set of functions with an upper bound. $O(f(N))$ is the set of all functions $g(N)$ such that there exist positive constants c and N_0 with $|g(N)| \leq c \cdot f(N)$ for $N \geq N_0$.
- The **"big Omega notation"** denotes a set of functions with an lower bound. $\Omega(f(N))$ is the set of all functions $g(N)$ such that there exist constants c and N_0 with $g(N) \geq c \cdot f(N)$ for $N \geq N_0$.
- The **"big Theta notation"** denotes a set of functions with both upper and lower bounds. $\Theta(f(N))$ means the set of all functions $g(N)$ such that there exist positive constants c_1, c_2, and N_0 with $c_1 \cdot f(N) \leq g(N) \leq c_2 \cdot f(N)$ for $N \geq N_0$.

We follow the traditional abuse of "=" in complexity notation to mean, depending on context, set membership or set inclusion. The "equality" $T(N) = O(f(N))$ really means the membership $T(N) \in O(f(N))$. That is equivalent to saying $T(N)$ is bounded from above by $c \cdot f(N)$ for sufficiently large c and N. Similarly, the "equality" $O(f(N)) = O(h(N))$ really means the set inclusion $O(f(N)) \subseteq O(h(N))$. So when we write $T(N) = O(N^2) = O(N^3)$, we really mean $T(N) \in O(N^2) \subseteq O(N^3)$, but the latter would depart from tradition.

In asymptotic analysis of serial programs, "O" is most common, because the usual intent is to prove an upper bound on a program's time or space. For parallel programs, "Θ" is often more useful, because you often need to prove that a *ratio*, such as a speedup, is above a lower bound, and this requires computing a lower bound on the numerator and an upper bound on the denominator. For example, you might need to prove that using P workers makes a parallel algorithm run at least $\sqrt{P}$ times faster than the serial version. That is, you want a lower bound ("Ω") on the speedup. That requires proving a lower bound ("Ω") on the serial time and an upper bound ("O") on the parallel time. When computing speedup, the parallel time appears in the denominator and the serial time appears in the numerator. A larger parallel time reduces speedup while a larger serial time increases speedup. However, instead of dealing with separate bounds like this for each measure of interest, it is often easier to deal with the "Θ" bound.

For a simple example of parallel asymptotic complexity, consider computing the dot product of two vectors of length N with P workers. This can be done by partitioning the vectors among the P workers so each computes a dot product of length N/P. These subproducts can be summed in a tree-like fashion, with a tree height of $\lg P$, assuming that $P \leq N$. Note that we use lg for the base 2 logarithm. Hence, the asymptotic running time is:

$$T_P(N) = \Theta(N/P + \lg P). \tag{2.12}$$

For now, consider what that equation says. As long as $\lg p$ is insignificant compared to N/P:

- For fixed P, doubling the input size doubles the time.

- For fixed N, doubling the number of workers halves the execution time.
- Doubling both the input size and workers keeps the execution time about the same. In other words, the code exhibits weak scaling.

The equation also warns you that if $\lg P$ is not insignificant compared to N, doubling the workers will *not* halve the execution time.

2.5.8 Asymptotic Speedup and Efficiency

Speedup and efficiency can be treated asymptotically as well, using a ratio of Θ complexities. For the previous dot product example, the **asymptotic speedup** is:

$$\frac{T_1}{T_P} = \frac{\Theta(N)}{\Theta(N/P + \lg P)}$$

$$= \Theta\left(\frac{N}{N/P + \lg P}\right).$$

When $\lg P$ is insignificant compared to N, the **asymptotic speedup** is $\Theta(P)$. The **asymptotic efficiency** is:

$$\frac{T_1}{P \cdot T_P} = \Theta\left(\frac{N}{N + P \lg P}\right). \tag{2.13}$$

When $N = \Theta(P \lg P)$, the **asymptotic efficiency** is $\Theta(1)$. Note that extra $\lg P$ factor. Merely scaling up the input by a factor of P is not enough to deliver $\Theta(1)$ weak scaling as P grows.

Remember that if there is a better serial algorithm that does not parallelize well, it is fairer to use that algorithm for T_1 when comparing algorithms. Do not despair if a parallelized algorithm does not get near 100% parallel efficiency, however. Few algorithms do. Indeed, an efficiency of $\Theta(1/\sqrt{P})$ is "break even" in a sense. At the turn of the century, speed improvements from adding transistors were diminishing, to the point where serial computer speed was growing as the square root of the number of transistors on a chip. So if the transistors for P workers were all devoted to making a single super-worker faster, that super-worker would speed up by about $\sqrt{P}$. That's an efficiency of only $1/\sqrt{P}$. So if your efficiency is significantly better than $1/\sqrt{P}$, your algorithm really is still benefitting from the parallel revolution.

2.5.9 Little's Formula

Little's formula relates the throughput and latency of a system to its **concurrency**. Consider a system in steady state that has items to be processed arriving at regular intervals, where the desired throughput rate is R items per unit time, the latency to process each item is L units of time, and the number of items concurrently in the system is C. Little's formula states the following relation between these three quantities:

$$C = R \cdot L. \tag{2.14}$$

Concurrency is similar but not identical to parallelism. In parallelism, all work is going on at the same time. Concurrency is the total number of tasks that are in progress at the same time, although they may not all be running simultaneously. Concurrency is a more general term that includes actual parallelism but also simulated parallelism, for example by time-slicing on a scalar processor.

Extra concurrency can be used to improve throughput when there are long latency operations in each task. For example, memory reads that miss in cache can take a long time to complete, relative to the speed at which the processor can execute instructions. While the processor is waiting for such long-latency operations to complete, if there is other work to do, it can switch to other tasks instead of just waiting. The same concept can be used to hide the latency of disk transactions, but since the latency is so much higher for disk transactions correspondingly more parallelism is needed to hide it.

Suppose a core executes 1 operation per clock, and each operation waits on one memory access with a latency L of 3 clocks. The latency is fully hidden when there are $C = R \cdot L = 1 \cdot 3$ operations in flight. To be in flight simultaneously, those operations need to be independent. Hardware often tries to detect such opportunities in a single thread, but often there are not enough to reach the desired concurrency C. Hardware multithreading can be used to increase the number of operations in flight, if the programmer specifies sufficient parallelism to keep the hardware threads busy. Most famously, the Tera MTA had 128 threads per processor, and each thread could have up to 8 memory references in flight [SCB+98]. That allowed it to hide memory latency so well that its designers eliminated caches altogether!

The bottom line is that parallelizing to hide latency and maximize throughput requires over-decomposing a problem to generate extra concurrency per physical unit.

Be warned, however, that hardware multithreading can worsen latency in some cases. The problem is that the multiple threads typically share a fixed-size cache. If n of these threads access disjoint sets of memory locations, each gets a fraction $1/n$ of the cache. If the concurrency is insufficient to fully hide the latency of the additional cache misses, running a single thread might be faster.

2.6 PITFALLS

Parallel programming entails additional pitfalls any time there are dependencies between parallel tasks. Dependencies between parallel tasks require **synchronization**. Too little synchronization can lead to **non-deterministic** behavior. Too much synchronization can unnecessarily limit scaling, or worse yet, cause **deadlock**.

2.6.1 Race Conditions

A **race condition** occurs when concurrent tasks perform operations on the same memory location without proper synchronization, and one of the memory operations is a write. Code with a race may operate correctly sometimes but fail unpredictably at other times. Consider the code in Table 2.2, where two tasks attempt to add 1 and 2 respectively to a shared variable X. The intended net effect is likely to be X += 3. But because of the lack of synchronization, two other net effects are possible: X += 1 or X += 2. To see how one of the updates could be lost, consider what happens if both tasks read X before either one writes to it. When the writes to X occur, the effect of the first write will be lost when the second write happens. Eliminating temporary variables and writing X += 1 and Y += 1 does not help, because the compiler might generate multiple instructions anyway, or the hardware might even break += into multiple operations.

Table 2.2 Two tasks race to update shared variable X. Interleaving can cause one of the updates to be lost.

Task A	Task B
a = X;	b = X;
a += 1;	b += 2;
X = a;	X = b;

Table 2.3 Race not explainable by serial interleaving. Assume that X and Y are initially zero. After both tasks complete, both a and b can be zero, even though such an outcome is impossible by serial interleaving of the instruction streams.

Task A	Task B
X = 1;	Y = 1;
a = Y;	b = X;

Race conditions are pernicious because they do not necessarily produce obvious failures and yet can lead to corrupted data [Adv10, Boe11]. If you are unlucky, a program with a race can work fine during testing but fail once it is in the customer's hands. Races are not limited to memory locations. They can happen with files and I/O too. For example, if two tasks try to print Hello at the same time, the output might look like HeHelllloo.

Surprisingly, analyzing all possible interleaving of instructions is *not* enough to predict the outcome of a race, because different hardware threads may see the same events occur in different orders. The cause is not relativistic physics, but the memory system. However, the effects can be equally counterintuitive. Table 2.3 shows one such example. It is representative of the key part of certain synchronization algorithms. Assume that X and Y are initially zero. After tasks A and B execute the code, what are the possible values for a and b? A naïve approach is to assume **sequential consistency**, which means that the instructions behave as if they were interleaved in some serial order. Figure 2.10 summarizes the possible interleavings. The first two graphs show two possible interleavings. The last graph shows a partial ordering that accounts for four interleavings. Below each graph is the final outcome for a and b.

Yet when run on modern hardware, the set of all possible outcomes can also include a = 0 and b = 0! Modern hardware is often *not* sequentially consistent. For example, the compiler or hardware may reorder the operations so that Task A sees Task B read Y before it writes X. Task B may see Task A similarly reordered. Each task sees that it executed instructions in the correct order and sees the other task deviate. Table 2.4 shows what the two tasks might see. Both are correct, because there is no global ordering of operations to different memory locations. There are system-specific ways to stop the compiler or hardware from reordering operations, called **memory fences** [AMSS10, Cor11a, TvPG06], but

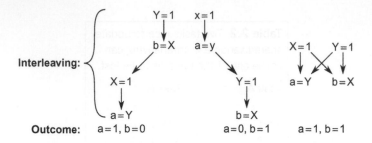

FIGURE 2.10

All sequentially consistent outcomes of Table 2.3. The graphs summarize all possible interleavings of instructions from Table 2.3, yet real hardware can deliver the outcome a = 0 and b = 0.

Table 2.4 No global ordering of operations to different locations. The hardware might reorder the operations from Table 2.3 so that different tasks see the operations happen in different orders. In each view, a task sees its own operations in the order specified by the original program.

Viewpoint of Task B	Viewpoint of Task A
a = Y	b = X
b = X	a = Y
Y = 1	X = 1
X = 1	Y = 1

these are beyond the scope of this book. Instead, we will emphasize machine-independent techniques to avoid races altogether.

The discussion here should impress upon you that races are tricky. Fortunately, the patterns in this book, as well as the programming models we will discuss, let you avoid races and not have to think about tricky memory ordering issues. This is a good thing because memory ordering is exactly the kind of thing that is likely to change with future hardware. Depending too much on the low-level implementation of current memory systems will likely lead to code that will be difficult to port to future processors.

2.6.2 Mutual Exclusion and Locks

Locks are a low-level way to eliminate races. This section explains what locks are and why they should be a means of last resort. Perhaps surprisingly, none of the examples in the rest of this book requires a lock. However, sometimes locks are the best way to synchronize part of a program.

Table 2.5 Mutex eliminates the race in Table 2.2. The mutex M serializes updates of X, so neither update corrupts the other one.

Task A	Task B
`extern tbb::mutex M;`	`extern tbb::mutex M;`
`M.lock();`	`M.lock();`
`a = X;`	`b = X;`
`a += 1;`	`b += 2;`
`X = a;`	`X = b;`
`M.unlock();`	`M.unlock();`

The race in Table 2.2 can be eliminated by a **mutual exclusion** region. Using mutual exclusion, the tasks can coordinate so they take turns updating X, rather than both trying to do it at once. Mutual exclusion is typically implemented with a **lock**, often called a **mutex**. A mutex has two states, locked and unlocked, and two operations:

Lock: Change the state from unlocked to locked.
Unlock: Change the state from locked to unlocked.

These operations are implemented atomically, meaning that they appear instantaneous to other tasks and are sequentially consistent.

The lock operation on an already locked mutex must wait until it becomes unlocked. Once a task completes a lock operation, it is said to *own the mutex* or *hold a lock* until it unlocks it. Table 2.5 shows how to use a mutex to remove the race in Table 2.2. Mutex M is presumed to be declared where X is declared. The lock–unlock operations around the updates of X ensure that the threads take their turn updating it. Furthermore, the lock–unlock pair of operations demarcate a "cage." Instruction reordering is prohibited from allowing instructions inside the cage to appear to execute outside the cage, preventing counterintuitive surprises. However, be aware that other threads might see instructions written *outside* the cage appear to execute inside the cage.

An important point about mutexes is that they should be used to *protect logical invariants*, not memory locations. In our example, the invariant is "the value of X is the sum of the values added to it." What this means is that the invariant is true outside the mutual exclusion region, but within the region we may have a sequence of operations that might temporarily violate it. However, the mutex groups these operations together so they can be treated essentially as a single operation that does not violate the invariant. Just using a mutex around each individual read or write would protect the memory location, but not the invariant. In particular, such an arrangement might expose temporary states in which the invariant is violated. In more complex examples, such as with data structures, a mutex protects an invariant among multiple locations. For example, a mutex protecting a linked list might protect the invariant "the next field of each element points to the next element in the list." In such a scheme, any time a task traverses the list, it must first lock the mutex; otherwise, it might walk next fields under construction by another task.

2.6.3 Deadlock

Deadlock occurs when at least two tasks wait for each other and each cannot resume until the other task proceeds. This happens easily when code requires locking of multiple mutexes at once. If Task A needs to lock mutexes M and N, it might lock M first and then try to lock N. Meanwhile, if Task B needs the same two locks but locks N first and then tries to lock M, both A and B will wait forever if the timing is such that each performs the first locking operation before attempting the second. This situation is called **deadlock**. The impasse can be resolved only if one task releases the lock it is holding.

There are several ways to avoid deadlock arising from mutexes:

Avoid mutexes when possible. Consider replicating the resource protected by the mutex. Alternatively, synchronize access to it using a higher-level pattern. For example, Section 12.2 shows how to use `tbb::pipeline` to serialize access to input and output files without any mutexes. In Intel Cilk Plus, hyperobjects (see Section 8.10) often eliminate the need for explicit mutual exclusion by way of implicit replication. The Intel ArBB programming model uses deterministic data-parallel patterns and manages without locks at all. In some cases, the TBB concurrent collections, which are based on atomic operations rather than locks, can be used for shared data structures.

Hold at most one lock at a time. An important corollary of this rule is *never call other people's code while holding a lock* unless you are certain that the other code never acquires a lock.

Always acquire locks on multiple mutexes in the same order. In the earlier example, deadlock is avoided if Task A and Task B both always try to lock mutex X first before trying to lock mutex Y.

Some common tactics for achieving the "same order" strategy include:

Stratify the mutexes. Assign each mutex a level such that two mutexes on the same level are never locked at the same time, then always acquire locks in level order. For example, in a tree where there is a mutex for each tree node, the levels might correspond to levels in a tree.

Sort the mutexes to be locked. If you always know the entire set of locks to be acquired before acquiring any of them, sort the mutex addresses and acquire the locks in that order. Note: if the memory allocations are not the same from run to run of the program, which might be accidental (non-deterministic memory allocation) or intentional (randomization of memory allocations for increased security), then the order may be different on different runs, complicating debugging and profiling.

Backoff. When acquiring a set of locks, if any lock cannot be acquired immediately, release all locks already acquired. This approach requires that the mutex support a "try lock" operation that immediately returns if the lock cannot be acquired.

Locks are not intrinsically evil. Sometimes they are the best solution to a synchronization problem. Indeed, TBB provides several kinds of mutexes for use with it and other programming models. But consider the alternatives to locks and avoid them if you can. If you must use locks, be careful to avoid situations that can cause deadlock.

Locks are not the only way to stumble into deadlock. Any time you write code that involves "wait until something happens," you need to ensure that "something" is not dependent on the current task doing anything else.

2.6.4 Strangled Scaling

Deadlock is not the only potential problem arising from synchronization. By definition, a mutex serializes execution and adds a potential Amdahl bottleneck. When tasks contend for the same mutex, the impact on scaling can be severe, even worse than if the protected code was serial. Not only does Amdahl bottleneck come into play, but the status of the protected memory locations must be communicated between cores, thus adding communication costs not paid by the serial equivalent.

Sometimes when profiling a piece of parallel code, the profiler reports that most of the time is spent in a lock operation. A common mistake is to blame the implementation of the mutex and say "if only I had a faster mutex." The real problem is using the mutex at all. It is just doing its job—serializing execution.

A mutex is only a *potential* bottleneck. If tasks rarely contend for the same mutex, the impact of the mutex on scaling is minor. Indeed, the technique of **fine-grain locking** replaces a single highly contended lock with many uncontended locks, and this can improve scalability by reducing contention. For example, each row of a matrix might be protected by a separate mutex, rather than a single lock for the entire matrix, if there are no invariants across different rows. As long as tasks rarely contend for the same row, the impact on scaling should be beneficial. Fine grain locking is tricky, however, and we do not discuss it further in this book. It is sometimes used inside the implementation of Intel Cilk Plus and Intel TBB, but you do not have to know that. The point is that mutexes can limit scalability if misused. The high-level patterns in the rest of this book let you avoid mutexes in most cases.

As a final note, you can sometimes use **atomic operations** in place of mutexes if the logical invariant involves a single memory location, and much of the synchronization constructs inside Intel Cilk Plus and Intel TBB are built with atomic operations. Atomic operations are discussed briefly in Section C.10.

2.6.5 Lack of Locality

Locality is the other key to scaling. Remember that work, span, and communication are the three key concerns. Locality refers to two bets on future memory accesses after a core accesses a location:

Temporal locality: The core is likely to access the *same* location again in the near future.
Spatial locality: The core is likely to access *nearby* locations in the near future.

Having good locality in a program means the hardware can win its bets since the above statements are more likely to be true. Hardware based on these assumptions being true can reduce communication. For example, as noted in Section 2.4.1, a memory access pulls an entire **cache line** (a small block of memory) around that memory location onto the chip and into the cache. Using the data on that line repeatedly while the cache line is resident is faster than pulling it in multiple times. To take advantage of this, programs should be written so they process data thoroughly and completely before moving to process other data. This increases the number of times the data will be found in cache, and will avoid reading the same data multiple times from off-chip memory. **Cache oblivious** algorithms [ABF05] (Section 8.8) are a formal way of exploiting this principle. Such algorithms are designed to have good locality at multiple scales, so it does not matter what specific size the cache line is.

Communication is so expensive and computation so cheap that sometimes it pays to increase the work in exchange for reducing communication. On current hardware, a cache miss can take up to the order of a hundred cycles. So it often pays to duplicate trivial calculations rather than try to do them in one place and share, and there is nascent research into **communication avoiding algorithms** [GDX08].

2.6.6 Load Imbalance

A **load imbalance** is the uneven distribution of work across workers. Figure 2.11 shows how load imbalance can impact scalability. In this figure, the parallel work was broken up into tasks, with one task per worker. The time taken by the longest-running task contributes to the span, which limits how fast the parallelized portion can run.

Load imbalance can be mitigated by **over-decomposition**, dividing the work into more tasks than there are workers. Like packing suitcases, it is easier to spread out many small items evenly than a few big items. This is shown in Figure 2.12. Some processors have fewer tasks than others. There is still a possibility that a very long task will get scheduled at the end of a run, but the parallel slack nonetheless improves the predictability of parallel execution times.

2.6.7 Overhead

Parallelization introduces additional overhead to launch and synchronize tasks, as shown in Figure 2.13. This overhead increases both work and span. The additional tasks incurred by overdecomposition tends to increase this overhead, since there is usually a fixed amount of overhead for managing every task. Making tasks too small can increase execution time and can also decrease **arithmetic intensity**. Therefore, there is a tension between providing sufficient overdecomposition to allow for balancing the load while still making tasks large enough to amortize synchronization overhead and maximize arithmetic intensity.

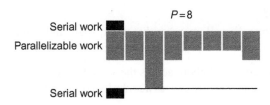

FIGURE 2.11

Load imbalance. Variation in the execution time of parallel tasks can reduce scalability.

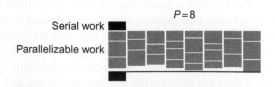

FIGURE 2.12

Overdecomposition can improve load balancing. Subdividing the parallel work into more tasks than workers permits the scheduler to pack tasks onto workers and improve load balance.

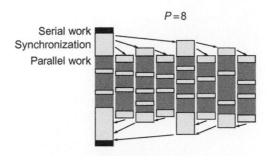

FIGURE 2.13

Overhead can reduce scalability. Distributing tasks to workers, starting tasks, and synchronizing completion adds to execution time. Tree-based schemes can reduce, but not eliminate, this overhead.

Careful synchronization design can reduce overhead, but cannot completely eliminate it. In the example in Figure 2.13, the overhead for launching and synchronizing a large number of independent tasks can use a tree structure, so that startup is logarithmic in the number of workers, instead of linear as would occur if all parallel tasks were launched from one task. Although the launching and synchronization time is logarithmic in the number of workers rather than linear, it nonetheless grows with the number of workers.

2.7 SUMMARY

This chapter covered a lot of theoretical and practical background. Although we do not want to dwell on computer architecture in this book, we have presented a simple summary of current trends in computer architecture as a basis for later discussion.

We also discussed many factors related to performance and presented some key definitions, including those of latency and throughput. Amdahl's Law and Gustafson's Law were presented and give bounds on performance, but we highly recommend the use of the work-span model for more accuracy. The work-span model not only accounts for imperfect parallelization but also gives a lower bound as well as an upper bound on speedup.

We also discussed several pitfalls that can lead to problems in parallel programs, from poor scalability to incorrect behavior. Race conditions and deadlock can be avoided with careful design. Assuming you achieve a correct program, of course you then want it to scale in performance. Scalability can be difficult to achieve, but here are some key rules of thumb:

- Make the available parallelism scale with the data.
- Keep the span short; avoid adding extra work for parallelism.
- Over-decompose to provide parallel slack.
- Minimize synchronization. Avoid locks.
- Use locality to minimize memory traffic. Be aware that the quantum of memory traffic is a cache line.
- Exploit both vector and thread parallelism if possible.

The rest of this book is about structured ways to achieve these goals.

Patterns

Patterns

3

Patterns have become popular recently as a way of codifying best practices for software engineering [GHJV95]. While patterns were originally applied to object-oriented software, the basic idea of patterns—identifying themes and idioms that can be codified and reused to solve specific problems in software engineering—also applies to parallel programming. In this book, we use the term **parallel pattern** to mean a recurring combination of task distribution and data access that solves a specific problem in parallel algorithm design.

A number of parallel patterns are described in this book. We will characterize and discuss various algorithms in terms of them. We give each pattern a specific name, which makes it much easier to succinctly describe, discuss, and compare various parallel algorithms. Algorithms are typically designed by composing patterns, so a study of patterns provides a high-level "vocabulary" for designing your own algorithms and for understanding other people's algorithms.

This chapter introduces all of the patterns discussed in this book in one place. We also introduce a set of serial patterns for comparison because parallel patterns are often composed with, or generalized from, these serial patterns. The serial patterns we discuss are the foundation of what is now known as structured programming. This helps make clear that the pattern-based approach to parallel programming used in this book can, to some extent, be considered an extension of the idea of structured programming.

It should be emphasized that patterns are universal. They apply to and can be used in *any* parallel programming system. They are not tied to any particular hardware architecture, programming language, or system. Patterns are, however, frequently embodied as mechanisms or features of particular systems. Systems, both hardware and software, can be characterized by the parallel patterns they support. Even if a particular programming system does not directly support a particular pattern it can usually, but not always, be implemented using other features.

In this book, we focus on patterns that lead to well-structured, maintainable, and efficient programs. Many of these patterns are in fact also **deterministic**, which means they give the same result every time they are executed. Determinism is a useful property since it leads to programs that are easier to understand, debug, test, and maintain.

We do not claim that we have covered all possible parallel patterns in this book. However, the patterns approach provides a framework into which you can fit additional patterns. We intend to document additional patterns online as a complement to this book, and you might also discover some new patterns on your own. In our experience many "new" patterns are in fact variations, combinations, or extensions of the ones we introduce here. We have focused in this book on the most useful and basic patterns in order to establish a solid foundation for further development.

We also focus on "algorithm strategy" patterns, sometimes called **algorithmic skeletons** [Col89, AD07]. These patterns are specifically relevant to the design of algorithm kernels and often appear as programming constructs in languages and other systems for expressing parallelism. Patterns have also been referred to as **motifs** and **idioms**. In more comprehensive pattern languages [MSM04, ABC+06], additional patterns and categories of patterns at both higher and lower levels of abstraction are introduced. The OUR pattern language in particular is quite extensive [Par11].

We have focused on the class of algorithm strategy patterns because these are useful in the design of machine-independent parallel algorithms. Algorithm strategy patterns actually have two parts, a semantics, which is *what* they accomplish, and an implementation, which is *how* they accomplish it. When designing an algorithm, you will often want to think only about the semantics of the pattern. However, when implementing the algorithm, you have to be aware of how to implement the pattern efficiently. The semantics are machine-independent but on different kinds of hardware there may be different implementation approaches needed for some of the patterns. We will discuss some of these low-level implementation issues in later chapters; in this chapter, we focus mostly on the semantics.

This chapter may seem a little abstract. In order to keep this chapter compact we do not give many examples of the use of each pattern here, since later chapters will provide many specific examples. If you would like to see more concrete examples first, we recommend that you skip or skim this chapter on first reading and come back to read it later.

3.1 NESTING PATTERN

The **nesting pattern** is the fundamental compositional pattern and appears in both serial and parallel programs. Nesting refers to the ability to hierarchically compose patterns.

The nesting pattern simply means that all "task blocks" in our pattern diagrams are actually locations within which general code can be inserted. This code can in turn be composed of other patterns. This concept is demonstrated in Figure 3.1.

Nesting allows other parallel patterns to be composed hierarchically, and possibly recursively. Ideally, patterns can be nested to any depth and the containing pattern should not limit what other patterns can be used inside it. Not all patterns support nesting. In this book, we focus on patterns that *do* support nesting since it is important for creating structured, modular code. In particular, it is hard to break code into libraries and then compose those libraries into larger programs unless nesting is supported. Programming models that do not support nesting likewise will have difficulties supporting modularity.

Figure 3.1 also demonstrates the graphical conventions we use to explain patterns generally. As previously described in Figure 2.1, tasks, which describe computations, are shown as sharp-cornered boxes, while data are indicated by round-cornered boxes. Grouped data is indicated by round-cornered enclosures, and grouped tasks are indicated by sharp-cornered polygonal enclosures. For some patterns we will introduce additional symbols in the form of various polygonal shapes.

Ordering dependencies are given by arrows. Time goes from top to bottom, and except when representing iteration we avoid having arrows go upward and therefore "backward" in time. In the absence of

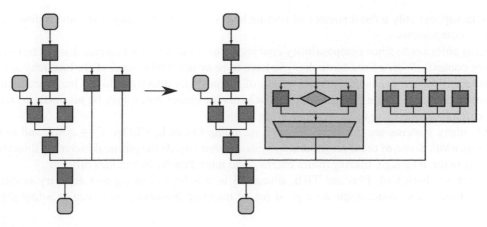

FIGURE 3.1

Nesting pattern. This is a compositional pattern that allows other patterns to be composed in a hierarchy. The definition of nesting is that any task block in a pattern can be replaced with a pattern with the same input and output configuration and dependencies.

such upward arrows, the height of a pattern diagram is a rough indication of the span (see Section 2.5.7) of a pattern. These graphical conventions are intentionally similar to those commonly associated with flow-charts.

The nesting pattern basically states that the interior of any "task box" in this notation can be replaced by any other pattern. Nesting can be static (related to the code structure) or dynamic (**recursion**, related to the dynamic function call stack). To support dynamic **data parallelism**, the latter is preferred, since we want the amount of parallelism to grow with problem size in order to achieve scalability. If static nesting is used, then nesting is equivalent to **functional decomposition**. In that case, nesting is an organizational structure for modularity but scaling will be achieved by the nested patterns, not by nesting itself.

Structured serial programming is based on nesting the **sequence**, **selection**, **iteration**, and **recursion** patterns. Likewise, we define structured parallel programming to be based on the composition of nestable parallel patterns. In structured serial programming, goto is avoided, since it violates the orderly arrangement of dependencies given by the nesting pattern. In particular, we want simple entry and exit points for each subtask and want to avoid jumping out of or into the middle of a task. Likewise, for "structured parallel programming" you should use only patterns that fit within the nesting pattern and avoid additional dependencies, both data and control, that break this model.

Nesting, especially when combined with recursion, can lead to large amounts of **potential parallelism**, also known as **parallel slack**. This can either be a good thing or a bad thing. For scalability, we normally want a large amount of parallel slack, as discussed in Section 2.5.

However, hardware resources are finite. It is not a good idea to blindly create threads for all of the potential parallelism in an application, since this will tend to oversubscribe the system. The implementation of a programming system that efficiently supports arbitrary nesting must intelligently map potential parallelism to actual physical parallelism. Since this is difficult, several programming models at present support only a fixed number of nesting levels and may even map these levels directly onto hardware components.

This is unfortunate since **composability** enables the use of libraries of routines that can be reused in different contexts. With a fixed hierarchy, you have to be aware at what level of the hierarchy any code you write will be used. Mapping the hierarchy of the program directly onto the hardware hierarchy also makes code less future-proofed. When new hardware comes out, it may be necessary to refactor the hierarchy of patterns to fit the new hardware.

Still, many systems are designed this way, including OpenCL, CUDA, C++ AMP, and to some extent OpenMP. Some of these programming systems even encode the physical hierarchy directly into keywords in the language, making future extension to more flexible hierarchies difficult.

In contrast, both Cilk Plus and TBB, discussed in this book, can support arbitrary nesting. At the same time, these systems can do a good job of mapping potential parallelism to actual physical parallelism.

3.2 STRUCTURED SERIAL CONTROL FLOW PATTERNS

Structured serial programming is based on four control flow patterns: **sequence**, **selection**, **iteration**, and **recursion**. Several parallel patterns are generalizations of these. In addition, these can be nested hierarchically so the compositional **"nesting"** pattern is also used.

We discuss these in some detail, even though they are familiar, to point out the assumptions that they make. It is important to understand these assumptions because when we attempt to parallelize serial programs based on these patterns, we may have to violate these assumptions.

3.2.1 Sequence

A **sequence** is a ordered list of tasks that are executed in a specific order. Each task is completed before the one after it starts. Suppose you are given the serial code shown in Listing 3.1. This code corresponds to Figure 3.2. Function f in line 1 will execute before function g in line 2, which will execute before function h in line 3. A basic assumption of the sequence pattern is that the program text ordering will be followed, even if there are no data dependencies between the tasks, so that side effects of the tasks such as output will also be ordered. For example, if task f outputs "He", task g outputs "llo " and task h outputs "World", then the above sequence will output "Hello World" even if there were no explicit dependencies between the tasks.

```
1  T = f(A);
2  S = g(T);
3  B = h(S);
```

LISTING 3.1

Serial sequence in pseudocode.

In Listing 3.2, data dependencies happen to restrict the order to be the same as the `texture` order. However, if the code happened to be as shown in Listing 3.2, the sequence pattern would still require executing g after f, as shown in Figure 3.3, even though there is no apparent reason to do so. This is so side effects, such as output, will still be properly ordered.

FIGURE 3.2

Sequence pattern. A serial sequence orders operations in the sequence in which they appear in the program text.

```
1   T = f(A);
2   S = g(A);
3   B = h(S,T);
```

LISTING 3.2

Serial sequence, second example, in pseudocode.

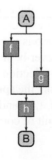

FIGURE 3.3

Sequence pattern, second example. A serial sequence orders operations in the sequence in which they appear in the program text, even if there are no apparent dependencies between tasks. Here, since g comes after f in the program text, the sequence pattern requires that they be executed in that order, even though there is no explicit dependency.

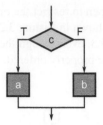

FIGURE 3.4

Selection pattern. One and only one of two alternatives a or b is executed based on a Boolean condition c.

```
1  if (c) {
2    a;
3  } else {
4    b;
5  }
```

LISTING 3.3

Serial selection in pseudocode.

There is a parallel generalization of sequence, the **superscalar sequence** discussed in Section 3.6.1, which removes the "code text order" constraint of the sequence pattern and orders tasks only by data dependencies. In fact, as discussed in Section 2.4, modern out-of-order processors do often reorder operations and do not strictly follow the sequence pattern.

3.2.2 Selection

In the **selection** pattern, a condition c is first evaluated. If the condition is true, then some task a is executed. If the condition is false, then task b is executed. There is a control-flow dependency between the condition and the tasks so neither task a nor b is executed before the condition has been evaluated. Also, exactly one of a or b will be executed, never both; this is another fundamental assumption of the serial selection pattern. See Figure 3.4. In code, selection will often be expressed as shown in Listing 3.3.

There is a parallel generalization of selection, the **speculative selection** pattern, which is discussed in Section 3.6.3. In speculative selection all of a, b, and c may be executed in parallel, but the results of one of a or b are discarded based on the result of computing c.

3.2.3 Iteration

In the **iteration** pattern, a condition c is evaluated. If it is true, a task a is evaluated, then the condition c is evaluated again, and the process repeats until the condition becomes false. This is diagrammed in Figure 3.5.

Unlike our other pattern diagrams, for iteration we use arrows that go "backward" in time. Since the number of iterations is data dependent, you cannot necessarily predict how many iterations will

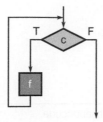

FIGURE 3.5

Serial iteration pattern. The task f is executed repeatedly as long as the condition c is true. When the condition becomes false, the tasks following this pattern are executed.

```
1  while (c) {
2    a;
3  }
```

LISTING 3.4

Iteration using a while loop in pseudocode.

```
1  for (i = 0; i < n; ++i) {
2    a;
3  }
```

LISTING 3.5

Iteration using a for loop in pseudocode.

take place, or if the loop will even terminate. You cannot evaluate the span complexity of an algorithm just by looking at the height of the diagram. Instead, you have to (conceptually) execute the program and look at the height of the trace of the execution.

This particular form of loop (with the test at the top) is often known as a while loop. The while loop can of course be expressed in code as shown in Listing 3.4.

There are various other forms of iteration but this is the most general. Other forms of looping can be implemented in terms of the while loop and possibly other patterns such as sequence.

The loop body a and the condition c normally have data dependencies between them; otherwise, the loop would never terminate. In particular, the loop body should modify some state that c uses for termination testing.

One complication with parallelizing the iteration pattern is that the body task f may also depend on previous invocations of itself. These are called **loop-carried dependencies**. Depending on the form of the dependency, loops may be parallelized in various ways.

One common form of loop is the counted loop, sometimes referred to simply as a for loop, which also generates a loop index, as shown in Listing 3.5.

```
1  i = 0;
2  while (i < n) {
3    a;
4    ++i;
5  }
```

LISTING 3.6

Demonstration of `while`/`for` equivalence in pseudocode.

This is equivalent to the `while` loop shown in Listing 3.6. Note that the loop body now has a loop-carried dependency on i. Even so, there are various ways to parallelize this specific form of loop, based on the fact that we know all the loop indices for every iteration in advance and can compute them in parallel. This particular loop form also has a termination condition based on a count n known in advance, so we can actually compute its complexity as a function of n.

Many systems for parallelizing loops, including Cilk Plus and OpenMP, prohibit modifications to i or n in the body of loops in the form of Listing 3.5; otherwise, the total number of iterations would not be known in advance. Serial loops do not have this prohibition and allow more general forms of termination condition and index iteration.

Several parallel patterns can be considered parallelizations of specific forms of loops include **map**, **reduction**, **scan**, **recurrence**, **scatter**, **gather**, and **pack**. These correspond to different forms of loop dependencies. You should be aware that there are some forms of loop dependencies that cannot be parallelized. One of the biggest challenges of parallelizing algorithms is that a single serial construct, iteration, actually maps onto many different kinds of parallelization strategies. Also, since data dependencies are not as important in serial programming as in parallel programming, they can be hidden.

In particular, the combination of iteration with random memory access and pointers can create complex hidden data dependencies. Consider the innocent-looking code in Listing 3.7. Can this code be parallelized or not?

The answer is ... maybe. In fact, the data dependencies are encoded in the arrays a, b, c, and d, so the parallelization strategy will depend on what values are stored in these arrays.[1] This code is, in fact, an interpreter for a simple "programming language" and can do relatively arbitrary computation. You have to decode the data dependency graph of the "program" stored in arrays a, b, c, and d before you know if the code can be parallelized! Such "accidental interpreters" are surprisingly common.

Other complications can arise due to pointers. For example, suppose we used the slightly different version of the code in Listing 3.8. The difference is that we output to a new argument y, in an attempt to avoid the data dependencies of the previous example. Can *this* version of the code be parallelized?

The answer is ... maybe. The array inputs x and y are really pointers in C. The code can be parallelized if x does not point to the same location as y (or overlapping locations). If they do, we say

---

[1] This is not a made-up example. One of the authors was once asked to parallelize code very similar to this ... without being provided with the input.

```
1  void engine(
2    int n,
3    double x[],
4    int a[],
5    int b[],
6    int c[],
7    int d[],
8  ) {
9    for (int i = 0; i < n; ++i)
10     x[a[i]] = x[b[i]] * x[c[i]] + x[d[i]];
11 }
```

LISTING 3.7

A difficult example in C. Can this code be parallelized?

```
1  void engine2(
2    int n,
3    double x[],
4    double y[],
5    int a[],
6    int b[],
7    int c[],
8    int d[],
9  ) {
10   for (int i = 0; i < n; ++i)
11     y[a[i]] = x[b[i]] * x[c[i]] + x[d[i]];
12 }
```

LISTING 3.8

Another difficult example in C. Can this code be parallelized?

the inputs are **aliased,** and this example has effectively the same data dependencies as Listing 3.7. So, now the parallelization of this function depends on how we call it. However, even if x and y point to distinct regions of memory, we still may not be able to parallelize safely if there are duplicate values in a, since race conditions can result from parallel writes to the same memory location. We will discuss the problem of parallel random writes in Section 3.5.5.

3.2.4 Recursion

Recursion is a dynamic form of nesting which allows functions to call themselves, directly or indirectly. It is usually associated with stack-based memory allocation or, if higher-order functions are supported, **closures** (see Section 3.4.4) which are objects allocated on the heap. **Tail recursion** is a special form of recursion that can be converted into iteration, a fact that is important in functional languages which often do not support iteration directly. In tail recursion, the calling function returns immediately after the recursive call and returns the value, if any, returned by the recursive call without modification.

3.3 PARALLEL CONTROL PATTERNS

Parallel control patterns extend the serial control patterns presented in Section 3.2. Each parallel control pattern is related to one or more of the serial patterns but relaxes the assumptions of the serial control patterns in various ways, or is intended for parallelizing a particular configuration of some serial control pattern.

3.3.1 Fork–Join

The **fork–join** pattern lets control flow fork into multiple parallel flows that rejoin later. Various parallel frameworks abstract fork–join in different ways. Some treat fork–join as a parallel form of a compound statement; instead of executing substatements one after the other, they are executed in parallel. Some like OpenMP's parallel region fork control into multiple threads that all execute the *same* statement and use other constructs to determine which thread does what.

Another approach, used in Cilk Plus, generalizes serial call trees to parallel call trees, by letting code **spawn** a function instead of calling it. A spawned call is like a normal call, except the caller can keep going without waiting for the callee to return, hence forking control flow between caller and callee. The caller later executes a join operation (called "sync" in Cilk Plus) to wait for the callee to return, thus merging the control flow. This approach can be implemented with an efficient mechanism that extends the stack-oriented call/return mechanism used for serial function calls.

Fork–join should not be confused with **barriers**. A barrier is a synchronization construct across multiple threads. In a barrier, each thread must wait for all other threads to reach the barrier before any of them leave. The difference is that after a barrier all threads continue, but after a join only one does. Sometimes barriers are used to imitate joins, by making all threads execute identical code after the barrier, until the next conceptual fork.

The fork–join pattern in Cilk Plus is structured in that the task graph generated is cleanly nested and planar, so the program can be reasoned about in a hierarchical fashion. When we refer to the fork–join pattern in this book we will be specifically referring to this structured form.

3.3.2 Map

As shown in Figure 3.6, the **map** pattern replicates a function over every element of an index set. The index set may be abstract or associated with the elements of a collection. The function being replicated is called an **elemental function** since it applies to the elements of an actual collection of input data. The map pattern replaces one specific usage of iteration in serial programs: a loop in which every iteration is independent, in which the number of iterations is known is advance, and in which every computation depends only on the iteration count and data read using the iteration count as an index into a collection. This form of loop is often used, like map, for processing every element of a collection with an independent operation. The elemental function must be **pure** (that is, without side-effects) in

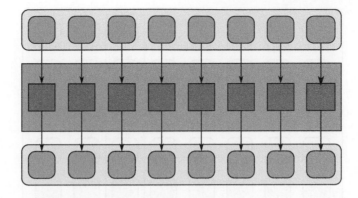

FIGURE 3.6

Map pattern. In a map pattern, a function is applied to all elements of a collection, usually producing a new collection with the same shape as the input.

order for the map to be implementable in parallel while achieving deterministic results. In particular, elemental functions must not modify global data that other instances of that function depend on.

Examples of use of the map pattern include gamma correction and thresholding in images, color space conversions, Monte Carlo sampling, and ray tracing.

3.3.3 Stencil

The **stencil** pattern is a generalization of the map pattern in which an elemental function can access not only a single element in an input collection but also a set of "neighbors." As shown in Figure 3.7, neighborhoods are given by set of relative offsets.

Optimized implementation of the stencil uses **tiling** to allow data reuse, as is discussed in detail in Section 7.3.

The stencil pattern is often combined with iteration. In this case, a stencil is repeated over and over to evolve a system through time or to implement an iterative solver. The combined pattern is equivalent to a space–time recurrence and can be analyzed and optimized using the techniques for the **recurrence** pattern, as discussed in Sections 3.3.6 and 7.5.

For the stencil pattern, boundary conditions on array accesses need to be considered. The edges of the input need require special handling either by modifying the indexing for out-of-bounds accesses or by executing special-case versions of the elemental function. However, the implementation should avoid using this special-case code in the interior of the index domain where no out-of-bounds accesses are possible.

The stencil pattern is used for image filtering, including convolution, median filtering, motion estimation in video encoding, and isotropic diffusion noise reduction. The stencil pattern is also used in simulation, including fluid flow, electromagnetic and financial partial differential equation (PDE) solvers, lattice quantum chromodynamics (QCD), and cellular automata (including lattice Boltzmann flow solvers). Many linear algebra operations can also be seen as stencils.

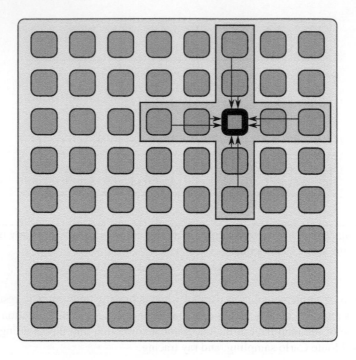

FIGURE 3.7

Stencil pattern. A collection of outputs is generated, each of which is a function of a set of neighbors in an input collection. The locations of the neighbors are located in a set of fixed offsets from each output. Here, only one neighborhood is shown, but in actuality the computation is done for all outputs in parallel, and different stencils can use different neighborhoods. Elements along the boundaries require special handling.

3.3.4 Reduction

A **reduction** combines every element in a collection into a single element using an associative **combiner function**. Given the associativity of the combiner function, many different orderings are possible, but with different spans. If the combiner function is also commutative, additional orderings are possible. A serial implementation of reduction, using addition as the combiner function and a sequential ordering, is given in Listing 3.9. The ordering of operations used in this code corresponds to Figure 3.8. Such a reduction can be used to find the sum of the elements of a collection, a very common operation in numerical applications.

Although Listing 3.9 uses a loop with a data dependency, Figure 3.9 shows how a reduction can be parallelized using a tree structure. The tree structure depends on a reordering of the combiner operations by associativity. Interestingly, tree parallelization of the reduction can be implemented using exactly the same number of operations as the serial version. A naïve tree reduction may require more intermediate storage than the serial version but at worst this storage is proportional to the available parallelism. In practice, it can be more efficient to perform local serial reductions over **tiles** and then combine the results using additional tile reductions. In other words, an efficient implementation might

```
1  double my_add_reduce(
2    const double a[], // input array
3    size_t n          // number of elements
4  ) {
5    double r = 0.0; // initialize with the identity for addition
6    for (int i = 0; i < n; ++i)
7      r += a[i];  // each iteration depends on the previous one
8    return r;
9  }
```

LISTING 3.9

Serial implementation of reduction.

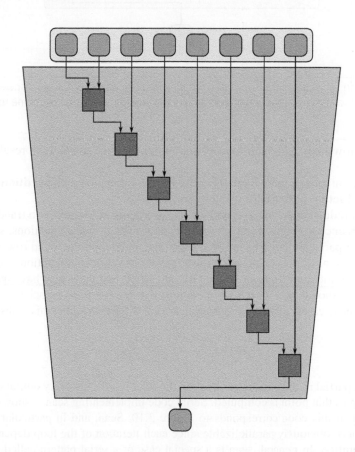

FIGURE 3.8

Serial reduction pattern. A reduction combines all the elements in a collection into a single element using an associative combiner function. Because the combiner function is associative, many orderings are possible. The serial ordering shown here corresponds to Listing 3.9. It has span n, so no parallel speedup is possible.

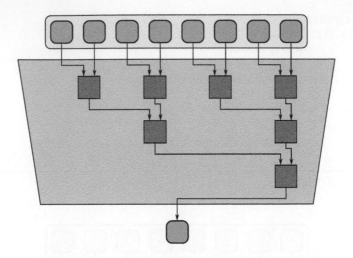

FIGURE 3.9

Tree reduction pattern. This diagram shows a tree ordering that has a span of $\lg n$, so a speedup of $n/\lg n$ is possible. Assuming the combiner function is associative, this ordering computes the same result as Figure 3.8 and Listing 3.9.

use relatively shallow trees with high fanouts and only use a tree to combine results from multiple workers.

There are some variants of this pattern that arise from combination with **partition** and **search** such as the **category reduction pattern** discussed in Section 3.6.8.

Applications of reduction are diverse, and include averaging of Monte Carlo (random) samples for integration; convergence testing in iterative solution of systems of linear equations, such as conjugate gradient; image comparison metrics as in video encoding; and dot products and row–column products in matrix multiplication. Reductions can also use operations other than addition, such as maximum, minimum, multiplication, and Boolean AND, OR, and XOR, and these also have numerous applications. However, you should be cautious of operations that are not truly associative, such as floating point addition. In these cases, different orderings can give different results; this is discussed further in Chapter 5.

3.3.5 Scan

Scan computes all partial reductions of a collection. In other words, for every output position, a reduction of the input up to that point is computed. Serial code implementing scan is shown in Listing 3.10. The ordering used in this code corresponds to Figure 3.10. Scan, and in particular the code shown in Listing 3.10, is not obviously parallelizable since each iteration of the loop depends on the output of the previous iteration. In general, scan is a special case of a serial pattern called a **fold**. In a fold, a **successor function** f is used to advance from the previous state to the current state, given some additional input. If the successor function is not associative we cannot, in fact, generally parallelize a fold. However, if the successor function *is* associative, we can reorder operations (and possibly add

```
1  void my_add_iscan(
2    const float a[],   // input array
3    float b[],         // output array
4    size_t n           // number of elements
5  ) {
6    if (n>0) b[0] = a[0];   // equivalent to assuming b[i−1] is zero
7    for (int i = 1; i < n; ++i)
8      b[i] = b[i−1] + a[i];   // each iteration depends on the previous one
9  }
```

LISTING 3.10

Serial implementation of scan.

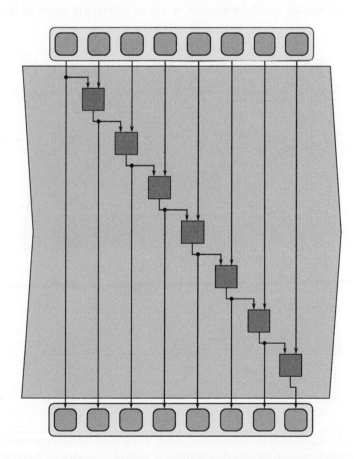

FIGURE 3.10

Serial scan pattern. This is one way of many possible to implement scan, but has a span of order $\Theta(n)$ and so is not parallelizable. This implementation of scan corresponds to the code in Listing 3.10.

some extra work) to reduce the span and allow for a parallel implementation. Associativity of the successor function is what distinguishes the special case of a scan from the general case of a fold. A parallelizable scan can be used in this example because the successor function is addition, which is associative.

One possible parallel implementation of scan when the successor function f is associative is shown in Figure 3.11. As you can see, parallelization of scan is less obvious than parallelization of reduction. We will consider various implementation alternatives in Section 5.4, but if the programming model supports scan as a built-in operation it may not be necessary to consider the details of the implementation.

However, it is worth noting that a parallel implementation of scan may require more work (evaluations of f) than is necessary in the serial case, up to twice as many, and also at best only has $\Theta(\lg n)$ span. Scan is a good example of an algorithm that is parallelizable but for which linear speedup is not possible and for which the parallel algorithm is not as efficient in terms of the total number of

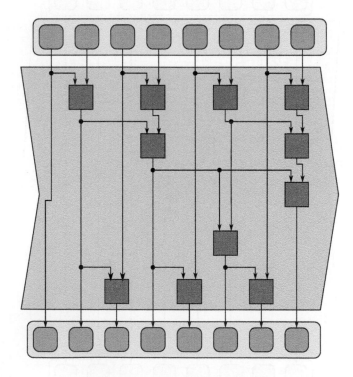

FIGURE 3.11

Parallel scan pattern. If the successor function is associative, many reorderings are possible with lower span. This is one of many possible ways to implement scan using a span of order $\Theta(\lg n)$. It consists basically of a reduction tree followed by some additional operations to compute additional intermediate partial reductions not computed by the tree. Notice, however, that the total amount of work is more than the algorithm used in Figure 3.10.

operations required as the serial implementation. Because of this, use of scan can limit scaling and alternative algorithms should be considered whenever possible.

Examples of the use of the scan pattern include integration, sequential decision simulations in option pricing, and random number generation. However, use of scan in random number generation is only necessary if one is forced to parallelize traditional sequential pseudorandom number generators, which are often based on successor functions. There are alternative approaches to pseudorandom number generation based on hashing that require only the map pattern [SMDS11]. For greater scalability, these should be used when possible.

Scan can also be used to implement **pack** in combination with **scatter**, but a pack operation is intrinsically deterministic, unlike scatter. Therefore, we have included pack as a separate pattern.

3.3.6 Recurrence

The map pattern results when we parallelize a loop where the loop bodies are all independent. A **recurrence** is also a generalization of iteration, but of the more complex case where loop iterations can depend on one another. We consider only simple recurrences where the offsets between elements are constant. In this case, recurrences look somewhat like stencils, but where the neighbor accesses can be to both inputs *and* outputs. A recurrence is like a map but where elements can use the outputs of adjacent elements as inputs.

There is a constraint that allows recurrences to be computable: They must be *causal*. That is, there must be a serial ordering of the recurrence elements so that elements can be computed using previously computed outputs. For recurrences that arise from loop nests, where output dependencies are really references to values computed in previous loop iterations, a causal order is given. In fact, it turns out that there are two cases where recurrences are parallelizable: (1) a 1D recurrence where the computation in the element is associative, (2) and a multidimensional recurrence arising from a nested loop body. The 1D case we have already seen: It is just the scan pattern in Section 3.3.5. In the nD case arising from nested loops, surprisingly, recurrences are always parallelizable over $n - 1$ dimensions by sweeping a hyperplane over the grid of dependencies [Lam74], an approach discussed in Section 7.5. This can be implemented using a sequence of stencils. Conversely, iterated stencils can be reinterpreted as recurrences over space–time.

Recurrences arise in many applications including matrix factorization, image processing, PDE solvers, and sequence alignment. Partial differentiation equation (PDE) solvers using iterated stencils, such as the one discussed in Chapter 10, are often converted into space–time recurrences to apply space–time **tiling**. Space–time tiling is an optimization technique for recurrences discussed in Section 7.5. Using this optimization can be more efficient than treating the stencil and the iteration separately, but it does require computing several iterations at once.

3.4 SERIAL DATA MANAGEMENT PATTERNS

Data can be managed in various ways in serial programs. Data management includes how storage of data is allocated and shared as well as how it is read, written, and copied.

3.4.1 **Random Read and Write**

The simplest mechanism for managing data just relies directly on the underlying machine model, which supplies a set of memory locations indexed by integers ("addresses"). Addresses can be represented in higher-level programming languages using pointers.

Unfortunately, pointers can introduce all kinds of problems when a program is parallelized. For example, it is often unclear whether two pointers refer to the same object or not, a problem known as **aliasing**. In Listing 3.8, we show how this can happen when variables are passed as function arguments. Aliasing can make vectorization and parallelization difficult, since straightforward approaches will often fail if inputs are aliased. On the other hand, vectorization approaches that are safe in the presence of aliasing may require extra data copies and may be considered unacceptably expensive. A common approach is to forbid aliasing or to state that vectorized functions will have undefined results if inputs are aliased. This puts the burden on the programmer to ensure that aliases do not occur.

Array indices are a slightly safer abstraction that still supports data structures based on indirection. Array indices are related to pointers; specifically, they represent offsets from some base address. However, since array indices are restricted to the context of a particular collection of data they are slightly safer. It is still possible to have aliases but at least the range of memory is restricted when you use array indices rather than pointers. The other advantage of using array indices instead of pointers is that such data structures can be easily moved to another address space, such as on a co-processor. Data structures using raw pointers are tied to a particular address space.

3.4.2 **Stack Allocation**

Frequently, storage space for data needs to be allocated dynamically. If data is allocated in a nested last in, first out (LIFO) fashion, such as local variables in function calls, then it can be allocated on a stack. Not only is **stack allocation** efficient, since an arbitrary amount of data can be allocated in constant time, it is also locality preserving.

To parallelize this pattern, typically each thread of control will get its own stack so locality is preserved. The function-calling conventions of Cilk Plus generalize stack allocation in the context of function calls so the locality preserving properties of stack allocation are retained.

3.4.3 **Heap Allocation**

In many situations, it is not possible to allocate data in a LIFO fashion with a stack. In this case, data is dynamically allocated from a pool of memory commonly called the heap. **Heap allocation** is considerably slower and more complex than stack allocation and may also result in allocations scattered all over memory. Such scattered allocations can lead to a loss in coherence and a reduction in memory access efficiency. Widely separated accesses are more expensive than contiguous allocations due to **memory subsystem** components that make locality assumptions, including caches, memory banks, and page tables. Depending on the algorithm used, heap allocation of large blocks of different sizes can also lead to fragmented memory [WJNB95]. When memory is fragmented, contiguous regions of address space may not be available even though enough unallocated memory is available in total. Fragmentation is less of a problem on machines with **virtual memory** because only the memory addresses actually in use will occupy physical memory, at least at the granularity of a page.

When parallelizing programs that use heap allocation, you should be aware that implicitly sharing the data structure used to manage the heap can lead to scalability problems. A parallelized heap allocator should be used when writing parallel programs that use dynamic memory allocation. Such an allocator maintains separate memory pools on each worker, avoiding constant access to global locks. Such a parallelized allocator is provided by TBB and can be used even if the other constructs of TBB are not.

For efficiency, many programs use simple custom allocators rather than the more general heap. For example, to manage the allocation of items that are all the same size, free items can be stored on a linked list and allocated in constant time. This also has the advantage of reducing fragmentation since elements of the same size are allocated from the same pool. However, if you implement your own allocation data structures, when the code is parallelized even a simple construct like a linked list can become a bottleneck if protected with a lock. Conversely, if it is not protected, it can be a race condition hazard.

3.4.4 Closures

Closures are function objects that can be constructed and managed like data. **Lambda functions** (see Appendix D.2) are simply unnamed closures that allow functions to be syntactically defined where and when needed. As we will see, the new C++ standard includes lambda functions that are used extensively by TBB. ArBB also allows closure objects to be constructed and compiled dynamically but does not require that lambda functions be supported by the compiler.

When closures are built, they can often be used to "capture" the state of non-local variables that they reference. This implicitly requires the use of dynamic memory allocation. Closures can also be generated dynamically or statically. If they are statically implemented, then the implementation may need to allow for a level of indirection so the code can access the data associated with the closure at the point it is created. If the code for the closure is dynamically constructed, as in ArBB, then it is possible to use the state of captured variables at the point of construction to optimize the generated code.

3.4.5 Objects

Objects are language constructs that associate data with the code to act on and manage that data. Multiple functions may be associated with an object and these functions are called the **methods** or **member functions** of that object. Objects are considered to be members of a class of objects, and classes can be arranged in a hierarchy in which subclasses inherit and extend the features of superclasses. All instances of a class have the same methods but have different state. The state of an object may or may not be directly accessible; in many cases, access to an object's state may only be permitted through its methods.

In some languages, including C++, subclasses can override member functions in superclasses. Overriding usually requires class and function pointers in the implementation, but function pointers in particular may not be supported on all hardware targets (specifically older GPUs). Some programming models, such as ArBB, partially avoid this problem by providing an additional stage of compilation at which the function pointers can be resolved so they do not have to be resolved dynamically during execution.

In parallel programming models objects have been generalized in various ways. For example, in Java, marking a method as `synchronized` adds a lock that protects an object's state from being modified by multiple methods at once. However, as discussed in Section 2.6.2, overuse of locks can be detrimental to performance.

Closures and objects are closely related. Objects can be fully emulated using just closures, for example, and the implementation of objects in Smalltalk [Kay96] was inspired in part by the implementation of nested functions in Algol and Simula [Per81, Nau81, Coh96].

3.5 PARALLEL DATA MANAGEMENT PATTERNS

Several patterns are used to organize parallel access to data. In order to avoid problems such as race conditions, it is necessary in parallel programs to understand when data is potentially shared by multiple workers and when it is not. It is especially important to know when and how multiple workers can modify the same data. For the most part the parallel data access patterns we will discuss in this book avoid modification of shared data or only allow its modification in a structured fashion. The exception is the **scatter** pattern, several variants of which can still be used to resolve or avoid race conditions. Some of these patterns are also important for data locality optimizations, such as **partition**, although these also have the affect of creating independent regions of memory that can safely be modified in parallel.

3.5.1 Pack

The **pack** pattern can be used to eliminate unused space in a collection. Elements of a collection are each marked with a Boolean value. Pack discards elements in the data collection that are marked with `false`. The remaining elements marked with `true` are placed together in a contiguous sequence, in the same order they appeared in the input data collection. This can be done either for each element of the output of a map or in a collective fashion, using a collection of Booleans that is the same shape as the data collection and is provided as an additional input. See Figure 3.12 for an illustration of the pack pattern with a specific set of input data.

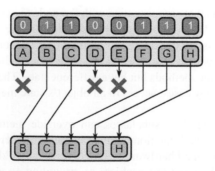

FIGURE 3.12

Pack pattern. Unused elements are discarded and the remainder packed together in a contiguous sequence.

Pack is especially useful when fused with map and other patterns to avoid unnecessary output from those patterns. When properly implemented, a programming system can use pack to reduce memory bandwidth. Pack can even be used as a way to emulate control flow on SIMD machines with good asymptotic performance [LLM08, HLJH09], unlike the masking approach.

An inverse of the pack operation, **unpack**, is also useful. The unpack operation can place elements back into a data collection at the same locations from which they were drawn with a pack. Both pack and unpack are deterministic operations. Pack can also be implemented using a combination of scan and scatter [Ble93].

Examples of the use of pack include narrow-phase collision detection pair testing when you only want to report valid collisions and peak detection for template matching in computer vision.

3.5.2 Pipeline

A **pipeline** pattern connects tasks in a **producer–consumer** relationship. Conceptually, all stages of the pipeline are active at once, and each stage can maintain state that can be updated as data flows through them. See Figure 3.13 for an example of a pipeline. A linear pipeline is the basic pattern but

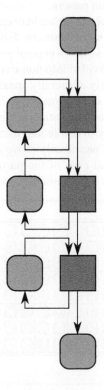

FIGURE 3.13

Pipeline pattern. Stages are connected in a producer–consumer relationship, and each stage can maintain state so that later outputs can depend on earlier ones.

more generally, a set of stages could be assembled in a directed acyclic graph. It is also possible to have parallel stages, as will be discussed in Chapter 9.

Pipelines are useful for serially dependent tasks like codecs for encoding and decoding video and audio streams. Stages of the pipeline can often be generated by using functional decomposition of tasks in an application. However, typically this approach results in a fixed number of stages, so pipelines are generally not arbitrarily scalable. Still, pipelines are useful when composed with other patterns since they can provide a multiplier on the available parallelism.

Examples of the use of the pipeline pattern include codecs with variable-rate compression, video processing and compositioning systems, and spam filtering.

3.5.3 Geometric Decomposition

The **geometric decomposition** pattern breaks data into a set of subcollections. In general these subcollections can overlap. See the middle example in Figure 3.14. If the outputs are partitioned into non-overlapping domains, then parallel tasks can operate on each subdomain independently without fear of interfering with others. See the rightmost example in Figure 3.14. We will call the special case of non-overlapping subregions the partition pattern.

The partition pattern is very useful for divide-and-conquer algorithms, and it can also be used in efficient parallel implementations of the **stencil** pattern. For the stencil pattern, typically the input is divided into a set of partially overlapping strips (a general geometric decomposition) so that neighbors can be accessed. However, the output is divided into non-overlapping strips (that is, a partition) so that outputs can be safely written independently. Generally speaking, if overlapping regions are used they should be for input, while output should be partitioned into non-overlapping regions.

An issue that arises with geometric decomposition is how boundary conditions are handled when the input or output domains are not evenly divisible into tiles of a consistent size.

A geometric decomposition does not necessarily move data. It often just provides an alternative "view" of the organization. In the special case of the partition pattern, a geometric decomposition makes sure that different tasks are modifying disjoint regions of the output.

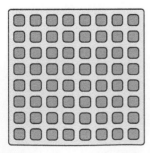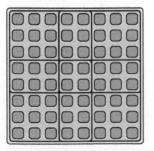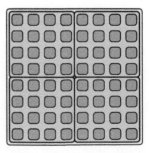

FIGURE 3.14

Geometric decomposition and the partition pattern. In the geometric decomposition pattern, the data is divided into potentially overlapping regions (middle, four 5 × 5 regions). The partition pattern is a special case of geometric decomposition where the domain is divided into non-overlapping regions (right, four 4 × 4 regions).

We have shown diagrams where the data is regularly arranged in an array and the decomposition uses regular subarrays. It would also be possible to have subcollections of different sizes, or for subcollections to be interleaved (for example, all the odd elements in one subcollection and all the even ones in the other). It is also possible to apply this pattern to less regular data structures, such as graphs. For example, a graph coloring might be used to divide the vertices of a graph into a subset of vertices that are not directly connected, or a graph might be divided into components in other ways.

The implementation of **stencil** operations, which are used in both image processing and simulation, are a good example of the use of geometric decomposition with overlapping input regions. When iterated stencils are implemented on distributed memory computers such as clusters, often one subdomain is assigned to each processor, and then communication is limited to only the overlap regions. Examples of the use of partition (with non-overlapping regions) include JPEG and other macroblock compression, as well as divide-and-conquer matrix multiplication.

3.5.4 **Gather**

The **gather** pattern reads a collection of data from another data collection, given a collection of indices. Gather can be considered a combination of map and random serial read operations. See Figure 3.15 for an example. The element type of the output collection is the same as the input data collection but the shape of the output collection is that of the index collection. Various optimizations are possible if the array of indices is fixed at code generation time or follows specific known patterns. For example, **shifting** data left or right in an array is a special case of gather that is highly coherent and can be accelerated using vector operations. The **stencil** pattern also performs a coherent form of gather in each element of a map, and there are specific optimizations associated with the implementation of such structured, local gathers.

Examples of gather include sparse matrix operations, ray tracing, volume rendering, proximity queries, and collision detection.

3.5.5 **Scatter**

The **scatter** pattern is the inverse of the gather pattern: A set of input data and a set of indices is given, but each element of the input is written at the given location, not read. The scatter can be considered equivalent to a combination of the map and random serial write patterns. Figure 3.16 illustrates a problem with scatter, however: What do we do if two writes go to the same location?

Unfortunately, in the naïve definition of scatter, race conditions are possible when there are duplicate write addresses. In general, we cannot even assume that either value is written properly. We will

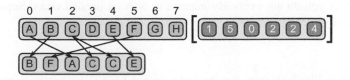

FIGURE 3.15

Gather pattern. A collection of data is read from an input collection given a collection of indices.

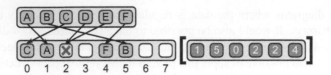

FIGURE 3.16

Scatter pattern. A collection of data is written to locations given by a collection of addresses. However, what do we do when two addresses are the same?

call such duplicates **collisions**. To obtain a full definition of scatter, we need to define what to do when such collisions occur. To obtain a deterministic scatter, we need rules to deterministically resolve collisions.

There are several possible solutions to the problem of collisions, including using associative operators to combine values, choosing one of the multiple values non-deterministically, and assigning priorities to values. These will be discussed in detail in Section 6.2.

3.6 OTHER PARALLEL PATTERNS

In this section we will discuss several additional patterns that often show up in practice, but for which we unfortunately do not have any specific code examples in this book. Please check online, as more details and examples for these patterns may be available there. Some of these patterns are extensions or elaborations of already discussed patterns.

3.6.1 Superscalar Sequences

In the **superscalar sequence** pattern, you write a sequence of tasks, just as you would for an ordinary serial sequence. As an example, consider the code shown in Listing 3.11. However, unlike the case with the sequence pattern, in a superscalar sequence tasks only need to be ordered by data dependencies [ERB+10, TBRG10, KLDB10]. As long as there are no side effects, the system is free to execute tasks in parallel or in a different order than given in the source code. As long as the data dependencies are satisfied, the result will be the same as if the tasks executed in the canonical order given by the source code. See Figure 3.17.

The catch here is the phrase "as long as the data dependencies are satisfied." In order to use this pattern, all dependencies need to be visible to the task scheduler.

This pattern is related to **futures**, discussed in Section 3.6.2. However, unlike with futures, for superscalar sequences you do not explicitly manage or wait on parallel tasks. Superscalar sequences are meant to be serially consistent.

3.6.2 Futures

The **futures** pattern is like fork–join, but the tasks do not have to be nested hierarchically. Instead, when a task is spawned, an object is returned—a *future*—which is used to manage the task. The most

```
1   D = f(A);
2   E = g(D);
3   F = h(B,E);
4   G = r(E);
5   P = p(D);
6   Q = q(D);
7   H = s(F,G);
8   C = t(H,P,Q);
```

LISTING 3.11

Superscalar sequence in pseudocode.

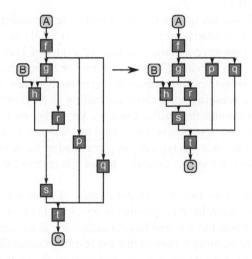

FIGURE 3.17

Superscalar sequence pattern. A superscalar sequence orders operations by their data dependencies only. On the left we see the timing given by a serial implementation of the code in Listing 3.11 using the sequence pattern. However, if we interpret this graph as a superscalar sequence, we can potentially execute some of the tasks simultaneously, as in the diagram on the right. Tasks in a superscalar sequence must not have any hidden data dependencies or side-effects not known to the scheduler.

important operation that can be done on a future is to wait for it to complete. Futures can implement the same hierarchical patterns as in fork–join but can also be used to implement more general, and potentially confusing, task graphs. Conceptually, fork–join is like stack-based allocation of tasks, while futures are like heap allocation of tasks.

Task **cancellation** can also be implemented on futures. Cancellation can be used to implement other patterns, such as the non-deterministic **branch-and-bound** pattern or **speculative selection**.

3.6.3 Speculative Selection

Speculative selection generalizes selection so that the condition and both alternatives can run in parallel. Compare Figure 3.4 with Figure 3.18. When the condition completes, the unneeded branch of the speculative selection is **cancelled**. Cancellation also needs to include the reversal of any side-effects. In practice, the two branches will have to block at some point and wait for the condition to be evaluated before they can commit any changes to state or cause any non-reversible side-effects. This pattern is inherently wasteful, as it executes computations that will be discarded. This means that it always increases the total amount of work.

It can be expensive to implement cancellation, especially if we have to worry about delaying changes to memory or side-effects. To implement this pattern, the underlying programming model needs to support task cancellation. Fortunately, TBB does support explicit task cancellation and so can be used to implement this pattern.

Speculative selection is frequently used at the very finest scale of parallelism in compilers for hiding instruction latency and for the simulation of multiple threads on SIMD machines.

In the first case, instructions have a certain number of cycles of latency before their results are available. While the processor is executing the instructions for the condition in an if statement, we might as well proceed with the first few instructions of one of the branches. In this case, the speculation pattern might not actually be wasteful, since those instruction slots would have otherwise been idle; however, we do not want to commit the results. Once we know the results of the condition, we may have to discard the results of these speculatively executed instructions. You rarely have to worry about the fine-scale use of this pattern, since it is typically implemented by the compiler or even the hardware. In particular, out-of-order hardware makes extensive use of this pattern for higher performance, but at some cost in power.

However, in the SIMT machine model, multiple threads of control flow are emulated on SIMD machines using masking, which is related to speculative selection. In order to emulate if statements in this model, the condition and both the true and false branches are all evaluated. However, the memory state is updated using masked memory writes so that the results of executing the true branch are only effective for the lanes where the condition was true and conversely for the false branch. This can be optimized if we find the condition is all true or all false early enough, but, like speculative selection, SIMT emulation of control flow is potentially wasteful since results are computed that are not used. Unlike the case with filling in unused instruction slots, using masking to emulate selection like this increases the total execution time, which is the sum of both branches, in addition to increasing the total amount of work.

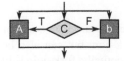

FIGURE 3.18

Speculative selection pattern. The speculative selection pattern is like the serial selection pattern, but we can start the condition evaluation and both sides of the selection at the same time. When the condition is finished evaluating, the unneeded branch is "cancelled."

A similar approach can also be used to emulate iteration on SIMD machines, but in the case of iteration the test for all-true or all-false is used to terminate the loop. In both cases, we may only use the SIMD model over small blocks of a larger workload and use a threading model to manage the blocks.

3.6.4 Workpile

The **workpile** pattern is a generalization of the map pattern where each instance of the elemental function can generate more instances and add them to the "pile" of work to be done. This can be used, for example, in a recursive tree search, where we might want to generate instances to process each of the children of each node of the tree.

Unlike the case with the map pattern with the workpile pattern the total number of instances of the elemental function is not known in advance, nor is the structure of the work regular. This makes the workpile pattern harder to vectorize than the map pattern.

3.6.5 Search

Given a collection, the **search** pattern finds data that meets some criteria. The criteria can be simple, as in an associative array, where typically the criteria is an exact match with some key. The criteria can also be more complex, such as searching for a set of elements in a collection that satisfy a set of logical and arithmetic constraints.

Searching is often associated with sorting, since to make searches more efficient we may want to maintain the data in sorted order. However, this is not necessarily how efficient searches need to be implemented.

Searching can be very powerful, and the relational database access language, SQL, can be considered a data-parallel programming model. The parallel **embedded language** LINQ from Microsoft uses generalized searches as the basis of its programming model.

3.6.6 Segmentation

Operations on collections can be generalized to operate on **segmented** collections. Segmented collections are 1D arrays that are subdivided into non-overlapping but non-uniformly sized partitions. Operations such as scan and reduce can then be generalized to operate on each segment separately, and map can also be generalized to operate on each segment as a whole (map-over-segments) or on every element as usual. Although the lengths of segments can be non-uniform, segmented scans and reductions can be implemented in a regular fashion that is independent of the distribution of the lengths of the segments [BHC+93]. Segmented collective operations are more expensive than regular reduction and scan but are still easy to load balance and vectorize.

The segmentation pattern is interesting because it has been demonstrated that certain recursive algorithms, such as quicksort [Ble90, Ble96], can be implemented using segmented collections to operate in a breadth-first fashion. Such an implementation has advantages over the more obvious depth-first parallel implementation because it is more regular and so can be vectorized. Segmented operations also arise in time-series analysis when the input data is segmented for some reason. This frequently occurs in financial, vision, and speech applications when the data is in fact segmented, such as into different objects or phonemes.

3.6.7 Expand

The **expand** pattern can be thought of as the pack pattern merged with map in that each element of a map can selectively output elements. However, in the expand pattern, each element of the map can output any number of elements—including zero. The elements are packed into the output collection in the order in which they are produced by each element of the map and in segments that are ordered by the spatial position of the map element that produced them. An example is shown in Figure 3.19.

Examples of the use of expand include broad-phase collision detection pair testing when reporting potentially colliding pairs, and compression and decompression algorithms that use variable-rate output on individually compressed blocks.

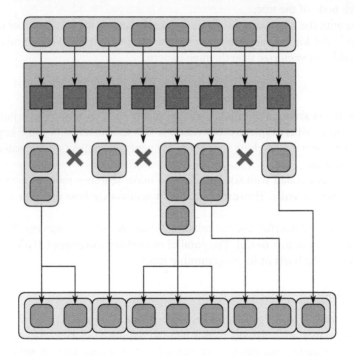

FIGURE 3.19

Expand pattern. Each element of a map can output zero or more elements, which are packed in the order produced and organized into segments corresponding to the location of the elements in the map that produced them.

3.6.8 Category Reduction

Given a collection of data elements each with an associated label, the **category reduction** pattern finds all elements with the same label and reduces them to a single element using an associative (and possibly commutative) operator. The category reduction pattern can be considered a combination of search and segmented reduction. An example is provided in Figure 3.20.

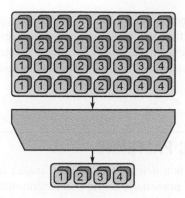

FIGURE 3.20

Category reduction pattern. Given an input collection with labels, all elements with the same label are collected and then reduced to a single element.

Searching and matching are fundamental capabilities and may depend indirectly on sorting or hashing, which are relatively hard to parallelize. This operation may seem esoteric, but we mention it because it is the form of "reduction" use in the Hadoop [Kon11, DG04] Map-Reduce programming model used by Google and others for highly scalable distributed parallel computation. In this model, a map generates output data and a set of labels, and a category reduction combines and organizes the output from the map. It should be emphasized that they do not call the reduction used in their model a category reduction. However, we apply that label to this pattern to avoid confusion with the more basic reduction pattern used in this book.

Examples of use of category reduction include computation of metrics on segmented regions in vision, computation of web analytics, and thousands of other applications implemented with Map-Reduce.

3.6.9 Term Graph Rewriting

In this book we have primarily focused on parallel patterns for imperative languages, especially C++. However, there is one very interesting pattern that is worth mentioning due to its utility in the implementation of functional languages: **term graph rewriting**.

Term graph rewriting matches patterns in a directed acyclic graph, specifically "terms" given by a head node and a sequence of children. It then replaces these terms with new subgraphs. This is applied over and over again, evolving the graph from some initial state to some final state, until no more substitutions are possible. It is worth noting that in this book we have used graphs to describe the relationships between tasks and data. However, in term graph rewriting, graphs *are* the data, and it is the evolution of these graphs over time that produces the computation.

Term graph rewriting is equivalent in power to the lambda calculus, which is usually used to define the semantics of functional languages. However, term graph rewriting is more explicit about data sharing since this is expressed directly in the graph, and this is important for reasoning about the memory usage of a functional program. Term graph rewriting can take place in parallel in different parts of the graph, since under some well-defined conditions term graph rewriting is confluent: It does not matter in which order the rewrites are done; the same result will be produced either way. A very interesting parallel functional language called Concurrent Clean has been implemented using this idea [PvE93, PvE99]. Many other parallel languages, including hardware simulation and synthesis languages, have been defined in terms of this pattern.

3.7　NON-DETERMINISTIC PATTERNS

Normally it is desirable to avoid non-determinism since it makes testing and debugging much more difficult. However, there are some potentially useful non-deterministic patterns.

We will discuss two non-deterministic patterns in this section, **branch and bound** and **transactions**. In some cases, such as search, the input–output behavior of the abstraction may be deterministic but the implementation may be non-deterministic internally. It is useful to understand when non-determinism can be contained inside some abstraction, and conversely when it affects the entire program.

3.7.1　Branch and Bound

The branch and bound pattern is often used to implement search, where it is highly effective. It is, however, a non-deterministic pattern and a good example of when non-determinism can be useful.

Suppose you have a set of items and you want to do an associative search over this set to find an item that matches some criteria. To do a parallel search, the simplest approach is to partition the set and search each subset in parallel. However, suppose we only need one result, and any data that satisfies the search criteria is acceptable. In that case, once an item matching the search criteria is found, in any one of the parallel subset searches, the searches in the other subsets can be cancelled.

The branch and bound strategy can actually lead to superlinear speedups, unlike many other parallel algorithms. However, if there are multiple possible matches, this pattern is non-deterministic because which match is returned depends on the timing of the searches over each subset. Since this form of non-determinism is fundamental in the definition of the result ("return the first result found that matches the criteria"), it is hard to remove this form of non-determinism. However, to get a superlinear speedup, the cancellation of in-progress tasks needs to be implemented in an efficient manner.

This pattern is also used for mathematical optimization, but with a few additional features. In mathematical optimization, you are given an objective function, some constraint equations, and a domain. The function depends on certain parameters. The domain and the constraint equations define legal values for the parameters. Within the given domain, the goal of optimization is to find values of the parameters that maximize (or minimize) the objective function.

Search and optimization are related in that in optimization we are searching for the location of the optimum, so one way to approach the problem is exactly like with search: Break up the domain into subdomains, search each region in parallel, and when a "good enough" value is found in one domain cancel the other parallel searches. But what conditions, exactly, allow us to cancel other searches?

We can cancel a search if we can prove that the optimum in a domain Y can be no better than y but we have already found a solution x better than y. In this case we can cancel any search in Y. Mathematically, we can compute bounds using techniques such as interval analysis [HW04] and often apply the subdivide-and-bound approach recursively.

What is interesting about this is that the global optima are fixed by the mathematical problem; therefore, they are unique. The code can be designed to return the same result every time it is run. Even though the algorithm might be non-deterministic internally, the output can be deterministic if implemented carefully.

The name "branch and bound" comes from the fact that we recursively divide the problem into parts, then bound the solution in each part. Related techniques, such as alpha-beta pruning [GC94], are also used in state-space search in artificial intelligence.

3.7.2 Transactions

Transactions are used when a central repository for data needs several different updates and we do not care what order the updates are done in, as long as the repository is kept in a consistent state. An example would be a database recording transactions on a bank account. We do not care too much in what order the deposits and withdrawals are recorded, as long as the balance at the end of the day is correct. In fact, in this special case, since deposits and withdrawals are using an associative operation (addition), the result is in fact deterministic. However, in general, transaction operations will be non-associative and in that case the outcome will not be deterministic if the order in which the individual operations are performed is non-deterministic.

For a concrete example that illuminates where transactions might be useful, suppose you are using a hash table. The kinds of operations you want to use on a hash table might involve inserting elements and searching for elements. Suppose that the hash table is implemented using a set of buckets with elements that map to the same bucket stored in a linked list. If multiple parallel tasks try to insert elements into the same bucket, we could use some implementation of the transaction pattern to make sure the linked lists are updated consistently. The order in which the elements are inserted into the linked lists may not be consistent from run to run. However, the overall program may still be deterministic if the internal non-determinism is not exposed outside the implementation of the pattern itself— that is, if hash table searches always return the same data no matter what the initial ordering of the lists was.

Implementing a deterministic hash table using non-deterministic mechanisms may require some additional effort, however. For example, suppose the same key is inserted twice with different data. In this case, suppose only one of the two possible data elements should be retained. If we retain the last element inserted, creating a dependency on timing, the hash table will be non-deterministic and this has the potential to make the whole program non-deterministic. On the other hand, if we use a rule to choose which of the two data elements to retain, such as picking the largest data element, then we can make the output deterministic.

The implementation of transactions is important. Of course, they could be implemented with locks, but a more scalable approach uses a commit and rollback protocol, as in a database transactions. When the term "transactions" is used it generally refers to this form of implementation.

3.8 PROGRAMMING MODEL SUPPORT FOR PATTERNS

Many of the patterns discussed in this chapter are supported directly in one or more of the programming models discussed in this book. By direct support, we mean that there is a language construct that corresponds to the pattern. Even if a pattern is not directly supported by one of the programming models we consider, it may be possible to implement it using other features.

In the following, we briefly describe the patterns supported by each of Cilk Plus, TBB, OpenMP, ArBB, and OpenCL. Patterns can be supported directly by a feature of the programming model, or they may be implementable using other features. A summary of serial pattern support is provided in Table 3.1, and a summary of parallel pattern support is provided in Tables 3.2 and 3.3. These tables use an F to indicate when a programming model includes an explicit feature supporting that pattern, an I if the pattern is implementable with that model, or a blank if there is no straightforward way to implement the pattern with that model. Some patterns are implementable with other patterns, and when an example of this is given in the book it is indicated with a P. Table 3.2 also includes section references to examples using or implementing that pattern. Table 3.3 indicates support for some additional patterns that are discussed in this book but for which, unfortunately, no suitable examples were available.

We additionally provide section references when an example is given in this book of a particular parallel pattern with a particular model. Unfortunately space does not permit us to give an example of every parallel pattern with every programming model, even when a pattern is implementable with that model. In other cases, common patterns (such as map) may show up in many different examples. Please refer to the online site for the book. Some additional examples will be made available there that can fill in some of these gaps.

Table 3.1 Summary of programming model support for the serial patterns discussed in this book. Note that some of the parallel programming models we consider do not, in fact, support all the common serial programming patterns. In particular, note that recursion and memory allocation are limited on some model.

Serial Pattern	TBB	Cilk Plus	OpenMP	ArBB	OpenCL
(Serial) Nesting	F	F	F	F	F
Sequence	F	F	F	F	F
Selection	F	F	F	F	F
Iteration	F	F	F	F	F
Recursion	F	F	F		?
Random Read	F	F	F	F	F
Random Write	F	F	F		F
Stack Allocation	F	F	F		?
Heap Allocation	F	F	F		
Closures				F	F
Objects	F	F	F(w/C++)	F	

Table 3.2 Summary of programming model support for the patterns discussed in this book. F: Supported directly, with a special feature. I: Can be implemented easily and efficiently using other features. P: Implementations of one pattern in terms of others, listed under the pattern being implemented. Blank means the particular pattern cannot be implemented in that programming model (or that an efficient implementation cannot be implemented easily). When examples exist in this book of a particular pattern with a particular model, section references are given.

Parallel Pattern	TBB	Cilk Plus	OpenMP	ArBB	OpenCL
Parallel nesting	F	F			
Map	F 4.2.3;	F 4.2.4;4.2.5;	F 4.2.6;	F 4.2.7;4.2.8;	F 4.2.9;
	4.3.3	4.3.4;4.3.5	4.3.6	4.3.7	4.3.8
	11	11			
Stencil	I 10	I 10	I	F 10	I
Workpile	F				I
Reduction	F 5.3.4	F 5.3.5	F 5.3.6	F 5.3.7	I
	11	11			
Scan	F 5.6.5	I 5.6.3	I 5.6.4	F 5.6.6	I
	14	P 8.11	P 5.4.4		
		14			
Fork–join	F 8.9.2	F 8.7;	I		
	13	8.9.1			
		13			
Recurrence		P 8.12			
Superscalar sequence				F	
Futures					
Speculative selection					
Pack	I 14	I 14	I	F	I
Expand	I	I	I	I	I
Pipeline	F 12	I 12	I		
Geometric decomposition	I 15	I 15	I	I	I
Search	I	I	I	I	I
Category reduction	I	I	I	I	I
Gather	I	F	I	F	I
Atomic scatter	F	I	I		I
Permutation scatter	F	F	F	F	F
Merge scatter	I	I	I	F	I
Priority scatter					

Table 3.3 Additional patterns discussed. F: Supported directly, with a special feature. I: Can be implemented easily and efficiently using other features. Blank means the particular pattern cannot be implemented in that programming model (or that an efficient implementation cannot be implemented easily).

Parallel Pattern	TBB	Cilk Plus	OpenMP	ArBB	OpenCL
Superscalar sequence	I	I	I		F
Futures	I	I	I		I
Speculative selection	I				
Workpile	F	I	I		I
Expand	I	I	I	I	I
Search	I	I	I	I	I
Category reduction	I	I	I	I	I
Atomic scatter	F	I	I		I
Permutation scatter	F	F	F	F	F
Merge scatter	I	I	I	F	I
Priority scatter					

3.8.1 Cilk Plus

The feature set of Cilk Plus is simple, based primarily on an efficient implementation of the fork–join pattern, but general enough that many other patterns can also be implemented in terms of its basic features. Cilk Plus also supports many of the other patterns discussed in this chapter as built-in features, with implementations usually built around fork–join. For some patterns, however, it may be necessary to combine Cilk Plus with components of TBB, such as if **atomic operations** or scalable parallel dynamic memory allocation are required. Here are the patterns supported directly by Cilk Plus.

Nesting, Recursion, Fork–Join

Nesting to arbitrary depth is supported by `cilk_spawn`. Specifically, this construct supports fork–join parallelism, which generalizes recursion. Support for other patterns in Cilk Plus are based on this fundamental mechanism and so can also be nested. As discussed later, fork–join in Cilk Plus is implemented in such a way that large amounts of **parallel slack** (the amount of potential parallelism) can be expressed easily but can be mapped efficiently (and mostly automatically) onto finite hardware resources. Specifically, the `cilk_spawn` keyword only marks opportunities for a parallel fork; it does not mandate it. Such forks only result in parallel execution if some other core becomes idle and looks for work to "steal."

Reduction

The reduction pattern is supported in a very general way by **hyperobjects** in Cilk Plus. Hyperobjects can support reductions based on arbitrary commutative and associative operations. The semantics of reduction hyperobjects are integrated with the fork–join model: new temporary accumulators are created at spawn points, and the associative combiner operations are applied at joins.

Map, Workpile

The map pattern can be expressed in Cilk Plus using `cilk_for`. Although a loop syntax is used, not all loops can be parallelized by converting them to `cilk_for`, since loops must not have loop-carried dependencies. Only loops with independent bodies can be parallelized, so this construct is in fact a map. This is not an uncommon constraint in programming models supporting "parallel for" constructs; it is also true of the "for" constructs in TBB and OpenMP. The implementation of this construct in Cilk Plus is based on recursive subdivision and fork–join, and so distributes the overhead of managing the map over multiple threads.

The map pattern can also be expressed in Cilk Plus using elemental functions, which when invoked inside an explicitly vectorized loop also give a "map" pattern. This form explicitly targets vector instructions. Because of this, it is more constrained than the `cilk_for` mechanism. However, these mechanisms can be composed.

The workpile pattern can be implemented in Cilk Plus directly on top of the basic fork–join model.

Scatter, Gather

The Cilk Plus array notations support scatter and gather patterns directly. The array notations also allow sequences of primitive map operations (for example, the addition of two arrays) to be expressed. Operations on entire arrays are supported with a special array slice syntax.

3.8.2 Threading Building Blocks

Threading Building Blocks (TBB) supports fork–join with a work-stealing load balancer as its basic model. In contrast with Cilk Plus, TBB is a portable ISO C++ library, not a compiler extension. Because TBB is not integrated into the compiler, its fork–join implementation is not quite as efficient as Cilk Plus, and it cannot directly generate vectorized code. However, TBB also provides implementations of several patterns not available directly in Cilk Plus, such as pipelines. Because it is a portable library, TBB is also available today for more platforms than Cilk Plus, although this may change over time.

In addition to a basic work-stealing scheduler that supports the fork–join model of parallelism, TBB also includes several other components useful in conjunction with other programming models, including a scalable parallel dynamic memory allocator and an operating-system-independent interface for atomic operations and locks. As previously discussed, locks should be used with caution and as a last resort, since they are non-deterministic and can potentially cause deadlocks and race conditions. Locks also make scheduling non-greedy, which results in sub-optimal scheduling.Here are the patterns supported directly by TBB.

Nesting, Recursion, Fork–Join

TBB supports nesting of tasks to arbitrary depth via the fork–join model. Like Cilk Plus, TBB uses work-stealing load balancing which is both scalable and locality-preserving. However, TBB can also support more general task graph dependencies than the planar graphs generated by the Cilk Plus fork–join implementation. These patterns are accessed by the `parallel_invoke` and task graph features of TBB.

Map

The map patterns is implemented in TBB using the `parallel_for` and `parallel_foreach` functions. Lambda functions can be used as arguments to these so that the required elemental function can be described as part of the call rather than being separately declared. As is clear from the names, these functions are useful for parallelizing `for` loops, but they do have some additional restrictions, so not all `for` loops can be parallelized. In particular, each invocation of the elemental function body needs to be independent, as we have described for the map pattern, and the number of iterations needs to be fixed and known in advance.

Workpile

The workpile pattern can be accessed from TBB using the `parallel_do` construct. This is similar to the `parallel_for` pattern, with the difference that the number of invocations does not need to be known in advance. In fact, additional invocations can be generated from inside the "body" of this construct.

Reduction

The reduction pattern can be accessed via the `parallel_reduce` construct. This construct allows the specification of an arbitrary combiner function. However, in order for the result to be computed deterministically the reduction function needs to be both associative and commutative (not just associative). If a deterministic reduction is needed, a `deterministic_parallel_reduce` function is provided.

Scan

The scan pattern can be accessed via the `parallel_scan` construct. An arbitrary successor function can be specified in order for the result to be deterministic. As with reduction, such a function must be both fully associative and commutative in order for the scan to be deterministic. There is no built-in deterministic scan in TBB but one can be implemented using other features of TBB.

Pipeline

The pipeline pattern can be specified directly with the `parallel_pipeline` construct, which can support not only linear pipelines but also directed acyclic graphs of pipeline stages. TBB's support for pipelines is demonstrated at length in Chapter 9.

Speculative Selection, Branch and Bound

TBB supports task cancellation, which can be used to implement many other patterns, including non-deterministic patterns such as branch and bound.

3.8.3 OpenMP

OpenMP is a standard interface for parallel programming based on annotating serial code so that certain constructs, in particular loops, can be reinterpreted as parallel constructs. The basic patterns it supports directly as features are map and reduce, although other patterns can also be implemented. In addition to the data-parallel map pattern, which also supports vectorization, recent versions of OpenMP also support a general task construct which allows other more irregular patterns to be implemented.

However, the implementation of OpenMP is usually based directly on threads, which raises various practical issues. In particular, nested use of OpenMP can lead to overdecomposition and OpenMP does not include a load balancer. Therefore, nesting is *not* listed as a pattern supported by OpenMP. Also, certain features in OpenMP that map units of work directly to threads preclude using an automatic task-based load balancer. OpenMP does not include generalized reductions but does include locks. Interestingly, a recent study [AF11] of OpenMP applications showed that the most common use of locks was to implement generalized reductions and load balancing. Inclusion of these features into the OpenMP standard would significantly reduce the need for locks.

One advantage of OpenMP over the other models discussed here is that it is also available for Fortran, as well as C and C++. Cilk Plus is available for both C and C++, while TBB is only available for C++.

Map, Workpile

OpenMP supports the map pattern by annotating a `for` loop (or `DO` loop in Fortran) to indicate to the compiler that the annotated loop should be interpreted as a parallel construct. Each iteration of the loop is executed in parallel in a different thread, and the end of the loop body implements a barrier.

The workpile pattern can also be implemented in OpenMP using its task model.

Reduction

When a loop body includes updates to variables declared outside the loop body with a predefined set of associative (or semi-associative floating point) operators, the variable may be marked as a reduction variable. In this case, OpenMP automatically implements a parallel reduction.

Fork–Join

OpenMP supports a general task model that can be used to implement the fork–join pattern. The task model can also be used to implement various other patterns discussed in this book. OpenMP is not a focus of this book, so we do not explore the OpenMP task model in depth, but the addition of tasks adds significant power to the OpenMP programming model.

Stencil, Geometric Decomposition, Gather, Scatter

There is no built-in support for directly expressing stencil, geometric decomposition, gather, or scatter in OpenMP, but many of the applications for which OpenMP is used also use these patterns. However, except for reduction variables, OpenMP generally does not manage data, so data access patterns are expressed through the base language functionality rather than through OpenMP itself.

3.8.4 Array Building Blocks

The basic building blocks of ArBB are based on many of the fundamental patterns discussed in this book. ArBB also supports automatic fusion of these basic building blocks and can generate vectorized code as well as code that runs on multiple cores. Unfortunately, ArBB at present does not support nesting or recursion. The patterns directly supported by ArBB include the following.

Map

The map patterns is supported using elemental functions, which must be separately declared and then invoked by a `map` operation over a collection or index set. Like the array notation of Cilk Plus, ArBB also supports arithmetic operations over entire collections (in other words, the vector operation style of map) but implements optimizations so that a sequence of such operations is as efficient as a map with an explicit elemental function.

Reduction, Scan

Reductions are supported but only over a set of known operators. Reductions over truly associative operations, such as modular integer addition and minimum and maximum, are both deterministic and repeatable.

The scan pattern is supported with **collective operations** scan and iscan, again for a fixed set of operators. The scan operation supports both exclusive scan, in which every output does not include the corresponding element of the input, and inclusive scan, in which every output does include the corresponding element of the input.

Although the reduction and scan operations in ArBB do not support custom combiner functions, the ArBB implementation supports automatic fusion of multiple map and reduction operations into a single operation. In practice, this can replace many of the uses of custom reduction and scan functions.

Unfortunately, in the current implementations of reduction and scan in ArBB, the results are not guaranteed to be deterministic if the combiner is not truly associative, in particular for floating-point operations. It is, however, possible to implement deterministic reductions and scans for these operations (as well as for custom combiner functions) using other features of ArBB.

Scatter, Gather

Random reads and writes can be implemented in ArBB using either scalar reads and writes inside maps, or with the collective operations gather and scatter. The scatter implementation only supports the **permutation scatter** pattern (see Section 6.2), which means it is only guaranteed to work correctly when there are no duplicate addresses. However, duplicates are only checked in a debugging mode. Whenever possible, scatter should be avoided since it is not checked in deployment mode and if used incorrectly could potentially lead to incorrect output.

Pack

The pack pattern is supported directly in ArBB with a collective operation, pack. The inverse of pack is also supported with unpack. Note that pack is a safe, deterministic operation that can be used in place of scatter in many situations.

3.8.5 OpenCL

The OpenCL programming model was designed to allow the use of **attached co-processors** with separate memories and using a tiled SIMD architecture, such as GPUs, to be accessed as computational devices. It also maps reasonably well onto CPUs with vector instructions.

OpenCL does not support full nesting but does provide two explicit levels of parallelism. One level (work-groups) maps onto the multiple cores in the devices; the other (work-items) maps onto SIMD lanes and multiple threads in each core.

The programming model of OpenCL is quite similar to that of CUDA, but since OpenCL is standardized and CUDA is not, we only give OpenCL examples in this book.

Map

When a kernel function is written in OpenCL and then executed on a device, it implements the map pattern. This is similar to the use of elemental functions in ArBB and Cilk Plus array notation. Each execution of a kernel executes a set of instances. Each instance is called a work item. When the map is executed, the work items are automatically tiled into sets of parallel work called work groups. Within each work-group, the implementation typically emulates control flow over multiple work items using masking over SIMD lanes. It is also possible to communicate using shared memory within a work group, but not between work groups. Generally, communication requires the insertion of a barrier, since a work group may be further decomposed into multiple chunks by the implementation that may run asynchronously. Barrier-free communication is possible within a single SIMD "chunk" within a work group on specific hardware but this is not standardized, and hence it is not advised.

Gather

Within an OpenCL kernel, random reads to memory can be performed. This can be done either to on-chip local memory (very fast and shared within a work group) or to global memory. On some processors supporting OpenCL, accesses to global memory are cached, but on others they are not. In the latter case, the implementation may use software pipelining to hide memory access latency. Multiple threads may also be used on multicore processors that support it. The global memory is still typically local to the co-processor, so OpenCL includes additional directives to do memory transfers to and from the host.

Note that with OpenCL maximizing throughput rather than minimizing latency is the goal. Multiple threads and software pipelining overlap memory access latency with additional computation; they do not eliminate the memory access latency. In fact, use of these techniques can increase latency overall. This style of "throughput" computation may also be used with other throughput-oriented programming models, such as ArBB and CUDA.

Scatter

Scatter is supported in OpenCL but some care is needed to deal with **collisions** (parallel writes to the same address). Recent versions of OpenCL include standardized **atomic operations**, and many processors targeted by OpenCL implementations support these efficiently in hardware.

Reduction, Scan, Pack, Expand

OpenCL does not support the reduction pattern directly as a feature but it is implementable. Typically, the array to be reduced is divided into tiles, each tile reduced using SIMD parallelism in a single work group, and then a final pass using a single work group is used to combine the results. However, there are several possible implementations, and the most efficient implementation does tend to depend on the device. The most efficient implementations use SIMD parallelism in a way that requires commutativity [Inc09b, Cat10].

Scan is also not built in, but there are several possible ways to implement it efficiently [Inc09a]. Since scan and gather/scatter can be implemented, pack can also be implemented. For efficiency, like scan and reduce, pack should be implemented directly in a tiled fashion. Likewise, with some overallocation of memory, it should be possible to implement a limited form of expand. However, OpenCL does not have dynamic memory allocation built-in. Dynamic memory allocation could be implemented using atomics in the same way as workpile. In Table 3.2, have marked "expand" as being imple-mentable although for efficiency it may have to be limited to finite expansion factors per element. It is notable that vertex shaders, implemented in DirectX (an API for graphics) on the same GPUs targeted by OpenCL, also implements the expand pattern, but limited to finite expansion factors.

Stencil
Stencil is not a built-in feature of OpenCL but can be implemented efficiently [Bor09]. Ideally, local shared memory should be used explicitly to support data reuse on devices without cache.

Workpile
OpenCL does not support the workpile pattern directly but it is possible to implement a work queue using atomics in CUDA, which has a similar programming model [GPM11]. Work queues are more limited than fork–join, so we have not marked fork–join as being implementable with OpenCL, although it might in theory be possible.

Superscalar Sequences
Multiple kernels can be queued up to execute asynchronously on OpenCL devices. Dependencies between kernels can be given declaratively in the form of events. OpenCL itself does not track data dependencies, but if appropriate events are created that correspond to data dependencies, then OpenCL can implement the superscalar sequence pattern.

The event/task-queue model of OpenCL is similar to futures, although it does not support all fea-tures that might be desirable in a futures implementation, such as cancellation. Therefore, we have not listed futures under the patterns supported by OpenCL, although this could change as the standard evolves.

Geometric Decomposition
Geometric decomposition is implementable on OpenCL, and in fact often necessary for performance. However, usually geometric decompositions are limited to one level of decomposition in order to map tiles onto shared local memory.

Closures
OpenCL is implemented using dynamic compilation so new kernels can in theory be implemented at runtime. The interface to this feature, however, is not as convenient as ArBB, since strings are used to define kernels.

Objects are not a built-in feature of OpenCL, since it is based on C. OpenCL also does not generally support a stack and recursion. Although some implementations may allow this, it is non-standard.

3.9 SUMMARY
In this chapter, we introduced the concept of patterns and gave a survey of a set of patterns useful in parallel programming. The types of patterns we focused on are also known as algorithmic skeletons, in that they tend to arise in the implementation of algorithms. We also related these patterns to the patterns of block control flow used in structured parallel programming. One very important pattern, nesting, appears in combination with both serial and parallel pattern and allows for hierarchical composition.

For serial patterns, the nesting pattern allows for nested control flow constructs, while in parallel programming it allows for nested parallelism.

Programming models can also be characterized by the patterns they support, either directly with a built-in feature or with other features that allow a straightforward and efficient implementation of a pattern. We have summarized the patterns supported, directly or indirectly, by the parallel programming models used in this book.

The remainder of this book goes into further detail on the most important patterns and gives many examples of the use of these patterns.

Map

4

This chapter goes into depth on the **map** pattern, introduced in Section 3.3.2. Both serial and parallel versions of this pattern are given in Figure 4.1. The map pattern compresses the time it takes to execute a loop, but it only applies when all instances of the loop body are independent.

Map applies a function to every element of a collection of data in parallel. More generally, map executes a set of function invocations, each of which accesses separate data elements. We will call the functions used in map **elemental functions**. The elemental functions used in a map should have no side effects to allow all the instances of the map to be able to execute in any order. This independence offers maximum concurrency with no need to synchronize between separate elements of the map, except upon completion. There is, however, no assumption or requirement that the instances of the map actually *will* be run simultaneously, or in any particular order. This provides the maximum flexibility for scheduling operations.

The map pattern is simple, being just a set of identical computations on different data, without any communication. It is so simple it is sometimes called **embarrassing parallelism**. However, while conceptually simple, map is the foundation of many important applications, and its importance should not be underestimated. It is important to recognize when map can be used since it is often one of the most efficient patterns. For example, if you do not have one problem to solve but many, your parallel solution may be as simple as solving several unrelated problems at once. This trivial solution can be seen as an instance of the map pattern.

Map is often combined with other patterns to make new patterns. For example, the **gather** pattern is really a combination of a serial random read pattern and the map pattern. Chapter 5 discusses a set of patterns that often combine with the map pattern, the **collectives**, including **reduction** and **scan**. Chapter 6 discusses various patterns for data reorganization, which also often combine with map. Often map is used for the basic parallel computation, and then it is combined with other patterns to represent any needed communication or coordination. Chapter 7 also discusses the **stencil** and **recurrence** patterns, which can be seen as generalizations of map to more complex input and output dependencies. Some additional generalizations, such as **workpile**, are also briefly discussed in this chapter.

Patterns have both semantic and implementation aspects. The semantics of the map pattern are simple, but achieving a scalable implementation often requires a surprising amount of care for best performance. For example, invoking a separate thread for each function invocation in a map is not a good idea if the amount of work each instance does is small. Threads provide **mandatory parallelism**, which is unnecessary in the case of a map, and potentially too heavyweight—a tasking model, which is lightweight but specifies only **optional parallelism**, is more suitable. It is also important to parallelize the overhead of synchronization at the beginning and end of the map and to deal with the fact that the functions invoked in each instance of the map may, in the general case, vary in the amount of

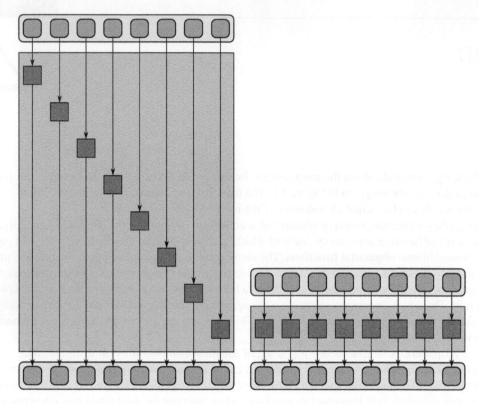

FIGURE 4.1

Serial and parallel execution of a map pattern. In the map pattern, an elemental function is applied to all elements of a collection, producing a new collection with the same shape as the input. In serial execution, a map is often implemented as a loop (with each instance of the loop body consisting of one invocation of the elemental function), but because there are no dependencies between loop iterations all instances can execute at the same time, given enough processors.

work they consume. Fortunately, the parallel programming models we use in this book include good implementations of the map pattern that take care of these details. For completeness we will discuss such implementation issues, but if you use a good programming model it will probably be unnecessary for you to worry about this yourself.

The map pattern is commonly used as the basis of **vectorization** as well as **parallelization**. To support full **nesting** of patterns, it is important to be able to support serial control flow and data access patterns inside a vectorized map. Again, these implementation details are (probably) not something you have to worry about yourself, if you are using a programming model that supports them, but the emulation of control flow in a vectorized map does have some performance implications.

In the following chapters, we will discuss some additional optimizations that are possible when combinations of map with other parallel patterns are considered. One particular combination of patterns, Map-Reduce, is at the heart of the success of Internet giant Google [DG04, Kon11]. Map-Reduce is used for thousands of computations on large distributed systems daily. This is a testament to the power of parallelism to process enormous quantities of data efficiently. Even after discussing only a small number of patterns it will be possible to understand the basis of such a system.

This is the first chapter where we will show code samples. We give examples demonstrating the map pattern in various programming models, including TBB, Cilk Plus, OpenMP, ArBB, and OpenCL. Unlike the cases in the later chapters, these code samples are not meant to showcase efficient implementations. Instead, these samples have been intentionally simplified to show the map pattern in its purest form, so they can be used as templates for building up more complex programs. Also, it should be noted that code samples in this book do not necessarily show all the wrapper code needed for a full application. However, full application source code, including all of the necessary wrapper code for each of the examples in this book, is available online. We also do not provide full documentation for each of the programming models used in this book, since such documentation is available online. However, for a summary of the features of the primary programming models used in this book and pointers to further reading, please see the appendices.

4.1 MAP

In the map pattern a function, which we will call an **elemental function**, is replicated and applied to different data. We can think of either applying the elemental function to each element of a collection of data or applying it to a set of indices that are then used to access different data for each of many instances of the function. The second approach is often used in some systems because map operations frequently access several sources of data and using a common set of indices is a convenient way to do this. We will call each parallel invocation of the elemental function on a different set of data, or portion of the index space, an **instance** of the elemental function.

The map pattern is closely associated with the **SIMD** model if there is no control flow in the function or the **SPMD** model if there is control flow in the function. The map pattern is also used with the **SIMT** model, which is just the SPMD model simulated on tiled SIMD hardware. These names were explained in Section 2.4.3. They do not refer to the map pattern itself, but to specific mechanisms for implementing it.

Instead of a single function, the map pattern may also be expressed indirectly as a sequence of vector operations. We will show in Section 4.4 that this form is semantically equivalent to the standard form using an elemental function. Since grouping operations is usually more efficient, implementations may try to convert sequences of vector operations into elemental functions automatically.

The map pattern corresponds to a parallelization of the serial iteration pattern in the special case that all iterations are independent. Therefore, the map pattern is often expressed in programming models using a "parallel for" construct. This is also equivalent to the elemental function form. In the case of the "parallel for," the loop body is the elemental function and the index variable in the parallel for construct generates an index space. Such "parallel for" constructs, being just alternative syntaxes for the map pattern, are significantly more restricted than regular `for` loops.

The map pattern assumes elemental functions have certain properties. In particular, elemental functions should not have side effects. Instances of elemental functions may read from other data in memory, as long as that data is not being modified in parallel. When we address data reorganization patterns in Chapter 6, we discuss the **gather** pattern. A gather is just a set of random reads inside a map. It is also possible to combine random write with a map, giving the **scatter** pattern, although this can cause **non-determinism** and **race conditions.** Therefore, we assume in a "pure" map that random reads from memory are permitted but not random writes. Instead of writing to random locations in memory, each element of a "pure" map can output a fixed number of results.

The map pattern is **deterministic** if side effects and hence interdependencies between elemental function instances are avoided. In the correct use of map, the outcome of the map does not depend on the order in which the various instances of the elemental function are executed.

As noted, the parameters to the instances of an elemental function can be either data itself or an index that is then used to access data using a random memory read. In the case that data itself is the input to a map, there are two kinds of arguments: data that is different for each instance of the map, and data that is the same. At least some of the data fed into each instance of a map should be different, of course; otherwise there would be no point in running multiple instances. However, it is frequently useful to "broadcast" to all instances of the map some common data that is the same in all instances. We will call data that is different for each instance of the map **varying** data, while data that is broadcast to each instance and is the same for every instance we will call **uniform** data.

4.2 SCALED VECTOR ADDITION (SAXPY)

We begin our discussion of map with a simple example: scaled vector addition of single-precision floating point data. This operation, called SAXPY, is an important primitive in many linear algebra operations.

We emphasize that, since SAXPY does very little work relative to the amount of data it produces and consumes, its scalability is limited. However, this example is useful for introducing map as well as the concepts of **uniform** and **varying** parameters, and our code samples show how these concepts are expressed in different parallel programming models.

4.2.1 Description of the Problem

The SAXPY operation scales a vector **x** by scalar value a and adds it to vector **y**, elementwise. Both vectors have length n. This operation shows up frequently in linear algebra operations, such as for row cancellation in Gaussian elimination. The name SAXPY is from the industry standard **BLAS** (Basic Linear Algebra Subprograms) library for the single-precision version of this operation. Double precision is DAXPY, complex is CAXPY, and double complex is ZAXPY.

The mathematical definition of SAXPY is:

$$\mathbf{y} \leftarrow a\mathbf{x} + \mathbf{y},$$

where vector **x** is used as an input and vector **y** is used for both input and output; that is, the old value of **y** is destroyed. Overwriting an input like this is not a fundamental mathematical requirement but is how it is defined in BLAS because it is the common use case. For our purposes, it lets us show how to use the same variable for both input and output in different programming models.

Alternatively, SAXPY operation can be described as a function acting over individual elements, and applying this function to every element of the input data. Suppose the ith element of **x** is x_i and the ith element of **y** is y_i. Then we can define

$$f(t,p,q) = tp + q,$$
$$\forall i: \ y_i \leftarrow f(a, x_i, y_i).$$

Function f is an example of an **elemental function** (Section 1.5.3). The variables t, p, and q are used here in the definition of the elemental function to emphasize that these are formal arguments, to be bound to individual elements of the input and output collections. The map pattern invokes the elemental function as many times as there are elements in its input. We call each such invocation an *instance* of the map.

As discussed in the introduction, elemental functions have two kinds of arguments. There are arguments like a that are the same in every invocation of the function, and those like x_i and y_i that are different for every invocation. Parameters like a will be called **uniform** parameters, since they are the same (uniform) in every invocation of the function. Those like x_i and y_i will be called **varying** parameters.

Because the **arithmetic intensity** of SAXPY is low, it probably will not scale very well. This operation, called SAXPY in the single-precision case, is a Level 1 BLAS routine. Level 2 BLAS routines perform matrix–vector operations, and Level 3 BLAS routines perform matrix–matrix operations. Higher level BLAS routines offer more opportunity for parallelism and hence scale better. There is simply not enough work in each unit of parallelism for most Level 1 BLAS routines relative to the cost of managing the parallelism and accessing memory. For more complex operations that do more work, however, the map pattern can scale very well, since there is no communication and synchronization only occurs at the end of the map.

Although the SAXPY example is simple, it does give us an opportunity to talk about several key concepts, and the examples can be used as a template for more complex applications of the map pattern.

We will demonstrate how to code the SAXPY example in both TBB and Cilk Plus, as well as OpenMP, ArBB, and OpenCL. In some cases, we will give multiple versions if there is more than one way to code the algorithm. The TBB version is explicitly **tiled** for better performance. We provide two Cilk Plus versions: one written using a parallel `cilk_for` and another using Cilk array notation.

Both TBB and Cilk Plus support the map pattern by a "parallel for" construct. Additionally, in Cilk Plus you can express the same operation using expressions over array sections. However, to start off with, we will show a serial implementation in order to provide a baseline.

4.2.2 Serial Implementation

As a basis for comparison, a serial implementation of the SAXPY operation is shown in Listing 4.1. The main algorithm is expressed as a loop that visits each element of the input and output arrays in turn and performs an operation on each element. Note that all the loop iterations are independent, which is what makes this algorithm a candidate for parallel implementation with the map pattern.

4.2.3 TBB

Listing 4.2 gives a TBB implementation of SAXPY. This implementation uses a **lambda function**, a feature introduced by the C++11 standard and widely available in new C++ compilers. We use lambda

```
1   void saxpy_serial(
2       size_t n,          // the number of elements in the vectors
3       float a,           // scale factor
4       const float x[],   // the first input vector
5       float y[]          // the output vector and second input vector
6   ) {
7       for (size_t i = 0; i < n; ++i)
8           y[i] = a * x[i] + y[i];
9   }
```

LISTING 4.1

Serial implementation of SAXPY in C.

```
1   void saxpy_tbb(
2       int n,        // the number of elements in the  vectors
3       float a,      // scale  factor
4       float x[],    // the  first  input vector
5       float y[]     // the  output  vector and second input  vector
6   ) {
7       tbb::parallel_for(
8           tbb::blocked_range<int>(0, n),
9           [&](tbb::blocked_range<int> r) {
10              for (size_t i = r.begin(); i != r.end(); ++i)
11                  y[i] = a * x[i] + y[i];
12          }
13      );
14  }
```

LISTING 4.2

Tiled implementation of SAXPY in TBB. Tiling not only leads to better **spatial locality** but also exposes opportunities for vectorization by the host compiler.

functions for brevity throughout the book, though they are not required for using TBB. Appendix D.2 discusses lambda functions and how to write the equivalent code by hand if you need to use an old C++ compiler.

The TBB code exploits **tiling**. The parallel_for breaks the half-open range $[0, n)$ into subranges and processes each subrange r with a separate task. Hence, each subrange r acts as a tile, which is processed by the serial for loop in the code. Here the range and subrange are implemented as blocked_range objects. Appendix C.3 says more about the mechanics of parallel_for.

TBB uses thread parallelism but does not, by itself, vectorize the code. It depends on the underlying C++ compiler to do that. On the other hand, tiling does expose opportunities for vectorization, so if the basic serial algorithm can be vectorized then typically the TBB code can be, too. Generally, the performance of the serial code inside TBB tasks will depend on the performance of the code generated by the C++ compiler with which it is used.

4.2.4 Cilk Plus

A basic Cilk Plus implementation of the SAXPY operation is given in Listing 4.3. The "parallel for" syntax approach is used here, as with TBB, although the syntax is closer to a regular for loop. In fact, an ordinary for loop can often be converted to a cilk_for construct if all iterations of the loop body are independent—that is, if it is a map. As with TBB, the cilk_for is not explicitly vectorized but the compiler may attempt to auto-vectorize. There are restrictions on the form of a cilk_for loop. See Appendix B.5 for details.

4.2.5 Cilk Plus with Array Notation

It is also possible in Cilk Plus to explicitly specify vector operations using Cilk Plus array notation, as in Listing 4.4. Here x[0:n] and y[0:n] refer to n consecutive elements of each array, starting with x[0] and y[0]. A variant syntax allows specification of a stride between elements, using x[start: length:stride]. Sections of the same length can be combined with operators. Note that there is no cilk_for in Listing 4.4.

```
1  void saxpy_cilk(
2     int n,       // the number of elements in the vectors
3     float a,     // scale factor
4     float x[],   // the first input vector
5     float y[]    // the output vector and second input vector
6  ) {
7     cilk_for (int i = 0; i < n; ++i)
8        y[i] = a * x[i] + y[i];
9  }
```

LISTING 4.3

SAXPY in Cilk Plus using cilk_for.

```
1  void saxpy_array_notation(
2     int n,       // the number of elements in the  vectors
3     float a,     // scale  factor
4     float x[],   // the input  vector
5     float y[]    // the output  vector and  offset
6  ) {
7     y[0:n] = a * x[0:n] + y[0:n];
8  }
```

LISTING 4.4

SAXPY in Cilk Plus using cilk_for and array notation for explicit vectorization.

Uniform inputs are handled by **scalar promotion:** When a scalar and an array are combined with an operator, the scalar is conceptually "promoted" to an array of the same length by replication.

4.2.6 OpenMP

Like TBB and Cilk Plus, the map pattern is expressed in OpenMP using a "parallel for" construct. This is done by adding a `pragma` as in Listing 4.5 just before the loop to be parallelized. OpenMP uses a "team" of threads and the work of the loop is distributed over the team when such a pragma is used. How exactly the distribution of work is done is given by the current scheduling option.

The advantage of the OpenMP syntax is that the code inside the loop does not change, and the annotations can usually be safely ignored and a correct serial program will result. However, as with the equivalent Cilk Plus construct, the form of the `for` loop is more restricted than in the serial case. Also, as with Cilk Plus and TBB, implementations of OpenMP generally do not check for incorrect parallelizations that can arise from dependencies between loop iterations, which can lead to race conditions. If these exist and are not correctly accounted for in the pragma, an incorrect parallelization will result.

4.2.7 ArBB Using Vector Operations

ArBB operates only over data stored in ArBB containers and requires using ArBB types to represent elements of those containers. The ArBB `dense` container represents multidimensional arrays. It is a template with the first argument being the element type and the second the dimensionality. The dimensionality default is 1 so the second template argument can be omitted for 1D arrays.

The simplest way to implement SAXPY in ArBB is to use arithmetic operations directly over `dense` containers, as in Listing 4.6. Actually, this gives a **sequence** of **maps**. However, as will be explained in Section 4.4, ArBB automatically optimizes this into a **map** of a **sequence**.

In ArBB, we have to include some extra code to move data into "ArBB data space" and to invoke the above function. Moving data into ArBB space is required for two reasons: **safety** and **offload**. Data stored in ArBB containers can be managed in such a way that race conditions are avoided. For example, if the same container is both an input and an output to a function, ArBB will make sure that

```
1  void saxpy_openmp(
2      int n,        // the number of elements in the vectors
3      float a,      // scale factor
4      float x[],    // the first input vector
5      float y[]     // the output vector and second input vector
6  ) {
7  #pragma omp parallel for
8      for (int i = 0; i < n; ++i)
9          y[i] = a * x[i] + y[i];
10  }
```

LISTING 4.5

SAXPY in OpenMP.

```
1  void saxpy_call_arbb(
2      f32 t,          // uniform input
3      dense<f32> p,   // varying input
4      dense<f32>& q   // uniform input and also output
5  ) {
6      q = t * p + q;
7  }
```

LISTING 4.6

SAXPY in ArBB, using a vector expression. One way the map pattern can be expressed in ArBB is by using a sequence of vector operations over entire collections.

```
1  void saxpy_arbb(
2      size_t n,         // number of elements
3      float a,          // uniform input
4      const float x[],  // varying input
5      float y[]         // varying input and also output
6  ) {
7      f32 aa = a;  // copy scalar to ArBB type
8      dense<f32> xx(n), yy(n); // ArBB storage for arrays
9      memcpy(&xx.write_only_range()[0], x, sizeof(float)*n);
10     memcpy(&yy.write_only_range()[0], y, sizeof(float)*n);
11     call(saxpy_call_arbb)(aa, xx, yy);
12     memcpy(y, &yy.read_only_range()[0], sizeof(float)*n);
13 }
```

LISTING 4.7

SAXPY in ArBB, using binding code for vector expression implementation. This code is necessary to move data in and out of ArBB data space.

the "alias" does not cause problems with the parallelization. Second, data stored in ArBB containers may in fact be maintained in a remote memory, such as on an **attached co-processor**, rather than in the host memory. Keeping data in ArBB containers for a sequence of operations allows ArBB to avoid copying data back to the host unnecessarily.

Listing 4.7 shows the necessary code to move data into ArBB space, to invoke the function given in Listing 4.6, and to move the result back out of ArBB space.

4.2.8 ArBB Using Elemental Functions

It is also possible to specify an **elemental function** for the map pattern directly in ArBB. Replicas of this function can then be applied in parallel to all elements of an ArBB collection using a map operation. The map operation can only be invoked from inside an ArBB call, so we need to define another function for the call. The call function, however, can have an entire sequence of map

```
1   void saxpy_map_arbb(
2       f32 t,  // input
3       f32 p,  // input
4       f32& q  // input and output
5   ) {
6       q = t * p + q;
7   }
```

LISTING 4.8

SAXPY in ArBB, using an elemental function. The `map` pattern can also be expressed in ArBB using an elemental function called through a `map` operation.

```
1   void saxpy_call2_arbb(
2       f32 a,           // uniform input
3       dense<f32> x,    // varying input
4       dense<f32>& y    // varying input and also output
5   ) {
6       map(saxpy_map_arbb)(a,x,y);
7   }
```

LISTING 4.9

SAXPY in ArBB, `call` operation. A `map` operation in ArBB can only be invoked from inside an ArBB context, so we have to use `call` first to open an ArBB context.

operations. It can also include vector operations and control flow, although we will not show that in this example. Listing 4.8 shows the definition of the elemental function for SAXPY, and Listing 4.9 shows the necessary call function. The binding code is identical to the previous example except for a change in the call function name.

When we define the elemental function used for the map in ArBB we do not have to decide at the point of definition of the function which parameters are uniform and which are varying. In ArBB, elemental functions are polymorphic and can be invoked with each parameter either being a scalar or being a collection. All the collections do have to be the same shape (dimensionality and number of elements), however.

4.2.9 OpenCL

Listing 4.10 gives kernel code for an OpenCL implementation of SAXPY. **Kernels** are equivalent to what we have been calling elemental functions, except that in OpenCL they always operate on the device and are given in a separate "kernel language" which is a superset (and a subset) of C99. Three OpenCL-specific keywords are used in this example: __kernel, __global, __constant. The __kernel keyword simply identifies a particular function as being invoked as an elemental

```
1   __kernel void
2   saxpy_opencl(
3       __constant float a,
4       __global float* x,
5       __global float* y
6   ) {
7       int i = get_global_id(0);
8       y[i] = a * x[i] + y[i];
9   }
```

LISTING 4.10

SAXPY in OpenCL kernel language.

function/kernel. The OpenCL programming model also includes multiple memory spaces, and __global and __constant identify the use of those spaces. In PCIe-based coprocessor implementations of OpenCL devices, global data is stored in the device's off-chip DRAM, while constant data is stored in a small on-chip memory. Access to data elements in the arrays is done explicitly with ordinary array indexing operations. In other programming models supporting elemental functions, such as ArBB, this indexing is handled by the system. In OpenCL the addresses are computed directly from the global ID, which is an element identifier for each instance of the kernel, with instances numbered starting from zero.

The host code (not shown, but available online) takes care of transferring the data to the device, invoking the computation, and transferring the data back. Since SAXPY is such a simple computation, offloading it alone to a co-processor will not be performant. More likely, the SAXPY kernel will be used as part of a larger computation. OpenCL provides a way to queue up a number of kernels to be executed in sequence to make this mode of operation more efficient.

4.3 MANDELBROT

The computation of the Mandelbrot set is a simple example that shows how the map pattern can include serial control flow and how elemental functions can be used to express this. It is also a good example of the kind of calculation that can lead to a **load imbalance**.

4.3.1 Description of the Problem

The Mandelbrot set is the set of all points c in the complex plane that do *not* go to infinity when the quadratic function $z \leftarrow z^2 + c$ is iterated. In practice, it is hard to prove that this recurrence will never diverge so we iterate up to some maximum number of times. We can also prove that once z leaves a circle of radius 2 it will be guaranteed to diverge. If this happens, we can terminate the computation early. In practice, we will compute the following function, up to some maximum value of K. We can then use a lookup table to map different counts to colors to generate an image.

$$z_0 = 0,$$

$$z_{k-1} = z_k^2 + c,$$

$$\text{count}(c) = \min_{0 \le k < K} (|z_k| \ge 2).$$

Computing the Mandelbrot set has little practical value. However, we are including it here because, while it can be implemented using the map pattern, it includes data-dependent control flow. This leads to a load imbalance: Different pixels in the computation can take different numbers of iterations to diverge. In fact, different regions of the complex plane will have different behaviors, because some regions are smooth while other regions require very different numbers of iterations for nearby pixels.

In other words, the SAXPY example in Section 4.2 could be implemented efficiently using SIMD mechanisms, but the Mandelbrot example is best implemented using SPMD or tiled SIMD mechanisms, including load balancing and early termination of finished tiles.

4.3.2 Serial Implementation

We provide a serial implementation of the Mandelbrot computation in Listing 4.11. We need to use complex numbers, and there are two options: the C99 `Complex`, and the C++ `std::complex`. In this section, we use `Complex` for the serial version, Cilk Plus, and TBB but will switch to `std::complex` for ArBB. Note that in this listing we use separate variables for the iteration index and the count. In some of the parallel versions we can remove this redundancy. We also break out the body of the Mandelbrot computation as a separate function, since it is this function that we will convert to an elemental function in the map pattern.

4.3.3 TBB

The TBB implementation of the Mandelbrot example follows exactly the same template as the example in Section 4.2.3. We can invoke the elemental function for each element in a block given by the `blocked_range` argument to the lambda function as shown in Listing 4.12.

4.3.4 Cilk Plus

Listing 4.13 gives a Cilk Plus implementation of the Mandelbrot example, using the `cilk_for` construct. Note that only the outer loop is parallelized. We could parallelize both loops but in this case parallelizing over only the rows will probably be sufficient, and leaving the inner loop serial will reduce the task management overhead. In addition, in the case of Mandelbrot the execution times for rows are more uniform than the execution times for pixels, making load balancing easier. However, there certainly might be applications that use two nested loops where we would want to parallelize both.

```
1   int mandel(
2       Complex c,
3       int depth
4   ) {
5       int count = 0;
6       Complex z = 0;
7       for (int k = 0; k < depth; k++) {
8           if (abs(z) >= 2.0) {
9               break;
10          }
11          z = z*z + c;
12          count++;
13      }
14      return count;
15  }
16
17  void serial_mandel(
18      int p[][],
19      int max_row,
20      int max_col,
21      int depth
22  ) {
23      for (int i = 0; i < max_row; ++i)
24          for (int j = 0; j < max_col; ++j)
25              p[i][j] = mandel(Complex(scale(i), scale(j)),
26                               depth);
27  }
```

LISTING 4.11

Serial implementation of Mandelbrot in C.

```
1   parallel_for( blocked_range<int>(0, max_row),
2       [&](blocked_range<int> r) {
3           for (size_t i = r.begin(); i != r.end(); ++i)
4               for (int j = 0; j < max_col; ++j)
5                   p[i][j] =
6                       mandel(Complex(scale(i), scale(j)), depth);
7       }
8   );
```

LISTING 4.12

Tiled implementation of Mandelbrot in TBB.

```
1   cilk_for (int i = 0; i < max_row; ++i)
2     for (int j = 0; j < max_col; ++j)
3       p[i][j] =
4           mandel(Complex(scale(i), scale(j)), depth);
```

LISTING 4.13

Mandelbrot using `cilk_for` in Cilk Plus.

4.3.5 Cilk Plus with Array Notations

The Mandelbrot set computation can also be implemented using Cilk Plus array notation. An implementation is shown in Listing 4.14. This actually combines thread parallelism over rows invoked with `cilk_for` with vector parallelism within each row, invoked with array notation. Within each row, we break the work up into chunks of 8 pixels.[1] Then, within each chunk, we invoke the `mandel` function. Within the `mandel` function, we now use an explicit SIMD implementation over the entire chunk, using vector operations. The `__sec_reduce_add` function computes the sum of all the elements in an array section—in this case, the results of the test. This is actually an instance of the reduction pattern, covered in detail in the next chapter. Note that the `break` will only be taken when *all* the pixels in a chunk have diverged. This implementation will therefore do more work than necessary, since all pixels in the chunk will have to be updated if even one needs to continue to iterate. However, if the pixels in a chunk have spatially coherent termination counts, this is often more efficient than serially computing each pixel.

4.3.6 OpenMP

Listing 4.15 shows the OpenMP parallelization of the Mandelbrot example. As with SAXPY in Section 4.2, in this case we are able to perform the parallelization with the addition of a single annotation. However, here we add a `collapse` attribute to the *pragma* annotation to indicate that we want to parallelize both loops at once. This allows OpenMP to parallelize the computation over the combined iteration space. This gives OpenMP more potential parallelism to work with. On the other hand, for systems with relatively small core counts, parallelizing over just the rows might be sufficient and might even have higher performance, as we have argued for the Cilk Plus implementation. If this is desired, the `collapse` clause can be omitted. To get the effect equivalent to the `collapse` clause in Cilk Plus, we would simply nest `cilk_for` constructs.

4.3.7 ArBB

For the ArBB version of Mandelbrot, we will switch to using `std::complex` and also specify the region of interest by giving two points in the complex plane. The implementation is given in Listings 4.16, 4.17, and 4.18. Listing 4.16 gives the elemental function, Listing 4.17 gives the call

---

[1]For simplicity, we do not show the extra code to handle partial chunks when the row length is not a multiple of 8.

```
1   void cilkplus_an_mandel(
2       int n,
3       std::complex c[n],
4       int count[n],
5       int max_count
6   ) {
7       std::complex z[n];
8       int test[n];
9       z[:] = 0;
10      for (int k = 0; k < max_count; k++) {
11          // test for divergence for all pixels in chunk
12          test[:] = (abs(z[:] < 2.0);
13          if (0 == __sec_reduce_add(test[:])) {
14              // terminates loop only if all have diverged
15              break;
16          }
17          // increment counts only for pixels that have not diverged
18          count[:] += test[:];
19          // unconditionally update state of iteration
20          z[:] = z[:]*z[:] + c[:];
21      }
22  }
23
24  void cilkplus_mandel(
25      int p[][],
26      int max_row,
27      int max_col,
28      int depth
29  ) {
30      // parallelize over rows
31      cilk_for (int i = 0; i < max_row; ++i)
32          // loop over the row in chunks of 8
33          for (int j = 0; j < max_col; j += 8)
34              // compute the Mandelbrot counts for a chunk
35              cilkplus_an_mandel(8, p[i]+j, points[i]+j, depth);
36  }
```

LISTING 4.14

Mandelbrot in Cilk Plus using `cilk_for` and array notation for explicit *vectorization*.

function (which also does a little bit of setup for the map), and Listing 4.18 invokes the call and synchronizes the result with the host.

The overall organization of the Mandelbrot code is similar to the elemental function version of SAXPY. However, control flow that depends on values computed by ArBB needs to be expressed in a special way. This is because ArBB is really an API for expressing computation at runtime and will

```
1   #pragma omp parallel for collapse(2)
2     for (int i = 0; i < max_row; i++)
3       for (int j = 0; j < max_col; j++)
4         p[i][j] = mandel(Complex(scale(i), scale(j)),
5                          depth);
```

LISTING 4.15

Mandelbrot in OpenMP.

```
1   void arbb_mandelbrot_map(
2     f64 x0, f64 y0, // lower left corner of region
3     f64 dx, f64 dy, // step size
4     i32 depth,    // maximum number of iterations
5     i32& output   // output: escape count
6   ) {
7     i32 i = 0;
8     // obtain stream index and cast from usize to f64
9     const array<f64, 2> pos = position<2>().as<f64>();
10    // use index to compute position of sample in the complex plane
11    const std::complex<f64> c(x0 + pos[0] * dx,
12                              y0 + pos[1] * dy);
13    std::complex<f64> z = c;
14    // if the loop reaches depth
15    // assume c is an element of the Mandelbrot set
16    _while (i < depth) {
17      _if (norm(z) > 4.0) {
18        _break; // escaped from a circle of radius 2
19      } _end_if;
20      z = z * z + c; // Mandelbrot recurrence
21      ++i;
22    } _end_while;
23    // record the escape count
24    output = i;
25  }
```

LISTING 4.16

Mandelbrot elemental function for ArBB `map` operation.

compile computations specified using this API to machine language. We have to differentiate between control flow used in the generation of the code from control flow meant to be included in the generated code. The _for, _if, etc. keywords are there to tell ArBB to insert data-dependent control flow into the code it generates. Other than this change in syntax, the logic of the ArBB elemental function is quite similar to that of the original serial version. However, the internal implementation will, in fact, be similar to that generated by the version given in Listing 4.14. ArBB will automatically block the

```
1   void arbb_mandelbrot_call(
2       f64 x0, f64 y0,          // lower left corner of region
3       f64 x1, f64 y1,          // upper right corner of region
4       i32 depth,               // maximum number of iterations
5       dense<i32, 2>& output    // output image (scaled escape count)
6   ) {
7       usize width = output.num_cols();
8       usize height = output.num_rows();
9       // step size for width by height equally spaced samples
10      f64 dx = (x1 - x0) / f64(width);
11      f64 dy = (y1 - y0) / f64(height);
12      // apply the map
13      map(arbb_mandelbrot_map)(x0, y0, dx, dy,
14                              depth, output);
15  }
```

LISTING 4.17

Mandelbrot call code for ArBB implementation. This code computes the pixel spacing and then maps the elemental function to compute the escape count for each pixel.

```
1   void arbb_mandelbrot(
2       double x0, double y0,
3       double x1, double y1,
4       int depth,
5       int width, int height,
6       int* result
7   ) {
8       // allocate buffer for result
9       dense<i32,2> output(width, height);
10      // compute the Mandelbrot set
11      call(arbb_mandelbrot_call)(f64(x0), f64(y0),
12                              f64(x1), f64(y1),
13                              i32(depth), output);
14      // synchronize and read back output
15      memcpy(result, &output.read_only_range()[0],
16          width * height * sizeof(int));
17  }
```

LISTING 4.18

Mandelbrot binding code for ArBB implementation. This code performs the call, then synchronizes the output with the host array.

work and emulate control flow using SIMD operations over chunks. It will also include any extra code needed to handle data misalignments at the edges of the arrays, for example, due to rows that are not a multiple of the hardware vector size.

4.3.8 OpenCL

An OpenCL implementation of the Mandelbrot computation is given in Listing 4.19. In this code, the necessary complex number operations are implemented manually. This kernel also includes an optimization that we could have used in the other implementations: We test the square of the magnitude of z for divergence, rather than the actual magnitude. This avoids a square root. Only the kernel code is shown here, although a complete application also requires host code using the OpenCL API to set up data, invoke the kernel, and read the results back.

The Mandelbrot computation allows for fine-grained 2D parallelization that is appropriate for the device's OpenCL targets. We do this here with a 2D kernel. Inside the kernel we can access the index from the appropriate dimension using the argument to `get_global_id` to select the argument. This

```
1   int mandel(
2       float cx, float cy,
3       int depth
4   ) {
5       int count = 0;
6       float zx = cx;
7       float zy = cy;
8       while (count < depth) {
9           if (zx*zx + zy*zy > 4.0)
10              break;
11          float zsqx = zx*zx - zy*zy;
12          float zsqy = 2*zx*zy;
13          zx = zsqx + cx;
14          zy = zsqy + cy;
15          count++;
16      }
17      return count;
18  }
19
20  __kernel void
21  do_mandel(
22      __global int* p,
23      float x0, float y0, float dx, float dy
24  ) {
25      int i = get_global_id(0);
26      int j = get_global_id(1);
27      float cx = x0 + i * dx;
28      float cy = y0 + j * dy;
29      int count = mandel(cx, cy, max_count);
30      p[j*width+i] = count;
31  }
```

LISTING 4.19

Mandelbrot kernel code for OpenCL implementation.

particular interface (using a numerical value to select the index component desired) was chosen because it provides a straightforward extension to higher dimensionalities.

4.4 SEQUENCE OF MAPS VERSUS MAP OF SEQUENCE

A **sequence of map** operations over collections of the same shape should be combined whenever possible into a single larger operation. In particular, vector operations are really map operations using very simple operations like addition and multiplication. Implementing these one by one, writing to and from memory, would be inefficient, since it would have low arithmetic intensity. If this organization was implemented literally, data would have to be read and written for each operation, and we would consume memory bandwidth unnecessarily for intermediate results. Even worse, if the maps were big enough, we might exceed the size of the cache and so each map operation would go directly to and from main memory.

If we fuse the operations used in a sequence of maps into a sequence inside a single map, we can load only the input data at the start of the map and keep intermediate results in registers rather than wasting memory bandwidth on them. We will call this approach **code fusion**, and it can be applied to other patterns as well. Code fusion is demonstrated in Figure 4.2.

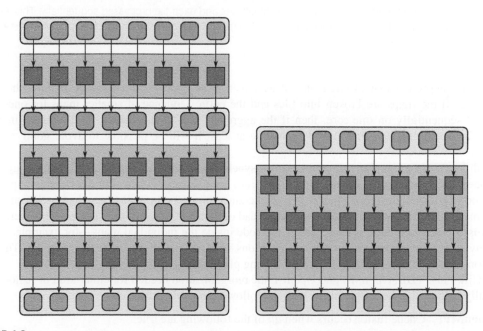

FIGURE 4.2

Code fusion optimization: Convert a sequence of maps into a map of sequences, avoiding the need to write intermediate results to memory. This can be done automatically by ArBB and explicitly in other programming models.

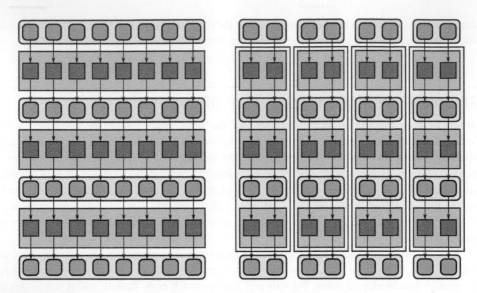

FIGURE 4.3

Cache fusion optimization: Process sequences of maps in small tiles sequentially. When code fusion is not possible, a sequence of maps can be broken into small tiles and each tile processed sequentially. This avoids the need for synchronization between each individual map, and, if the tiles are small enough, intermediate data can be held in cache.

Another approach that is often almost as effective as code fusion is **cache fusion**, shown in Figure 4.3. If the maps are broken into tiles and the entire sequence of smaller maps for one tile is executed sequentially on one core, then if the aggregate size of the tiles is small enough intermediate data will be resident in cache. In this case at least it will be possible to avoid going to main memory.

Both kinds of fusion also reduce the cost of synchronization, since when multiple maps are fused only one synchronization is needed after all the tiles are processed, instead of after every map. However, code fusion is preferred when it is possible since registers are still faster than cache, and with cache fusion there is still the "interpreter" overhead of managing the multiple passes. However, cache fusion is useful when there is no access to the code inside the individual maps—for example, if they are provided as precompiled user-defined functions without source access by the compiler. This is a common pattern in, for example, image processing plugins.

In Cilk Plus, TBB, OpenMP, and OpenCL the reorganization needed for either kind of fusion must generally be done by the programmer, with the following notable exceptions:

OpenMP: Cache fusion occurs when *all* of the following are true:

- A single parallel region executes all of the maps to be fused.
- The loop for each map has the same bounds and chunk size.
- Each loop uses the `static` scheduling mode, either as implied by the environment or explicitly specified.

TBB: Cache fusion can be achieved using `affinity_partitioner`, as explained in Appendix 3.2.

Cilk Plus: Sequences of vector operations expressed using array notation may, in some implementations, be code-fused into efficient elemental functions.

In ArBB, not only will vector operations be fused together whenever possible, but ArBB will also code-fuse sequences of map operations using different elemental functions. This reorganization used by code fusion can be seen as an application of associativity between map and sequence. This is one of many possible high-level optimizations achieved by algebraically manipulating patterns. We will discuss other such optimizations in later chapters.

4.5 COMPARISON OF PARALLEL MODELS

As we have seen, Cilk Plus, TBB, and OpenMP use parallel `for` loop constructs to implement the map pattern, ArBB uses either vector operations or elemental functions, and OpenCL uses elemental functions. Both TBB and Cilk Plus can also use elemental functions (in fact, the TBB syntax is really implemented this way), but the need for separate declaration of these functions can be avoided through use of lambda functions in C++. Cilk Plus also supports the map pattern through sequences of vector operations. In ArBB and Cilk Plus, the fusion of sequences of vector operations is important for performance.

4.6 RELATED PATTERNS

There are several patterns related to map. We discuss three of them here: **stencil, workpile,** and **divide-and-conquer**. Stencil in particular is extremely common in practice. Chapter 7 discusses the stencil pattern in more detail, and a detailed example is given in Chapter 10. Divide-and-conquer is the basis of many recursive algorithms that can in turn be parallelized using the **fork–join** pattern.

4.6.1 Stencil

The **stencil** pattern is a map, except each instance of the elemental function accesses neighbors of its input, offset from its usual input. A **convolution** uses the stencil pattern but combines elements linearly using a set of weights. Convolutions are common, but generally the computation performed on the set of neighbors gathered in the stencil pattern need not be linear. Many forms of non-linear stencil exist—for example, the median filter for reducing impulse noise in images.

A stencil is still a map since the operations do not depend on each other. All that has been done is generalize the way that input is read. However, the stencil pattern is worth calling out for two reasons: It is common in imaging and PDE solvers, and many machine-dependent optimizations are possible for it.

Efficient implementation of the stencil pattern seeks to take advantage of data reuse. Adjacent invocations of the elemental function tend to reuse some number of inputs. The number of elements reused depends on the exact set of neighbors specified by the stencil but generally it is beneficial to **tile** the input domain into subdomains and slide a "window" across each subdomain so that data can be reused. This is complicated to implement well in practice, and the optimal shape of the window can be machine dependent, as well as being dependent on the stencil shape.

In Cilk Plus, TBB, and OpenMP the stencil pattern can be implemented using random access. The sliding window optimization can be implemented as part of an overall tiling strategy. These three systems would then depend on the cache and perhaps the hardware prefetcher to take advantage of the spatial and temporal locality of the stencil. In OpenCL, the overall organization is the same, but depending on the hardware it may be necessary to manage data in on-chip "shared" memory explicitly. In ArBB, stencils are specified declaratively: Neighbors of an input can be accessed using the `neighbor` function inside a map. This allows ArBB to implement sliding windows internally, using a strategy appropriate for the machine being targeted without complicating the user's code.

4.6.2 Workpile

The **workpile** pattern is an extension of the map pattern in which work items can be added to the map while it is in progress, from inside elemental function instances. This allows work to grow and be consumed by the map. The workpile pattern terminates when no more work is available.

The workpile pattern is supported natively in TBB, but not presently in ArBB, OpenMP, OpenCL, or Cilk Plus. It could be implemented in OpenCL and OpenMP using explicit work queues. Its implementation in ArBB might be possible but would probably not be efficient enough to be useful at present. In Cilk Plus, the implementation would be straightforward in terms of fork–join and work stealing.

4.6.3 Divide-and-conquer

The **divide-and-conquer** pattern is related to the **partition** pattern discussed in Chapter 6. Basically, the divide-and-conquer pattern applies if a problem can be divided into smaller subproblems recursively until a base case is reached that can be solved serially. Divide-and-conquer can be implemented by combining the partition and map patterns: the problem is partitioned and then a map is applied to compute solutions to each subproblem in the partition.

Recursive divide-and-conquer is extremely natural in Cilk Plus and TBB since they use the **fork–join** pattern extensively, and this pattern is easy to implement with fork–join. The fork–join pattern is discussed in Chapter 8. In OpenMP recursive divide-and-conquer can be implemented using the tasking model. It is extremely difficult to implement recursive divide-and-conquer in OpenCL and ArBB since these do not at present support nested parallelism, although it could probably (with great difficulty and probably inefficiently) be emulated with work queues. However, non-recursive partitioning is the basis of many algorithms implementable in OpenMP, OpenCL, and ArBB. In fact, the partitioned memory model of OpenCL practically demands at least one level of partitioning for most problems.

Recursive divide-and-conquer is used to implement map itself in Cilk Plus and TBB, and therefore indirectly in ArBB, since the latter uses TBB for task management. When implementing a map, we do not want to try and create all tasks from the task invoking the map since that would place all the task creation overhead in the invoking task. Instead, we split the problem domain into a small number of partitions and then recursively subdivide in each resulting task as needed.

4.7 **SUMMARY**

This chapter has described the map pattern, which is the simplest parallel pattern. We have described some important optimizations of the map pattern, including the fusion of a sequence of maps into a map of sequences. In some cases, this optimization can be done automatically; in other cases, it must be done manually. We have also introduced some patterns closely related to map: **stencil**, **workpile**, and **divide-and-conquer** patterns.

Chapter 5 discusses **collective** operations, including **reduction** and **scan**, and Chapter 6 discusses data reorganization patterns. These two classes of patterns either are often combined with map or, in the case of data reorganization, result from the combination of specific serial data access patterns with map. The **stencil** and **recurrence** patterns are important generalizations of the map pattern and are discussed in Chapter 7. **Divide-and-conquer** is discussed in more detail in Chapter 8.

Collectives

In Chapter 4, we introduced the **map** pattern, which describes **embarrassing parallelism**: parallel computations on a set of completely independent operations. However, obviously we need other patterns to deal with problems that are not completely independent.

The **collective** operations are a set of patterns that deal with a collection of data as a whole rather than as separate elements. The **reduce** pattern allows data to be summarized; it combines all the elements in a collection into a single element using some associative **combiner** operator. The **scan** pattern is similar but reduces every subsequence of a collection up to every position in the input. The usefulness of reduce is easy to understand. One simple example is summation, which shows up frequently in mathematical computations. The usefulness of scan is not so obvious, but partial summarizations do show up frequently in **serial** algorithms, and the parallelization of such serial algorithms frequently requires a scan. Scan can be thought of as a discrete version of integration, although in general it might not be linear.

As we introduce the reduce and scan patterns, we will also discuss their implementations and various optimizations particularly arising from their combination with the map pattern.

Not included in this chapter are operations that just reorganize data or that provide different ways to view or isolate it, such as partitioning, scatter, and gather. When data is shared between tasks these operations can also be used for communication and will be discussed in Chapter 6.

5.1 REDUCE

In the **reduce** pattern, a **combiner** function $f(a,b) = a \otimes b$ is used to combine all the elements of a collection pairwise and create a summary value. It is assumed that pairs of elements can be combined in different orders, so multiple implementations are possible. Possible implementations of reduce are diagrammed in Figure 5.1. The left side of this figure is equivalent to the usual naïve serial implementation for reducing the elements of a collection. The code given in Listing 5.1 implements the serial algorithm for a collection a with n elements.

The identity of the combiner function is required by this implementation. This is so that the reduction of an empty collection is meaningful, which is often useful for boundary conditions in algorithms. In this implementation the identity value could also be interpreted as the initial value of the reduction, although in general we should distinguish between initial values and identities. If we do not need to worry about empty collections, we can define the reduce pattern using Listing 5.2.

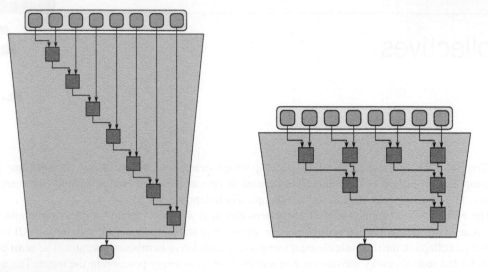

FIGURE 5.1

Serial and tree implementations of the reduce pattern for 8 inputs.

```
1   template<typename T>
2   T reduce(
3     T (*f)(T,T), // combiner function
4     size_t n, // number of elements in input array
5     T a[],      // input array
6     T identity // identity of combiner function
7   ) {
8     T accum = identity;
9     for (size_t i = 0; i < n; ++i) {
10       accum = f(accum, a[i]);
11    }
12    return accum;
13  }
```

LISTING 5.1

Serial reduction in C++ for 0 or more elements.

5.1.1 Reordering Computations

To parallelize reduction, we have to reorder the operations used in the serial algorithm. There are many ways to do this but they depend on the combiner function having certain algebraic properties.

To review some basic algebra, a binary operator $\otimes$ is considered to be **associative** or **commutative** if it satisfies the following equations:

Associative: $(a \otimes b) \otimes c = a \otimes (b \otimes c)$.
Commutative: $a \otimes b = b \otimes a$.

```
1   template<typename T>
2   T reduce(
3       T (*f)(T,T), // combiner function
4       size_t n, // number of elements in input array
5       T a[]       // input array
6   ) {
7       assert(n > 0);
8       T accum = a[0];
9       for (size_t i = 1; i < n; i++) {
10          accum = f(accum, a[i]);
11      }
12      return accum;
13  }
```

LISTING 5.2

Serial reduction in C++ for 1 or more elements.

Associativity and commutativity are not equivalent. While there are common mathematical operations that are both associative and commutative, including addition; multiplication; Boolean AND, OR, and XOR; maximum; and minimum (among others), there are many useful operations that are associative but not commutative. Examples of operations that are associative but not commutative include matrix multiplication and quaternion multiplication (used to compose sequences of 3D rotations). There are also operations that are commutative but not associative, an example being saturating addition on signed numbers (used in image and signal processing). More seriously, although addition and multiplication of real numbers are both associative and commutative, floating point addition and multiplication are only approximately associative. Parallelization may require an unavoidable reordering of floating point computations that will change the result.

To see that *only* associativity is required for parallelization, consider the following:

$$s = a_0 \otimes a_1 \otimes a_2 \otimes a_3 \otimes a_4 \otimes a_5 \otimes a_6 \otimes a_7$$

$$= (((((((a_0 \otimes a_1) \otimes a_2) \otimes a_3) \otimes a_4) \otimes a_5) \otimes a_6) \otimes a_7)$$

$$= (((a_0 \otimes a_1) \otimes (a_2 \otimes a_3)) \otimes ((a_4 \otimes a_5) \otimes (a_6 \otimes a_7))).$$

The first grouping shown is equivalent to the left half of Figure 5.1, the second grouping to the right right half of Figure 5.1. Another way to look at this is that associativity allows us to use any order of pairwise combinations as long as "adjacent" elements are intermediate sequences. However, the second "tree" grouping allows for parallel scaling, but the first does not.

A good example of a non-associative operation is integer arithmetic with saturation. In saturating arithmetic, if the result of an operation is outside the representable range, the result is "clamped" to the closest representable value rather than overflowing. While convenient in some applications, such as image and signal processing, saturating addition is not associative for signed integers.

The following example shows that saturating addition is not associative for signed bytes. Let $\oplus$ be the saturating addition operation. A signed byte can represent an integer between -128 and 127

inclusive. Thus, a saturating addition operation $120 \oplus 78$ yields 127, not 198. Consider reduction with $\oplus$ of the sequence $[120, 78, -90, -50]$. Serial left-to-right order yields:

$$s_1 = (((120 \oplus 77) \oplus -90) \oplus -50)$$
$$= ((127 \oplus -90) \oplus -50)$$
$$= (37 \oplus -50)$$
$$= -13.$$

Tree order yields a different result:

$$s_2 = ((120 \oplus 77) \oplus (-90 \oplus -50))$$
$$= (127 \oplus -128)$$
$$= -1.$$

In contrast, modular integer addition, where overflow wraps around, is fully associative. A result greater than 127 or -128 is brought in range by adding or subtracting 256, which is equivalent to looking at only the low-order 8 bits of the binary representation of the algebraic result. Here is the serial reduction with modular arithmetic on signed bytes:

$$s_1 = (((120 + 77) + -90) + -50)$$
$$= ((-59 + -90) + -50)$$
$$= (107 + -50)$$
$$= 57.$$

Tree ordering gives the same result:

$$s_2 = ((120 + 77) + (-90 + -50))$$
$$= (-59 + 116)$$
$$= 57.$$

5.1.2 Vectorization

There are useful reorderings that also require commutativity. For example, suppose we want to vectorize a reduction on a processor with two-way SIMD instructions. Then we might want to combine all the even elements and all the odd elements separately, as in Figure 5.2, then combine the results.

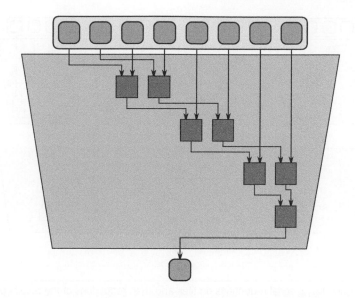

FIGURE 5.2

A reordering of serial reduction that requires commutativity. Commutativity of the combiner operator is not required for parallelization but enables additional reorderings that may be useful for vectorization. This example reduces eight inputs using two serial reductions over the even and odd elements of the inputs then combines the results. This reordering is useful for vectorization on SIMD vector units with two lanes.

However, this reordering requires commutativity:

$$s = a_0 \otimes a_1 \otimes a_2 \otimes a_3$$
$$= a_0 \otimes a_2 \otimes a_1 \otimes a_3$$
$$= (a_0 \otimes a_2) \otimes (a_1 \otimes a_3).$$

Note that a_1 and a_2 had to be swapped before we could group the operations according to this pattern.

5.1.3 Tiling

In practice, we want to **tile**[1] computations and use the serial algorithm for reduction when possible. In a tiled algorithm, we break the work into chunks called **tiles** (or blocks), operate on each tile separately, and then combine the results. In the case of reduce, we might want to use the simple serial reduce algorithm within each tile rather than the tree ordering. This is because while the tree and serial reduce algorithms use the same number of applications of the combiner function, the simplest implementation of the tree ordering requires $O(n)$ storage for intermediate results while the serial ordering requires only $O(1)$ storage.

---

[1]This is also called "block," but since that term can be confused with synchronization we avoid it here.

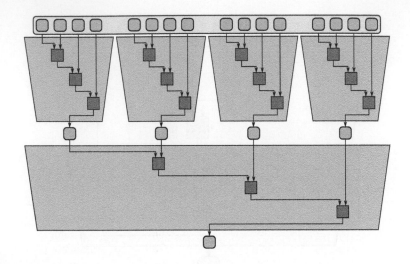

FIGURE 5.3

A reordering of reduction using serial reductions on tiles and then reductions of the results of those reductions. This can be generalized to a two-phase approach to implementing reduce in general.

This is shown in Figure 5.3 for 16 inputs with four tiles of four inputs each, followed by a "global reduction" with four inputs. In practice, since synchronization is expensive, it is common for reductions to have only two phases: a local phase over tiles and a global phase combining the results from each tile. We may also use a vectorized implementation within the tiles as discussed in Section 5.1.2, although this usually requires further reordering.

> **WARNING**
>
> The issues of associativity and commutativity matter mostly when the combiner function may be user defined. Unfortunately, it is hard for an automated system to prove that an arbitrary function is associative or commutative, although it is possible to do so in specific cases—for example, when forming expressions using known associative operators [FG94]. Generally, though, these properties have to be asserted and validated by the user. Therefore, you need to make sure that when using user-defined reductions the functions you are providing satisfy the required properties for the implementation. If you violate the assumptions of the implementation it may generate incorrect and/or non-deterministic results. It is also necessary for the implementor of a reduction taking arbitrary combiner functions to document whether or not commutativity is assumed. The issue does not arise when only built-in operations with known properties are provided by the reduction implementor.

5.1.4 Precision

Another issue can arise with large reductions: *precision*. Large summations in particular have a tendency to run out of bits to represent intermediate results. Suppose you had an array with a million single-precision floating point numbers and you wanted to add them up. Assume that they are all approximately the same magnitude. Single-precision floating point numbers only have about six or seven digits of precision. What can happen in this scenario if the naïve serial algorithm is used is that the partial sum can grow very large relative to the new values to be added to it. If the partial sum grows large enough, new values added to it will be less than the smallest representable increment and their summation will have no effect on the accumulator. The increments will be rounded to zero. This means that part of the input will effectively be ignored and the result will of course be incorrect.

The tree algorithm fares better in this case. If all the inputs are about the same size, then all the intermediate results will also be about the same size. This is a good example of how reassociating floating point operations can change the result. Using a tiled tree will retain most of the advantages of the tree algorithm if the tiles and the final pass are of reasonable sizes.

The tree algorithm is not perfect either, however. We can invent inputs that will break any specific ordering of operations. A better solution is to use a larger precision accumulator than the input. Generally speaking, we should use double-precision accumulators to sum single-precision floating point inputs. For integer data, we need to consider the largest possible intermediate value.

Converting input data to a higher-precision format and then doing a reduce can be considered a combination of a map for the conversion and a reduce to achieve the higher-precision values. Fusion of map and reduce for higher performance is discussed in Section 5.2.

5.1.5 Implementation

Most of the the programming models used in this book, except OpenCL, include various built-in implementations of reduce. TBB and Cilk Plus in addition support reduce with user-defined combiner functions. However, it your responsibility to ensure that the combiner function provided is associative. If the combiner function is not fully associative (for example if it uses floating point operations), you should be aware that many implementations reassociate operations non-deterministically. When used with combiner functions that are not fully associative, this can change the result from run to run of the program. At present, only TBB provides a guaranteed deterministic reduce operation that works with user-defined combiner functions that are not fully associative.

OpenCL

Reduce is not a built-in operation, but it is possible to implement it using a sequence of two kernels. The first reduces over blocks, and the second combines the results from each block. Such a reduction would be deterministic, but optimizations for SIMD execution may also require commutativity.

TBB

Both deterministic and non-deterministic forms of reduce are supported as built-in operations. The basic form of reduce is `parallel_reduce`. This is a fast implementation but may non-deterministically reassociate operations. In particular, since floating point operations are not truly associative, using this construct with floating point addition and multiplication may lead to non-determinism. If determinism is required, then the `parallel_deterministic_reduce` construct may be used. This may result in lower performance than the non-deterministic version. Neither of these implementations commutes operations and so they can both safely be used with non-commutative combiner functions.

Cilk Plus

Two forms of reduce are provided: __sec_reduce for array slices, and reducer hyperobjects. Both of these support user-defined combiner functions and assume associativity. Neither form assumes commutativity of a user-defined combiner. Either of these reductions may non-deterministically reassociate operations and so may produce non-deterministic results for operations that are not truly associative, such as floating point operations. It is possible to implement a deterministic tree reduction in a straightforward fashion in Cilk Plus using fork–join, although this may be slower than the built-in implementations.

ArBB

Only reductions using specific associative and commutative built-in operations are provided. Floating point addition and multiplication are included in this set. The implementation currently does not guarantee that the results of floating point reductions will be deterministic. If a deterministic reduce operation is required, it is possible to implement it using a sequence of map operations, exactly as with OpenCL.

OpenMP

Only reductions with specific associative and commutative built-in operations are provided. More specifically, when a variable is marked as a reduction variable, at the start of a parallel region a private copy is created and initialized in each parallel context. At the end of the parallel region the values are combined with the specified operator.

5.2 FUSING MAP AND REDUCE

A map followed by a reduce can be optimized by fusing the map computations with the initial stages of a tree-oriented reduce computation. If the map is **tiled**, this requires that the reduction be tiled in the same way. In other words, the initial reductions should be done over the results of each each map tile and then the reduce completed with one or more additional stages. This is illustrated in Figure 5.4.

This optimization avoids the need for a synchronization after the map and before the reduce, and it also avoids the need to write the output of the map to memory if it is not used elsewhere. If this is the case, the amount of write bandwidth will be reduced by a factor equal to the tile size. The synchronization can also be avoided in sophisticated systems that break the map and reduce into tiles and only schedule dependencies between tiles. However, even such systems will have overhead, and fusing the computations avoids this overhead.

5.2.1 Explicit Fusion in TBB

The map and reduce patterns can be fused together in TBB by combining their implementations and basically combining the first step of the reduce implementation with some preprocessing (the map) on the first pass. In practice, this can be accomplished through appropriate use of the tiled reduction constructs in TBB, as we show in Section 5.3.4.

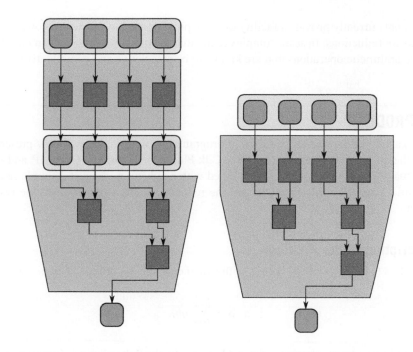

FIGURE 5.4

Optimization of map and reduce by fusion. When a map feeds directly into a reduction, the combination can be implemented more efficiently by combining the map with the initial stage of the reduce.

5.2.2 Explicit Fusion in Cilk Plus

In Cilk Plus map and reduce can be fused by combining their implementations. The map and initial stages of the reduce can be done serially within a tile, and then the final stages of the reduce can be done with **hyperobjects**. We show an example of this in Section 5.3.5.

5.2.3 Automatic Fusion in ArBB

A map followed by a reduce is fused automatically in ArBB. You do not have to do anything special, except ensure that the operations are in the same `call`. Technically, ArBB does a code transformation on the sequence of operations that within serial code generation is often called **loop fusion**. In ArBB, however, it is applied to parallel operations rather than loop iterations.

The map and reduce operations do not have to be adjacent in the program text either, as opportunities for fusion are found by analyzing the computation's data dependency graph. The system will also find multiple fusion opportunities—for example, a map followed by multiple different reductions on the same data. If the output of the map is the same shape as that used by the reduce operations, the fusion will almost always happen. However, intermediate random-memory access operations such as gather and scatter will inhibit fusion, so they should be used with this understanding.

ArBB does not currently provide a facility to allow programmers to define their own arbitrary combiner functions for reductions. Instead, complex reductions are built up by fusing elementary reductions based on basic arithmetic operations that are known to be associative and commutative.

5.3 DOT PRODUCT

As a simple example of the use of the different programming models, we will now present an implementation of the inner or "dot" product in TBB, Cilk Plus, SSE **intrinsics**, OpenMP, and ArBB. Note that this is actually an example of a map combined with a reduction, not just a simple reduction. The map is the initial pairwise multiplication, and the reduction is the summation of the results of that multiplication.

5.3.1 Description of the Problem

Given two vectors (1D arrays) **a** and **b** each with n elements, the dot product **a** · **b** is a scalar given by:

$$\mathbf{a} \cdot \mathbf{b} = \sum_{i=0}^{n-1} a_i b_i.$$

where a_i and b_i denote the ith elements of **a** and **b**, respectively. Subscripts run from 0 to $n-1$ as usual in C and C++.

It is unlikely that a **scalable speedup** will be obtained when parallelizing such a simple computation. As with SAXPY in Section 4.2, a simple operation such as dot product is likely to be dominated by memory access time. The dot product is also the kind of computation where calling a library routine would probably be the best solution in practice, and tuned implementations of the dot product do indeed appear in BLAS libraries. However, dot product is simple and easy to understand and also shows how a map can be combined with reduce in practice.

As map and reduce are a common combination, you can use these examples as templates for more complex applications. We will also use this example to demonstrate some important optimizations of this combination without getting caught up in the complexities of the computation itself.

5.3.2 Serial Implementation

For reference, a serial implementation of dot product is provided in Listing 5.3. There is nothing special here. However, note that the usual serial expression of reduce results in loop-carried dependencies and would not be parallelizable if implemented in exactly the order specified in this version of the algorithm. You have to recognize, abstract, and extract the reduce operation to parallelize it. In this case, the serial reduce pattern is easy to recognize, but when porting code you should be alert to alternative expressions of the same pattern.

This example assumes that n is small, so the reduction accumulator can have type `float`. For large reductions this is unwise since single-precision floating point values may not be able to represent partial sums with sufficient precision as explained in Section 5.1.4. However, the same type for the

```
1   float sprod(
2       size_t n,
3       const float a[],
4       const float b[]
5   ) {
6       float res = 0.0f;
7       for (size_t i = 0; i < n; i++) {
8           res += a[i] * b[i];
9       }
10      return res;
11  }
```

LISTING 5.3

Serial implementation of dot product in C++. The reduction in this example is based on a loop-carried dependency and is not parallelizable without reordering the computation.

accumulator, the input, and the output has been used in order to simplify the example. In some of the implementations we will show how to use a different type for performing the accumulations.

5.3.3 SSE Intrinsics

Listing 5.4 gives an explicitly vectorized version of the dot product computation. This example uses SSE **intrinsics**. SSE stands for Streaming **SIMD** Extensions and is an instruction set extension supported by Intel and AMD processors for explicitly performing multiple operations in one instruction. It is associated with a set of registers that can hold multiple values. For SSE, these registers are 128 bits wide and can store two double-precision floating point values or four single-precision floating point values.

When using SSE intrinsics, special types are used to express pairs or quadruples of values that may be stored in SSE registers, and then functions are used to express operations performed on those values. These functions are recognized by the compiler and translated directly into machine language.

Use of intrinsics is not quite as difficult as writing in assembly language since the compiler does take care of some details like register allocation. However, intrinsics are definitely more complex than the other programming models we will present and are not as portable to the future. In particular, SIMD instruction sets are subject to change, and intrinsics are tied to specific instruction sets and machine parameters such as the width of vector registers.

For (relative) simplicity we left out some complications so this example is not really a full solution. In particular, this code does not handle input vectors that are not a multiple of four in length.

Some reordering has been done to improve parallelization. In particular, this code really does four serial reductions at the same time using four SSE register "lanes", and then combines them in the end. This uses the implementation pattern for reduce discussed in Section 5.1.2, but with four lanes. Like the other examples that parallelize reduce, some reordering of operations is required, since the exact order given in the original serial implementation is not parallelizable. This particular ordering assumes commutativity as well as associativity.

```
1   float sse_sprod(
2       size_t n,
3       const float a[],
4       const float b[]
5   ) {
6       assert(0 == n % 4);  // only works for N a multiple of 4
7       __m128 res, prd, ma, mb;
8       res = _mm_setzero_ps();
9       for (size_t i = 0; i < n; i += 4) {
10          ma = _mm_loadu_ps(&a[i]);  // load 4 elements from a
11          mb = _mm_loadu_ps(&b[i]);  // load 4 elements from b
12          prd = _mm_mul_ps(ma,mb);  // multiple 4 values elementwise
13          res = _mm_add_ps(prd,res);  // accumulate partial sums over 4–tuples
14      }
15      prd = _mm_setzero_ps();
16      res = _mm_hadd_ps(res, prd);  // horizontal addition
17      res = _mm_hadd_ps(res, prd);  // horizontal addition
18      float tmp;
19      _mm_store_ss(&tmp, res);
20      return tmp;
21  }
```

LISTING 5.4

Vectorized dot product implemented using SSE intrinsics. This code works only if the number of elements in the input is a multiple of 4 and only on machines that support the SSE extensions. This code is not parallelized over cores.

Other problems with the SSE code include the fact that it is machine dependent, verbose, hard to maintain, and it only takes advantage of vector units, not multiple cores. It would be possible to combine with code with a Cilk Plus or TBB implementation in order to target multiple cores, but that would not address the other problems. In general, machine dependence is the biggest problem with this code. In particular, new instruction set extensions such as AVX are being introduced that have wider vector widths, so it is better to code in a way that avoids dependence on a particular vector width or instruction set extension.

5.3.4 TBB

Listing 5.5 uses TBB's algorithm template parallel_reduce. This template recursively decomposes a reduction into smaller subreductions and reduces each base case using a functor provided by the user. Here that functor uses std::inner_product to do serial reduction, which the compiler may be able to automatically vectorize. The base case code can also be used for map–reduce fusion, as done here: the std::inner_product call in the base case does both the multiplications and a reduction over the tile it is given. The user must also provide a functor to combine the results of the base cases, which here is the functor std::plus<float>.

```
1   float tbb_sprod(
2       size_t n,
3       const float *a,
4       const float *b
5   ) {
6       return tbb::parallel_reduce(
7           tbb::blocked_range<size_t>(0,n),
8           float(0),
9           [=]( // lambda expression
10              tbb::blocked_range<size_t>& r,
11              float in
12          ) {
13              return std::inner_product(
14                  a+r.begin(), a+r.end(),
15                  b+r.begin(), in );
16          },
17          std::plus<float>()
18      );
19  }
```

LISTING 5.5

Dot product implemented in TBB.

The template `parallel_reduce` also requires the identity of the combiner function. In this case, the identity of floating point addition is `float(0)`. Alternatively, it could be written as `0.f`. The f suffix imbues the constant with type `float`. It is important to get the type right, because the template infers the type of the internal accumulators from the type of the identity. Writing just `0` would cause the accumulators to have the type of a literal `0`, which is `int`, not the desired type `float`.

The template `parallel_reduce` implements a flexible reduce pattern which can be instantiated in a variety of ways. For example, Listing 5.6 shows an instantiation that does accumulation using a precision higher than the type of the input, which is often important to avoid overflow in large reductions. The type used for the multiplication is also changed, since this is a good example of a fused map operation. These modifications change `float` in Listing 5.5 to `double` in several places:

1. The return type is `double`.
2. The identity element is `double(0)`, so that the template uses `double` as the type to use for internal accumulators.
3. The parameter `in` is declared as `double`, not only because it might hold a partial accumulation, but because `std::inner_product` uses this type for *its* internal accumulator.
4. To force use of double-precision + and * by `std::inner_product`, there are two more arguments, `std::plus<double>()` and `std::multiplies<double>()`. An alternative is to write the base case reduction with an explicit loop instead of `std::inner_product`.
5. The combining functor is `std::plus<double>`.

```
1   double tbb_sprod2(
2       size_t n,
3       const float *a,
4       const float *b
5   ) {
6       return tbb::parallel_reduce(
7           tbb::blocked_range<size_t>(0,n),
8           double(0),
9           [=]( // lambda expression
10              tbb::blocked_range<size_t>& r,
11              double in
12          ) {
13              return std::inner_product(
14                  a+r.begin(), a+r.end(),
15                  b+r.begin(), in,
16                  std::plus<double>(),
17                  std::multiplies<double>() );
18          },
19          std::plus<double>()
20      );
21  }
```

LISTING 5.6

Modification of Listing 5.5 with double-precision operations for multiplication and accumulation.

5.3.5 Cilk Plus

Listing 5.7 expresses the pairwise multiplication and reduction using Cilk Plus array notation. A good compiler can generate code from it that is essentially equivalent to the hand-coded SSE in Listing 5.4, except that the Cilk Plus version will correctly handle vector widths that are not a multiple of the hardware vector width. In fact, it is not necessary to know the hardware vector width to write the Cilk Plus code. The Cilk Plus code is not only shorter and easier to understand and maintain, it's portable.

An explicitly thread parallel and vector parallel dot product can be expressed as shown in Listing 5.8. The variable res has a special type called a reducer. Here the reducer res accumulates the correct reduction value even though there may be multiple iterations of the cilk_for running in parallel. Even though the code looks similar to serial code, the Cilk Plus runtime executes it using a tree-like reduction pattern. The cilk_for does tree-like execution (Section 8.3) and parts of the tree executing in parallel get different views of the reducer. These views are combined so at the end of the cilk_for there is a single view with the whole reduction value. Section 8.10 explains the mechanics of reducers in detail.

Our code declares res as a reducer_opadd<float> reducer. This indicates that the variable will be used to perform + reduction over type float. The constructor argument (0) indicates the variable's initial value. Here it makes sense to initialize it with 0, though in general a reducer can be

```
1   float cilkplus_sprod(
2       size_t n,
3       const float a[],
4       const float b[]
5   ) {
6       return __sec_reduce_add(a[0:n] * b[0:n]);
7   }
```

LISTING 5.7

Dot product implemented in Cilk Plus using array notation.

```
1   float cilkplus_sprod_tiled(
2       size_t n,
3       const float a[],
4       const float b[]
5   ) {
6       size_t tilesize = 4096;
7       cilk::reducer opadd<float> res(0);
8       cilk_for (size_t i = 0; i < n; i+=tilesize) {
9           size_t m = std::min(tilesize,n-i);
10          res += __sec_reduce_add(a[i:m] * b[i:m]);
11      }
12      return res.get_value();
13  }
```

LISTING 5.8

Dot product implementation in Cilk Plus using explicit *tiling*.

initialized with any value, because this value is not assumed to be the identity. A reducer_opadd<T> assumes that the identity of + is T(), which by C++ rules constructs a zero for built-in types. The min expression in the code deals with a possible partial "boundary" tile, so the input does not have to be a multiple of the tile size.

Listing 5.8 shows how to modify the reduction to do double-precision accumulation. The casts to double-precision are also placed to result in the use of double-precision multiplication. These casts, like the multiplication itself, are really examples of the map pattern that are being fused into the reduction. Of course, if you wanted to do single-precision multiplication, you could move the cast to after the __sec_reduce_add. Doing the multiplication in double precision may or may not result in lower performance, however, since a dot product will likely be performance limited by memory *bandwidth*, not computation. Likewise, doing the accumulation in double precision will likely not be a limiting factor on performance. It might increase communication slightly, but for reasonably large tile sizes most of the memory bandwidth used will result from reading the original input.

5.3.6 OpenMP

An OpenMP implementation of dot product is shown in Listing 5.10. In OpenMP, parallelization of this example is accomplished by adding a single line annotation to the serial implementation. However, the annotation must specify that res is a **reduction variable**. It is also necessary to specify the combiner operator, which in this case is (floating point) addition.

What actually happens is that the scope of the loop specifies a parallel region. Within this region local copies of the reduction variable are made and initialized with the identity associated with the reduction operator. At the end of the parallel region, which in this case is the end of the loop's scope, the various local copies are combined with the specified combiner operator. This code implicitly does map–reduce fusion since the base case code, included within the loop body, includes the extra computations from the map.

```
1   double cilkplus_sprod_tiled2(
2       size_t n,
3       const float a[],
4       const float b[]
5   ) {
6       size_t tilesize = 4096;
7       cilk::reducer_opadd<double> res(0);
8       cilk_for (size_t i = 0; i < n; i+=tilesize) {
9           size_t m = std::min(tilesize,n-i);
10          res += __sec_reduce_add(double(a[i:m]) * double(b[i:m]));
11      }
12      return res.get_value();
13  }
```

LISTING 5.9

Modification of Listing 5.8 with double-precision operations for multiplication and accumulation.

```
1   float openmp_sprod(
2       size_t n,
3       const float *a,
4       const float *b
5   ) {
6       float res = 0.0f;
7   #pragma omp parallel for reduction(+:res)
8       for (size_t i = 0; i < n; i++) {
9           res += a[i] * b[i];
10      }
11      return res;
12  }
```

LISTING 5.10

Dot product implemented in OpenMP.

OpenMP implementations are not required to inform you if the loops you annotate have reductions in them. In general, you have to identify them for yourself and correctly specify the reduction variables. OpenMP 3.1 provides reductions only for a small set of built-in associative and commutative operators and intrinsic functions. User-defined reductions have to be implemented as combinations of these operators or by using explicit parallel implementations. However, support for user-defined reductions is expected in a future version of OpenMP, and in particular is being given a high priority for OpenMP 4.0, since it is a frequently requested feature.

5.3.7 ArBB

Listing 5.11 gives the kernel of a dot product in ArBB. This function operates on ArBB data, so the additional code in Listing 5.12 is required to move data into ArBB space, invoke the function in

```
1  void arbb_sprod_kernel(
2     dense<f32> a,
3     dense<f32> b,
4     f32 &res
5  ) {
6     res = sum(a * b);
7  }
```

LISTING 5.11

Dot product implemented in ArBB. Only the kernel is shown, not the binding and calling code, which is given in Listing 5.12.

```
1  float arbb_sprod(
2     size_t n,        // number of elements
3     const float x[], // varying input
4     const float y[]  // varying input
5  ) {
6     dense<f32> xx(n), yy(n); // ArBB storage for arrays
7     memcpy(&xx.write_only_range()[0], // copy in data
8          x, sizeof(float)*n);
9     memcpy(&yy.write_only_range()[0], // copy in data
10         y, sizeof(float)*n);
11    f32 res;
12    call(arbb_sprod_kernel)(xx,yy,res);
13    return value(res); // convert result back to C++ value
14 }
```

LISTING 5.12

Dot product implementation in ArBB, using wrapper code to move data in and out of ArBB data space and invoke the computation.

```
1  void arbb_sprod_kernel2(
2      dense<f32> a,
3      dense<f32> b,
4      f64 &res
5  ) {
6      dense<f64> aa = dense<f64>(a);
7      dense<f64> bb = dense<f64>(b);
8      res = sum(aa * bb);
9  }
```

LISTING 5.13

High-precision dot product implemented in ArBB. Only the kernel is shown.

Listing 5.11 with `call`, and retrieve the result with `value`. Internally, ArBB will generate tiled and vectorized code roughly equivalent to the implementation given in Listing 5.8.

To avoid overflow in a very large dot product, intermediate results should be computed using double precision. The alternative kernel in Listing 5.13 does this. The two extra data conversions are, in effect, additional map pattern instances. Note that in ArBB multiple maps are fused together automatically as are maps with reductions. This specification of the computation produces an efficient implementation that does not write the intermediate converted high-precision input values to memory.

5.4 SCAN

The **scan** collective operation produces all partial reductions of an input sequence, resulting in a new output sequence. There are two variants: inclusive scan and exclusive scan. For inclusive scan, the nth output value is a reduction over the first n input values; a serial and one possible parallel implementation are shown in Figure 5.5. For exclusive scan, the nth output value is a reduction over the first $n - 1$ input values. In other words, exclusive scan excludes the nth input value. The C++ standard library template `std::partial_sum` is an example of an inclusive scan. Listings 5.14 and 5.15 show serial routines for inclusive scan and exclusive scan, respectively.

Each of the routines takes an initial value to be used as part of the reductions. There are two reasons for this feature. First, it avoids the need to have an identity element when computing the first output value of an exclusive scan. Second, it makes serial scan a useful building block for writing tiled parallel scans.

At first glance, the two implementations look more different than they really are. They could be almost identical, because another way to write an exclusive scan is to copy Listing 5.14 and swap lines 10 and 11. However, that version would invoke `combine` one more time than necessary.

Despite the loop-carried dependence, scan can be parallelized. Similar to the parallelization of reduce, we can take advantage of the associativity of the combiner function to reorder operations. However, unlike the case with reduce, parallelizing scan comes at the cost of redundant computations. In exchange for reducing the span from $O(N)$ to $O(\lg N)$, the work must be increased, and in many algorithms nearly doubled. One very efficient approach to parallelizing scan is based on the **fork–join**

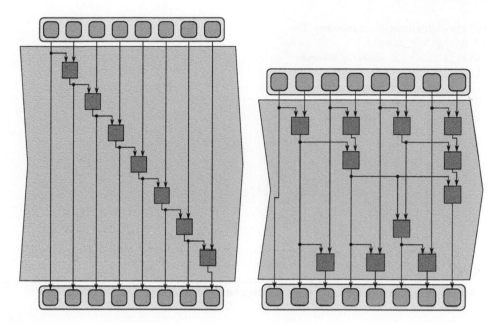

FIGURE 5.5

Serial and parallel implementations of the (inclusive) scan pattern.

```
1  template<typename T, typename C>
2  void inclusive_scan(
3      size_t n,      // number of elements
4      const T a[],   // input collection
5      T A[],         // output collection
6      C combine,     // combiner functor
7      T initial      // initial value
8  ) {
9      for (size_t i=0; i<n; ++i) {
10         initial = combine(initial,a[i]);
11         A[i] = initial;
12     }
13 }
```

LISTING 5.14

Serial implementation of inclusive scan in C++, using a *combiner* functor and an initial value.

pattern. The fork–join pattern is covered in Chapter 8, and this approach is explained in Section 8.11 along with an implementation in Cilk Plus. Section 5.4 presents another implementation of scan using a three-phase approach and an implementation using OpenMP.

```
1   template<typename T, typename C>
2   void exclusive_scan(
3       size_t n,      // number of elements
4       const T a[],   // input  collection
5       T A[],         // output  collection
6       C combine,     // combiner functor
7       T initial      // initial  value
8   ) {
9       if( n>0 ) {
10          for (size_t i=0; i<n-1; ++i) {
11              A[i] = initial;
12              initial = combine(initial,a[i]);
13          }
14          A[n-1] = initial;
15      }
16  }
```

LISTING 5.15

Serial implementation of exclusive scan in C++. The arguments are similar to those in Listing 5.14.

Scan is a built-in pattern in both TBB and ArBB. Here is a summary of the characteristics of these implementations at the point when this book was written. We also summarize the interface and characteristics of the scan implementation we will present for Cilk Plus and give a three-phase implementation of scan in OpenMP.

5.4.1 Cilk Plus

Cilk Plus has no built-in implementation of scan. Section 8.11 shows how to implement it using the fork–join pattern. The interface to that implementation and its characteristics are explained here, however, so we can use it in the example in Section 5.6.

Our Cilk Plus implementation performs a tiled scan. It abstracts scan as an operation over an index space and thus makes no assumptions about data layout. The template interface is:

```
template<typename T, typename R, typename C, typename S>
void cilk_scan(size_t n, T initial, size_t tilesize,
               R reduce, C combine, S scan);
```

The parameters are as follows:

- n is the size of the index space. The index space for the scan is the half-open interval $[0,n)$.
- initial is the initial value for the scan.
- tilesize is the desired size of each tile in the iteration space.
- reduce is a functor such that reduce($i,size$) returns a value for a reduction over indices in $[i, i + size)$.
- combine is a functor such that combine(x,y) returns $x \oplus y$.

- scan is a functor such that scan(*i*,*size*,*initial*) does a scan over indices in [*i*, *i* + *size*) starting with the given initial value. It should do an exclusive or inclusive scan, whichever the call to cilk_scan is intended to do.

The actual access to the data occurs in the reduce and scan functors. The implementation is deterministic as long as all three functors are deterministic.

In principle, doing the reduction for the last tile is unnecessary, since the value is unused. However, not invoking reduce on that tile would prevent executing a fused map with it, so we still invoke it. Note that the results of such an "extra" map tile may be needed later, in particular in the final scan, even if it is not needed for the initial reductions. Technically, the outputs of the map (which need to be stored to memory for later use) is a side-effect, but the data dependencies are all accounted for in the pattern. The Cilk Plus implementation of the integration example in Section 5.6.3 demonstrates this.

5.4.2 TBB

TBB has a parallel_scan construct for doing either inclusive or exclusive scan. This construct may non-deterministically reassociate operations, so for non-associative operations, such as floating point addition, the result may be non-deterministic.

The TBB construct parallel_scan abstracts scan even more than cilk_scan. It takes two arguments: a recursively splittable range and a body object.

```
template<typename Range, typename Body>
void parallel_scan( const Range& range, Body& body );
```

The range describes the index space. The body describes how to do the reduce, combine, and scan operations in a way that is analogous to those described for the Cilk Plus interface.

5.4.3 ArBB

Built-in implementations of both inclusive and exclusive scans are supported, but over a fixed set of associative operations. For the fully associative operations, the results are deterministic. However, for floating point multiplication and addition, which are non-associative, the current implementation does not guarantee the results are deterministic.

5.4.4 OpenMP

OpenMP has no built-in parallel scan; however, OpenMP 3.x tasking can be used to write a tree-based scan similar to the fork–join Cilk Plus code in Section 8.11. In practice, users often write a three-phase scan, which is what we present in this section. The three-phase scan has an asymptotic running time of $T_P = \Theta(N/P + P)$. When $P \ll N$, the N/P term dominates the P term and speedup becomes practically linear. For fixed N, the value of $N/P + P$ is minimized when $P = \sqrt{N}$.[2] Thus,

---

[2]Proof: The arithmetic mean of two positive values is always greater than or equal to their geometric mean, and the means are equal only when the two values are equal. The geometric mean of N/P and P is $\sqrt{N}$, and their arithmetic mean is $\frac{N/P + P}{2}$. Thus, the latter is minimized when $N/P = P$; that is, $P = \sqrt{N}$.

the maximum asymptotic speedup is:

$$\frac{T_1}{T_P} = \Theta\left(\frac{N}{N/P + P}\right) = \Theta\left(\frac{N}{N/\sqrt{N} + \sqrt{N}}\right) = \Theta(\sqrt{N}).$$

Although this is not as asymptotically good as the tree-based scan that takes $O(\lg N)$ time, constant factors may make the three-phase scan attractive. However, like other parallel scans, the three-phase scan requires around twice as many invocations of the combiner function as the serial scan.

The phases are:

1. Break the input into tiles of equal size, except perhaps the last. Reduce each tile in parallel. Although the reduction value for the last tile is unnecessary for step 2, the function containing the tile reduction is often invoked anyway. This is because a map may be fused with with the reduction function, and if so the outputs of this map are needed in step 3.
2. Perform an exclusive scan of the reduction values. This scan is always exclusive, even if the overall parallel scan is inclusive.
3. Perform a scan on each of the tiles. For each tile, the initial value is the result of the exclusive scan from phase 2. Each of these scans should be inclusive if the parallel scan is inclusive, and exclusive if the parallel scan should be exclusive. Note that if the scan is fused with a map, it is the output of the map that is scanned here.

Figure 5.6 diagrams the phases, and Listing 5.16 shows an OpenMP implementation.

Like many OpenMP programs, this code exploits knowing how many threads are available. The code attempts to use one tile per thread. Outside the parallel region the code computes how many threads to *request*. The clause `num_threads(t)` specifies this request. There is no guarantee that the full request will be granted, so inside the parallel region the code recomputes the tile size and number of tiles based on how many threads were granted. Our code would still be correct if it did not recompute these quantities, but it might have a load imbalance and therefore be slower, because some threads would execute more tiles than other threads.

Each phase waits for the previous phase to finish, but threads do *not* join between the phases. The first and last phases run with one thread per tile, which contributes $\Theta(N/P)$ to the asymptotic running time. The middle phase, marked with `omp single`, runs on a single thread. This phase contributes $\Theta(P)$ to the running time. During this phase, the other m threads just wait while this phase is running. Making threads wait like this is both good and bad. The advantage is that the threads are ready to go for the third phase, and the mapping from threads to tiles is preserved by the default scheduling of `omp for` loops. This minimizes memory traffic. The disadvantage is that the worker threads are committed when entering the parallel region. No additional workers can be added if they become available, and no committed workers can be removed until the parallel region completes.

5.5 FUSING MAP AND SCAN

As with reduce, scan can be optimized by fusing it with adjacent operations.

Consider in particular the three-phase implementation of scan. Suppose such a scan is preceded by a map and followed by another map. Then, as long as the tiles are the same size, the tiles in the

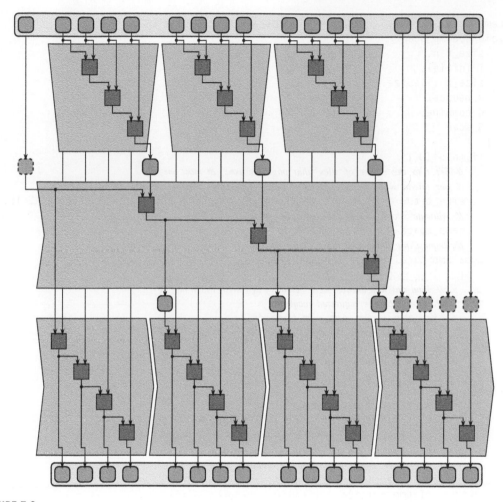

FIGURE 5.6

Three-phase tiled implementation of inclusive scan, including initial value.

first map can be combined with the serial reductions in the first phase of the scan, and the tiled scan in the third phase can be combined with the following tiled map. This is shown in Figure 5.7. This creates more arithmetically intense code blocks and can cut down significantly on memory traffic and synchronization overhead.

It would also be possible to optimize a scan by fusing it with following reductions or three-phase scans since the first part of a three-phase scan is a tile reduction. However, if a reduction follows a scan, you can get rid of the reduction completely since it is available as an output of the scan, or it can be made available with very little extra computation.

```
1   template<typename T, typename R, typename C, typename S>
2   void openmp_scan(
3       size_t n,
4       T initial,
5       size_t tilesize,
6       R reduce,
7       C combine,
8       S scan
9   ) {
10      if (n > 0) {
11          // Set t to the number of tiles  that might be used, at most one tile
12          // per thread with no tile  smaller than the requested  tilesize
13          size_t t = std::min( size_t(omp_get_max_threads()), (n-1)/tilesize+1 );
14          // Allocate space to hold the reduction value of each tile
15          temp_space<T> r(t);
16          // Request one thread per  tile
17  #pragma omp parallel num_threads(t)
18          {
19              // Find out how threads were  actually  delivered, which may be
20              // fewer than the requested  number
21              size_t p = omp_get_num_threads();
22              // Recompute tilesize  so there  is one tile  per actual  thread
23              tilesize = (n+p-1)/p;
24              // Set m to index of last  tile
25              size_t m = p-1;
26  #pragma omp for
27              // Set r[i] to reduction of the ith  tile
28              for ( size_t i = 0; i <= m; ++i )
29                  r[i] = reduce(i*tilesize, i==m ? n-m*tilesize : tilesize);
30  #pragma omp single
31              // Use single  thread  to do in-place exclusive  scan on r
32              for ( size_t i = 0; i <= m; ++i ) {
33                  T tmp = r[i];
34                  r[i] = initial;
35                  initial = combine(initial,tmp);
36              }
37  #pragma omp for
38              // Do scan over each  tile, using r[i] as  initial  value
39              for ( size_t i = 0; i <= m; ++i )
40                  scan(i*tilesize, i==m ? n-m*tilesize : tilesize, r[i]);
41          }
42      }
43  }
```

LISTING 5.16

Three-phase tiled implementation of a scan in OpenMP. The interface is similar to the Cilk Plus implementation explained in Section 5.4, except that `tilesize` may be internally adjusted upward so that the number of tiles matches the number of threads. Listing 8.7 on page 227 has the code for template class `temp_space`.

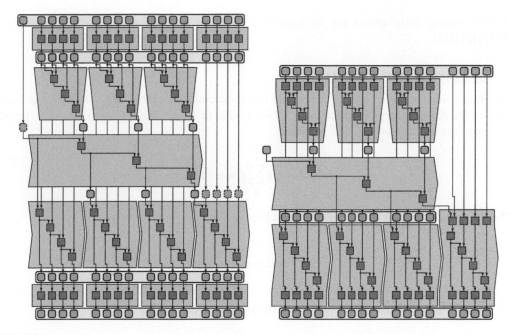

FIGURE 5.7

Optimization of map and three-phase scan by fusion. The initial and final phases of the scan can be combined with maps appearing in sequence before and after the scan. There is also an opportunity to fuse an initial map with the scan and final map of the last tile, but it is only a boundary case and may not always be worth doing.

5.6 INTEGRATION

Scan shows up in a variety of unexpected circumstances, and is often the key to parallelizing an "unparallelizable" algorithm. However, here we show a simple application: integrating a function. The scan of a tabulated function, sometimes known as the cumulation of that function, has several applications. Once we have computed it, we can approximate integrals over any interval in constant time. This can be used for fast, adjustable box filtering. A two-dimensional version of this can be used for antialiasing textures in computer graphics rendering, an approach known as summed area tables [Cro84].

One disadvantage of summed-area tables in practice, which we do not really consider here, is that extra precision is needed to make the original signal completely recoverable by differencing adjacent values. If this extra precision is not used, the filtering can be inaccurate. In particular, in the limit as the filter width becomes small we would like to recover the original signal.

As another important application, which we, however, do not discuss further in this book, you can compute random numbers with the distribution of a given probability density by computing the cumulation of the probability density distribution and inverting it. Mapping a uniform random number through this inverted function results in a random number with the desired probability distribution. Since the cumulation is always monotonic for positive functions, and probability distributions are always positive, this inversion can be done with a binary search. Sampling according to arbitrary probability density distributions can be important in Monte Carlo (random sampling) integration methods [KTB11].

5.6.1 Description of the Problem

Given a function f and interval $[a,b]$, we would like to precompute a table that will allow rapid computation of the definite integral of f over any subinterval of $[a,b]$. Let $\Delta x = (b-a)/(n-1)$. The table is a running sum of samples of f, scaled by Δx:

$$\text{table}_i = \Delta x \sum_0^i f(a+i\Delta x).$$

The integral of f over $[c,d]$ can be estimated by:

$$\int_c^d f(x)dx \approx interp(d) - interp(c),$$

where $interp(x)$ denotes linear interpolation on the table.

5.6.2 Serial Implementation

Listing 5.17 shows a serial implementation of the sampling and summation computation. It has a loop-carried dependence, as each iteration of the loop depends on the previous one.

Sometimes you will want to use a generic function defined in a function template as in Listing 5.18. To pass such a function as an argument, it is helpful to first instantiate it with particular types as in Listing 5.19.

Listing 5.20 shows how to compute the definite integral from two samples. It defines a helper function `serial_sample` that does linearly interpolated lookup on the array. Out of bounds subscripts are handled as if the original function is zero outside the bounds, which implies that the integral is zero to the left of the table values and equal to `table[n−1]` to the right of the table.

5.6.3 Cilk Plus

Listing 5.21 shows the Cilk Plus code for preparing the integration table. The initial mapping of the function is fused into the functor for doing tile reductions. The final scaling of the scan is fused in the functor for doing tile scans.

Scan is not a built-in operation in Cilk Plus, but we discuss its interface in Section 5.4 and its implementation in Section 8.11.

5.6.4 OpenMP

Listing 5.21 can be translated to OpenMP by making two changes:

- Replace `cilk_scan` with `openmp_scan` (Listing 5.16).
- Replace the array notation with a loop.

```
1   template<typename X, typename Y, typename F>
2   void serial_prepare_integral_table(
3       X a,          // start position of sampling
4       X b,          // end position of sampling
5       size_t n,     // number of samples to take
6       Y table[],    // destination for table samples
7       F f           // function parameter
8   ) {
9       // Handle empty request
10      if (n==0) return;
11      // Compute sample spacing
12      const X dx = (b-a)/X(n-1);
13      // Store scaled running sum of sample points in table [0:n]
14      Y sum = Y(0);
15      for ( size_t i = 0; i < n; ++i ) {
16          sum += f(a+dx*i); //f: X \maps to Y
17          table[i] = sum * dx;
18      }
19  }
```

LISTING 5.17

Serial integrated table preparation in C++. The code has a single loop that samples function f provided as an argument, performs an inclusive scan, and scales the results of the scan by dx.

```
1   template <typename Y, typename X>
2   Y generic_f(X x) {
3       return Y(abs(sqrt(x) * sin(X(0.12) * x + x*x)));
4   }
```

LISTING 5.18

Generic test function for integration.

```
1   float f(float x) {
2       return generic_f<float,float>(x);
3   }
```

LISTING 5.19

Concrete instantiation of test function for integration.

The second change is optional, since OpenMP plus Cilk Plus array notation can be an effective way to exploit both thread and vector parallelism. Of course, this requires a compiler that supports both.

Scan is not a built-in operation in OpenMP, but we discuss its implementation using a three-phase approach in Section 5.4.

```
1   template <typename Y, typename X>
2   Y serial_sample(
3       size_t n,
4       Y table[],
5       X x
6   ) {
7       // Compute integer part of sample position
8       X i = floor(x);
9       // Look up samples at i and i+1
10      // for out of bound indices, use 0 on left and table [n−1] on right
11      Y y0 = i < X(0) ? Y(0)
12          : table[i < X(n) ? size_t(i) : n−1];
13      Y y1 = i+1 < X(0) ? Y(0)
14          : table[i+1 < X(n) ? size_t(i+1) : n−1];
15      // Linearly interpolate between samples
16      return y0+(y1−y0)*(x−i);
17  }
18
19  template <typename X, typename Y>
20  Y serial_integrate(
21      size_t n, // number of samples in table
22      Y table[], // cumulative samples
23      X a,        // lower bound of function domain
24      X b,        // upper bound of function domain
25      X x0,       // lower bound of integral
26      X x1        // upper bound of integral
27  ) {
28      // Compute scale for convering x0 and x1 to table indices
29      X scale = X(n−1)/(b−a);
30      // Look up interpolated values of indefinite integral
31      Y y0 = serial_sample(n, table, scale*(x0−a));
32      Y y1 = serial_sample(n, table, scale*(x1−a));
33      // Compute integral
34      return y1−y0;
35  }
```

LISTING 5.20

Serial implementation of integrated table lookup in C++. Two linearly interpolated samples of the table are taken and interpolated. Out-of-bounds indices are handled as if the original function (not the integral) is zero outside the bounds.

5.6.5 TBB

The TBB `parallel_scan` algorithm template has an internal optimization that lets it avoid calling the combiner function twice for each element when no actual parallelism occurs. Unfortunately, this optimization prevents fusing a map with the reduce portion of a scan. Consequently, the TBB implementation of the integration example must compute each sample point on both passes through a tile. The second pass has no easy way to know if the first pass occurred and so there is no point in the

```
1   template<typename X, typename Y, typename F>
2   void cilk_prepare_integral_table(
3       X a,        // start position of sampling
4       X b,        // end position of sampling
5       size_t n,   // number of samples to take
6       Y table[],  // destination for table samples
7       F f         // function that maps X → Y
8   ) {
9       // Handle empty request
10      if (n == 0) return;
11      // Compute sample spacing
12      const X dx = (b−a)/(n−1);
13      // Do parallel scan
14      cilk_scan(
15          n, Y(0),
16          1024, // tile size
17          [=,&table]( size_t i, size_t m ) −> Y {
18              Y sum = Y(0);
19              for ( ; m>0; −−m, ++i )
20                  sum += (table[i] = f(a + dx*i));
21              return sum;
22          },
23          std::plus<Y>(),
24          [=,&table]( size_t i, size_t m, Y initial ) {
25              // Store running sum of sample points in table[i:m]
26              for ( ; m>0; −−m, ++i ) {
27                  initial += table[i];
28                  table[i] = initial*dx;
29              }
30          }
31      );
32  }
```

LISTING 5.21

Integrated table preparation in Cilk Plus. The code implements the interface discussed in Section 5.4.

first pass storing the samples. If the samples are expensive to compute, to avoid the extra computation we can precompute the samples and store them in a table before calling the scan. Here we assume the samples are relatively inexpensive to compute.

Listing 5.22 shows the code. In the TBB implementation a single templated operator() serves as both a *both* tiled reduce and a tiled scan. The idea behind this is that the code may have full or partial information about preceding iterations. The value of the expression tag.is_final_scan() distinguishes these two cases:

true: The state of the Body is the same as if all iterations of the loop preceding subrange r. In this case, operator() does a serial scan over the subrange. It leaves the Body in a state suitable for continuing beyond the current subrange.

```
1   template<typename X, typename Y, typename F>
2   struct Body {
3       const X a, dx;
4       Y* const table;
5       F f;
6       // Running sum
7       Y sum;
8       // Reduction or scan of a tile
9       template<typename Tag>
10      void operator()( tbb::blocked_range<size_t> r, Tag tag ) {
11          for ( size_t i = r.begin(); i != r.end(); ++i ) {
12              sum += f(a + dx*i);
13              if ( tag.is_final_scan() )
14                  table[i] = sum*dx;
15          }
16      }
17      // Initial body
18      Body( X a_, X dx_, Y* table_, F f_ )
19          : a(a_), dx(dx_), table(table_), f(f_), sum(0) {}
20      // Body created for look-ahead reduction
21      Body( Body& body, tbb::split )
22          : a(body.a), dx(body.dx), table(body.table), f(body.f), sum(0) {}
23      // Merge bodies for two consecutive ranges.
24      void reverse_join( Body& body ) {sum = body.sum + sum;}
25      // Assign *this = final body state from final tile
26      void assign( Body& body ) {sum = body.sum;}
27  };
28
29  template<typename X, typename Y, typename F>
30  void tbb_prepare_integral_table(
31      X a,        // start position of sampling
32      X b,        // end position of sampling
33      size_t n,   // number of samples to take
34      Y table[],  // destination for table samples
35      F f         // function that maps X → Y
36  ) {
37      // Handle empty request
38      if (n==0) return;
39      // Compute sample spacing
40      const X dx = (b-a)/(n-1);
41      // Initialize body for scan
42      Body<X,Y,F> body(a,dx,table,f);
43      // Do the scan
44      tbb::parallel_scan( tbb::blocked_range<size_t>(0,n), body );
45  }
```

LISTING 5.22

Integrated table preparation in TBB. Class Body defines all the significant actions required to do a scan.

false: The state of the Body represents the effect of zero or more consecutive iterations preceding subrange r, but not all preceding iterations. In this case, operator() updates the state to include reduction of the current subrange.

The second case occurs only if a thread actually steals work for the parallel_scan.

Method reverse_join merges two states of adjacent subranges. The "reverse" in its name comes from the fact that *this is the state of the *right* subrange, and its argument is the *left* subrange. The left subrange can be either a partial state or a full state remaining after a serial scan.

Method assign is used at the very end to update the original Body argument to tbb::parallel_scan with the Body state after the last iteration.

5.6.6 ArBB

Listing 5.23 shows the ArBB code for generating the table and Listing 5.24 shows the ArBB code for computing the integral by sampling this table.

```
1   // wrapper for test function
2   //   instantiate template and modify interface :
3   //   ArBB map functions need to return void
4   void arbb_f(
5       f32& y,  // output
6       f32 x  // input
7   ) {
8       y = generic_f<f32,f32>(x);  // instantiate template
9   }
10
11  template <typename Y, typename X>
12  void arbb_precompute_table(
13      X a,            // start position to sample
14      X b,            // end position to sample
15      usize n,        // number of samples
16      dense<Y>& table  // accumulated samples
17  ) {
18      // compute scale factor to convert domains
19      X dx = (b-a)/X(n-1);
20      // generate sample positions
21      dense<X> positions =
22        a + dx * dense<X>(indices(usize(0),n,usize(1)));
23      // sample function (arbb_f is a non-local)
24      dense<Y> samples;
25      map(arbb_f)(samples, positions);
26      // compute cumulative table
27      table = add_iscan(dx*samples);
28  }
```

LISTING 5.23

Integrated table preparation in ArBB. This simply invokes the built-in collective for inclusive scan using the addition operator. Templating the code provides generality.

```
1    template <typename Y, typename X>
2    void arbb_sample(
3        Y& y,
4        dense<Y> table,
5        X x
6    ) {
7        // get number of samples
8        isize n = isize(table.length());
9        // compute integer part of sample position
10       X i = floor(x);
11       // look up samples at i and i+1
12       // for out of bound indices, use 0 on left and table [n−1] on right.
13       Y y0 = select(i < X(0), Y(0),
14           table[select(i < X(n), isize(i), n−1)]);
15       Y y1 = select(i+X(1) < X(0), Y(0),
16           table[select(i+X(1) < X(n), isize(i)+1, n−1)]);
17       // Linearly interpolate between samples
18       y = y0+(y1−y0)*Y(x−X(i));
19   }
20
21   template <typename Y, typename X>
22   void arbb_integrate(
23       Y& integral,
24       dense<Y> table, // cumulative samples
25       X a,             // lower bound of function domain
26       X b,             // upper bound of function domain
27       X x0,            // lower bound of integral
28       X x1             // upper bound of integral
29   ) {
30       // Compute scale for convering x0 and x1 to table indices.
31       usize n = table.length();
32       X scale = X(n−1)/(b−a);
33       // Look up interpolated values of indefinite integral
34       Y y0, y1;
35       arbb_sample(y0, table, scale*(x0−a));
36       arbb_sample(y1, table, scale*(x1−a));
37       // compute integral
38       integral = y1−y0;
39   }
```

LISTING 5.24

Integrated table lookup in ArBB. Two linearly interpolated samples of the table are taken and interpolated. Various other operations are required to avoid reading out of bounds on the arrays. This code is similar to the serial code, except for changes in types. The ? operator used in the serial code also has to be replaced with `select`. Unfortunately, the ? operator is not overloadable in ISO C++.

Listing 5.23 uses a special function to generate a set of integers. Vector arithmetic converts these integers into sample positions and then uses a map to generate all the samples. Finally, a scan function computes the cumulative table. The ArBB implementation will actually fuse all these operations together. In particular, the computation of sample positions, the sampling of the function, and the first phase of the scan will be combined into a single parallel operation.

Given the table, the integral can be computed using the function given in Listing 5.24. This function can be used to compute a single integral or an entire set if it is called from a `map`. This code is practically identical to the serial code in Listing 5.20. The templates take care of most of the type substitutions so the only difference is the use of an ArBB collection for the table.

5.7 SUMMARY

This chapter discussed the collective reduce and scan patterns and various options for their implementation and gave some simple examples of their use. More detailed examples are provided in later chapters.

Generally speaking, if you use TBB or Cilk Plus, you will not have to concern yourself with many of the implementation details for reduce discussed in this chapter. These details have been introduced merely to make it clear why associative operations are needed in order to parallelize reduce and why commutativity is also often useful.

Scan is built into TBB and ArBB but not Cilk Plus or OpenMP. However, we provide an efficient implementation of scan in Cilk Plus in Section 8.11. This chapter also presented a simple three-phase implementation of scan in OpenMP, although this implementation is not as scalable as the one we will present later based on fork–join.

Reduce and scan are often found together with map, and they can be optimized by fusing their implementations or parts of their implementation with an adjacent map, or by reversing the order of map and reduce or scan. We discussed how to do this in TBB and Cilk Plus and provided several examples, whereas ArBB does it automatically.

Data Reorganization

6

This chapter will discuss patterns for data organization and reorganization. The performance bottleneck in many applications is just as likely, if not more likely, to be due to data movement as it is to be computation. For data-intensive applications, it is often a good idea to design the data movement first and the computation around the chosen data movements. Some common applications are in fact mostly data reorganization: searching and sorting, for instance.

In a parallel computer, additional considerations arise. First, there may be additional costs for moving data between processors and for reorganizing data for **vectorization**. Changes to data layout for vectorization may affect how data structures are declared and accessed. Second, scalability may depend on **cache** blocking and avoidance of issues such as **false sharing**. These issues also have data layout and possibly algorithmic implications.

Gather and **scatter** patterns arise from the combination of random read and write, respectively, with the **map** pattern. For gather, there are some special cases that can be implemented more efficiently than a completely random gather. **Shifts** are gathers where the data accesses are offset by fixed distances. Shifts can sometimes be implemented using vector instructions more efficiently than completely random gathers. In Chapter 7 we will also discuss the special case of the **stencil** pattern, which is a combination of map with a local gather over a fixed set of offsets and so can be implemented using shifts.

Gather is usually less expensive than scatter, so in general scatters should be converted to gathers when possible. This is usually only possible when the scatter addresses are known in advance for some definition of "in advance."

Scatter raises the possibility of a **collision** between write locations and, with it, **race conditions**. We will discuss situations under which the potential for race conditions due to scatter can be avoided, as well as some **deterministic** versions of scatter, extending the introduction to this topic in Chapter 3.

Scatter can also be combined with local reductions which leads to a form of scatter useful for combining data that we will call **merge scatter**. Certain uses of scatter can also be replaced with deterministic patterns such as **pack** and **expand**. Pack and expand are also good candidates for fusion with the map pattern, since the fused versions can have significantly reduced write **bandwidth**. In fact, it is easiest to understand the expand pattern as an extension of a map fused with pack.

Divide-and-conquer is a common strategy for designing algorithms and is especially important in parallel algorithms, since it tends to lead to good **data locality**. **Partitioning** data, also known as **geometric decomposition**, is a useful strategy for parallelization. Partitioning also maps nicely onto memory hierarchies including non-uniform memory architectures. Partitioning is related to some of the optimization strategies we will discuss for **stencil** in Chapter 7.

Finally, we present some memory layout optimizations—in particular, the conversion of **arrays of structures** into **structures of arrays**. This conversion is an important data layout optimization for vectorization. The **zip** and **unzip** patterns are special cases of gather that can be used for such data layout reorganization.

6.1 GATHER

The **gather** pattern, introduced in Section 3.5.4, results from the combination of a map with a random read. Essentially, gather does a number of independent random reads in parallel.

6.1.1 General Gather

A defining serial implementation for a general gather is given in Listing 6.1. Given a collection of locations (addresses or array indices) and a source array, gather collects all the data from the source array at the given locations and places them into an output collection. The output data collection has the same number of elements as the number of indices in the index collection, but the elements of the output collection are the same type as the input data collection. If multidimensional index collections are supported, generally the output collection has the same dimensionality as the index collection, as well. A diagram showing an example of a specific gather on a 1D collection (using a 1D index) is given in Figure 6.1.

The general gather pattern is simple but there are many special cases which can be implemented more efficiently, especially on machines with vector instructions. Important special cases include **shift** and **zip**, which are diagrammed in Figures 6.2 and 6.3. The inverse of zip, **unzip**, is also useful.

```
1  template<typename Data, typename Idx>
2  void gather(
3      size_t n,   // number of elements in data  collection
4      size_t m,   // number of elements in index  collection
5      Data a[],   // input data collection  (n elements)
6      Data A[],   // output data collection  (m elements)
7      Idx idx[]   // input index collection  (m elements)
8  ) {
9      for (size_t i = 0; i < m; ++i) {
10         size_t j = idx[i];   // get ith index
11         assert(0 <= j && j < n);   // check array bounds
12         A[i] = a[j];   // perform random read
13     }
14 }
```

LISTING 6.1

Serial implementation of gather in pseudocode. This definition also includes bounds checking (assert) during debugging as an optional but useful feature.

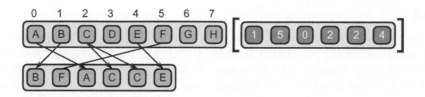

FIGURE 6.1

Gather pattern. A collection of data is read from an input collection given a collection of indices. This is equivalent to a map combined with a random read in the map's elemental function.

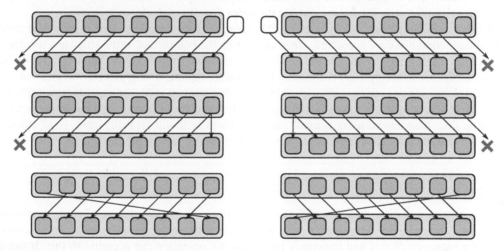

FIGURE 6.2

Shifts are special cases of gather. There are variants based on how boundary conditions are treated. Boundaries can be duplicated, rotated, reflected, a default value can be used, or most generally some arbitrary function can be used. Unlike a general gather, however, shifts can be efficiently implemented using vector instructions since in the interior, the data access pattern is regular.

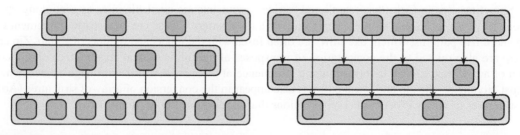

FIGURE 6.3

Zip and unzip (special cases of gather). These operations can be used to convert between array of structures (AoS) and structure of arrays (SoA) data layouts.

6.1.2 Shift

In a 1D array, the **shift** pattern moves data to the left or right in memory or, equivalently, to lower or higher locations, assuming we number locations from left to right. In higher dimensional arrays, shift may offset data by different amounts in each dimension. There are a few variants of shift that depend on how boundary conditions are handled, since by nature shift requires data that is "out of bounds" at the edge of the array. This missing data can be replaced with a default value, the edge value can be duplicated, or the data from the other side of the input array can be used. The last pattern is often called a **rotate**. It is also possible to extend the shift pattern to higher-dimensional collections to shift by larger amounts and to support additional boundary conditions, including arbitrary user-defined boundary conditions. For example, the latter can be supported by allowing arbitrary code to be executed to compute values for samples that are outside the index domain of the input collection.

Efficient implementations of shift are possible using vector operations. This is true even if complex boundary conditions are supported, since away from the boundaries, shifts still use a regular data access pattern. In this case, chunks of the input can be read into registers using vector loads, realigned using vector instructions (typically combining two separate input chunks), and then written out. More efficient implementations are typically possible if the shift amount is known at code generation time. A vectorized implementation is not strictly necessary for efficiency. Since a shift has good data locality, reading data from cache using normal read operations will still typically have good efficiency. However, vectorizing the shift can reduce the number of instructions needed.

6.1.3 Zip

The **zip** pattern interleaves data. A good example arises in the manipulation of complex numbers. Suppose you are given an array of real parts and an array of imaginary parts and want to combine them into a sequence of real and imaginary pairs. The zip operation can accomplish this. It can also be generalized to more elements—for example, forming triples from three input arrays. It can also be generalized to zipping and unzipping data of unlike types, as long as arrays of structures are supported in the programming model. The **unzip** pattern is also useful. Unzip simply reverses a zip, extracting subarrays at certain offsets and strides from an input array. For example, given a sequence of complex numbers organized as pairs, we could extract all the real parts and all the imaginary parts into separate arrays. Zip and unzip are diagrammed in Figure 6.3.

Sometimes, as in Cilk Plus, "start" and "stride" arguments are available in array sectioning operations or views, or as part of the specification of a map pattern. These can be used to implement the zip and unzip patterns, which, like shift, are often fused with the inputs and outputs of a map. Zip and unzip are also related to the computation of transposes of multidimensional arrays. Accessing a column of a row-major array involves making a sequence of memory accesses with large strides, which is just zip/unzip. The zip and unzip patterns also appear in the conversion of array of structures (AoS) to structures of arrays (SoA), data layout options that are discussed in Section 6.7.

6.2 SCATTER

The **scatter** pattern was previously discussed in Section 3.5.5. Scatter is similar to gather, but write locations rather than read locations are provided as input. A collection of input data is then written in parallel to the write locations specified. Unfortunately, unlike gather, scatter is ill-defined when duplicates appear in the collection of locations. We will call such duplicates **collisions**. In the case of a collision, it is unclear what the result should be since multiple output values are specified for a single output location.

The problem is shown in Figure 6.4. Some rule is needed to resolve such collisions. There are at least four solutions: **permutation scatter**, which makes collisions illegal (see Figure 6.6); **atomic scatter**, which resolves collisions non-deterministically but atomically (see Figure 6.5); **priority scatter**, which resolves collisions deterministically using priorities (see Figure 6.8); and **merge scatter**, which resolves collisions by combining values (see Figure 6.7).

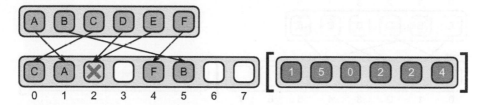

FIGURE 6.4

Scatter pattern. Unfortunately, the result is undefined if two writes go to the same location.

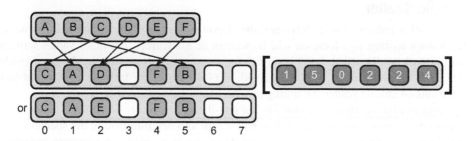

FIGURE 6.5

Atomic scatter pattern.

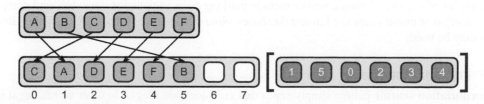

FIGURE 6.6

Permutation scatter pattern. Collisions are illegal.

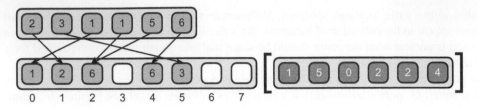

FIGURE 6.7

Merge scatter pattern. Associative and commutative operators are used to combine values upon collision.

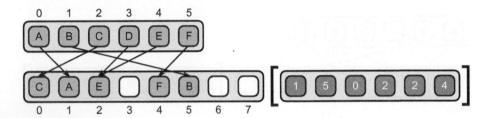

FIGURE 6.8

Priority scatter pattern. Every element is assigned a priority, which is used to resolve collisions.

6.2.1 Atomic Scatter

The **atomic scatter** pattern is **non-deterministic**. Upon collision, in an atomic scatter one and only one of the values written to a location will be written in its entirety. All other values written to the same location will be discarded. See Figure 6.5 for an example. Note that we do not provide a rule saying which of the input items will be retained. Typically, it is the last one written but in parallel implementations of atomic scatter the timing of writes is non-deterministic.

This pattern resolves collisions atomically but non-deterministically. Use of this pattern may result in non-deterministic programs. However, it is still useful and deterministic in the special case that all input data elements written to the same location have the same value. A common example of this is the writing of `true` Boolean flags into an output array that has initially been cleared to `false`. In this case, there is an implicit OR merge between the written values, since only one of the writes needs to update the output location to turn it into a `true`, and the result is the same whichever write succeeds.

Examples of the use of atomic scatter include marking pairs in collision detection, and computing set intersection or union as are used in text databases. Note that these are both examples where Boolean values may be used.

6.2.2 Permutation Scatter

The **permutation scatter** pattern simply states that collisions are illegal; in other words, legal inputs should not have duplicates. See Figure 6.6 for an example of a legal permutation scatter. Permutation scatters can always be turned into gathers, so if the addresses are known in advance, this optimization should be done. Checking for collisions, to report them as errors, can be expensive but can be done in a debugging-only mode if necessary.

The danger with permutation scatter is that programmers will use it when addresses do in fact have collisions. The resulting program may work but would depend upon undefined behavior exhibited by a particular implementation. Later on, when the implementation changes, this behavior may change and the program will be "broken." That is why it is better for implementations to actually check for collisions and report them, at least in debug mode.

Of course this problem is true for any program that depends on any undefined behavior. The issues with undefined behavior here are similar to the safety issues that arise with out-of-bounds array accesses in some programming languages. A program with an out-of-bounds access may work fine on some implementations but produce incorrect results on other implementations or simply crash. Therefore, some languages introduce array-bounds checking, but this can be expensive.

Examples of use of the permutation scatter include FFT scrambling, matrix/image transpose, and unpacking. Note that the first two of these could be (and usually should be) implemented with an equivalent gather.

6.2.3 Merge Scatter

In the **merge scatter** pattern, associative and commutative operators are provided to merge elements in case of a collision. Both properties are required, normally, since scatters to a particular location could occur in any order. In Figure 6.7, an example is shown that uses addition as the merge operator.

One problem with this pattern is that it, as with the reduction pattern, depends on the programmer to define an operator with specific algebraic properties. However, the pattern could be extended to support non-deterministic, but atomic, read–modify–write when used with non-associative operators. Such an extension would be a simple form of the **transaction** pattern.

Merge scatter can be used to implement histograms in a straightforward way by using the addition operation. Merge scatter can also be used for the computation of mutual information and entropy, as well as for database updates. The examples given earlier for atomic scatter of Boolean values could be interpreted as merge scatters with the OR operation.

6.2.4 Priority Scatter

In the **priority scatter** pattern, an example of which is given in Figure 6.8, every element in the input array for a scatter is assigned a priority based on its position. This priority is used to decide which element is written in case of a collision. By making the priorities higher for elements that would have been written later in a serial ordering of the scatter, the scatter is made not only deterministic but also consistent with serial semantics.

Consider the serial defining implementation of scatter in Listing 6.2. If there is a **collision** (two addresses writing the to same location) in the serial implementation of scatter, this is not normally considered a problem. Later writes will overwrite previous writes, giving a deterministic result.

Priorities for the priority scatter can be chosen to mimic this behavior, also discussed in Listing 6.2, making it easier to convert serial scatters into parallel scatters.

Another interesting possibility is to combine merge and priority scatter so that writes to a given location are guaranteed to be ordered.

```
1   template<typename Data, typename Idx>
2   void scatter(
3       size_t n,  // number of elements in output data   collection
4       size_t m,  // number of elements in input data and index   collection
5       Data a[],  // input data collection  (m elements)
6       Data A[],  // output data collection (n elements)
7       Idx idx[]  // input index collection (m elements)
8   ) {
9       for (size_t i = 0; i < m; ++i) {
10          size_t j = idx[i]; // get ith index
11          assert(0 <= j && j < n); // check output array bounds
12          A[j] = a[i]; // perform random write
13      }
14  }
```

LISTING 6.2

Serial implementation of scatter in pseudocode. Array bounds checking is included in this implementation for clarity but is optional.

This combined priority merge pattern is, in fact, fundamental to a massively parallel system available on nearly every personal computer: 3D graphics rendering. The pixel "fragments" written to the framebuffer are guaranteed to be in the same order that the primitives are submitted to the graphics system and several operations are available for combining fragments into final pixel values.

6.3 CONVERTING SCATTER TO GATHER

Scatter is more expensive than gather for a number of reasons. For memory reads, the data only has to be read into cache. For memory writes, due to cache line blocking, often a whole cache line has to be read first, then the element to be modified is updated, and then the whole cache line is written back. So a single write in your program may in fact result in both reads *and* writes to the memory system.

In addition, if different cores access the same cache line, then implicit communication and synchronization between cores may be required for cache coherency. This needs to be done by the hardware even if there are no actual collisions if writes from different cores go to the same cache line. This can result in significant extra communication and reduced performance and is generally known as **false sharing**.

These problems can be avoided if the addresses are available "in advance." All forms of scatter discussed in Section 6.2 can be converted to gathers if the addresses are known in advance. It is also possible to convert the non-deterministic forms of scatter into deterministic ones by allocating cores to each output location and by making sure the reads and processing for each output location are done in a fixed serial order.

However, a significant amount of processing is needed to convert the addresses for a scatter into those for a gather. One way to do it is to actually perform the scatter, but scatter the source addresses rather than the data. This builds a table that can then be used for the gather. The values in such a table will be deterministic if the original scatter was deterministic. Atomic scatters can be converted to priority scatters in this step, which will affect only the process of building the table, not the performance of the gather.

Since extra processing is involved, this approach is most useful if the same pattern of scatter addresses will be used repeatedly so the cost can be amortized. Sometimes library functions include an initialization or "planning" process in which the configuration and size of the input data are given. This is a good place to include such computation.

6.4 PACK

The **pack** pattern is used to eliminate unused elements from a collection. The retained elements are moved so that they are contiguous in memory which can improve the performance of later memory accesses and vectorization. Many common uses of the scatter pattern can be converted to packs. One advantage of a pack over a scatter is that a pack is deterministic by nature, unlike the case with scatter.

Pack can be implemented by combining scan and a conditional scatter. First, convert the input array of Booleans into integer 0's and 1's, and then perform an exclusive scan of this array with an initial value of 1 and the addition operation. This produces a set of offsets into an output array where each data input to be kept should be written. This can be done with a permutation scatter since locations will not be duplicated. Note, however, that the scatter should be conditional, since only the locations with a true flag should result in a write. An example of the pack operation is diagrammed in Figure 6.9.

The inverse of the pack operation is **unpack**, which, given the same data on which elements were kept and which were discarded, can place elements back in their original locations. Since the discarded values are unknown, a default value can be used for these locations. An example of the unpack pattern is diagrammed in Figure 6.10.

A generalization of the pack pattern is the **split** pattern. This pattern is shown in Figure 6.11. Rather than discarding elements as with pack, in the split operation elements are moved to either the upper or lower half of an output collection based on the value of some per-element predicate. Of

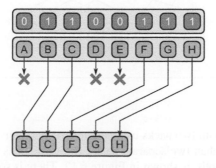

FIGURE 6.9

Pack pattern.

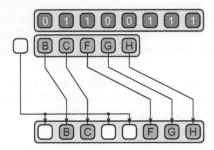

FIGURE 6.10

Unpack pattern.

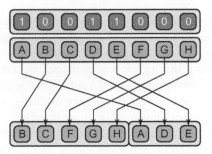

FIGURE 6.11

Split pattern.

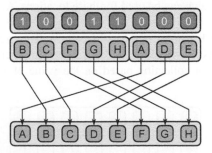

FIGURE 6.12

Unsplit pattern.

course, split can be emulated with two packs using complementary conditions, but split can usually be implemented more efficiently than two separate packs. Split also does not lose information like pack does. The inverse of split, **unsplit**, is shown in Figure 6.12. There is some relationship between these patterns and zip and unzip discussed in Section 6.1.3, but zip and unzip are specific patterns that can usually be implemented more efficiently than the more general split and unsplit patterns.

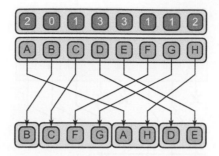

FIGURE 6.13

The bin pattern generalizes the split pattern to multiple categories.

Interestingly, control flow can be emulated on a SIMD machine given pack and unpack operations or, better yet, split and unsplit operations [LLM08, HLJH09]. Unlike the case with masking, such control flow actually avoids work and does not suffer from a reduction in coherency for divergent control flow. However, without hardware support it does have higher overhead, so most implementations emulating control flow on SIMD machines use the masking approach.

Split can be generalized further by using multiple categories. The Boolean predicate can be considered as a classification of input elements into one of two categories. It is also reasonable to generalize split to support more than two categories. Support for multiple categories leads to the **bin** pattern, shown in Figure 6.13 for four categories. The bin pattern appears in such algorithms as radix sort and pattern classification and can also be used to implement **category reduction**.

Note in the case of both the split and bin patterns that we would like to have, as a secondary output from these operations, the number of elements in each category, some of which may be empty. This is also useful for the pack pattern. In the case of pack this is the size of the output collection. Note that the output of the pack pattern might be empty!

Normally we want both split and bin to be stable, so that they preserve the relative order of their inputs. This allows these operations to be used to implement radix sort, among other applications.

One final generalization of pack, the **expand** pattern, is best understood in the context of a pack fused with a map operation (see Figure 6.15). When pack is fused with map, each element can output zero or one element. This can be generalized so that each element can output any number of elements, and the results are fused together in order.

6.5 FUSING MAP AND PACK

Pack can be fused to the output of a map as shown in Figure 6.14. This is advantageous if most of the elements of the map are discarded.

For example, consider the use of this pattern in a collision detection problem. In such a problem, we have a large number of objects and want to detect which pairs overlap in space. We will call each overlapping pair a collision, and the output of the algorithm is a list of all the collisions. We might have a large number of potentially colliding pairs of objects, but only a few that actually collide.

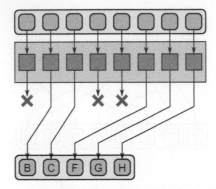

FIGURE 6.14

Fusion of map and pack patterns.

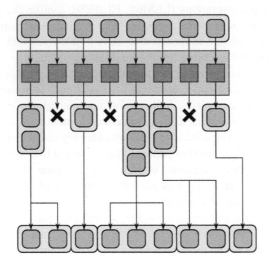

FIGURE 6.15

Expand pattern. This permits the implementation of applications that result in data amplification. It also provides a form of dynamic memory allocation.

Fusing a map to check pairs for collision, with a pack to store only actual collisions, will reduce the total amount of output bandwidth to be proportional to the results reported and not the number of pairs tested.

The **expand** pattern is best understood in the context of a pack fused with a map operation. Compare Figure 6.14 with Figure 6.15. When pack is fused with map, each element can output zero or one element. This is generalized in the expand pattern so that each element can output any number of elements, and the results are output in order.

For example, suppose you wanted to create a parallel implementation of L-system substitution. In L-system substitution, the input and output are strings of characters. Every element of the input string might get expanded into a new string of characters, or deleted, according to a set of rules. Such a pattern is often used in computer graphics modeling where the general approach is often called *data amplification*. In fact, this pattern is supported in current graphics rendering pipelines in the form of *geometry shaders*. To simplify implementation, the number of outputs might be bounded to allow for static memory allocation, and this is, in fact, done in geometry shaders. This pattern can also be used to implement variable-rate output from a map, for example, as required for lossless compression.

As with pack, fusing expand with map makes sense since unnecessary write bandwidth can then be avoided. The expand pattern also corresponds to the use of `push_back` on C++ STL collections in serial loops.

The implementation of expand is more complex than pack but can follow similar principles. If the scan approach is used, we scan integers representing the number of outputs from each element rather than only zeros and ones. In addition, we should **tile** the implementation so that, on a single processor, a serial "local expand" is used which is trivial to implement.

6.6 GEOMETRIC DECOMPOSITION AND PARTITION

A common strategy to parallelize an algorithm is to divide up the computational domain into sections, work on the sections individually, and then combine the results. Most generally, this strategy is known as **divide-and-conquer** and is also used in the design of recursive serial algorithms. The parallelization of the general form of divide-and-conquer is supported by the **fork–join** pattern, which is discussed extensively in Chapter 8.

Frequently, the data for a problem can also be subdivided following a divide-and-conquer strategy. This is obvious when the problem itself has a spatially regular organization, such as an image or a regular grid, but it can also apply to more abstract problems such as sorting and graphs. When the subdivision is spatially motivated, it is often also known as **geometric decomposition**.

As a special case of geometric decomposition, the data is subdivided into uniform non-overlapping sections that cover the domain of computation. We will call this the **partition** pattern. An example of a partition in 1D is shown in Figure 6.16. The partition pattern can also be applied in higher dimensions as is shown in Figure 6.17.

The sections of a partition are non-overlapping. This is an important property to avoid write conflicts and race conditions. A partition is often followed by a map over the set of sections with each instance of the elemental function in the map being given access to one of the sections. In this case, if we ensure that the instance has exclusive access to that section, then within the partition serial scatter patterns, such as random writes, can be used without problems with race conditions. It is also possible to apply the pattern recursively, subdividing a section into subsections for nested parallelism. This can be a good way to map a problem onto hierarchically organized parallel hardware.

FIGURE 6.16

Partitioning. Data is divided into non-overlapping, equal-sized regions.

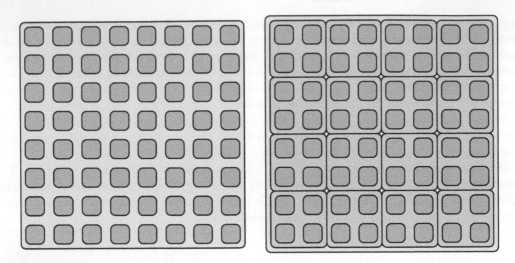

FIGURE 6.17

Partitioning in 2D. The partition pattern can be extended to multiple dimensions.

These diagrams show only the simplest case, where the sections of the partition fit exactly into the domain. In practice, there may be boundary conditions where partial sections are required along the edges. These may need to be treated with special-purpose code, but even in this case the majority of the sections will be regular, which lends itself to vectorization. Ideally, to get good memory behavior and to allow efficient vectorization, we also normally want to partition data, especially for writes, so that it aligns with cache line and vectorization boundaries. You should be aware of how data is actually laid out in memory when partitioning data. For example, in a multidimensional partitioning, typically only one dimension of an array is contiguous in memory, so only this one benefits directly from spatial locality. This is also the only dimension that benefits from alignment with cache lines and vectorization unless the data will be transposed as part of the computation. Partitioning is related to strip-mining the **stencil** pattern, which is discussed in Section 7.3.

Partitioning can be generalized to another pattern that we will call **segmentation**. Segmentation still requires non-overlapping sections, but now the sections can vary in size. This is shown in Figure 6.18. Various algorithms have been designed to operate on segmented data, including segmented versions of scan and reduce that can operate on each segment of the array but in a perfectly load-balanced fashion, regardless of the irregularities in the lengths of the segments [BHC+93]. These segmented algorithms can actually be implemented in terms of the normal scan and reduce algorithms by using a suitable combiner function and some auxiliary data. Other algorithms, such as quicksort [Ble90, Ble96], can in turn be implemented in a vectorized fashion with a segmented data structure using these primitives.

In order to represent a segmented collection, additional data is required to keep track of the boundaries between sections. The two most common representations are shown in Figure 6.19. Using an array

FIGURE 6.18

Segmentation. If data is divided into non-uniform non-overlapping regions, it can be referred to as *segmentation* (a generalization of partitioning).

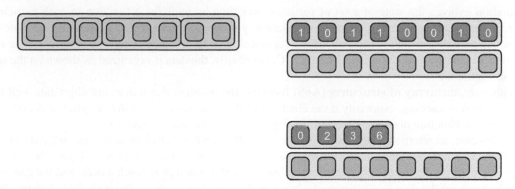

FIGURE 6.19

Segmentation representations. Various representations of segmented data are possible. The start of each segment can be marked using an array of flags. Alternatively, the start point of each segment can be indicated using an array of integers. The second approach allows zero-length segments; the first does not.

of Boolean flags to mark the start point of each segment is convenient and is useful for efficient implementation of segmented scans and reductions. The Boolean flags can be stored reasonably efficiently using a packed representation. However, this representation does not allow zero-length segments which are important for some algorithms. Also, it may be space inefficient if segments are very long on average. An alternative approach is to record the start position of every segment. This approach makes it possible to represent empty segments. Note that differences of adjacent values also give the length of each segment. The overall length of the collection can be included as an extra element in the length array to make this regular and avoid a special case.

Many of the patterns we have discussed could output segmented collections. For example, the output of the expand, split, and bin patterns, discussed in Section 6.4, could be represented as a segmented collection. Of course it is always possible to discard the segment start data and so "flatten" a segmented collection. It would also be possible to support nested segmentation, but this can always be represented, for any given maximum nesting depth, using a set of segment-start auxiliary arrays [BHC+93, Ble90]. It is possible to map recursive algorithms, such as quicksort, onto such data representations [Ble96, Ble90].

Various extensions to multidimensional segmentations are possible. For example, you could segment along each dimension. A kD-tree-like generalization is also possible, where a nested segmentation rotates among dimensions. However, the 1D case is probably the most useful.

6.7 ARRAY OF STRUCTURES VS. STRUCTURES OF ARRAYS

For vectorization, data layout in memory may have to be modified for optimal performance.

The usual approach to data abstraction is to declare structures representing some object and then create collections of that structure. For example, suppose we want to simulate a collection of particles. Every particle will have a state with a collection of values, such as velocity, mass, color, etc. You would normally declare a structure containing all the state variables needed for one particle. A particle simulation evolves the state of a set of particles over time by applying a function to each particle's state, generating a new state. For such a simulation, you would need a collection holding the state of the set of particles, which is most obviously represented by defining an array of structures. Code for this data organization is shown in Listing 6.3. Conceptually, the data is organized as shown on the left side of Figure 6.20.

However, the **array of structures (AoS)** form has the problem that it does not align data well for vectorization or caching, especially if the elements of the structure are of different types or the overall length of the structure does not lend itself to alignment to cache line boundaries.

In this case, an alternative approach is to use one collection for each element of state in the structure, as on the right side of Figure 6.20. This is known as the *structure of arrays*, or SoA, layout. Now if we apply the map pattern to this, vectorization of an elemental function is much easier, and we can also cleanly break up the data to align to cache boundaries. It is also easier to deal with data elements that vary in size.

Unfortunately, in languages like C and Fortran, changing the data layout from AoS to SoA results in significant changes to data structures and also tends to break data encapsulation. Listing 6.4 shows the reorganization required to convert the data structures declared in Listing 6.3 to SoA form.

Figure 6.21 shows how these two options lay out data in memory and how padding can be added to help with cache alignment in both cases. For AoS form, we can add padding to each structure to maintain cache alignment and avoid false sharing but this can add a significant amount of overhead to each structure. If we do not add this padding, misalignments may significantly increase computation time and will also complicate vectorization. In SoA form, padding is not really needed, but even if we do include it, it tends to be only required at the boundaries. If the collections are large, then SoA form has large internal regions of coherently organized data that can be efficiently vectorized even without internal padding.

```
1   struct Particle {
2       float vel[3];
3       float pos[3];
4       float temp;
5       char color[3];
6       int type;
7   };
8   vector<Particle> particles(N);
```

LISTING 6.3

Array of structures (AoS) data organization.

```
1   struct Particles {
2       float* vel[3];
3       float* pos[3];
4       float* temp;
5       char* color[3];
6       int* type[];
7       // constructor, allocates arrays for each component
8       Particles(int n) {
9           vel[0] = new float[n];
10          vel[1] = new float[n];
11          vel[2] = new float[n];
12          pos[0] = new float[n];
13          pos[1] = new float[n];
14          pos[2] = new float[n];
15          temp = new float[n];
16          color[0] = new char[n];
17          color[1] = new char[n];
18          color[2] = new char[n];
19          type = new int[n];
20      }
21      // destructor, deallocates arrays for each component
22      ~Particles () {
23          delete[] vel[0];
24          delete[] vel[1];
25          delete[] vel[2];
26          delete[] pos[0];
27          delete[] pos[1];
28          delete[] pos[2];
29          delele[] temp;
30          delete[] color[0];
31          delete[] color[1];
32          delete[] color[2];
33          delete[] type;
34      }
35  };
36  Particles particles(N);
```

LISTING 6.4

Structure of arrays (SoA) data organization.

Unfortunately, the SoA form is not ideal in all circumstances. For random or incoherent circumstances, gathers are used to access the data and the SoA form can result in extra unneeded data being read into cache, thus reducing performance. In this case, use of the AoS form instead will result in a smaller working set and improved performance. Generally, though, if the computation is to be vectorized, the SoA form is preferred.

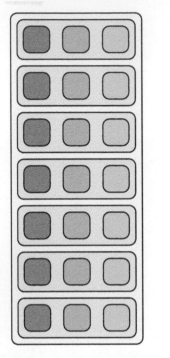
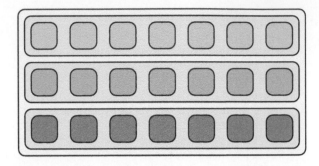

FIGURE 6.20

Array of structures (AoS) versus structure of arrays (SoA). SoA form is typically better for vectorization and avoidance of false sharing. However, if the data is accessed randomly, AoS may lead to better cache utilization.

Array of Structures (AoS), padding at end

Array of Structures (AoS), padding after each structure

Structure of Arrays (SoA), padding at end

Structure of Arrays (SoA), padding after each component

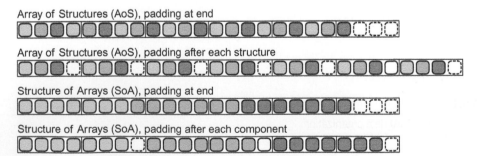

FIGURE 6.21

Data layout options for arrays of structures and structures of arrays. Data can be laid out structure-by-structure, structure-by-structure with padding per structure, or, for structure of array, array-by-array or array-by-array with padding. The structure of array form, either with or without padding, makes vectorization much easier.

6.8 SUMMARY

We have presented some data reorganization patterns and discussed some important issues around data layout.

Data reorganization patterns include scatter and gather, both of which have several special cases. Gather is a pattern that supports a set of parallel reads, while scatter supports a set of parallel writes. Shift and zip, as well as zip's inverse, unzip, are special cases of gather that can be more efficiently vectorized. Scatter has a potential problem when multiple writes to the same location are attempted. This problem can be resolved in several ways. Atomic scatters ensure that upon such collisions correct data is written, but the order is still non-deterministic. Permutation scatters simply declare collisions to be illegal and the result undefined, but it can be expensive to check for collisions, so this is usually only supportable in a debug mode. Priority scatters order the writes by priority to mimic the behavior of a random write in a loop, while merge scatters use an associative and commutative operation to combine the values involved in a collision. All forms of scatter are more expensive than gather, so scatters should normally be converted to gathers whenever possible. This is always possible if the scatter locations are known in advance.

The pack pattern can replace many uses of scatter but has the advantage that it is deterministic. The pack pattern has several generalizations, including the split, bin, and expand patterns.

A poor data layout can negatively impact performance and scalability, so it should be considered carefully. Unfortunately, some of the optimizations considered in this chapter are not always applicable. In particular, the effectiveness of the structure of arrays (SoA) form depends on how many operations over the data can be vectorized versus how often the data is accessed randomly. Cache effects such as false sharing can also dramatically affect performance, and many other computer architecture issues come to play in practice. See Appendix A for suggestions of additional reading on this topic.

Stencil and Recurrence

In this chapter, we discuss a special case of the **map** pattern, the **stencil** pattern, which has a regular data access pattern. We will also discuss the **recurrence** pattern, which is a generalization of the map pattern that supports more complex data dependencies but which can still be efficiently parallelized.

The stencil pattern results when the inputs to every instance of a map pattern are based on regular access to an input data collection using a fixed set of offsets. In other words, every output of a stencil is a function of some neighborhood of elements in an input collection.

Stencils are common in practice. There are also several specific optimizations that can be applied to their implementation. In particular, the neighborhood structure of stencils exposes opportunities for data reuse and optimization of data locality. The regular structure of the memory reads also means that vectorized **elemental functions** can use **shifts**, rather than general **gathers**, for accessing input data. Efficient implementation of multidimensional stencils also requires attention to cache effects.

Stencils access a neighborhood of input data using a set of offsets. Recurrences are similar but access a neighborhood of *outputs*. Unlike a map, instances of a recurrence can depend on the values computed by other instances. In serial code, recurrences appear as loop-carried dependencies in which iterations of a loop can depend on previous iterations. We limit our discussion to cases where the output dependencies follow a regular pattern based on a set of offsets.

In Chapter 5, we discussed recurrences in one-dimensional loops, which can be parallelized as scans, but only if the instance operations are associative. In this chapter, we show that n-dimensional recurrences with $n > 1$ (those arising from loop nests) can always be parallelized over $n - 1$ dimensions whether or not the operations are associative. In fact, you do not require any special properties for the operations in the recurrence. All that matters is that the pattern of data dependencies is regular. In this chapter, we discuss a simple way to parallelize recurrences based on hyperplane sweeps, while in Chapter 8 we discuss another way to parallelize recurrences based on recursive **divide-and-conquer**.

7.1 STENCIL

A **stencil** is a map in which each output depends on a "neighborhood" of inputs specified using a set of fixed offsets relative to the output position. A defining serial implementation is given in Listing 7.1 and is diagrammed in Figure 7.1. The data access patterns of stencils are regular and can be implemented either using a set of random reads in each elemental function or as a set of shifts, as discussed in Section 7.2.

```
1   template<
2       int NumOff,      // number of  offsets
3       typename In,     // type of input  locations
4       typename Out,    // type of output  locations
5       typename F       // type of function / functor
6   >
7   void stencil(
8       int n,           // number of elements  in  data  collection
9       const In a[],    // input data collection  (n elements)
10      Out r[],         // output  data  collection  (n elements)
11      In b,            // boundary value
12      F func,          // function / functor from  neighborhood inputs  to  output
13      const int offsets[] // offsets (NumOffsets elements)
14  ) {
15      // array to hold neighbors
16      In neighborhood[NumOff];
17      // loop over all  output  locations
18      for (int i = 0; i < n; ++i) {
19          // loop over all  offsets  and gather neighborhood
20          for (int j = 0; j < NumOff; ++j) {
21              // get index of jth  input  location
22              int k = i+offsets[j];
23              if (0 <= k && k < n) {
24                  // read input  location
25                  neighborhood[j] = a[k];
26              } else {
27                  // handle boundary case
28                  neighborhood[j] = b;
29              }
30          }
31          // compute output value from  input  neighborhood
32          r[i] = func(neighborhood);
33      }
34  }
```

LISTING 7.1

Serial implementation of stencil. This code is generic, so it calls `func` for doing the actual processing after reading the neighborhood.

Stencils are important in many applications. In image and signal processing, the convolution operation is fundamental to many operations. In a convolution, the input samples are combined using a weighted sum with specific fixed weights associated with each offset input. Convolution is a linear operation but not all stencils are linear. Bilateral filtering is a powerful noise-reduction filter that uses non-linear operations to avoid smoothing over edges [TM98]. It is non-linear but follows the stencil pattern.

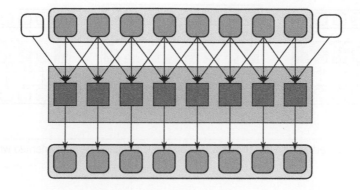

FIGURE 7.1

Stencil pattern. The stencil pattern combines a local, structured gather with a function to combine the results into a single output for each input neighborhood.

Stencils also arise in solvers for partial differential equations (PDEs) over regular grids. PDE solvers are important in many scientific simulations, in computer-aided engineering, and in imaging. Imaging applications include photography, satellite imaging, medical imaging, and seismic reconstruction. Seismic reconstruction is one of the major workloads in oil and gas exploration.

Stencils can be one dimensional, as shown in Figure 7.1, or multidimensional. Stencils also have different kinds of neighborhoods from square compact neighborhoods to sparse neighborhoods. The special case of a convolution using a square compact neighborhood with constant weights is known as a *box filter* and there are specific optimizations for it similar to that for the scan pattern. However, these optimizations do not apply to the general case. Stencils reuse samples required for neighboring elements, so stencils, especially multidimensional stencils, can be further optimized by taking cache behavior into account as discussed in Section 7.3. Stencils, like shifts, also require consideration of boundary conditions. When subdivided using the partition pattern, presented in Section 6.6, boundary conditions can result in additional communication between cores, either implicit or explicit.

7.2 IMPLEMENTING STENCIL WITH SHIFT

The regular data access pattern used by stencils can be implemented using shifts. For a group of elemental functions, a vector of inputs for each offset in the stencil can be collected by shifting the input by the amount of the offset. This is diagrammed in Figure 7.2.

Implementing a stencil in this way is really only beneficial for one-dimensional stencils or the memory-contiguous dimension of a multidimensional stencil. Also, it does not reduce total memory traffic to external memory since, if random scalar reads are used, data movement from external memory will still be combined into block reads by the cache. Shifts, however, allow vectorization of the data reads, and this can reduce the total number of instructions used. They may also place data in vector registers ready for use by vectorized elemental functions.

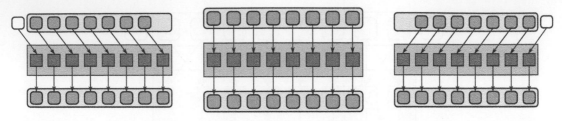

FIGURE 7.2

Stencil pattern implemented with shifts. The offsets of a stencil can each be implemented with a shift and then combined.

7.3 TILING STENCILS FOR CACHE

When parallelizing multidimensional stencils where the data is laid out in a row-by-row fashion, there is a tension between optimizing for cache line data locality and minimizing the size of the working set. Figure 7.3 demonstrates the approach used to optimize stencils for cache known as **strip-mining**.

Assume the data for a two-dimensional array is laid out in a row-by-row fashion so that all data in a row is contiguous in memory. That means that horizontal offsets access data that is close by, but vertical offsets access data that is far away. Therefore, horizontally accessed data will tend to be in the same cache line, but vertically accessed data will tend to be in different cache lines.

When breaking up the work over multiple cores, rectangular regions are assigned to each core. Assigning rows to each core would make good use of horizontal data locality. However, this approach would tend to read data redundantly since each core will need data from adjacent rows, assuming there are vertical offsets in the stencil. Conversely, assigning columns to each core would redundantly read data in the same cache line. Even worse, multiple cores would then write to the same cache line and cause false sharing and less than impressive performance.

If there are a significant number of vertical offsets, the right solution is often to assign a "strip" to each core. The strip is a multiple of cache lines wide, to avoid false sharing on output and to avoid significant redundancy on reads, and the height of the array vertically. Within each core, a strip is processed serially, from top to bottom. This organization of the computation should give good temporal coherence and reuse of data in the cache. The width of the strip should be small enough so that the working set of the stencil for the strip will fit in the cache.

There are two other memory system effects that can occur with memory systems when processing stencils. First, if the row size is a power of two, sometimes data from different rows can map to the same "sets" in set-associative caches, causing false cache conflicts. Whether this happens depends on a number of memory subsystem design issues including the number of sets in the cache and the size of the cache lines. This pathological case, if it occurs, can usually be avoided by padding array rows with unused elements to avoid row lengths that are powers of two. You should also take the strip width and stencil height into account to determine a padding amount that avoids conflicts anywhere in the working set. The second problem is TLB misses. For very large stencils, enough different pages may have to be touched that there are not enough entries in the TLB cache to manage the virtual-to-physical address translation. This can cause TLB cache thrashing, in which constant misses in the TLB cache will severely degrade performance. If the TLB miss rate is high, the data may have to be

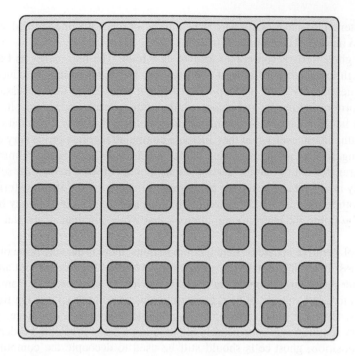

FIGURE 7.3

Tiling stencils for cache using strip-mining. Strips are assigned to each core. The strips are a multiple of a cache line wide, wide enough to avoid too much unused data being read into cache, and the height of the array. Processing goes top to bottom within a strip to minimize the working set and maximize reuse of the data in the cache. The strip alignment with cache lines prevents false sharing between adjacent strips. Reads may come from adjacent input strips, but writes are from separate cores and are always in separate strips.

reorganized into tiles and processing order changed to avoid needing to access more pages at once than are supported by the memory system.

The partition and geometric decomposition patterns, discussed in Section 6.6, are related to strip-mining. When strip-mining, the output partitions are non-overlapping but the input footprints of each partition overlap. That is, the input is a more general geometric decomposition, not a partition.

7.4 OPTIMIZING STENCILS FOR COMMUNICATION

The stencil pattern is often used inside an iterative loop—for example, in partial differential equation (PDE) solvers. The output of each stencil application is used as the input for the next iteration. In this case, synchronization is required between iterations so that the overlapping regions can be updated. These overlapping regions, often called "ghost cells" in this context, may have to be explicitly communicated between nodes when the pattern is used in a distributed system [KS10]. It is generally better to replicate these ghost cells in each local memory and swap them at the end of each iteration when using an iterated stencil than to try and share the memory for them at a fine-grained level. Fine-grained sharing can lead to increased communication costs.

The set of all ghost cells is sometimes known as a **halo**. The halo needs to be large enough to contain all the neighbors needed for at least one iteration. It is also possible to reduce communication to only every nth iteration by using a "deep halo" that is n times larger than necessary. However, this does require performing additional redundant computation in each node. This should be used only when the limiting factor is latency of communication, not bandwidth or computation. Optimizations that reduce communication, even when they increase computation, often prove very effective. General trends in computing, toward more processing cores, increasingly favor such optimizations. However, like any program transformation that increases the total amount of work to increase scalability, the code should be carefully analyzed and tested for performance to determine if the transformation is actually beneficial. Many other optimizations are possible in this pattern, including **latency hiding**, which can be accomplished by doing the interior computations first while simultaneously waiting for ghost cell updates.

In the context of iterative update of stencil computations, there is also the issue of double buffering to consider. For most iterated stencils, it is necessary to make a copy of the input and generate a new output buffer, rather than doing an update in place. However, for some stencils, namely, those that are *causal* (the offsets to input values can be organized to always point "backward in time" to previously processed samples, for some serial ordering), it is possible to do updates in place. This optimization can reduce memory requirements considerably but assumes a serial processing order. When used with geometric decomposition, ghost cells should still be used to decouple the computations, and some additional memory will still be required for the ghost cells.

Iterated stencils are really a special case of recurrences, discussed in Section 7.5. Thinking about iterated stencils as recurrences exposes the option of space-time blocking, which can significantly improve **arithmetic intensity**, the ratio of computation to communication.

7.5 RECURRENCE

When several loops are nested and have data dependencies between them, even though the loop iterations are not independent it is still possible to parallelize the entire loop nest. Consider Figure 7.4. In this figure, the arrows represent data dependencies where each output b[i][j] depends on the outputs from elements to the left and above. Such data dependencies result from the double loop nest shown in Listing 7.2. In the diagram, inputs are only shown at the boundaries (implemented by initializing appropriate elements of b) but in general there could be other inputs at every element, represented in the code with array a, and we also actually have outputs at every element.

You can parallelize such a loop nest even if the function f has no special properties. The trick is to find a plane that cuts through the grid of intermediate results so that all references to previously computed values are on one side of the plane. Such a plane is called a *separating hyperplane*. You can then sweep (iterate) through the data in a direction perpendicular to this plane and perform all the operations on the plane at each iteration in parallel. This is equivalent to skewing the elements of Figure 7.4 so that all dataflow arrows correctly point downward and forward in time. After you do this, the implementation looks like the diagram in Figure 7.5, where we have also shown all data elements

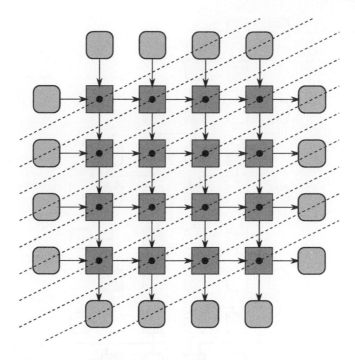

FIGURE 7.4

Recurrence pattern, definition. A multiply nested loop can be parallelized if the data dependencies are regular by finding a separating hyperplane and sweeping it through the lattice. Here, one possible separating hyperplane sweep is shown using a sequence of dotted lines.

```
1   void my_recurrence(
2       size_t v,        // number of elements  vertically
3       size_t h,        // number of elements  horizontally
4       const float a[v][h], // input 2D array
5       float b[v][h]    // output 2D array (boundaries already  initialized )
6   ) {
7       for (int i=1; i<v; ++i)
8           for (int j=1; j<h; ++j)
9               b[i][j] = f(b[i-1][j], b[i][j-1], a[i][j]);
10  }
```

LISTING 7.2

Serial 2D recurrence. For syntactic simplicity, the code relies on the C99 feature of variable-length arrays.

consumed and computed for clarity. Leslie Lamport showed [Lam74] that a hyperplane can always be found if the dependencies are constant offsets. Note that as the plane sweeps through the array, the amount of parallelism is small at first, grows to a maximum value, and then shrinks again. This

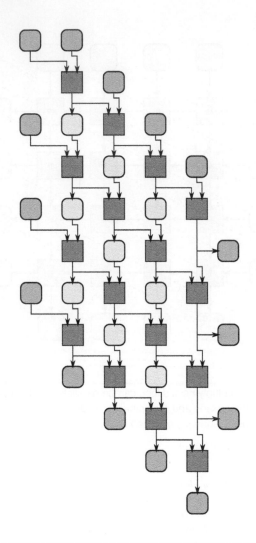

FIGURE 7.5

Recurrence pattern, implementation. A hyperplane sweep can also be seen as a skew of the elements of the recurrence so that all data dependencies are oriented forward in time.

approach to parallelization can be generalized to higher-dimensional loop nests as well as loop nests whose inner loop bounds depend on indices of outer loops. This generalization is called *polyhedral theory* [VBC06].

Such a parallelization can be challenging to implement, especially in higher dimensions, since the transformation of the indices and proper handling of the boundary conditions can get quite complicated. Different choices of the hyperplane can lead to different parallelizations with different performances as well. In the above example, consider the case where the horizontal size h is large and the vertical size v is small, and vice versa. You may want to "slant" the hyperplane in different directions to get optimal performance in these two cases.

Both parallel and serial implementations of recurrences are also often combined with **tiling**. Tiling is especially beneficial for recurrences since it improves the ratio of data access to computation. In this approach, the recurrence is broken into a grid of tiles, and the data dependencies between the tiles lead to a new recurrence. Within the tiles, however, a serial implementation of the recurrence can be used. Such tiling is often so beneficial that it is useful to convert iterated stencils to recurrences so that this approach can be used. Tiling can be applied using either a static decomposition or a **divide-and-conquer** strategy under programming models supporting **fork–join**. The fork–join approach is discussed at greater length in Section 8.12.

Examples of the use of the recurrence pattern include infinite impulse response filters, dynamic programming (such as that used for sequence alignment in the Smith–Waterman algorithm), option pricing by the binomial lattice algorithm, and matrix factorization.

7.6 SUMMARY

In this chapter, we have discussed two related patterns, stencils and recurrences. These are very common in practice, in everything from simulation to image processing. What these two patterns have in common is a regular pattern of communication and data access. To obtain high performance with these patterns, this regularity needs to be used to improve efficiency both by reuse of data (reducing the necessary bandwidth to off-chip memory) and by vectorization.

In both stencil and recurrence, it is possible to convert a set of offset memory accesses to shifts, but this is really only useful if vectorization is also used. Stencils can also use strip-mining to make effective use of the cache.

The other challenge with recurrences in particular (which also arise when stencils are iterated) is implementing space-time tiling. While this is an effective technique, picking the right size of tile involves a tradeoff between higher arithmetic intensity and working set. Chapter 8 introduces a recursive approach to tiling a recurrence, which Chapter 10 elaborates upon in the context of a practical example. The recursive approach tiles the recurrence at many different levels, so that at some level the tiles become the right size to fit in cache.

Fork–Join

When you come to a fork in the road, take it.

(Yogi Berra, 1925–)

This chapter describes the **fork–join** pattern and gives several examples, including its use to implement other patterns such as **map**, **reduce**, **recurrence**, and **scan**. Applied recursively, fork–join can generate a high degree of **potential parallelism**. This can, in turn, be efficiently scheduled onto **actual parallelism** mechanisms by the Cilk Plus and Intel Threading Building Blocks (TBB) **work-stealing** schedulers.

Many serial **divide-and-conquer** algorithms lend themselves to parallelization via fork–join. However, the limits on **speedup** noted in Section 2.5 need to be taken into account. In particular, most of the work should be pushed as deep into the recursion as possible, where the parallelism is high.

This chapter starts with the basic concept of fork and join and introduces the Cilk Plus, TBB, and OpenMP syntaxes for it. Section 8.3 shows how the map pattern can be implemented efficiently using recursive fork–join, which is indeed how Cilk Plus and TBB implement it. Both Cilk Plus and TBB use a parallel iteration idiom for expressing the map pattern, although the TBB interface can also be thought of as using an **elemental function** syntax. The recursive approach to parallelism needs split and merge operations as well as a base case. Section 8.4 covers how to select the base case for parallel recursion. Section 8.5 explains how the work-stealing schedulers in Cilk Plus and TBB automatically balance load. It also details the subtle differences in work-stealing semantics between the two systems and the impact of this on program behavior—in particular, memory usage. Section 8.6 shows a common cookbook approach to analyzing the work and span of fork–join, particularly the recursive case. To demonstrate this approach and to give a concrete example of recursive parallelism, Section 8.7 presents an implementation of Karatsuba multiplication of polynomials. Section 8.8 touches on the subject of **cache-oblivious** algorithms. Cache-oblivious algorithms [ABF05] optimize for the **memory hierarchy** without knowing the structure or size of that hierarchy by having **data locality** at many different scales. Section 8.9 presents parallel Quicksort in detail, because it exposes subtle implementation issues that sometimes arise in writing efficient parallel divide-and-conquer algorithms. Parallel Quicksort also highlights the impact of the differences in Cilk Plus versus TBB work-stealing semantics. Section 8.10 shows how Cilk Plus **hyperobjects** can simplify writing reductions in the fork–join context. Section 8.11 shows how the scan pattern can be implemented efficiently with fork–join. Section 8.12 shows how fork–join can be applied to recurrences and, in particular, recursive **tiled** recurrences.

8.1 DEFINITION

In **fork–join** parallelism, control flow *forks* (divides) into multiple flows that *join* (combine) later. After the fork, one flow turns into two separate flows. Each flow is independent, and they are not constrained to do similar computation. After the join, only one flow continues.

For example, consider forking to execute B() and C() in parallel and then joining afterwards. The execution of a fork–join can be pictured as a directed graph, as in Figure 8.1. This figure also demonstrates the graphical notation we will use for the fork and join operations.

Often fork–join is used to implement recursive **divide-and-conquer** algorithms. The typical pattern looks like this:

```
void DivideAndConquer( Problem P ) {
    if( P is base case ) {
        Solve P;
    } else {
        Divide P into K subproblems;
        Fork to conquer each subproblem in parallel;
        Join;
        Combine subsolutions into final solution;
    }
}
```

It is critical that the subproblems be independent, so that they can run in parallel. Nesting K-way fork–join this way to N levels permits K^N-way parallelism. Figure 8.2 shows three-level, two-way nesting, resulting in eight parallel flows at the innermost level. The algorithm should be designed to put the vast majority of work deep in the nest, where parallelism is high. Section 8.6 shows how to formally analyze the speedup of fork–join.

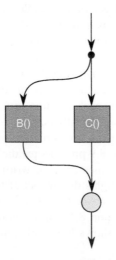

FIGURE 8.1

Fork–join control flow.

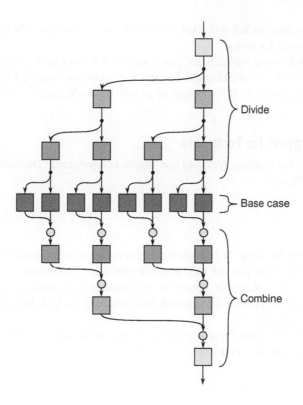

FIGURE 8.2

Nested fork–join control flow in a divide-and-conquer algorithm. For good speedup, it is important that most of the work occur deep in the nesting (more darkly shaded boxes), where parallelism is high.

Selecting the size of the base case for parallel divide-and-conquer can be critical in practice. It should allow the recursion to go deep enough to permit plenty of parallelism. However, the recursion should not be *too* deep; in particular, it should not result in subproblems so fine grained that scheduling overheads dominate. Section 8.4 offers more guidance on this point. Also, the problem division and combine operations which appear before and after the fork and join operations should be as fast as possible, so they do not dominate the asymptotic complexity and strangle speedup.

8.2 PROGRAMMING MODEL SUPPORT FOR FORK–JOIN

Programming model support for fork–join has to express where to fork and where to join. Cilk Plus, TBB, and OpenMP express fork–join differently. Cilk Plus uses a syntactic extension, TBB uses a library, and OpenMP uses **pragma** markup, but the fundamental parallel control flow is the same for all. There are, however, subtle differences about *which* **threads** execute a particular part of the parallel control flow, as Section 8.5 will explain. As long as you do not rely on thread-local storage, the difference is immaterial for now.

When reading the following subsections, pay attention not only to the different ways of expressing fork–join but also to how variables outside the fork–join are captured and referenced. This is particularly relevant when there is an increment of an index variable, such as ++i in the example.

8.2.1 Cilk Plus Support for Fork–Join

Cilk Plus has keywords for marking fork and join points in a program. The control flow in Figure 8.1 can be written in Cilk Plus as:

```
cilk_spawn B();
C();
cilk_sync;
```

The cilk_spawn marks the fork. It indicates that the caller can continue asynchronously without waiting for B() to return. The precise fork point occurs *after* evaluation of any actual arguments. The cilk_sync marks an explicit join operation. It indicates that execution must wait until all calls **spawned** up to that point by the current function have returned. In Cilk Plus there is also an explicit join at the end of every function.

Note in our example above that there is *not* a cilk_spawn before C(). The example could also be written as the following, which would work:

```
cilk_spawn B();
cilk_spawn C();
/* nil */
cilk_sync;
```

However, this is redundant and considered bad style in Cilk Plus, because it specifies two forks, as in Figure 8.3. The second fork is pointless overhead—it runs /* nil */ (that is, nothing) in the spawning task in parallel with C(). You should put some of the work in the spawned task and some in the spawning task instead.

Multiway forks are possible. For example, the following code forks four ways:

```
cilk_spawn A();
cilk_spawn B();
cilk_spawn C();
D();          // Not spawned, executed in spawning task
cilk_sync;    // Join
```

The matching of cilk_spawn and cilk_sync is dynamic, not lexical. A cilk_sync waits for all spawned calls in the current function to return. Spawning within a loop, or conditional spawning, can be handy on occasion. The following fragment does both: It spawns f(a[i]) for nonzero a[i]:

```
for ( int i=0; i<n; ++i )
    if ( a[i]!=0 )
        cilk_spawn f(a[i]);
cilk_sync;
```

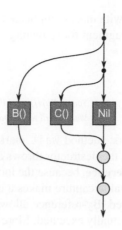

FIGURE 8.3

Bad style for fork–join. Spawning every subtask in Cilk Plus is unnecessary overhead. In general, work should also be computed by the spawning task.

Be warned, however, that spawning many tasks from a loop is often less efficient than using recursive forking, because the loop itself may become a serial bottleneck. The cilk_for construct uses recursive forking even though it looks like a loop. The cilk_sync can be conditional, too, although none of the examples in this book uses that capability. As mentioned previously, there is always an implicit cilk_sync (join) at the end of a function. Therefore, when a function returns, you can be sure that any Cilk Plus parallelism created in it has finished. Note, too, that because forking occurs *after* evaluation of any actual arguments, each spawned call in this example receives the intended value of a[i] as an argument, even as the loop continues to increment i.

8.2.2 **TBB Support for Fork–Join**

TBB has two high-level algorithm templates for fork–join, one for simple cases and one for more complicated cases. For simple cases, the function template parallel_invoke does an *n*-way fork for small *n*. It also waits for all tasks that it forks to complete; that is, it joins all the tasks before returning. Here is an example for $n = 2$:

```
tbb::parallel_invoke( B, C );
```

In the current TBB implementation, the parallel_invoke template accepts up to 10 arguments.

The arguments should be function objects, sometimes called *functors*, each with a method void operator()()const that takes no arguments. Passing parameters to the functor is done by capturing them during construction. Typically the function objects are constructed by **lambda expressions**, which give a more convenient syntax for constructing functors, especially for capturing parameters. For example, here is a hypothetical fragment for walking two subtrees in parallel:

```
tbb::parallel_invoke( [=]{Walk(node->left);},
                      [=]{Walk(node->right);} );
```

The class tbb::task_group deals with more complicated cases, and in particular provides a more explicit join operation. Here is a TBB fragment for spawning f(a[i]) for nonzero a[i]:

```
task_group g;
for ( int i=0; i<n; ++i )
    if ( a[i] != 0 )
        g.run( [=,&a]{f(a[i]);} );   // Spawn f(a[i]) as child task
g.wait();                            // Wait for all tasks spawned from g
```

Method run marks where a fork occurs; method wait marks a join. The wait is required before destroying the task_group; otherwise, the destructor throws an exception missing_wait. Note that i must be captured **by value**, not **by reference**, because the loop might increment the original variable i before the functor actually runs. By-value capture makes a copy of non-local variable references at the point where the lambda is constructed. By-reference allows the lambda to refer to the state of the non-local variable when the lambda is actually executed. More details on this are given in Section D.2. The general by-value capture given by the "=" argument to the lambda ensures that the value of i at the point of the invocation of g.run is used for that task. The notation &a specifies that a is captured by reference, since C++ does not allow capturing arrays by value.

8.2.3 OpenMP Support for Fork–Join

OpenMP 3.0 also has a fork–join construct. Here is an OpenMP fragment for the fork–join control flow from Figure 8.1:

```
#pragma omp task
B();
C();
#pragma omp taskwait
```

The construct task indicates that the subsequent statement can be independently scheduled as a task. In the example, the statement "B();" is run in parallel. The statement could also be a compound statement—that is, a group of statements surrounded by braces. The work in C() is performed by the spawning task, and finally the construct omp taskwait waits for all child tasks of the current task.

There is a catch peculiar to OpenMP: Parallelism happens only inside parallel regions. Thus, for the example to actually fork there must be an enclosing OpenMP parallel construct, either in the current routine or further up the call chain.

Variable capture needs attention. OpenMP tasks essentially capture global variables by reference and local variables by value. In OpenMP parlance, these capture modes are respectively called shared and firstprivate. Sometimes these defaults must be overridden, as the following fragment illustrates:

```
int foo( int i ) {
    int x, y;
#pragma omp task shared(x)
    x = f(i);
    ++i;
    y = g(i);
#pragma omp taskwait
    return x+y;
}
```

The `shared` clause requests that x be captured by reference. Without it, x would be captured by value, and the effect of the assignment x = f(i) would be lost.

8.3 RECURSIVE IMPLEMENTATION OF MAP

One of the simplest, but most useful, patterns to implement with fork–join is **map**. Although both Intel TBB and Cilk Plus have concise ways to express map directly, the map pattern is nonetheless a good starting example for parallel **divide-and-conquer**, because it implements a familiar pattern. It also gives some insight into how Cilk Plus and TBB implement their map constructs. They really do use the divide-and-conquer approach to be described, because it efficiently exploits the underlying work-stealing mechanism explained in Section 8.5. Furthermore, you may eventually need to write a version of the map pattern with features beyond the built-in capabilities—for example, when fusing it with other patterns—so knowledge of how to implement map efficiently using fork–join is useful.

Consider the following Cilk Plus code:

```
cilk_for( unsigned i=lower; i<upper; ++i )
    f(i);
```

The `cilk_for` construct can be implemented by a divide-and-conquer routine `recursive_map`, which is called like this:

```
if( lower<upper )
    recursive_map(lower,upper,grainsize,f)
```

The conditional eliminates needing to deal with the empty case inside the routine. Listing 8.1 shows the `recursive_map` routine. The parameter `grainsize` controls the size of the base case. In Cilk Plus, the compiler and runtime choose the size of the base case based on considerations that will be discussed in Section 8.4.

```
1   template<typename Func>
2   void recursive_map( unsigned lower, unsigned upper, unsigned grainsize, Func f ) {
3       if( upper−lower<=grainsize )
4           // Parallel base case
5           for( unsigned i=lower; i<upper; ++i )
6               f(i);
7       else {
8           // Divide and conquer
9           unsigned middle = lower+(upper−lower)/2u;
10          cilk_spawn recursive_map( lower, middle, grainsize, f );
11          recursive_map( middle, upper, grainsize, f );
12      }
13      // Implicit  cilk_sync when function  returns
14  }
```

LISTING 8.1

Recursive implementation of the map pattern in Cilk Plus.

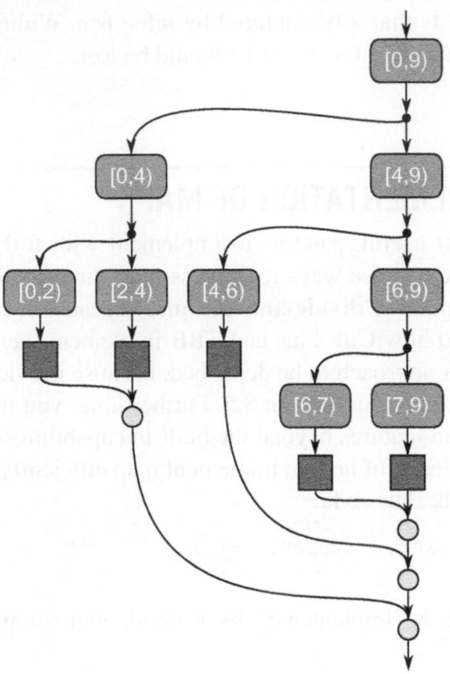

FIGURE 8.4

Execution of `recursive_map(0,9,2,f)` using the implementation in Listing 8.1.

Figure 8.4 illustrates the execution of `recursive_map(0,9,2,f)`, which maps f over the half-open interval $[0,9)$ with no more than two iterations per **grain**. Arcs are labeled with [*lower*, *upper*) to indicate the corresponding arguments to `recursive_map`.

Now consider an optimization. In Listing 8.1, no explicit `cilk_sync` is necessary because every function with `cilk_spawn` performs an implicit `cilk_sync` when it returns. Except for this implicit `cilk_sync`, the routine does nothing after its last call. Hence, the last call is what is known as a **tail call**. In serial programming, as long as local variables can be overwritten before the last call, a tail call can be optimized away by the following transformation:

1. Update the parameters to be the values required for the callee.
2. Jump to the top of the routine.

Applying these rules literally to the previous example yields the code in Listing 8.2. This code can be cleaned up by removing redundant updates and structuring the `goto` as a `while` loop, resulting in the concise code in Listing 8.3.

Similar tricks for converting tail calls to iteration applies to TBB, as will be shown in Listings 8.12 and 8.13 of Section 8.9.2.

```
1  template<typename Func>
2  void recursive_map( unsigned lower, unsigned upper, unsigned grainsize, Func f ) {
3  retry:
4      if( upper−lower<=grainsize )
5          for( unsigned i=lower; i<upper; ++i )
6              f(i);
7      else {
8          unsigned middle = lower+(upper−lower)/2u;
9          cilk_spawn recursive_map(lower, middle, grainsize, f);
10         // Set parameters to be values required for callee
11         lower = middle;
12         upper = upper;
13         grainsize = grainsize;
14         // Jump into the callee
15         goto retry;
16     }
17     // Implicit cilk_sync when function returns
18 }
```

LISTING 8.2

Modification of Listing 8.1 that changes tail call into a goto.

```
1  template<typename Func>
2  void recursive_map( unsigned lower, unsigned upper, unsigned grainsize, Func f ) {
3      while( upper−lower>grainsize ) {
4          unsigned m = lower+(upper−lower)/2u;
5          cilk_spawn recursive_map( lower, m, grainsize, f );
6          lower = m;
7      }
8      for( unsigned i=lower; i<upper; ++i )
9          f(i);
10     // Implicit cilk_sync when function returns
11 }
```

LISTING 8.3

Cleaned-up semi-recursive map in Cilk Plus.

8.4 CHOOSING BASE CASES

In parallel divide-and-conquer, there are often *two* distinct base cases to consider:

- A base case for stopping parallel recursion
- A base case for stopping serial recursion

They sometimes differ because they are guided by slightly different overhead considerations. The alternative to parallel recursion is serial recursion, which avoids parallel scheduling overheads. The alternative to serial recursion is a serial iterative algorithm, which avoids calling overheads. However, these two overheads are often at different scales so the optimal sizes for the base cases are often different.

For example, in the Quicksort example detailed later in Section 8.9, serial recursion continues only until there are about 7 elements to sort. It stops at a relatively short sequence because the iterative alternative is a quadratic sort, which has a higher asymptotic complexity but less overhead and a lower constant factor. However, in the same example, parallel recursion stops at about 500 elements. The parallel recursion stops for a much bigger base case problem size because the alternative is serial recursive Quicksort, which is still quite efficient at this size but avoids parallel overheads.

Given a machine with P hardware threads, it is tempting to choose a parallel base case such that there are exactly P leaves in the tree of spawned functions. However, doing so often results in poor performance, because it gives the scheduler no flexibility to balance load, as noted in Section 2.6.6. Even if the leaves have nominally equal work and processors are nominally equivalent, system effects such as page faults, cache misses, and interrupts can destroy the balance. Thus, it is usually best to **overdecompose** the problem to create **parallel slack** (Section 2.5.6). As the next section explains, the underlying work-stealing scheduler in Cilk Plus and TBB makes unused parallel slack cheap for fork–join parallelism.

Of course, overdecomposition can go too far, causing scheduling overheads to swamp useful work, just as ordinary function calls can swamp useful work in serial programs. A rough rule of thumb is that a `cilk_spawn` costs on the order of 10 non-inlined function calls, and a TBB spawn costs on the order of 30 non-inlined function calls, excluding the cost of data transfer between workers if parallelism actually occurs. Basic intuitions for amortizing call overhead still apply—only the relative expense of the call has changed.

When the leaves dominate the work, you should also consider whether **vector parallelism** can be applied, as in the Karatsuba multiplication example (Listing 8.6).

8.5 LOAD BALANCING

Cilk Plus and TBB efficiently balance the load for fork–join automatically, using a technique called **work stealing**. Indeed, as remarked earlier, the work-stealing technique is so effective for **load balancing** that both frameworks implement their map operations (`cilk_for` and `tbb::parallel_for`) using fork–join algorithms.

In a basic work-stealing scheduler, each thread is called a **worker**. Each worker maintains its own double-ended queue (deque) of tasks. Call one end of the deque the "top" and the other end the "bottom." A worker treats its own deque like a stack. When a worker spawns a new task, it pushes that task onto the top of its own deque. When a worker finishes its current task, it pops a task from the *top* of its own deque, unless the deque is empty.

When a worker's deque is empty, a worker chooses a random victim's deque and steals a task from the *bottom* of that deque. Because that is the last task that the owner of the deque would touch, this approach has several benefits:

- The thief will be grabbing work toward the beginning of the call tree. This tends to be a big piece of work that will keep the thief busy longer than a small piece would.

- In the case of recursive decomposition of an index space, the work stolen will have indices that are consecutive but will tend to be distant from those that the victim is working on. This tends to avoid cache conflicts when iterating over arrays.

Overall, the net effect is that workers operate serially depth-first by default, until more actual parallelism is required. Each steal adds a bit of parallel breadth-first execution, just enough to keep the workers busy. The "just enough" part is important. Always doing breadth-first execution leads to space exponential in the spawning depth, and the worst **spatial locality** imaginable! Cilk Plus formalizes the "just enough" notion into some strong guarantees about time and space behavior.

Before going into the Cilk Plus guarantees, it is worth understanding why they will not always apply to TBB also. Cilk Plus and TBB differ in their concept of what is a stealable task. The code fragments in Listing 8.4 will be used to show the difference. The Cilk Plus and TBB fragments show poor style, because the code will probably perform much better if written as a map instead of a serial loop that creates tasks. But it serves well to illustrate the stealing issue, and sometimes similar code has to be written when access to the iteration space is inherently sequential, such as when a loop traverses a linked list.

For each spawned f(i), there are *two* conceptual tasks:

- A child task f(i).
- Continuation of executing the caller. This task, which has no name, is naturally called a **continuation**.

A key difference between Cilk Plus and TBB is that in Cilk Plus, thieves steal *continuations*. In TBB, thieves steal *children*.

Figure 8.5 diagrams the difference, assuming there are plenty of workers to steal work. The left side shows Cilk Plus execution, which uses *steal-continuation* semantics. The initial worker sets i=0 and spawns f(0). The worker immediately starts executing f(0), leaving the continuation available to

```
1   // Serial
2   for( int i=0; i<n; ++i )
3      f(i);
4
5   // Cilk Plus
6   for( int i=0; i<n; ++i )
7      cilk_spawn f(i);
8   cilk_sync;
9
10  // TBB
11  tbb::task_group g;
12  for( int i=0; i<n; ++i )
13     g.run( [=]{f(i);} );  // Must capture i by value.
14  g.wait();
```

LISTING 8.4

Three loop forms illustrating *steal-continuation* versus *steal-child semantics for work-stealing*. This is generally a poor way to parallelize a loop but is useful for discussing differences in stealing. Note that the TBB code needs to capture i by value, before the next ++i happens.

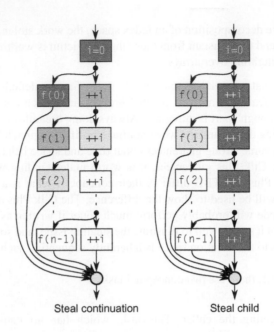

Steal continuation   Steal child

FIGURE 8.5

Steal continuation vs. steal child. The diagrams show the execution of the routines in Listing 8.4. Each task is shaded according to which worker executes it if there are plenty of workers. In *steal-continuation* semantics, a thief steals the continuation, and the original worker executes the child. *Steal-child* semantics are the other way around.

steal. Then another worker steals that continuation and continues execution of the loop. It updates i and executes f(1). The next worker steals the further continuation of the loop and executes f(2). The key point is that the loop advances only when there is a worker ready to execute another iteration of it.

The right side shows TBB execution, which uses *steal-child* semantics. The initial worker sets i=0 and spawns f(0). It leaves f(0) available to steal and proceeds to go around the loop again. It thus executes *all* iterations of the loop before attending to spawned work. Furthermore, if it does pick up an iteration afterward, f(n−1) is topmost on its deque, so it executes f(n−1) first, the reverse order of the serial code.

This difference has a major impact on stack space guarantees. In the Cilk Plus execution, each worker is working on a call chain in a state that would have existed in the serial program. Thus, Cilk Plus can guarantee that, if a program takes stack space S_1 for serial execution, it takes no more than stack space PS_1 when executed by P workers.[1] However, if run with a single worker, the TBB code creates a state where the for loop completes, but none of the calls to f(i) has yet started, a nonsensical state for the original program. Assuming each spawned call takes $\Theta(1)$ space to represent on the stack, the TBB program takes $\Theta(n)$ stack space, *even if no parallelism is being exploited.*

---

[1] TBB cannot make the same guarantee unless the code is written in continuation-passing style, an example of which is given in Section 8.9.2.

The example also illustrates another difference. In the TBB code, the worker that enters the loop is the worker that continues execution after `f(i)` finishes. If that worker executes `g.wait()` and not all `f(i)` are finished, it tries to execute some of the outstanding `f(i)` tasks. If none of those is available, it either idly waits or goes off on an errand to find temporary work to keep it busy. If, in the meantime, the other spawned `f(i)` finishes, further progress is blocked until the original worker returns from its errand. Thus, TBB scheduling is not always greedy (Section 2.5.6), which in turn means that, strictly speaking, the lower bound on speedup derived in Chapter 2 does not apply.

In the Cilk Plus code, workers never wait at a `cilk_sync`. The *last* worker to reach the `cilk_sync` is the worker that continues execution afterwards. Any worker that reaches the `cilk_sync` earlier abandons the computation entirely and tries to randomly steal work elsewhere. Though random stealing deviates from ideal greediness, in practice as long as there is plenty of parallel slack the deviation is insignificant and Cilk Plus achieves the time bound in Equation 2.9 (page 64).

TBB can implement steal-continuation semantics, and achieve the Cilk Plus space and time guarantees, if continuations are represented as explicit task objects. This is called **continuation passing style**. Unfortunately, it requires some tricky coding, as Section 8.9.2 will show.

Cilk Plus and TBB have different semantics because they are designed with different tradeoffs in mind. Cilk Plus has nicer properties but requires special compiler support to deal with stealing continuations, and it is limited to a strict fork–join model. TBB is designed as a plain library that can be run by any C++ compiler and supports a less strictly structured model.

The stealing semantics for OpenMP are complex and implementation dependent. The OpenMP rules [Boa11] imply that *steal-child* must be the default but permits *steal-continuation* if a task is annotated with an `untied` clause. However, the rules do not *require* continuation stealing, so the benefits of these semantics are not guaranteed even for `untied` tasks in OpenMP.

8.6 COMPLEXITY OF PARALLEL DIVIDE-AND-CONQUER

Computing the **work** and **span** of the basic fork–join pattern is straightforward. Suppose execution forks along multiple paths and rejoins. The total work T_1 is the sum of the work along each path. The span T_∞ is the maximum span of any path.

More formally, let $B\|C$ denote the fork–join composition of B and C, as introduced earlier in Figure 8.1. The overall work and span are:

$$T_1(B\|C) = T_1(B) + T_1(C),$$

$$T_\infty(B\|C) = \max(T_\infty(B), T_\infty(C)).$$

Realistically, there will be some overhead for forking and joining. The burdened span (see Section 2.5.6) includes this overhead, typically a small constant addition for the synchronization plus the cost of communicating **cache lines** between hardware threads.

Since parallel divide-and-conquer is a recursive application of fork–join composition, analyzing the work and span in a recursive divide-and-conquer algorithm is a matter of defining recurrence relations for T_1 and T_∞ and solving them. Typically, the recurrences for T_1 and T_∞ have similar form but differ in constant factors, which can cause them to have quite different asymptotic solutions. Though solving arbitrary recurrence relations can be difficult, the relations for divide-and-conquer programs often have a form for which a closed-form solution is already known.

The following discussion presents a simplified form of the Master method [CLRS09], which suffices for the most common cases. It assumes that the problem to be solved has a size N and the recursion has these properties:

- The recursion step solves a subproblems, each of size N/b.
- The divide and merge steps take time cN^d.
- The base case is $N = 1$ and can be solved in time e.

Here time means either T_1 or T_∞, depending on context, so to explain the generic math an unadorned T will be used.

Let $T(N)$ denote the time required to execute a divide-and-conquer algorithm with the aforementioned properties. The recurrence relations will be:

$$T(N) = aT(N/b) + cN^d \quad \text{if } N > 1,$$
$$T(1) = e.$$

There are three asymptotic solutions to this recurrence:

$$T(N) = \Theta(N^{\log_b a}) \quad \text{if } \log_b a > d, \tag{8.1}$$

$$T(N) = \Theta(N^d \lg N) \quad \text{if } \log_b a = d, \tag{8.2}$$

$$T(N) = \Theta(N^d) \quad \text{if } \log_b a < d. \tag{8.3}$$

None of the solutions mentions c or e directly—those are scale factors that disappear in the Θ notation. What is important is the value of $\log_b a$ relative to d.

The intuition behind these solutions is as follows. A full proof is given in Cormen et al. [CLRS09]. Start by partitioning the program's recursive call tree level by level, with the levels labeled, from top to bottom, as N, N/b, N/b^2, N/b^3, and so on. The three cases in the solution correspond to which levels dominate the work. Let r be the work at level N/b divided by the work at level N. Each problem has a subproblems that are proportionately smaller by $1/b$. Each problem will require cN^d work itself and have a children requiring $c(N/b)^d$ work on the next level down. So, $r = ac(N/b)^d/(cN^d) = b^d/a$. Three distinct cases arise, as illustrated in the diagrams in Figure 8.6 for some specific values of a and b, with $c = d = e = 1$. The general cases and their corresponding illustrations are:

Case 1. If $\log_b a > d$, then $r > 1$. The work at each level exponentially increases with depth, so levels near the bottom dominate.
Case 2. If $\log_b a = d$, then $r = 1$. The work at each level is about the same, so the work is proportional to the work at the top level times the number of levels.
Case 3. If $\log_b a < d$, then $r < 1$. The work at each level exponentially decreases with depth. So levels near the top dominate.

A useful intuition for effective parallelization can be drawn from these general notions. Ideally, the subproblems are independent and can be computed in parallel, so only one of the subproblems

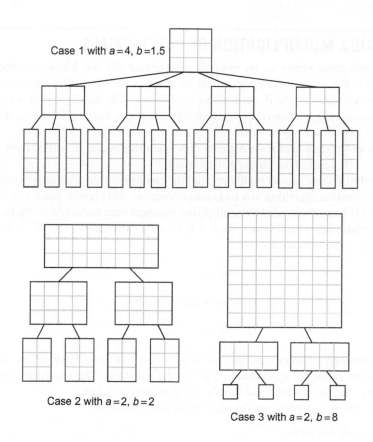

FIGURE 8.6

The three cases in the Master method. Each grid square represents a unit of work.

contributes to T_∞. So $a = 1$ in the recurrences for T_∞, and consequently $\log_b a = 0$. Since $d \geq 0$ for any real program, only two of the closed-form solutions apply to T_∞:

$$T_\infty(N) = \Theta(\lg N) \quad \text{if } d = 0,$$
$$T_\infty(N) = \Theta(N^d) \quad \text{if } d > 0.$$

Thus, for divide-and-conquer algorithms that fit our assumptions, T_∞ can be logarithmic at best, and only if the divide and combine steps take constant time.

Sometimes, as for the Merge Sort in Chapter 13, constant-time divide and combine is not practical, but logarithmic time is. The recurrences for such algorithms replace the cN^d term with a more complicated term and are beyond the scope of this discussion. See Cormen et al. [CLRS09] for a more general form of the recurrences and their closed-form solution, and Akra and Bazzi [AB98] for an even more general form.

8.7 KARATSUBA MULTIPLICATION OF POLYNOMIALS

Polynomial multiplication serves as an example of applying the the Master method to real code. Before delving into the fork–join algorithm and its analysis, let's consider the basic flat algorithm for multiplying polynomials A and B, each with n coefficients. The flat algorithm is essentially grade-school multiplication, except no carries propagate between terms. Listing 8.5 shows the flat algorithm implemented with Cilk Plus array notation.

Input arrays a and b each hold n coefficients of polynomials A and B, respectively. Output array c holds the $2n - 1$ coefficients of the output polynomial C.

The flat algorithm is concise and highly parallel for large n, but unfortunately creates $\Theta(n^2)$ work. Karatsuba's multiplication algorithm is a fork–join alternative that creates much less work. A slightly different form of it is sometimes used for multiplying numbers with hundreds of digits. Both forms are based on the observation that $(a_1 K + a_0) \cdot (b_1 K + b_0)$ can be expanded to $a_1 b_1 K^2 + (a_1 b_0 + a_0 b_1)K + a_0 b_0$ using only three multiplications:

$$t_0 = a_0 \cdot b_0,$$

$$t_1 = (a_0 + a_1) \cdot (b_0 + b_1),$$

$$t_2 = a_1 \cdot b_1.$$

The final expansion can be calculated as $t_2 K^2 + (t_1 - t_0 - t_2)K + t_0$. Each of the three multiplications can be done by recursive application of Karatsuba's method. The recursion continues until the multiplications become so small that the flat algorithm is more efficient.

The interpretation of K depends on the meaning of *multiplication*:

- For convolution, K is a shift.
- For multiplication of polynomials in x, K is a power of x.
- For multiplication of numerals, K is a power of the radix.

For example, to do the radix 10 multiplication problem $1234 \cdot 5678$, K is initially 100, so the problem can be written as $(12(100) + 34) \cdot 56(100) + 78$. The three requisite multiplications are:

$$t_0 = 34 \cdot 78,$$

$$t_1 = (12 + 34) \cdot (56 + 78),$$

$$t_2 = 12 \cdot 56.$$

```
1  void simple_mul( T c[], const T a[], const T b[], size_t n ) {
2      c[0:2*n-1] = 0;
3      for (size_t i=0; i<n; ++i)
4          c[i:n] += a[i]*b[0:n];
5  }
```

LISTING 8.5

Flat algorithm for polynomial multiplication using Cilk Plus array notation.

```
1   void karatsuba( T c[], const T a[], const T b[], size_t n ) {
2       if( n<=CutOff ) {
3           simple_mul( c, a, b, n );
4       } else {
5           size_t m = n/2;
6           // Set c[0:n−1] = t₀
7           cilk_spawn karatsuba( c, a, b, m );
8           // Set c[2*m:n−1] = t₂
9           cilk_spawn karatsuba( c+2*m, a+m, b+m, n−m );
10          temp_space<T> s(4*(n−m));
11          T *a_=s.data(), *b_=a_+(n−m), *t=b_+(n−m);
12          a_[0:m] = a[0:m]+a[m:m];
13          b_[0:m] = b[0:m]+b[m:m];
14          if( n&1 ) {
15              a_[m] = a[2*m];
16              b_[m] = b[2*m];
17          }
18          // Set t = t₁
19          karatsuba( t, a_, b_, n−m );
20          cilk_sync;
21          // Set t = t₁ − t₀ − t₂
22          t[0:2*m−1] -= c[0:2*m−1] + c[2*m:2*m−1];
23          // Add (t₁ − t₀ − t₂)K into final product
24          c[2*m−1] = 0;
25          c[m:2*m−1] += t[0:2*m−1];
26          if( n&1 )
27              c[3*m−1:2] += t[2*m−1:2] − c[4*m−1:2];
28      }
29  }
```

LISTING 8.6

Karatsuba multiplication in Cilk Plus.

Each of these can be done via Karatsuba's method with $K = 10$. Carry propagation can be deferred to the very end or done on the fly using carry-save addition.

Listing 8.6 shows Cilk Plus code for Karatsuba multiplication. Translation to TBB is a matter of using `task_group` instead of `cilk_spawn`/`cilk_sync`, and it is possible to translate this code to OpenMP using tasking constructs.

The parameters are similar to those in Listing 8.5. The type `temp_space`, described in more detail in Section 8.7.1, holds scratch space for computing $t_1 = (a_0 + a_1) \cdot (b_0 + b_1)$. The statements conditional on n&1 do a little extra work required for odd-length sequences and can be ignored to get the general idea of the algorithm.

A coding point worth mentioning is that $t_1 - t_0 - t_2$ is computed separately before adjusting the final product in c. The reason why is that t_0 and t_2 are stored in array c. It would be incorrect to merge lines 22 and 25 into a single line like this:

```
c[m:2*m−1] += t[0:2*m−1] − c[0:2*m−1] − c[2*m:2*m−1]; // Wrong!
```

because then there would be *partial* overlap of the source and destination array sections. In Cilk Plus, no overlap or exact overlap is okay, but partial overlap causes undefined behavior as explained in Section B.8.5. Line 27 avoids the partial overlap issue because $m \geq 2$; thus, the array sections c[3*m-1:2] and c[4*m-1:2] never overlap.

To use the code for *n*-digit integer multiplication, make T an integral type large enough to hold *n* products of digits. Do the convolution, and then normalize the resulting numeral by propagating carries.

The extra work for when N is odd is insignificant, so assume N is even. Serial execution recurses on three half-sized instances. The additions and subtractions take time linear in N. The relations for T_1 are:

$$T_1(N) = 3T_1(N/2) + cN,$$
$$T_1(1) = \Theta(1).$$

This is case 1 in the Master method. Plugging in the closed-form solution yields:

$$T_1(N) = \Theta(N^{\log_2 3}) \approx \Theta(N^{1.58\cdots}).$$

The recurrence relations for T_∞ differ in the coefficient. There are three subproblems being solved in parallel. Since they are all similar, T_∞ is as if two of the subproblems disappeared, because their execution overlaps solution of the other subproblem. So the recurrence is:

$$T_\infty(N) = T_\infty(N/2) + O(N),$$
$$T_\infty(1) = \Theta(1).$$

This is case 3, with solution $T_\infty(N) = \Theta(N)$.

The speedup limit is $T_1/T_\infty = \Theta(N^{1.58\cdots})/\Theta(N) = \Theta(N^{0.58\cdots})$, so the speedup limit grows a little faster than $\sqrt{N}$.

The formulae also enable a ballpark estimate for a good parallel base case. We want the base case to have at least 1000 operations for Cilk Plus. Since the operation count grows as $N^{1.58\cdots}$, that indicates that $n = 100$ is the right order of magnitude for the parallel base case.

The space complexity of Karatsuba multiplication can also be derived from recurrences. Let S_1 be the space for serial execution. The recurrence for S_1 is

$$S_1(N) = S_1(N/2) + \Theta(N),$$
$$S_1(1) = \Theta(1).$$

This is case 3, with solution $S_1(N) = \Theta(N)$.

Finally, consider S_∞, the space required if an infinite number of threads were available:

$$S_\infty(N) = 3S_\infty(N/2) + \Theta(N),$$
$$S_\infty(1) = \Theta(1),$$

which has the solution $S_\infty(N) = \Theta(N^{\log_2 3})$. Though a machine with an infinite number of threads is theoretical, there is a real, practical lesson here: Parallelizing divide-and-conquer by creating a new

```
1   template<typename T>
2   class temp_space {
3       static const size_t n = 4096/sizeof(T);
4       T temp[n];
5       T* base;
6   public:
7       T* data() {return base;}
8       T& operator[]( size_t k ) {return base[k];}
9       temp_space( size_t size ) {
10          base = size<=n ? temp : new T[size];
11      }
12      ~temp_space() {
13          if( base!=temp )
14              delete[] base;
15      }
16  };
```

LISTING 8.7

Type for scratch space. It is optimized for allocating short arrays of a type T with a trivial constructor and destructor.

---

thread for each spawn can result in an exponential space explosion. Fortunately, there is a better way. As Section 8.5 shows, Cilk Plus work-stealing guarantees that $S_p \leq S_1 P$, which enables Karatsuba multiplication to run in space $S_P = O(NP)$, much better than exponential space.

8.7.1 Note on Allocating Scratch Space

The Karatsuba multiplication algorithm in Listing 8.6 could use a std::vector<T> for scratch space. But that would introduce the overhead of dynamic memory allocation even for relatively short arrays near the leaves of the computation, which dominate the execution time. Hence, the code uses the class temp_space shown in Listing 8.7 for scratch space.

For simplicity, this class always allocates n elements in temp and hence is suboptimal if type T has a non-trivial constructor or destructor. More complex implementations can remove this overhead.

At the time of this writing, C99 variable-length arrays or alloca cannot be used in a function that has cilk_spawn. This is because these features allocate space on the current stack. The continuation after a cilk_spawn may be run on a stack different from the original stack of the caller, and this new stack disappears after a cilk_sync. Hence, anything allocated on that stack would be unsafe to access after the cilk_sync.

8.8 CACHE LOCALITY AND CACHE-OBLIVIOUS ALGORITHMS

Although work and span analysis often illuminates fundamental limits on speedup, it ignores memory **bandwidth** constraints that often limit speedup. When memory bandwidth is the critical resource, it is important to reuse data from cache as much as possible instead of fetching it from main memory. Because the size of caches and the number of levels of cache vary between platforms, tailoring algorithms to cache properties can be complicated. A solution is a technique called **cache-oblivious programming**. It is really cache-*paranoid* programming because the code is written to work reasonably well regardless of the actual structure of the cache. In practice, there are possibly multiple levels of cache, and when you write the code you are oblivious to their actual structure and size.

Optimizing for an unknown cache configuration sounds impossible at first. The trick is to apply recursive divide-and-conquer, resulting in good data locality at multiple scales. As a problem is chopped into finer and finer pieces, eventually a piece fits into outer-level cache. With further subdivision, pieces may fit into a smaller and faster cache.

An example of cache-oblivious programming is dense matrix multiplication. The obvious non-recursive code for such multiplication uses three nested loops. Although choosing the right loop order can help somewhat, for sufficiently large matrices the three-loop approach will suffer when the matrices do not fit in cache. The cache-oblivious algorithm divides a matrix multiplication into smaller matrix multiplications using divide-and-conquer, until at some point the matrices fit in cache. Better yet, the divide-and-conquer structure gives us an obvious place to insert fork–join parallelism.

Assume that A, B, and C are matrices, and we want to compute $C = C + A \times B$. A divide-and-conquer strategy is:

- If the matrices are small, use serial matrix multiplication.
- If the matrices are large, divide into two matrix multiplication problems.

There are three ways to do the division, based on the following three identities:

$$\begin{bmatrix} A \end{bmatrix} \times \begin{bmatrix} B_0 & B_1 \end{bmatrix} = \begin{bmatrix} A \times B_0 & A \times B_1 \end{bmatrix}, \tag{8.4}$$

$$\begin{bmatrix} A_0 \\ A_1 \end{bmatrix} \times \begin{bmatrix} B \end{bmatrix} = \begin{bmatrix} A_0 \times B \\ A_1 \times B \end{bmatrix}, \tag{8.5}$$

$$\begin{bmatrix} A_0 & A_1 \end{bmatrix} \times \begin{bmatrix} B_0 \\ B_1 \end{bmatrix} = \begin{bmatrix} A_0 \times B_0 + A_1 \times B_1 \end{bmatrix}. \tag{8.6}$$

Choosing the identity that splits the longest axis is a good choice, because then the submatrices will tend toward being square. That tends to maximize cache locality during multiplication.[2]

To see this, suppose A has dimensions $m \times k$, and B has dimensions $k \times n$. The total work T_1 to multiply the matrices is $O(mnk)$. The total space S to hold all three matrices is $O(mk + kn + mn)$. This sum is minimal for a given product mnk when $m = n = k$. Hence, striving to make the matrices square improves the chance that the result fits within some level of cache.

Listing 8.8 shows a pseudocode implementation. The informal notations rows(X) and cols(X) denote the number of rows and columns, respectively, of a matrix X. The first two recursive pairs

---

[2] Splits could be quantized to the cache line **granularity**, though then the code would no longer be completely cache oblivous.

```
1   void MultiplyAdd( Matrix& C, const Matrix& A, const Matrix& B ) {
2     assert( cols(A)==rows(B) );
3     if ( less than M operations are required to compute C ) {
4         Compute C+=A*B using non-recursive algorithm.
5     } else if ( cols(B)>=max(rows(A),rows(B)) ) {
6         Partition C into [ C0  C1 ] and B into [ B0  B1 ]
7         cilk_spawn MultiplyAdd( C0, A, B0 );
8         MultiplyAdd( C1, A, B1 ); //No spawn
9         cilk_sync;
10    } else if ( rows(A)>=rows(B) ) {
11        Partition C into [ C0 / C1 ] and A into [ A0 / A1 ]
12        cilk_spawn MultiplyAdd( C0, A0, B );
13        MultiplyAdd( C1, A1, B ); //No spawn
14        cilk_sync;
15    } else {
16        Partition A into [ A0  A1 ] and B into [ B0 / B1 ]
17        MultiplyAdd( C, A0, B0 );
18        MultiplyAdd( C, A1, B1 );
19    }
20  }
```

LISTING 8.8

Pseudocode for recursive matrix multiplication.

of calls do parallel fork–join. They can be written in TBB using `tbb::parallel_invoke`. They are safe to execute in parallel because they update separate parts of matrix C. But the last recursive pair cannot execute in parallel, because both calls update the same matrix.

Since the last case is serial and equivalent to a single `MultiplyAdd`, it is tempting to write `MultiplyAdd` in a way that uses only the first two of our splitting identities. Doing so would not affect the parallelism but could seriously raise consumption of memory bandwidth. To see this, consider what would happen in the base case: A and B would be very skinny, with A wide and B tall. In extreme, A would be an m-element column matrix and B would be an n-element row matrix. Their product would be an $m \times n$ matrix, requiring one store to memory for each multiplication.

The asymptotic complexity is:

$$T_1 = \Theta(\text{rows}(C) \cdot \text{rows}(B) \cdot \text{cols}(C)),$$

$$T_\infty = \Theta(\lg \text{rows}(C) + \text{rows}(B) + \lg \text{cols}(C)). \qquad (8.7)$$

For practical purposes, rows(B) is usually much larger than either of the lg factors, so the speedup limit is $\Theta(\text{rows}(C)\text{cols}(C))$; that is, the speedup is proportional to the size of the output matrix. To see this directly from the code, observe that the code is essentially doing a fork–join recursion over the output matrix and computing inner products for each output element. Thus, it is asymptotically equivalent to computing each element of C in parallel. But writing the code to directly do that would result in poor cache behavior, because each inner product would be consuming an entire row of A and column of B at once.

It is possible to raise the speedup limit by using temporary storage, so that the serial pair of recursive calls can run in parallel, like this:

```
Matrix tmp = [0];
cilk_spawn MultiplyAdd( C, A0, B0 );
MultiplyAdd( tmp, A1, B1 ); // No spawn
C += tmp;
```

Then $T_\infty = \Theta(\lg\text{rows}(C) + \lg\text{rows}(B) + \lg\text{cols}(C))$, which is significantly lower than the bound in Equation 8.7. However, in practice the extra operations and memory bandwidth consumed by the final += make it a losing strategy in typical cases, particularly if the other fork–join parts introduce sufficient parallelism to keep the machine busy. In particular, the extra storage is significant. For example, suppose the top-level matrices A and B are square $N \times N$ matrices. The temporary is allocated every time the inner dimension splits. So the recurrences for the serial execution space S are:

$$S_1(N) = S_1(N/2) + \Theta(N^2),$$

$$S_1(1) = c,$$

which has the solution:

$$S_1(N) = \Theta(N^2).$$

Since Cilk Plus guarantees that $S_P \leq PS_1$, the space is at worst $O(PN^2)$. That is far worse than the other algorithm, which needs no temporary matrices and thus requires only $O(\lg N)$ space.

There are other recursive approaches to matrix multiplication that reduce T_1 at the expense of complexity or space. For example, Strassen's method [Str69] recurses by dividing A, B, and C each into quadrants and uses identities similar in spirit to Karatsuba multiplication, such that only 7 quadrant multiplications are required, instead of the obvious 8. Strassen's algorithm runs in $O(N^{\lg 7}) \approx O(N^{2.807\cdots})$ for multiplying $N \times N$ matrices, and the quadrant multiplications can be computed in parallel.

8.9 QUICKSORT

Quicksort is a good example for studying how to parallelize a non-trivial divide-and-conquer algorithm. In its simplest form, it is naturally expressed as a recursive fork–join algorithm. More sophisticated variants are only partially recursive. This section will show how parallel fork–join applies to both the simple and sophisticated variants, demonstrating certain tradeoffs.

Serial Quicksort sorts a sequence of keys by recursive partitioning. The following pseudocode outlines the algorithm:

```
void Quicksort( sequence ) {
    if( sequence is short ) {
        Use a sort optimized for short sequences
    } else {
        // Divide
        Choose a partition key K from the sequence.
        Permute the sequence such that:
            Keys to the left of K are less than K.
            Keys to the right of K are greater than K.
        // Conquer
        Recursively sort the subsequence to the left of K.
        Recursively sort the subsequence to the right of K.
    }
}
```

The two subsorts are independent and can be done in parallel, thus achieving some speedup. As we shall see, the speedup will be limited by the partitioning step.

The Quicksort examples all share the code shown in Listing 8.9, which defines the *divide* step. Issues for writing a good serial Quicksort carry over into its parallel counterparts. Two points of the code so far that are worth noting are:

1. A median of medians is used to choose the partition key, which greatly improves the probability that the partition will not be grossly imbalanced [BM93].
2. The special case of equal keys is detected, so the Quicksort can quit early. Otherwise, Quicksort takes quadratic time in this case, because the partition would be extremely imbalanced, with no keys on the left side of the partition.

The Cilk Plus and TBB versions of Quicksort are largely similar. The difference is in the details of how the parallel conquer part is specified.

8.9.1 Cilk Plus Quicksort

Serial Quicksort can be parallelized with Cilk Plus by spawning one of the subsorts, as shown in Listing 8.10. With the cilk_... keywords removed, the code is identical to a serial Quicksort, except that the choice of a base case is different. Though the parallel code could use the same base case as for serial Quicksort, it would result in very fine-grained tasks whose scheduling overhead would swamp useful work. Thus, the base case for parallel recursion is much coarser than where a serial Quicksort would stop. However, the serial base case is likely a serial recursive Quicksort, which will recurse further on down to a serial base case.

There is no explicit cilk_sync here because there is nothing to do after the subsorts complete. The implicit cilk_sync when the function returns suffices, just as it did in Listing 8.1.

Serial Quicksort is notorious for working well in the average case but having pathological behavior in the worst case. These problems carry over into the parallel version, so they are worth attention. In

```
1    // Size of parallel base case
2    ptrdiff_t QUICKSORT_CUTOFF = 500;
3
4    // Choose median of three keys
5    T* median_of_three(T* x, T* y, T* z) {
6        return *x<*y ? *y<*z ? y : *x<*z ? z : x
7            : *z<*y ? y : *z<*x ? z : x;
8    }
9
10   // Choose a partition key as median of medians
11   T* choose_partition_key( T* first, T* last ) {
12       size_t offset = (last−first)/8;
13       return median_of_three(
14           median_of_three(first, first+offset, first+offset*2),
15           median_of_three(first+offset*3, first+offset*4, last−(3*offset+1)),
16           median_of_three(last−(2*offset+1), last−(offset+1), last−1 )
17       );
18   }
19
20   // Choose a partition key and partition [ first ... last ) with it
21   // Returns pointer to where the partition key is in partitioned sequence
22   // Returns NULL if all keys in [ first ... last ) are equal
23   T* divide( T* first, T* last ) {
24       // Move partition key to front
25       std::swap( *first, *choose_partition_key(first,last) );
26       // Partition
27       T key = *first;
28       T* middle = std::partition( first+1, last, [=](const T& x) {return x<key;} )
                 − 1;
29       if( middle!=first ) {
30           // Move partition key to between the partitions
31           std::swap( *first, *middle );
32       } else {
33           // Check if all keys are equal
34           if( last==std::find_if( first+1, last, [=](const T& x) {return key<x;} ) )
35               return NULL;
36       }
37       return middle;
38   }
```

LISTING 8.9

Code shared by Quicksort implementations.

particular, even if the choice of partition key is made carefully, in the worst case sorting N keys will cause recursing to depth N, possibly causing stack overflow. In serial Quicksort, a solution is to recurse on the smaller subproblem and iterate on the bigger subproblem. The same technique applies to parallel

```
1   void parallel_quicksort( T* first, T* last ) {
2       if( last-first<=QUICKSORT_CUTOFF ) {
3           std::sort(first,last);
4       } else {
5           // Divide
6           if( T* middle = divide(first,last) ) {
7               // Conquer subproblems in parallel
8               cilk_spawn parallel_quicksort( first, middle );
9               parallel_quicksort( middle+1, last );
10              // No cilk_sync needed here because of implicit one later
11          }
12      }
13      // Implicit cilk_sync when function returns
14  }
```

LISTING 8.10

Fully recursive parallel Quicksort using Cilk Plus.

Quicksort, as shown in Listing 8.11. The recursion depth is now bounded by lg N since each recursion shrinks N by a factor of two or more.

8.9.2 TBB Quicksort

TBB versions of Quicksort can be coded similarly to the Cilk Plus versions, except that the mechanics differ. A version similar to Listing 8.10 can be written using `tbb::parallel_invoke` to invoke pairs of recursive calls. A version similar to Listing 8.11 can be written using `tbb::task_group` as shown in Listing 8.12. Though in practice this code has reasonable performance most of the time, it has a a worst-case space problem. The problem is that the Cilk Plus guarantees on space and time are not generally true in TBB, because TBB has *steal-child* semantics, and the guarantees depend on *steal-continuation* semantics (Section 8.5). In particular, if the smaller problem is consistently a single element, then $\Theta(N)$ tasks are added to `task_group g`, and none is executed until `g.wait()` executes. Thus, the worst case space is $\Theta(N)$, even though the algorithm recurses only $O(\lg N)$ deep. This is a general problem with steal-child semantics: Many children may be generated before any are run.

The solution is to not generate a new child until it is needed. This can be done by simulating steal-continuation semantics in TBB, by writing the code using **continuation-passing style**. There are two common reasons to use continuation-passing style in TBB:

- Avoiding waiting—Instead of waiting for predecessors of a task to complete at a join point, the code specifies a continuation task to run after the join point.
- Avoiding premature generation of tasks—Instead of generating a bunch of tasks and then executing them, the code generates one task and executes it, and leaves behind a continuation that will generate the next task.

The rewritten example will have an example of each. The `empty_task` will represent execution after a join point. The `quicksort_task` will leave behind a continuation of itself.

```
1   void parallel_quicksort( T* first, T* last ) {
2     while( last-first>QUICKSORT_CUTOFF ) {
3       // Divide
4       T* middle = divide(first,last);
5       if( !middle ) return;
6
7       // Now have two subproblems: [ first .. middle) and (middle .. last )
8       if( middle-first < last-(middle+1) ) {
9         // Left problem [ first .. middle) is smaller, so spawn it
10        cilk_spawn parallel_quicksort( first, middle );
11        // Solve right subproblem in next iteration
12        first = middle+1;
13      } else {
14        // Right problem (middle .. last ) is smaller, so spawn it
15        cilk_spawn parallel_quicksort( middle+1, last );
16        // Solve left subproblem in next iteration
17        last = middle;
18      }
19    }
20    // Base case
21    std::sort(first,last);
22  }
```

LISTING 8.11

Semi-recursive parallel Quicksort using Cilk Plus. There is no `cilk_sync` before the base case because the base case is independent of the spawned subproblems.

Continuation-passing tasking requires using TBB's low-level tasking interface, class `tbb::task`, which is designed for efficient implementation of divide-and-conquer. An instance of class `task` has the following information:

- A reference count of predecessor tasks that must complete before running this task. The count may include an extra one if the task is explicitly waited on. The Quicksort example does not have the wait, so the count will be exactly the number of predecessors.
- A virtual method that executes when the predecessors finish. The method may also specify the next task to execute.
- A pointer to its successor. After the method executes, the scheduler decrements the successor's reference count. If the count becomes zero, the successor is automatically spawned.

The general steps for using it to write recursive fork–join are:

- Create a class *D* representing the divide/fork actions. Derive it from base class `tbb::task`.
- Override virtual method `tbb::task::execute()`. The definition should perform the divide/fork actions. It should return `NULL`, or return a pointer to the next task to execute.
- Create a top-level wrapper function that creates a root task and executes it using `tbb::task::spawn_root_and_wait`.

```
1   void quicksort( T* first, T* last ) {
2       tbb::task_group g;
3       while( last−first>QUICKSORT_CUTOFF ) {
4           // Divide
5           T* middle = divide(first,last);
6           if( !middle ) {
7               g.wait();
8               return;
9           }
10
11          // Now have two subproblems: [ first .. middle) and [middle+1.. last )
12          if( middle−first < last−(middle+1) ) {
13              // Left problem ( first .. middle) is smaller, so spawn it .
14              g.run([=]{quicksort( first, middle );});
15              // Solve right subproblem in next iteration .
16              first − middle+1;
17          } else {
18              // Right problem (middle.. last ) is smaller, so spawn it .
19              g.run([=]{quicksort( middle+1, last );});
20              // Solve left subproblem in next iteration .
21              last = middle;
22          }
23      }
24      // Base case
25      std::sort(first,last);
26      g.wait();
27  }
```

LISTING 8.12

Semi-iterative parallel Quicksort using TBB.

Because of the desire to lazily generate child tasks, the Quicksort code is a little trickier than TBB code for typical fork–join situations. Listing 8.13 shows the code. Overall, the logic is similar to the Cilk Plus version in Listing 8.11, but the parallel mechanics differ. These mechanics will now be explained in detail.

The top-level routine is `quicksort`, which creates the root task and runs it. The root task can be viewed as the gateway from normal calling to the continuation-passing world. Instances of class `task` must always be allocated using an overloaded `new`, with an argument returned by one of the methods beginning with `tbb::task::allocate`. There are several of these methods, each specific to certain usages.

Class `quicksort_task` is a task for sorting. What were function parameters in the Cilk Plus version become class members, so that the values can be remembered between the time the task is created and when it actually runs. The override of `task::execute()` has the algorithm. If the task represents a base case, it does a serial sort and returns `NULL`. The `NULL` indicates that the scheduler should use its normal work-stealing algorithm for choosing the next task to execute.

```
1   class quicksort_task: public tbb::task {
2       /*override*/tbb::task* execute();
3       T *first, *last;
4       bool has_local_join;
5       void prepare_self_as_stealable_continuation();
6   public:
7       quicksort_task( T* first_, T* last_ ) : first(first_), last(last_),
            has_local_join(false) {}
8   };
9
10  void quicksort_task::prepare_self_as_stealable_continuation() {
11      if( !has_local_join ) {
12          task* local_join = new( allocate_continuation() ) tbb::empty_task();
13          local_join->set_ref_count(1);
14          set_parent(local_join);
15          has_local_join = true;
16      }
17      recycle_to_reexecute();
18  }
19
20  tbb::task* quicksort_task::execute() {
21      if( last-first<=QUICKSORT_CUTOFF ) {
22          std::sort(first,last);
23          // Return NULL continuation
24          return NULL;
25      } else {
26          // Divide
27          T* middle = divide(first,last);
28          if( !middle ) return NULL;
29
30          // Now have two subproblems: [ first .. middle) and [middle+1.. last )
31
32          // Set up current task object as continuation of itself
33          prepare_self_as_stealable_continuation();
34
35          // Now recurse on smaller subproblem
36          tbb::task* smaller;
37          if( middle-first < last-(middle+1) ) {
38              // Left problem ( first .. middle) is smaller
39              smaller = new( allocate_additional_child_of(*parent()) ) quicksort_task(
                      first, middle );
40              // Continuation will do larger subproblem
41              first = middle+1;
42          } else {
43              // Right problem (middle.. last ) is smaller
44              smaller = new( allocate_additional_child_of(*parent()) ) quicksort_task(
                      middle+1, last );
45              // Continuation will do larger subproblem
46              last = middle;
```

```
47            }
48            // Dive into smaller subproblem
49            return smaller;
50        }
51    }
52
53    void quicksort( T* first, T* last ) {
54        // Create root task
55        tbb::task& t = *new( tbb::task::allocate_root() )
                 quicksort_task( first, last );
56        // Run it
57        tbb::task::spawn_root_and_wait(t);
58    }
```

LISTING 8.13

Quicksort in TBB that achieves Cilk Plus space guarantee.

If the task represents a recursive case, then it operates much like the task_group example, except that the while loop has been converted to continuation-passing style. The recursive part has been turned into the return of task smaller. The scheduler will cause the current thread to execute that task next. Sometimes this trick is used simply as an optimization to bypass the task scheduler, but here it is doing more, by forcing the current thread to dive into the smaller subproblem, just as the semi-recursive Cilk Plus version does. Meanwhile, the current task is destructively updated to become the larger subproblem. The call recycle_to_reexecute() causes it to be visible to thieves after it returns from method execute(). TBB restrictions require that this idiom be used instead of directly respawning it, because the latter could cause it to be reentrantly executed by a second thread before the first thread is done with it.

8.9.3 Work and Span for Quicksort

The average case is a bit tricky to analyze, but it turns out to be asymptotically the same as the ideal case, so the ideal case is presented here. Though ideal, it will reveal a limitation of our parallelization.

The recurrences for the ideal case, where partitioning creates subproblems of equal size, are:

$$T_1(N) = 1 + 2T_1(N/2),$$
$$T_\infty(N) = N + T_\infty(N/2).$$

The closed form solutions from the Master method are:

$$T_1(N) = \Theta(N \lg N),$$
$$T_\infty(N) = N.$$

Thus, the **speedup** limit in the ideal case is:

$$T_1(N)/T_\infty = \Theta(N \lg N)/\Theta(N) = \lg(N).$$

So, the best we can expect is a logarithmic improvement in performance, no matter how many processors we throw at it.

The limit on speedup arises from the partition steps near the top levels of the recursion. In particular, the first partition step requires $O(N)$ time. Therefore, even if the rest of the sort ran in zero time, the total time would still be $O(N)$. To do any better, we need to parallelize the partition step, as in Sample Sort (Chapter 14), or choose a different kind of sort such as Merge Sort (Chapter 13).

However, Quicksort does have some advantages over the other sorts mentioned.

- Quicksort is an in-place algorithm. The other two sorts are not and thus have twice the cache footprint.
- Quicksort spends most of its time in `std::partition`, which is friendly to cache and prefetch mechanisms.
- Quicksort always moves keys via `std::swap`. It never copies keys. For some key types, such as reference-counted objects, swapping keys can be far faster than moving keys.

Thus, even though the other sorts have higher **scalability** in theory, they sometimes perform worse than Quicksort. For low core counts, parallel Quicksort may be a good choice.

8.10 REDUCTIONS AND HYPEROBJECTS

The recursive implementation of the **map** pattern can be extended to do **reduction**. Listing 8.14 shows such an extension of Listing 8.1 for doing a sum reduction of $f(i)$ for i from `lower` (inclusive) to `upper` (exclusive).

```
1   template<typename T, typename Func>
2   T sum_of( unsigned lower, unsigned upper, unsigned grainsize, Func f ) {
3       if( upper−lower<=grainsize ) {
4           // Parallel base case
5           T sum = T();
6           for( unsigned i=lower; i<upper; ++i )
7               sum += f(i);
8           return sum;
9       } else {
10          // Divide and conquer
11          unsigned middle = lower+(upper−lower)/2u;
12          T sum1 = cilk_spawn sum_of<T>( lower, middle, grainsize, f);
13          T sum2 = sum_of<T>( middle, upper, grainsize, f );
14          cilk_sync;
15          return sum1+sum2;
16      }
17  }
```

LISTING 8.14

Recursive implementation of parallel reduction in Cilk Plus.

The approach extends to any operation that is **associative**, even if the operation is not **commutative**. Using explicit fork–join for reduction is sometimes the best approach, but other times it can be a nuisance on several counts:

- The partial reduction value has to be explicit in the function prototype, either as a return value or a parameter specifying where to store it. It cannot be a global variable because that would introduce races.
- It requires writing fork–join in cases where otherwise a `cilk_for` would do and be easier to read.

Cilk Plus **hyperobjects** are an elegant way to avoid these drawbacks. A hyperobject is an object for which each Cilk Plus **strand** gets its own view. A strand is a portion of Cilk Plus execution with no intervening fork or join points. The hyperobjects described here are called **reducers** because they assist doing reductions. There are other kinds of hyperobjects, such as **holders** and **splitters**, that are sometimes useful, too [FHLLB09]. Listing 8.15 shows a simple example of using a hyperobject to avoid a race.

If `sum` were an ordinary variable of type `float`, the invocations of `f(1)` and `f(2)` could race updating it and not have the correct net effect, but the code is safe because variable `sum` is declared as a reducer. The calls `f(1)` and `f(2)` are on different strands and so each gets its own view of `sum` to update.

The summation of the two views happens automatically at the `cilk_sync`. The Cilk Plus runtime knows to add the views because `sum` was declared as a `reducer_opadd`. Method `get_value` gets the value of the view. It is a method, and not an implicit conversion, so you have to be explicit about getting the value. Be sure that all strands that contribute to the value are joined before getting the value; otherwise, you may get only a partial sum.

```
1  #include <iostream>
2  #include <cilk/cilk.h>
3  #include <cilk/reducer_opadd.h>
4
5  cilk::reducer_opadd<float> sum(4);
6
7  void f( int m ) {
8      sum += m;
9  }
10
11 int main() {
12     cilk_spawn f(1);
13     f(2);
14     cilk_sync;
15     std::cout << sum.get_value() << std::endl;
16     return 0;
17 }
```

LISTING 8.15

Using a hyperobject to avoid a race in Cilk Plus. Declaring `sum` as a reducer makes it safe to update it from separate strands of execution. The `cilk_sync` merges the updates, so the code always prints 7.

There are other reducers built into Cilk Plus for other common reduction operations. For instance, `reducer_opxor` performs exclusive OR reduction. Section B.7 lists the predefined reducers. You can define your own reducer for any data type and operation that form a mathematical **monoid**, which is to say:

- The operation is associative.
- The operation has an identity element.

For example, the data type of strings forms a monoid under concatenation, where the identity element is the empty string. Cilk Plus provides such a reducer for C++ strings, called `reducer_basic_string`. Section 11.2.1 walks through the steps of building your own reducer.

Generating many views would be inefficient, so there are internal optimizations that reduce the number of views constructed. These optimizations guarantee that no more than $3P$ views of a hyper-object exist at any one time, where P is the total number of workers. Furthermore, new views are generated lazily, only when a steal occurs. Since steals are rare in properly written Cilk Plus code, the number of views constructed tends to be low.

Figure 8.7 illustrates this point for the example from Listing 8.15. Views are distinguished by subscripts. The left graph shows the stolen case and how only one new view has to be created. Initially variable `sum` has a single view sum_1. If the continuation that calls `f(2)` is stolen, Cilk Plus creates a new view sum_2 and initializes it to `T()`, which by convention is assumed to be the identity element. The other strand after the fork uses sum_1 instead of constructing a new view. Now `f(1)` and `f(2)` can safely update their respective views. At the join point, sum_2 is folded into sum_1, and (not pictured) destroyed. Afterwards, sum_1 has the intended total.

The right graph shows the unstolen case, in which *no* new views have to be created. Since the calls `f(1)` and `f(2)` run consecutively, not in parallel, a single view sum_1 suffices. This is another

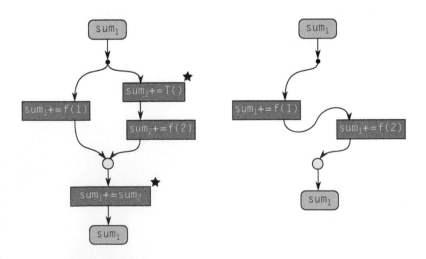

FIGURE 8.7

Hyperobject views in Cilk Plus. A hyperobject constructs extra view sum_2 only if actual parallelism occurs. The actions marked with stars are implicit and not written by the programmer.

```
1  #include <cilk/reducer_opadd.h>
2
3  template<typename T, typename Func>
4  T sum_of( unsigned lower, unsigned upper, unsigned grainsize, Func f ) {
5      cilk::reducer_opadd<T> sum;
6      cilk_for( unsigned i=lower; i<upper; ++i )
7          sum += f(i);
8      return sum.get_value();
9  }
```

LISTING 8.16

Using a local reducer in Cilk Plus.

demonstration of a general principle behind Cilk Plus: Extra effort for parallelism is expended only if the parallelism is real, not merely **potential parallelism**.

Hyperobjects are handy because they are *not* lexically bound to parallelism constructs. They can be global variables that are updated by many different strands. The runtime will deal with reducing the updates into final correct value.

Hyperobjects are also useful as local variables, as shown in Listing 8.16, which is another way to implement the reduction from Listing 8.14.

It is important to remember that hyperobjects eliminate races between strands of Cilk Plus execution, not races between arbitrary threads. If multiple threads not created by the Cilk Plus runtime *do* concurrently access a hyperobject, they will race and thus possibly introduce **non-determinism**.

8.11 IMPLEMENTING SCAN WITH FORK–JOIN

This section shows how to use fork–join to implement the **scan** pattern using the interface presented in Section 5.4. The code examples are Cilk Plus. The TBB template `parallel_scan` uses a similar implementation technique but with a twist described later.

The parallel scan algorithm [Ble93] operates as if the data are the leaves of a tree as shown in Figure 8.8. In the picture, the input consists of the sequence $r_0, r_1, \ldots, r_7$ and an initial value *initial*, and the output sequence is an exclusive scan $s_0, s_1, \ldots, s_7$. The algorithm makes two sweeps over the tree, one upward and one downward. The upsweep computes a set of partial reductions of the input over **tiles**. The downsweep computes the final scan by combining the partial reduction information. Though the number of tiles in our tree illustration is a power of two, the example code works for any number of tiles.

Figure 8.9 shows the internal structure of a tree node. Let $\oplus$ denote the combiner operation. The term *subscan* here means a subsequence of the final scan sequence. The node shown computes values related to the subscan for $r_i, r_{i+1}, \ldots, r_{i+m-1}$. The subsequence is split into two halves: a leading subsequence of k elements and a trailing subsequence of $m - k$ elements. Let $r_{i:m}$ denote a reduction over m consecutive elements of the sequence, starting at index i. During the upsweep, the node computes $r_{i:m} = r_{i:k} \oplus r_{i+k:m-k}$. Let s_i denote the initial value required for computing the subscan starting

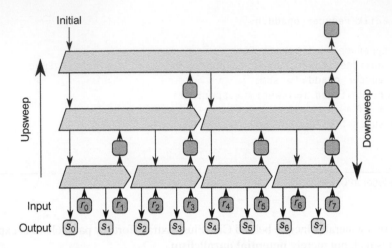

FIGURE 8.8

Tree for parallel scan. Parallel scan does two passes over the tree, one upward and one downward. See Figure 8.9 for the internal structure of the pentagonal tree nodes.

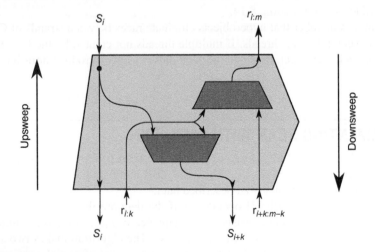

FIGURE 8.9

Node in the parallel scan tree in Figure 8.8. Each operation costs one invocation of the combining functor. For an n-ary tree, the node generalizes to performing an n-element reduction during the upsweep and a n-element exclusive scan on the downsweep.

at index i. In other words, $s_i = initial \oplus r_{0:i}$. During the downsweep, the node gets s_i from its parent, passes it downward, and computes $s_{i+k} = s_i \oplus r_{i:k}$. These are the initial values for computing the subscans for the two half subsequences.

```
1   template<typename T, typename R, typename C, typename S>
2   void cilk_scan( size_t n, T initial, size_t tilesize,
        R reduce, C combine, S scan ) {
3       if( n>0 ) {
4           size_t m = (n−1)/tilesize;
5           temp_space<T> r(m+1);
6           upsweep(0, m+1, tilesize, r.data(),
7                   n−m*tilesize, reduce, combine);
8           downsweep(0, m+1, tilesize, r.data(),
9                   n−m*tilesize, initial, combine, scan);
10      }
11  }
```

LISTING 8.17

Top level code for tiled parallel scan. This code is actually independent of the parallel framework. It allocates temporary space for partial reductions and does an upsweep followed by a downsweep.

The tree computes an untiled exclusive scan. A **tiled** exclusive scan for an operation ⊕ can be built from it as follows. Label the tiles $b_1, b_2, \ldots, b_{N-1}$. Conceptually, the steps are:

1. Compute each r_k as the ⊕ reduction of tile b_k.
2. Do upsweep and downsweep to compute each s_k.
3. Compute the exclusive scan of tile b_k using s_k as the initial value.

In practice, Steps 1 and 3 are not separate passes, but embedded into the upsweep and downsweep passes, respectively. For an inclusive scan, change the last step to be an inclusive scan over each tile.

Listing 8.17 shows the top-level code for a tiled scan. The parameters are explained in Section 5.4 on page 164. As noted in that section, the reduction is done for the last tile even though its return value is unnecessary in order to permit fusion optimization.

Listing 8.18 shows the code for routine upsweep. It performs the upsweep for the index range i:m. The base case invokes the tile reduction functor reduce. The recursive case chooses where to split the index space, using function split (not shown), which should return the greatest power of two less than m:

$$\text{split}(m) = 2^{\lfloor \lg m - 1 \rfloor}.$$

The function serves to embed an implicit binary tree onto the index space. The if at the end of routine upsweep checks whether there is a tree node summarizing the index space. When m is not a power of two, there is no such node. Conceptually the missing node is for summarizing an index space larger than the requested space.

Listing 8.19 shows the code for routine downsweep. Most of the parameters are similar to those in the other routines. Parameter lastsize is the size of the rightmost tile, which might be a partial tile. Its structure closely resembles the structure of upsweep because it is walking the same tree, only it does its real work before the fork, not after the join as in upsweep. Consequently, tail recursion optimization (Section 8.3) can be applied to downsweep but not upsweep.

```
1   template<typename T, typename R, typename C>
2   void upsweep( size_t i, size_t m, size_t tilesize, T r[], size_t lastsize,
        R reduce, C combine ) {
3       if( m==1 ) {
4           r[0] = reduce(i*tilesize, lastsize);
5       } else {
6           size_t k = split(m);
7           cilk_spawn upsweep(i, k, tilesize, r, tilesize, reduce, combine);
8           upsweep(i+k, m-k, tilesize, r+k, lastsize, reduce, combine);
9           cilk_sync;
10          if( m==2*k )
11              r[m-1] = combine(r[k-1], r[m-1]);
12      }
13  }
```

LISTING 8.18

Upsweep phase for tiled parallel scan in Cilk Plus.

```
1   template<typename T, typename C, typename S>
2   void downsweep( size_t i, size_t m, size_t tilesize, const T r[], size_t lastsize
        , T initial, C combine, S scan ) {
3       if( m==1 ) {
4           scan(i*tilesize, lastsize, initial);
5       } else {
6           size_t k = split(m);
7           cilk_spawn downsweep(i, k, tilesize, r, tilesize, initial, combine, scan);
8           initial = combine(initial, r[k-1]);
9           downsweep(i+k, m-k, tilesize, r+k, lastsize, initial, combine, scan);
10          // Implicit cilk_sync;
11      }
12  }
```

LISTING 8.19

Downsweep phase for tiled parallel scan in Cilk Plus.

The work is proportional to the number of nodes in the tree, and the span is proportional to the height of the tree. So the asymptotic **work-span** bounds are

$$T_1 = \Theta(n),$$

$$T_\infty = \Theta(\lg n).$$

Unfortunately the asymptotic bounds hide a constant factor of 2 in the work, and in practice this factor of 2 can undo much of the gains from parallelization. A serial scan makes a single pass over the data, but a parallel scan makes two passes: upsweep and downsweep. Each pass requires reading the data. Hence, for large scans where data does not fit in cache, the communication cost is double that for a serial scan. Therefore, when communication bandwidth is the limiting resource for a serial scan, a parallel scan will run half as fast. Even if it does fit in the total aggregate cache, there is a communication problem, because greedy scheduling arbitrarily assigns workers to the tile reductions and scan reductions. Thus, each tile is often transferred from the cache of the worker who reduced it to the cache of the worker who scans it.

The implementation of TBB's `tbb::parallel_scan` attempts to mitigate this issue through a trick that dynamically detects whether **actual parallelism** is available. The TBB interface requires that each tile scan return a reduction value as well. This value is practically free since it is computed during a scan anyway. During the upsweep pass, the TBB implementation uses the tile scan instead of a reduction whenever it has already computed all reductions to the left of the tile. This enables skipping the downsweep pass for all tiles to the left of all tiles processed by work-stealing thieves. In other words, execution is equivalent to a tiled serial scan until the point is reached where actual parallelism forks the control flow. This way, if two workers are available, typically only the right half of the tree needs two passes, thus averaging 1.5 passes over the data. For more available workers, the benefit starts to diminish. The trick is dynamic—`tbb::parallel_scan` pays the 2× overhead for parallelism only if *actual* parallelism is being applied to the scan.

One elegant feature of our Cilk Plus interface for scan is that sometimes the scan values can be consumed without actually storing them. For example, consider implementing the **pack** pattern using a scan followed by a conditional scatter, as described in Section 6.4. Listing 8.20 shows the code.

```
1   template<typename T, typename Pred>
2   size_t pack( const T a[], size_t n, T b[], Pred p ) {
3       size_t result;
4       cilk_scan( n, size_t(0), 10000,
5           [&]( size_t i, size_t m ) -> T {
6               size_t sum=0;
7               for( size_t j=1; j<i+m; ++j )
8                   if( p(a[j]) )
9                       sum++;
10                  return sum;
11          },
12          std::plus<T>(),
13          [&]( size_t i, size_t m, T sum ) {
14              for( size_t j=i; j<i+m; ++j )
15                  if( p(a[j]) )
16                      b[sum++] = a[j];
17              if( i+m==n )
18                  // Save result from last tile
19                  result = sum;
20          }
21      );
22      return result;
23  }
```

LISTING 8.20

Implementing pack pattern with `cilk_scan` from Listing 8.17.

It fills an array b with the elements of array a that satisfy predicate p and returns the number of such elements found. It calls `parallel_scan` to compute a running sum of how many elements satisfy predicate p. A standalone scan of the sum operation would have to store the partial sums in an array. That is not necessary here, because each partial sum is consumed immediately by the assignment `b[sum++] = a[j]`.

The scan tree in Figure 8.8 generalizes to trees of higher degree. For an N-ary scan tree, the node performs an N-ary serial reduction during the upsweep and an N-element serial exclusive scan on the downsweep. Indeed, some implementations do away with recursion altogether and use a single serial scan, as was shown by the OpenMP implementation of scan in Section 5.4. That saves synchronization overhead at the expense of increasing the span. If such a degenerate single-node tree is used for a tiled scan with tiles of size $\sqrt{N}$, the span is $\Theta(\sqrt{N})$. Though not as good as the $\Theta(\lg N)$ span using a binary tree, it is an improvement over the $\Theta(N)$ time for a serial scan, and constant factors can put it ahead in some circumstances.

8.12 APPLYING FORK–JOIN TO RECURRENCES

Recurrences, described in Section 7.5, result when a loop nest has loop-carried dependencies—that is, data dependencies on outputs generated by earlier iterations in the serial execution of a loop. We explained how this can always be parallelized with a hyperplane sweep. However, sometimes a recurrence can also be evaluated using fork–join by recursively partitioning the recurrence, an approach that can have useful data locality properties. This section explores some tradeoffs for recursive partitioning.

For example, consider the "binomial lattice" recurrence in Figure 8.10. For the sake of a familiar example, the values shown are binomial coefficients, organized as in Pascal's triangle. However, this particular pattern of dependencies shows up in far more sophisticated applications such as pricing models for stock options, infinite impulse response image processing filters, and in dynamic programming problems. A good example of the last is the Smith–Waterman algorithm for sequence alignment, which is used extensively in bioinformatics [SW81].

This data dependency graph is an obvious candidate for the superscalar or "fire when ready" approach, but using this approach would give up the locality and space advantages of fork–join.

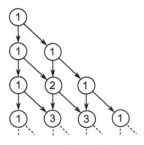

FIGURE 8.10

Directed acyclic data dependency graph for binomial lattice.

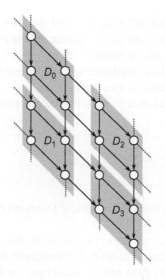

FIGURE 8.11

Decomposing a diamond subgraph into subdiamonds.

A recursive fork–join decomposition of this recurrence will be explored as an alternative, and its advantages and disadvantages analyzed.

Consider a diamond-shaped subgraph where the number of points along an edge is a power of two, such as the example in Figure 8.11. The diamond can be decomposed into four subdiamonds, labeled D_0, D_1, D_2, and D_3. Diamonds D_2 and D_3 can be evaluated in parallel. Furthermore, the same approach can be applied recursively to the four subdiamonds.

The parallel base case occurs when the current diamond is so small that fork–join overheads become significant. At that point, vector parallelism can be exploited by serially iterating over the diamond from top to bottom and computing each row of points in parallel.

Here is a pseudocode sketch for the recursive pattern:

```
void recursive_diamond( diamond D ) {
    if( D is small ) {
        base_diamond( D );
    } else {
        divide D into subdiamonds D₀, D₁, D₂, D₃;
        recursive_diamond(D₀);
        cilk_spawn recursive_diamond(D₁);
        /* nospawn */recursive_diamond(D₂);
        cilk_sync;
        recursive_diamond(D₃)
    }
}
```

The effort for turning this sketch into efficient code mostly concerns manipulation of memory. There is a fundamental tradeoff between parallelism and worst-case memory space, because in order to avoid a race operations occurring in parallel must record their results into separate memory locations. For the binomial lattice, one extreme is to use a separate memory location for each lattice point. This is inefficient. For a diamond with a side of width w, it requires $\Theta(w^2)$ space.

At the other extreme, it is possible to minimize space by mapping an entire column of lattice points to a single memory location. Unfortunately this mapping requires serial execution, to avoid overwriting a location with a new value before all uses of its old value complete, as shown below:

```
void base_diamond( diamond D ) {
    for each row R in D do
        for each column i in row R from right to left
            A[i]=f(A[i−1],A[i]);
}
```

This **serialization** extends to the recursive formulation: Diamond D_1 must be evaluated before D_2, and hence fork–join parallelism could not be used.

The solution is to double the space and have two locations for each lattice point. Organize the locations into two arrays, A and B. A location in array A corresponds to a column of the lattice. A location in array B corresponds to a diagonal of the lattice. Subscripts for B start at zero and go downward for the sake of improving **vectorization** of the base case, as explained later.

Figure 8.12 shows the parameterized description of a diamond subgraph:

- a points to the element of A holding the leftmost column value.
- b points to the element of B holding the topmost diagonal value.

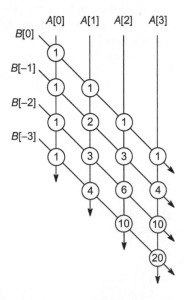

FIGURE 8.12

Parameters for diamond subgraph.

```
1   template<typename T, typename F>
2   void base_diamond( T* a, T* b, size_t w, int s, size_t n, const F& f ) {
3       size_t kfinish = std::min( 2*w-1, n );
4       for( size_t k=s; k<kfinish; ++k ) {
5           int m = std::min(k+1,2*w-1-k);
6           T* as = a+std::max(w,k+1)-w;
7           T* bs = b-std::min(k,w-1);
8           as[0:m] = f( bs[0:m], as[0:m] );
9           bs[0:m] = as[0:m];
10      }
11  }
```

LISTING 8.21

Base case for evaluating a diamond of lattice points.

- w is the number of points along a side of the diamond.
- s and n describe clipping limits on the diamond. The rows to be processed, relative to the top corner, are rows with indices in the half-open interval $[s,n)$.

Listing 8.21 shows the code for the row updates, using vector parallelism across each row. The two vector updates can in theory be chained together. However, at the time of writing, Cilk Plus did not allow chaining of such assignments, though they will be allowed in the future.

With a positive coordinate convention for B, the vector update would look something like:

```
as[0:m] = f( bs[0:m:-1], as[0:m] );
bs[0:m:-1] = as[0:m];
```

with pointer `bs` being calculated slightly differently. Though the code would work, it would be less efficient because the compiler would have to insert permutation instructions to account for the fact that `as` and `bs` have strides in different directions.

Listing 8.22 shows the rest of the code. It assumes that only the topmost diamond is clipped.

One final note: Additional performance can be gained by turning off denormalized floating point ("*denormals*") numbers. Their use can severely impact performance. Floating point numbers consist of a mantissa and exponent; the normalized format has a mantissa that always has a leading one (value $=$ 1.mantissa^{exponent}), whereas a denormalized format has a leading zero (value $=$ 0.mantisssa^{exponent}). Denormalized floating point numbers are so small (close to zero) that the exponent would underflow in the normal representation without this additional "denormal" format. Denormalized numbers help preserve important algebraic properties such as the equivalence of the equality tests $x - y = 0$ and $x = y$. Alas, denormalized numbers often require extra cycles to process. A common case of f in our example is a function that averages its inputs, which will result in the output being a bell curve. The tails of the curve will have values that asymptotically approach zero and consequently contain many denormalized floating-point values. Using options that flush denormalized numbers to zero, such as `/Qftz` with the Intel compiler, can greatly improve the performance of this example. This is very useful if the value of the extra numerical range is not worth the performance loss to your program. It is common to use such flush-to-zero options in high-performance code.

```
1   template<typename T, typename F>
2   void recursive_diamond( T* a, T* b, size_t w, int s, size_t n, const F& f ) {
3       if( w<=CUT_OFF ) {
4           base_diamond( a, b, w, s, n, f );
5       } else {
6           size_t h = w/2;
7           recursive_diamond( a, b, h, s, n, f );
8           if( h<n ) {
9               cilk_spawn recursive_diamond( a+h, b, h, 0, n-h, f );
10              recursive_diamond( a, b-h, h, 0, n-h, f );
11              if( w<n ) {
12                  cilk_sync;
13                  recursive_diamond( a+h, b-h, h, 0, n-2*h, f );
14              }
15          }
16      }
17  }
18
19  template<typename T, typename F>
20  void parallel_lattice( T* a, size_t n, F f ) {
21      T* b = new T[n];
22      std::reverse_copy( a, a+n, b );
23      size_t w=1;
24      while( w<n ) w*=2;
25      recursive_diamond( a, b+n-1, w, 1, n, f );
26      delete[] b;
27  }
```

LISTING 8.22

Code for parallel recursive evaluation of binomial lattice in Cilk Plus.

8.12.1 Analysis

The work T_1 for the diamond lattice is $\Theta(N^2)$. The corresponding span T_∞ for the same algorithm is $\Theta(N^{\lg 3}) \approx \Theta(N^{1.585})$. Taking the ratio of these two results in a speedup of $\Theta(N^{0.415})$. By inspection, it is easy to see that if the recurrence was executed directly by following graph edges, then the span is only $\Theta(N)$ and speedup is $\Theta(N)$. The point is that imposing the recursive diamond structure has improved data locality but lengthened the asymptotic span. The practical impact will depend on the number P of available processors. If P is significantly less than $N^{0.415}$, the impact will be relatively small; otherwise, it may be large compared to the direct solution. However, constant factors due to the better **arithmetic intensity** (and therefore better cache behavior) of the tiled version may allow it to perform better in practice. Unfortunately, which is better will depend on the magnitude of the relevant constant factors on a particular architecture, so the best solution often involves selecting an implementation and tuning its parameters by experimentation.

```
1  template<typename T, typename F>
2  void striped_lattice( T* a, size_t n, F f ) {
3    T* b = new T[n];
4    std::reverse_copy( a, a+n, b );
5    size_t w=CUT_OFF;
6    for( size_t i=0; i<n; i+=w )
7      cilk_for( size_t j=0; j<=i; j+=w )
8        base_diamond( a+j, b+n-1-(i-j), w, i?0:1, n-i, f );
9    delete[] b;
10 }
```

LISTING 8.23

Marching over diamonds in Cilk Plus. This is an example of a hyperplane sweep parallelization of the binomial lattice recurrence.

8.12.2 Flat Fork–Join

Another solution to consider is to march over the lattice from top to bottom and execute a row of diamonds in parallel using a hyperplane sweep. This is row-by-row application of the map pattern, and is discussed in Section 7.5. Listing 8.23 shows the code for this approach, which uses routine base_diamond from Listing 8.21.

A cilk_for with K iterations takes time $\Theta(\lg K)$. Thus, $T_\infty = \Theta(N \lg N)$, which for large N is a significant improvement over $\Theta(N^{0.415})$ and only a factor of $\lg N$ away from the optimal span of $\Theta(N)$.

8.13 SUMMARY

In this chapter we presented the fork–join pattern, which is a natural fit for parallel divide-and-conquer algorithms. Parallel divide-and-conquer generates independent subproblems, solves them in parallel, and then combines the results. Algorithms based on recursive divide-and-conquer often have very good space behavior, locality, and load-balancing properties when executed by a fork–join implementation that uses work-stealing. Speedup may, however, be limited by the speed of the divide or combine steps or by uneven division of work.

We presented the Master method for computing the asymptotic complexity of the work and span. These can be used to predict the speedup of a divide-and-conquer algorithm. Karatsuba polynomial multiplication and Quicksort were given as examples, which also demonstrated practical issues with memory allocation.

Cache-oblivious algorithms using matrix multiplication as an example were discussed, and we also presented fork–join implementations of scan and the binomial lattice recurrence.

Pipeline

Online algorithms are important for modern computing. In an online algorithm, processing starts before all the input is available, and the output starts to be written before all processing is complete. In other words, computing and I/O take place **concurrently**. Often the input is coming from real-time sources such as keyboards, pointing devices, and sensors. Even when all the input is available, it is often on a file system, and overlapping the algorithm with input/output can yield significant improvements in performance. A **pipeline** is one way to achieve this overlap, not only for I/O but also for computations that are mostly parallel but require small sections of code that must be serial.

This chapter covers a simple pipeline model embodied in the TBB `parallel_pipeline` template. It shows the mechanics of using that template, as well as how to imitate it in Cilk Plus in limited circumstances. This chapter also touches on the general issue of **mandatory parallelism** versus **optional parallelism**, which becomes important when pipelines are generalized beyond the simple model. In particular, care must be taken to avoid producer/consumer deadlock when using optional parallelism to implement a pipeline.

9.1 BASIC PIPELINE

A **pipeline** is a linear sequence of stages. Data flows flows through the pipeline, from the first stage to the last stage. Each stage performs a transform on the data. The data is partitioned into pieces that we call items. A stage's transformation of items may be one-to-one or may be more complicated. A serial stage processes one item at a time, though different stages can run in parallel.

Pipelines are appealing for several reasons:

- Early items can flow all the way through the pipeline before later items are even available. This property makes pipelines useful for soft real-time and online applications. In contrast, the **map** pattern (Chapter 4) has stronger synchronization requirements: All input data must be ready at the start, and no output data is ready until the map operation completes.
- Pipeline composition is straightforward. The output of a pipeline can be fed into the input of a subsequent pipeline.
- A serial pipeline stage maps naturally to a serial I/O device. Even random-access devices such as disks behave faster when access to them is serial. By having separate stages for computation and I/O, a pipeline can be an effective means of overlapping computation and I/O.

- Pipelines deal naturally with resource limits. The number of items in flight can be throttled to match those limits. For example, it is possible for a pipeline to process large amounts of data using a fixed amount of memory.
- The linear structure makes it it easy to reason about **deadlock** freedom, unlike topologies involving cycles or merges.
- With some discipline, each stage can be analyzed and debugged separately.

A pipeline with only serial stages has a fundamental speedup limit similar to **Amdahl's law**, but expressed in terms of **throughput**. The throughput of the pipeline is limited to the throughput of the slowest serial stage, because every item must pass through that stage one at a time. In asymptotic terms, $T_P = \Theta(T_1)$, so pipelines provide *no* asymptotic **speedup**! Nonetheless, the hidden constant factor can make such a pipeline worth the effort. For example, a pipeline with four perfectly balanced stages can achieve a speedup of four. However, this speedup will not grow further with more processors: It is limited by the number of serial stages, as well as the balance between them.

9.2 PIPELINE WITH PARALLEL STAGES

Introducing parallel stages can make a pipeline more **scalable**. A parallel stage processes more than one item at a time. Typically it can do so because it has no mutable state. A parallel stage is different from a serial stage with internal parallelism, because the parallel stage can process multiple input items at once and can deliver the output items out of order.

The introduction of parallel stages introduces a complication to serial stages. In a pipeline with only serial stages, each stage receives items in the same order. But when a parallel stage intervenes between two serial stages, the later serial stage can receive items in a different order from the earlier stage. Some applications require consistency in the order of items flowing through the serial stages, and usually the requirement is that the final output order be consistent with the initial input order. The data compression example in Chapter 12 is a good example of this requirement.

Intel TBB deals with the ordering issue by defining three kinds of stages:

- `parallel`: Processes incoming items in parallel
- `serial_out_of_order`: Processes items one at a time, in arbitrary order
- `serial_in_order`: Processes items one at a time, in the same order as the other `serial_in_order` stages in the pipeline

The difference in the two kinds of serial stages has no impact on asymptotic speedup. The throughput of the pipeline is still limited by the throughput of the slowest stage. The advantage of the `serial_out_of_order` kind of stage is that by relaxing the order of items, it can improve **locality** and reduce **latency** in some scenarios by allowing an item to flow through that would otherwise have to wait for its predecessor.

The simplest common sequence of stages for `parallel_pipeline` is serial–parallel–serial, where the serial stages are in order. There are two ways to picture such a pipeline. The first is to draw each stage as a vertex in a graph and draw edges indicating the flow of data. Figure 9.1 pictures a serial–parallel–serial pipeline this way. The parallel stage is distinguished by not having a feedback loop like the two serial stages do. This way of drawing a pipeline is concise and intuitive, though it departs from

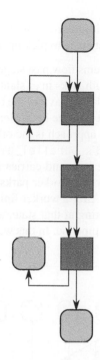

FIGURE 9.1

Serial–parallel–serial pipeline. The two serial stages have feedback loops that represent updating their state. The middle stage is stateless; thus multiple invocations of it can run in parallel.

the diagrams in other sections because a single vertex handles a sequence of data items and not a single piece of data.

An alternative is to show one vertex per stage invocation, as in Figure 9.2. The parallel stage is distinguished by not having any horizontal dependencies in the picture. It gives an intuitive analysis of the **work** and **span**. For example, assume each serial **task** in the picture takes unit time, and each parallel task takes four units of time. For n input items, the work T_1 is $6n$ since each item requires two serial tasks and one parallel task. The span T_∞ is $n + 5$, because the longest paths through the graph pass through some combination of $n + 1$ serial tasks before and after passing through one parallel task. Speedup is thus limited to $\frac{6n}{n+5}$, which approaches 6 as n approaches ∞. This sort of picture is not possible if the pipeline computation has `serial_out_of_order` stages, which are beyond the **DAG** model of computation (Section 2.5.6).

9.3 IMPLEMENTATION OF A PIPELINE

There are two basic approaches to implementing a pipeline:

- A worker is bound to a stage and processes items as they arrive. If the stage is parallel, it may have multiple workers bound to it.

- A worker is bound to an item and carries the item through the pipeline [MSS04]. When a worker finishes the last stage, it goes to the first stage to pick up another item.

The difference can be viewed as whether items flow past stages or stages flow past items. In Figure 9.2, the difference is whether a worker deals with tasks in a (slanted) row or tasks in a column.

The two approaches have different locality behavior. The bound-to-stage approach has good locality for internal state of a stage, but poor locality for the item. Hence, it is better if the internal state is large and item state is small. The bound-to-item approach is the other way around.

The current implementation of TBB's `parallel_pipeline` uses a modified bind-to-item approach. A worker picks up an available item and carries it through as many stages as possible. If a stage is not ready to accept another item, the worker parks the item where another worker can pick it up when the stage is ready to accept it. After a worker finishes applying a serial stage to an item, it checks if there is a parked input item waiting at that state, and if so **spawns** a task that unparks that item and continues carrying it through the pipeline. In this way, execution of a serial stage is serialized without a mutex.

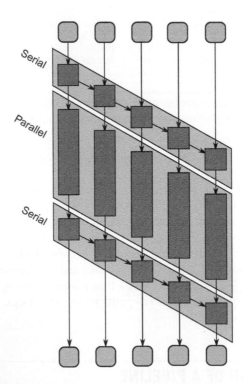

FIGURE 9.2

DAG model of pipeline in Figure 9.1. This picture shows the DAG model of computation (Section 2.5.6) for the pipeline in Figure 9.1, assuming there are five input items. To emphasize the opportunity for parallelism, each box for a parallel task is scaled to show it taking four times as much time as a serial task.

The parking trick enables **greedy scheduling**—no worker waits to run a stage while there is other work ready to do. But it has the drawback of eliminating any implicit space bounds. Without the parking trick, a pipeline with *P* workers uses at most about *P* more space than serial execution, since the space is no worse than *P* copies of the serial program running. But the parking trick is equivalent to creating suspended copies of the serial program, in addition to the *P* running copies. TBB addresses the issue by having the user specify an upper bound on the number of items in flight.

9.4 PROGRAMMING MODEL SUPPORT FOR PIPELINES

Understanding the various syntaxes for pipelines is not only good for using them but also reveals some design issues. Our running example is a serial–parallel–serial pipeline. The three stages run functors f, g, and h, in that order. Listing 9.1 shows the serial code. Functions f and h are assumed to require serial in-order stages, and g is assumed to be okay to run as a parallel stage.

9.4.1 Pipeline in TBB

The TBB `parallel_pipeline` template requires that a stage map one input item to one output item. The overall steps for building a pipeline in TBB are:

- Construct a `filter_t<X,Y>` for each stage. Type *X* is the input type; type *Y* is the output type. The first stage must have type `filter_t<void,...>`. The last stage must have type `filter_t <...,void>`.
- Glue the stages together with `operator&`. The output type of a stage must match the input type of the next stage. The type of a `filter_t<X,Y>` glued to a `filter_t<Y,Z>` is a `filter_t<X, Z>`. From a type system perspective, the result acts just like a big stage. The top-level glued result must be a `filter_t<void,void>`.
- Invoke `parallel_pipeline` on the `filter_t<void,void>`. The call must also provide an upper bound on the number of items in flight.

Listing 9.2 shows a TBB implementation of our running example. It illustrates the details of constructing stages. Function `make_filter` builds a `filter_t` object. Its arguments specify the kind of stage and the mapping of items to items. For example, the middle stage is a parallel stage that uses functor g to map input items of type T to output items of type U.

```
1  void serial_pipeline() {
2      while( T t = f() ) {
3          U u = g(t);
4          h(u);
5      }
6  }
```

LISTING 9.1

Serial implementation of a pipeline, with stages f, g, and h.

```
1   void tbb_sps_pipeline( size_t ntoken ) {
2       tbb::parallel_pipeline (
3           ntoken,
4           tbb::make_filter<void,T>(
5               tbb::filter::serial_in_order,
6               [&]( tbb::flow_control& fc ) -> T{
7                   T item = f();
8                   if( !item ) fc.stop();
9                   return item;
10              }
11          ) &
12          tbb::make_filter<T,U>(
13              tbb::filter::parallel,
14              g
15          ) &
16          tbb::make_filter<U,void>(
17              tbb::filter::serial_in_order,
18              h
19          )
20      );
21  }
```

LISTING 9.2

Pipeline in TBB. It is equivalent to the serial pipeline in Listing 9.1, except that the stages run in parallel and the middle stage processes multiple items in parallel.

The first and last stages use side effects to communicate with the rest of the program, and the corresponding input/output types are void. The last stage is declared as mapping items from U to void and uses side effects to output items. Conversely, the first stage is declared as mapping items from void to T and uses side effects to input items.

The first stage is also special because each time it is invoked it has to return an item or indicate that there are no more items. The TBB convention is that it takes an argument of type flow_control&. If it has no more items to output, it calls method stop on that argument, which indicates that there are no more items, and the currently returned item should be ignored.

9.4.2 Pipeline in Cilk Plus

Pipelines with an arbitrary number of stages are not expressible in Cilk Plus. However, clever use of a reducer enables expressing the common case of a serial–parallel–serial pipeline. The general approach is:

1. Invoke the first stage inside a serial loop.
2. Spawn the second stage for each item produced by the first stage and feed its output to a *consumer reducer*.
3. Invoke the third stage from inside the consumer reducer, which enforces the requisite serialization.

```
1   // Function for third stage
2   extern void h_( HState*, U u );
3   // Mutable state for third stage
4   HState s;
5   // Reducer for third stage
6   reducer_consume<HState,U> sink( &s, h_ );
7
8   void Stage2( T t ) {
9       U u = g(t);  // Second stage
10      sink.consume(u);  // Feed item to third stage
11  }
12
13  void cilk_sps_pipeline() {
14      while( T t = f() )  // First stage is serial
15          cilk_spawn Stage2(t);  // Spawn second stage
16      cilk_sync;
17  }
```

LISTING 9.3

Pipeline in Cilk Plus equivalent to the serial pipeline in Listing 9.1. This version uses function h_ instead of functor h for reasons explained in the text.

Though the template for the consumer reducer could be written for our functor h, doing so complicates writing the template. So, to simplify exposition, we assume that the third stage is defined by a function h_ that takes two arguments: a pointer to its mutable state and the value of an input item. These assumptions work nicely for the bzip2 example (Section 12.4).

Listing 9.3 shows the mechanics of writing the pipeline. The intra-stage logic is close to that in Listing 9.2. All that differs is how the stages communicate. Whereas in the TBB code stages communicate through arguments and return values, here the communication is ad hoc. The second stage of the TBB version returned its result value u to send it on to the third stage. Its Cilk Plus equivalent sends u to the third stage by invoking sink.consume(u). Unlike the TBB version, the first stage does not really need any wrapper at all. It is just a serial loop that gets items and spawns the second stage.

Now reducer_consume can be explained. Recall how Section 8.10 described reducers in terms of algebraic **monoids**. The reducer here is manipulating side effects, namely updates to HState. At first glance, this imperative nature seems contrary to a algebraic monoid, but there is a monoid lurking behind reducer_consumer: list concatenation, or what mathematicians call the *free monoid*. Suppose all processing by the third stage function h_ could be deferred until after the cilk_sync. Then each view could be a list of U. Two views could be joined by concatenating their lists, and since concatenation is **associative**, the final list of U would be independent of whether execution really forked or not.

The implementation described so far is mathematically clean but has two drawbacks:

- It loses **potential parallelism** by not overlapping invocations of h_ with invocations of the other stages.
- The list of U might be prohibitively large to store.

Indeed, the latter objection is severe for the bzip2 example, because each item is a pointer to a compressed block of data waiting to be written to disk. Retaining all those blocks in memory would limit how big a file bzip2 can process. However, observe that the list in the leftmost view can be fed to h_ immediately. There is no reason to build a list for the leftmost view. Only lists in other views need to be deferred.

So reducer_consumer joins views using the following rules:

- If the left view is leftmost, its list is empty. Process the list of the right view.
- Otherwise, concatenate the lists.

Listing 9.4 shows the implementation. The list is non-empty only if **actual parallelism** occurs, since only then is there is a non-leftmost view. Section 11.2.1 explains the general mechanics of creating a View and Monoid for a cilk::reducer.

```
1   #include <cilk/reducer.h>
2   #include <list>
3   #include <cassert>
4
5   template<typename State, typename Item>
6   class reducer_consume {
7   public:
8       // Function that consumes an Item to update a State object
9       typedef void (*func_type)(State*,Item);
10  private:
11      struct View {
12          std::list<Item> items;
13          bool is_leftmost;
14          View( bool leftmost=false ) : is_leftmost(leftmost) {}
15          ~View() {}
16      };
17
18      struct Monoid: cilk::monoid_base<View> {
19          State* state;
20          func_type func;
21          void munch( const Item& item ) const {
22              func(state,item);
23          }
24          void reduce(View* left, View* right) const {
25              assert( !right->is_leftmost );
26              if( left->is_leftmost )
27                  while( !right->items.empty() ) {
28                      munch(right->items.front());
29                      right->items.pop_front();
30                  }
31              else
32                  left->items.splice( left->items.end(), right->items );
33          }
34          Monoid( State* s, func_type f ) : state(s), func(f) {}
35      };
```

```
36
37    cilk::reducer<Monoid> impl;
38
39    public:
40        reducer_consume( State* s, func_type f ) :
41            impl(Monoid(s,f), /*leftmost=*/true)
42        {}
43
44        void consume( const Item& item ) {
45            View& v = impl.view();
46            if( v.is_leftmost )
47                impl.monoid().munch( item );
48            else
49                v.items.push_back(item);
50        }
51    };
```

LISTING 9.4

Defining a reducer for serializing consumption of items in Cilk Plus.

From a mathematical perspective, the fields of View are monoid values:

- View::items is a value in a list concatenation monoid.
- View::is_leftmost is a value in a monoid over boolean values, with operation $x \otimes y \rightarrow x$.

Both of these operations are **associative** but not **commutative**.

9.5 MORE GENERAL TOPOLOGIES

Pipelines can be generalized to non-linear topologies, and stages with more complex rules. TBB 4.0 has such a framework, in namespace tbb::flow. This framework also lifts the restriction that each stage map exactly one input item to one output item. With more complex topologies comes power, but more programmer responsibility.

The additional power of the TBB 4.0 tbb::flow framework comes with additional responsibility. The framework lifts most of the restrictions of parallel_pipeline while still using a modified bound-to-item approach that avoids explicit waiting. It allows stages to perform one-to-many and many-to-one mappings, and topologies can be non-linear and contain cycles. Consequently, designing pipelines in that framework requires more attention to potential deadlock if cycles or bounded buffers are involved.

9.6 MANDATORY VERSUS OPTIONAL PARALLELISM

Different potential implementations of a pipeline illustrate the difference between **optional parallelism** and **mandatory parallelism**. Consider a two-stage pipeline where the producer puts items into a bounded buffer and the consumer takes them out of the buffer. There is no problem if the producer and consumer run in parallel. But serial execution is tricky. If a serial implementation tries to run the producer to completion before executing the consumer, the buffer can become full and block further progress of the producer. Alternatively, trying to run the consumer to completion before executing the producer will hang. The parallelism of the producer and consumer is mandatory: The producer and consumer *must* interleave to guarantee forward progress. Programs with mandatory parallelism can be much harder to debug than serial programs.

The TBB `parallel_pipeline` construct dodges the issue by restricting the kinds of pipelines that can be built. There is no explicit waiting—a stage is invoked only when its input item is ready, and must emit exactly one output item per invocation. Thus, serial operation of `parallel_pipeline` works by carrying one item at a time through the entire pipeline. No buffering is required. Parallel operation does require buffering where a parallel stage feeds into a serial stage and the serial stage is busy. Because `parallel_pipeline` requires the user to specify its maximum number n of items in flight level, the buffer can be safely bounded to n.

9.7 SUMMARY

The pipeline pattern enables parallel processing of data to commence without having all of the data available, and it also allows data to be output before all processing is complete. Thus, it is a good fit for soft real-time situations when data should be processed as soon as it becomes available. It also allows overlap of computation with I/O and permits computations on data that may not fit in memory in its entirety. The weakness of pipelines is scalability—the throughput of a pipeline is limited to the throughput of its slowest serial stage. This can be addressed by using parallel pipeline stages instead of serial stages to do work where possible. The TBB implementation uses a technique that enables greedy scheduling, but the greed must be constrained in order to bound memory consumption. The user specifies the constraint as a maximum number of items allowed to flow simultaneously through the pipeline. Simple pipelines can be implemented in Cilk Plus by creative use of reducers.

Examples

Forward Seismic Simulation

Reflection seismology is the imaging of the Earth's subsurface structure using sound waves. It is widely used in the oil and gas industry to determine where to find hydrocarbons and most efficiently extract them. *Reverse time migration* (RTM) is one approach to imaging that yields high quality images but requires much computation, and hence is desirable to parallelize.

The example here is not the entire RTM algorithm, but the key part that dominates the computational burden. The obvious parallelization with the **stencil** pattern (Section 4.6.1) suffers from low **arithmetic intensity**, even when using **tiling** for cache (Section 7.3). However, the arithmetic intensity can be raised much further by recognizing that the problem involves not only a stencil in space but also a **recurrence** (Section 7.5) in space–time, since the stencil is iterated. This is a common pattern in solvers for partial differential equations. Using recursive subdivision on this space–time recurrence results in an efficient **cache-oblivious** algorithm with good arithmetic intensity.

10.1 BACKGROUND

A reflection seismology survey consists of collecting data in the field and processing it to generate a subsurface image. The collection step involves sending acoustic waves from *sources* into the Earth and recording the echoes at *receivers*. Examples of land sources are explosives or trucks with massive thumper/vibrator machinery. Water sources are typically devices called *air guns* that pop out compressed air. Receivers are microphones staked into the ground or towed behind a boat. Often a line or grid of receivers record the echoes from a single shot.

Reflection seismology works because different kinds of rock have different velocities and acoustical impedances. Where sound crosses between rocks of varying impedance, some of the sound is reflected from the boundary. The waveform recorded by the receiver is a superposition of reflections from the shot, along many paths in the subsurface, including paths with multiple reflections. For further information, see the program Seismic Duck (http://sourceforge.net/projects/seismic-duck/), which provides an animated introduction to reflection seismology.

Reverse time migration is a way of generating a subsurface image from the source/receiver data. RTM starts by modeling acoustic waves both forward and backward in time. Because of symmetries in the underlying physics, the two directions are essentially the same computation and differ only in boundary conditions:

- The forward model includes sources running forward in time as a boundary condition.
- The reverse model includes receivers running backward in time as boundary condition.

Each model computes a time-varying acoustic signal at each point in the subsurface volume. RTM generates an image such that the value of each point in the image is the time correlation of the signals at that point from the forward and reverse models. The intuition behind doing this is that a rock transition reflects the signal from the source to the receiver. At a reflection point the signals from the forward model and reverse model will match and generate a high correlation value. There may be points where coincidental correlations happen. Summing images for many different shot and receiver locations dilutes the effect of these coincidental matches.

Wavefield models vary in sophistication and computational burden. Our example will use a simple model, the acoustic wave equation, which accounts only for pressure effects. More complex models, such as the elastic wave equation, account for shear effects, at the cost of significantly more memory and arithmetic operations. The physics for the acoustic wave equation involves two fields over points (x, y, z) in the subsurface volume:

- $A_t(x, y, z)$ is the pressure at point (x, y, z) at time t.
- $V(x, y, z)$ is the velocity of sound at point (x, y, z).

Field V is independent of time, but precisely knowing it requires knowing the kind of rock at point (x, y, z). For example, the value of V is much higher for salt than sandstone. This might seem like a hopelessly circular problem—you need to know the rock structure before you can image it! Fortunately, an iterative process works. Start with a rough initial guess for V and generate an approximate RTM image. Use the resulting image to refine the estimate of V, and rerun RTM. This process can be repeated until the image seems reasonable to a geophysicist.

10.2 STENCIL COMPUTATION

Our example code focuses on computing the forward and reverse models of the wavefield, because those are the computationally intensive steps in RTM. The acoustic wave equation is:

$$\frac{\partial^2 A}{\partial t^2} = V^2 \nabla^2 A, \tag{10.1}$$

where the Laplacian $\nabla^2 A$ is defined as:

$$\nabla^2 A = \frac{\partial^2 A}{\partial x^2} + \frac{\partial^2 A}{\partial y^2} + \frac{\partial^2 A}{\partial z^2}. \tag{10.2}$$

Our example code discretizes A and V into three-dimensional (3D) grids and approximates the Laplacian $\nabla^2 A$ with a stencil. Here is the discretized version of the equations:

$$A_{t+1} = 2A_t - A_{t-1} + V^2(C * A_t), \tag{10.3}$$

where t is a time index and $C * A_t$ denotes the convolution of a stencil C with the value of field A at time t. As a minor optimization, the code stores a field V^2 instead of V in an array. The code stores field A in a four-dimensional array, with $A_{t,x,y,z}$ stored in A[t&1][z][y][x]. The expression t&1 computes t modulo two. Storing two snapshots of A in time suffices because at each time step, the value A_{t+1}

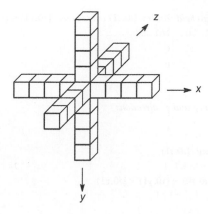

FIGURE 10.1

Structure of stencil for estimating Laplacian.

depends only upon A_t and A_{t-1}. Thus, the location of $A_{t-1}(x,y,z)$ can be overwritten with the value of $A_{t+1}(x,y,z)$.

Figure 10.1 shows the structure of the stencil C. Each pair of opposite arms estimates the second partial derivative in that direction. For example, the arms pointing in the $+x$ and $-x$ directions estimate $\frac{\partial^2 A}{\partial x^2}$. The six arms differ only in direction and thus there are only five independent coefficients, which the code stores in an array C. Listing 10.1 shows code for using the stencil serially.

10.3 IMPACT OF CACHES ON ARITHMETIC INTENSITY

One way to parallelize the code in Listing 10.1 is to use the geometric decomposition pattern (Section 6.6). There is a large amount of available parallelism, because for a given value of t, the inner three loops can all be parallel. Grids in RTM tend to be as big as memory will allow. For exposition, assume that the spatial grid is $500 \times 500 \times 500$, for a total of 125×10^6 grid points. For single-precision values, that works out to 1.0 GByte for A and 0.5 GByte for V. That is potential 125×10^6-way parallelism! In fact, just changing the z loop to a cilk_for enables 500-way thread parallelism, and marking the x loop with #pragma simd enables 500-way vector parallelism. Here is what the changed code looks like:

```
        ...
        // Apply stencil over [x0,x1) × [y0,y1) × [z0,z1)
        cilk_for (int z=z0; z < z1; ++z)
            for (int y=y0; y < y1; ++y)
#pragma simd
                for (int x=x0; x < x1; ++x) {
                    ...
                }
```

```
1    // Time-domain simulation of wavefield for t ∈ [t0,t1) over volume [x0,x1) × [y0,y1) × [z0,z1)
2    void serial_stencil( int t0, int t1,
3        int x0, int x1,
4        int y0, int y1,
5        int z0, int z1)
6    {
7        // Compute array strides for y and z directions
8        int sy = Nx;
9        int sz = Nx*Ny;
10       // March through time interval [t0,t1)
11       for( int t=t0; t<t1; ++t) {
12           // Apply stencil over [x0,x0) × [y0,y1) × [z0,z1)
13           for (int z=z0; z<z1; ++z)
14               for (int y=y0; y<y1; ++y)
15                   for (int x=x0; x<x1; ++x) {
16                       int s = z * sz + y * sy + x;
17                       // a points to A_t(x,y,z)
18                       float *a = &A[t&1][s];
19                       // a_flip points to A_{t-1}(x,y,z)
20                       float *a_flip = &A[(t+1)&1][s];
21                       // Estimate ∇²A_t(x,y,z)
22                       float laplacian = C[0] * a[0]
23                           + C[1] * ((a[1] + a[-1]) +
24                               (a[sy] + a[-sy]) +
25                               (a[sz] + a[-sz]))
26                           + C[2] * ((a[2] + a[-2]) +
27                               (a[2*sy] + a[-2*sy]) +
28                               (a[2*sz] + a[-2*sz]))
29                           + C[3] * ((a[3] + a[-3]) +
30                               (a[3*sy] + a[-3*sy]) +
31                               (a[3*sz] + a[-3*sz]))
32                           + C[4] * ((a[4] + a[-4]) +
33                               (a[4*sy] + a[-4*sy]) +
34                               (a[4*sz] + a[-4*sz]));
35                       // Compute A_{t+1}(x,y,z)
36                       a_flip[0] = 2*a[0] - a_flip[0] + Vsquared[s] * laplacian;
37                   }
38       }
39   }
```

LISTING 10.1

Serial code for simulating wavefield.

Though the changes usually speed up the code, they usually fall far short of the hardware capabilities. The problem is *arithmetic intensity*, as defined in Section 2.4.2. Consider the floating-point arithmetic and memory operations required for one point update:

- 29 memory operations:
    - 25 reads from a for the stencil.
    - 1 read for a_flip[0].
    - 1 write to A_flip[0].
    - 1 read from Vsquared.
  The duplicate read of a[0] does not count, since either the compiler or cache will turn it into a single read.
- 33 floating-point operations:
    - 25 additions
    - 1 subtraction
    - 7 multiplications

Hence, the arithmetic intensity is $33/29 \approx 1.14$. This intensity is about an order of magnitude lower than what would keep arithmetic units busy on typical current hardware.

A cache hierarchy helps raise the intensity by eliminating some reads from main memory. This effect happens along several axes. As the inner x loop advances, the stencil reads some locations that were read by the previous iteration. Figure 10.2 visualizes this. Each x iteration moves the stencil along the x axis, leaving the ghost of its former locations in cache. Any parts overlapping the ghost are already in cache. Only the parts with exposed faces on the right side contribute to memory loads. So the cache has automatically removed 8 loads, raising the arithmetic intensity to $33/(29 - 8) \approx 1.57$.

In fact, a similar thing happens on the y-arms. If the cache is big enough, then most of the loads for the y-arm will be loads from cache because they overlap ghosts of former loads, except for the load of a[4*sy]. The elimination of most of the loads along the x-arm and y-arms raises the arithmetic intensity to $33/(29 - 8 - 7) \approx 2.36$, about twice the uncached version.

Is caching of y-arm loads a reasonable assumption for Listing 10.1? To analyze this, consider what one iteration of the y loop would load into cache:

- A row of a corresponding to each cube with a dark face in Figure 10.2. That is a total of 17 rows. The rows corresponding to the z-arms do not really need to be kept in cache, but the hardware does not know that.

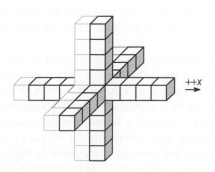

FIGURE 10.2

Reuse of memory when stencil steps along the x axis.

- A row of a_flip.
- A row of Vsquared.

That is 19 rows of 500 elements each, or $19 \times 500 \times 4$bytes $= 38$ KBytes. Allowing for imperfect associativity and imperfect approximations of least recently used (LRU), this will certainly fit in cache, though perhaps not in the innermost cache.

> **WARNING**
>
> If the x and y grid dimensions are exactly powers of two, there is a risk that the y-arm and z-arm will all map to the same associative set, possibly exceeding the size of the associative set of the cache and thus force premature evictions, which can cause slowdown.

What about caching of the z-arms? If the z-arm loads could be cached long enough to be reused, then each array element has to be loaded only once, and the arithmetic intensity increases significantly to $33/4 = 8.25$. That requires about 198 KByte of ideal cache for our problem dimensions, for a single thread. That is well within the size of caches on modern CPUs, though not the innermost and fastest cache. However, if the cache is shared by multiple threads, there might not be enough cache to go around. As coded, the problem is reaching the limits of the free benefit from caches.

10.4 RAISING ARITHMETIC INTENSITY WITH SPACE–TIME TILING

But there is another way to code the problem that raises the arithmetic intensity much higher. A fourth dimension in the problem is a recurrence in time. Suppose the code runs for 10 timesteps. Imagine a cache that is big enough to hold all of the arrays across all timesteps. Then the arithmetic intensity grows by a factor of 10! Alas, that requires a 1.5×10^9 byte cache, several orders of magnitude beyond current offerings and surely not the innermost cache.

Fortunately, there is a trick that gets most of the benefit without a behemoth cache. Chop the problem into cache-sized subproblems. Each subproblem will simulate the wavefield over a chunk of space–time. This chunking is possible because for any value $A_t(x, y, z)$, its influence on the rest of the simulation propagates at a top speed of four grid units per time step, because the longest stencil arm is four grid points. This upper limit on propagation of information acts as a "speed of light" for the simulation.

By way of analogy, consider the impact of the real speed of light on a simulation of the Earth. The Earth could be simulated for an 8-minute chunk of time, starting with the state of space within 8 light-minutes of Earth, without knowing the state of the rest of the universe. For example, the state of the sun, even if it blew up, would be irrelevant for such a simulation time-frame because the sun is 8.3 light minutes away. The principle is similar for our simulation—the upper bound on the speed of information propagation bounds what state information is necessary to know to model a region over a limited time interval. The limit on information propagation in the seismic simulation has a similar effect, though there is a slight geometric difference. The propagation of information in the code follows

```
1  for( int t=t0; t<t1; ++t )
2    for( int i=i0; i<i1; ++i ) {
3      float* b = &B[t&1][i];
4      float* b_flip = &B[t+1 & 1][i];
5      b_flip[0] = f(b[-1],b[0],b[1],b_flip[0]).
6    }
```

LISTING 10.2

Code for one-dimensional iterated stencil. The code marches a one-dimensional field B through time, using a flip-flop indexing scheme similar to the one in Listing 10.1.

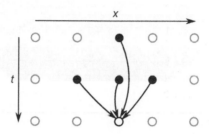

FIGURE 10.3

Dependence of value in space–time for one-dimensional problem in Listing 10.2. Computing the value of $B_{t+1,x}$ requires knowing only four other values in space–time: $B_{t,x-1}$, $B_{t,x}$, $B_{t,x+1}$, and $B_{t-1,x}$.

"taxicab geometry"; thus, the set of points within a given distance forms an octohedron instead of a sphere.

Space-time geometry is a bit tricky to visualize for four dimensions, so we explain the details for a one-dimensional (1D) problem first, using a three-point stencil, and then extend it to multiple dimensions. Listing 10.2 shows the code for the 1D problem, which abstracts the stencil as a function f. Figure 10.3 shows the dependencies for each point in space–time. To update a point does *not* require the value of all points for the previous timestep. It requires only the values of its neighbors in the previous timestep. Thus, a subgrid cells can be updated multiple steps into the future without updating the entire grid, as shown in Figure 10.4.

Choosing a trapezoid small enough to fit in cache raises arithmetic intensity, because:

- The arithmetic operations will be proportional to its area.
- The cache misses will be proportional to the length of its top or bottom, whichever is longer.

So **tiling** space-time with trapezoids can raise the arithmetic intensity significantly.

Explicitly choosing the **tile** size based on the cache size could be done but requires knowing the cache size. Furthermore, there are typically multiple levels of cache. So a better approach is to adopt a **cache-oblivious** strategy of recursive tiling. Trapezoids decompose into trapezoids, and some of the subtrapezoids can be evaluated in parallel, similar to the way that diamonds were decomposed into

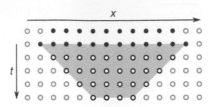

FIGURE 10.4

Trapezoidal space–time region for one-dimensional stencil. All points in the trapezoid can be computed from its top points, without knowing the value of any other points.

FIGURE 10.5

Decomposing a space–time trapezoid.

diamonds in Section 8.12. Figure 10.5 shows such a decomposition. Horizontal cuts are cuts in time; slanted cuts are cuts in space. The first level of recursion did a time cut. The numerical labels indicate order of evaluation. Trapezoids with the same label can be evaluated in parallel. Note that the triangles are trapezoids with zero-length tops, so they can also be decomposed. Further recursive decomposition of the triangles and trapezoids creates recursive parallelism.

10.5 CILK PLUS CODE

The trapezoid trick of the previous section works in multiple dimensions. The only change is that the trapezoids are now four dimensional. Space cuts can be in any of the three spatial dimensions. It is difficult to visualize, but not difficult to extrapolate from the 1D case. A space–time trapezoid in the 1D case can be represented by four integers: x0, x1, dx0, dx1, where:

- [x0,x1) is the half-open interval representing the top of the trapezoid.
- dx0 and dx1 are the corresponding slopes of the sides with respect to t.

In the 1D example where the stencil arms extend only one unit, the slopes are usually 1 or −1, and 0 at a boundary of the grid. For the 3D example, the arms extend four units, so the slopes are usually 4 or −4, and 0 at boundaries of the grid.

Listing 10.3 shows the base case code. It is almost identical to Listing 10.1, except that after each time step it adjusts the boundaries of the spatial hyperplane by the corresponding slope values. It also adds a #pragma simd that gives the compiler permission to vectorize the inner loop.

```
1   void base_trapezoid(int t0, int t1,
2       int x0, int dx0, int x1, int dx1,
3       int y0, int dy0, int y1, int dy1,
4       int z0, int dz0, int z1, int dz1 )
5   {
6       // Compute array strides for y and z directions
7       int sy = Nx;
8       int sz = Nx*Ny;
9       // March through time [t0,t1)
10      for (int t=t0; t < t1; ++t) {
11          // Apply stencil over [x0,x0) × [y0,y1) × [z0,z1)
12          for (int z=z0; z < z1; ++z)
13              for (int y=y0; y < y1; ++y)
14  #pragma simd
15                  for (int x=x0; x < x1; ++x) {
16                      // Update one point. The code here is the same as the
17                      // body of the x loop in Listing 10.1.
18                      ...
19                  }
20          // Slide down along the trapezoid
21          x0 += dx0; x1 += dx1;
22          y0 += dy0; y1 += dy1;
23          z0 += dz0; z1 += dz1;
24      }
25  }
```

LISTING 10.3

Base case for applying stencil to space–time trapezoid.

Listing 10.4 shows the recursive code. It biases cutting towards using the longest spatial axis that permits a cut into K trapezoids. A value of $K = 2$ works well in practice. The three space cuts are essentially the same logic, only reoriented along a different spatial axis. Time cuts are used as a last resort, since they do not directly introduce parallelism, though they may open opportunities for more space cuts of the resulting subtrapezoids. See Section 8.8 for a similar situation for the choice of cuts in recursive matrix multiplication.

The strategy shown requires two synchronizations for each split along an axis, one after each cilk_for loop. Thus, splitting each dimension once adds six synchronizations to the span. It turns out that splitting all three dimensions at once enables using only four synchronizations [TCK+11], thus enabling greater parallelism. The logic is substantially more complicated to code, so it seems like a technique best left to "stencil compilers" such as Pochoir [TCK+11].

The gain from the space–time restructuring can help even sequential code. On one of the author's machines, just the cache-oblivious algorithm without #pragma simd yielded a $1.6 \times$ speed improvement, using just a *single* thread!

```
1   const int ds = 4; // Slant of a space cut (in grid units per time step)
2
3   #define TRAPEZOID(u0,u1) \
4       u0+i*w,                     /* left side */ \
5       ds,                         /* left slope */ \
6       i<K-1 ? u0+(i+1)*w : u1,    /* right side */ \
7       -ds                         /* right slope */
8
9   #define TRIANGLE(u0,du0,u1,du1) \
10      i<K ? u0+i*w : u1,          /* left side */ \
11      i==0 ? du0 : -ds,           /* left slope */ \
12      i<K ? u0+i*w : u1,          /* right side */ \
13      i<K? ds : du1               /* right slope */
14
15  void recursive_trapezoid(int t0, int t1,
16          int x0, int dx0, int x1, int dx1,
17          int y0, int dy0, int y1, int dy1,
18          int z0, int dz0, int z1, int dz1 )
19  {
20      int dt = t1-t0;
21      if( dt>1 ) {
22          int dx = x1-x0, dy = y1-y0, dz v z1-z0;
23          if (dx >= dx_threshold && dx >= dy && dx >= dz && dx >= 2*ds*dt*K) {
24              int w = dx / K;
25              cilk_for (int i=0; i<K; ++i)
26                  recursive_trapezoid(t0, t1,
27                      TRAPEZOID(x0,x1),
28                      y0, dy0, y1, dy1,
29                      z0, dz0, z1, dz1);
30              cilk_for (int i=K; i>=0; --i)
31                  recursive_trapezoid(t0, t1,
32                      TRIANGLE(x0,dx0,x1,dx1),
33                      y0, dy0, y1, dy1,
34                      z0, dz0, z1, dz1);
35              return;
36          }
37          if (dy >= dyz_threshold && dy >= dz && dy >= 2*ds*dt*K) {
38              int w = dy / K;
39              cilk_for (int i=0; i<K; ++i)
40                  recursive_trapezoid(t0, t1,
41                      x0, dx0, x1, dx1,
42                      TRAPEZOID(y0,y1),
43                      z0, dz0, z1, dz1);
44              cilk_for (int i=K; i>=0; --i)
45                  recursive_trapezoid(t0, t1,
46                      x0, dx0, x1, dx1,
47                      TRIANGLE(y0,dy0,y1,dy1),
```

```
48                    z0, dz0, z1, dz1);
49              return;
50          }
51          if (dz >= dyz_threshold && dz >= 2*ds*dt*K) {
52              int w = dz / K;
53              cilk_for (int i=0; i<K; ++i)
54                  recursive_trapezoid(t0, t1,
55                      x0, dx0, x1, dx1,
56                      y0, dy0, y1, dy1,
57                      TRAPEZOID(z0,z1));
58              cilk_for (int i=K; i>=0; --i)
59                  recursive_trapezoid(t0, t1,
60                      x0, dx0, x1, dx1,
61                      y0, dy0, y1, dy1,
62                      TRIANGLE(z0,dz0,z1,dz1));
63              return;
64          }
65          if (dt > dt_threshold) {
66              int halfdt = dt / 2;
67              recursive_trapezoid(t0, t0 + halfdt,
68                  x0, dx0, x1, dx1,
69                  y0, dy0, y1, dy1,
70                  z0, dz0, z1, dz1);
71              recursive_trapezoid(t0 + halfdt, t1,
72                  x0 + dx0*halfdt, dx0, x1 + dx1*halfdt, dx1,
73                  y0 + dy0*halfdt, dy0, y1 + dy1*halfdt, dy1,
74                  z0 + dz0*halfdt, dz0, z1 + dz1*halfdt, dz1);
75              return;
76          }
77      }
78      base_trapezoid(t0, t1,
79          x0, dx0, x1, dx1,
80          y0, dy0, y1, dy1,
81          z0, dz0, z1, dz1);
82  }
```

LISTING 10.4

Parallel cache-oblivious trapezoid decomposition in Cilk Plus. The code applies a stencil to recursively divide a space–time trapezoid.

10.6 ARBB IMPLEMENTATION

The discussion so far has focused on aggressive hand restructuring of the serial code. ArBB offers a competitive approach based on the premise that if you specify the computation at a sufficiently high level then the ArBB runtime can take care of the optimizations.

```
1   void rtm_stencil(arbb::dense<arbb::f32> Acoef,
2       arbb::f32 in, arbb::f32& out, arbb::f32 vsq)
3   {
4       using namespace arbb;
5       f32 laplacian = coef[0] * in;
6
7       for (int n = 1; n <= 4; ++n) {
8           laplacian += Acoef[n] *
9               (neighbor(in, -n, 0, 0) + neighbor(in, n, 0, 0) +
10               neighbor(in, 0, -n, 0) + neighbor(in, 0, n, 0) +
11               neighbor(in, 0, 0, -n) + neighbor(in, 0, 0, n));
12      }
13      out = 2 * in - out + vsq * laplacian;
14  }
15
16  void arbb_stencil(arbb::usize t0, arbb::usize t1, arbb::dense<arbb::f32> coef,
17      arbb::dense<arbb::f32, 3> Ac, arbb::dense<arbb::f32, 3>& An, arbb::dense<arbb
            ::f32, 3> vsq)
18  {
19      using namespace arbb;
20
21      _for (usize t = t0, t < t1, ++t) {
22          _if (t % 2 == 0) {
23              map(rtm_stencil)(coef, Ac, An, vsq);
24          }
25          _else {
26              map(rtm_stencil)(coef, An, Ac, vsq);
27          } _end_if;
28      } _end_for;
29  }
```

LISTING 10.5

ArBB code for simulating a wavefield.

The ArBB implementation of the stencil given in Listing 10.5 is simple because ArBB supports stencils as a built-in pattern, internally implementing many of the stencil optimizations discussed in Section 7.3, in particular strip mining. However, it does not currently implement the recursive space–time trapezoid decomposition, discussed in the previous section.

Syntactically, in the **elemental functions** used for map operations in ArBB, not only can the current element be used as an input but also offset inputs can be accessed using the neighbor function, which takes an offset. The offset must be a normal C++ type, not an ArBB type, which means it can be computed at ArBB function definition time, but not at runtime. As far as ArBB is concerned, neighbor offsets are constants, and the stencil shape is a constant.

Using offsets means that at the boundaries of a collection, some offsets will be outside the bounds of the input collection. In ArBB, such accesses always return 0. If a different treatment of boundaries is needed, the current position can be found using a `position` call and the stencil computation modified accordingly. There is no requirement that the stencil computation be linear or uniform, as it can be a function of the position as well. However, the compiler for ArBB is smart enough that if conditional statements are given that are linear functions of the position, which is the case when we only want to modify the stencil within some fixed distance of the boundary, then these conditional statements will only be evaluated near the boundaries of the input collection and not everywhere in the interior.

10.7 SUMMARY

Stencils are an effective approach to solving the wave equation in the time domain. Memory bandwidth, not hardware threads, can easily become the limiting resource if the stencil is parallelized in the obvious way, because the arithmetic intensity will be low. Caches ameliorate the problem somewhat, though greater gains can be obtained by tiling. The iterated stencil problem is a stencil pattern in space and recurrence pattern in time, so the tiles have a trapezoidal shape in space–time. The slopes of the sides relate to the stencil dimensions. Tiling recursively enables a cache-oblivious algorithm, which optimizes for all possible levels and sizes of cache while being oblivious to which really exist. Because the resulting code uses cache more efficiently, it often runs faster, even when run with a single thread, than the original serial code runs.

K-Means Clustering

The k-means algorithm [Mac67], also called Lloyd's algorithm [Llo82], is a way of finding clusters in a dataset. It is popular because it is simple to implement. Parallelizing it with the **map** (Chapter 4) and **reduce** (Section 5.1) patterns is straightforward. However, a little cleverness can reduce the number of synchronizations by manipulating the code so that the map and reduce patterns can be fused. The parallel k-means implementation involves a reduction over a "heavy" type. The Cilk Plus implementation illustrates the mechanics of defining reducer hyperobjects for such reductions, when the predefined reducers do not suffice. The TBB implementation shows how to use thread-local storage in TBB.

11.1 ALGORITHM

The standard algorithm for k-means [Mac67, Llo82] starts by creating initial clusters and then iteratively updating them. Each update performs the two steps shown in Figure 11.1:

1. Compute the centroid of each cluster.
2. Reassign points to be in the cluster with the closest centroid.

In some situations, a cluster becomes empty. One common repair, which is used in the example, is to assign the point farthest from its current cluster to the empty cluster.

Each of the two steps can be parallelized along two dimensions, across points or across clusters. However, usually the number of points is large enough to provide sufficient **parallel slack** (Section 2.5.6), and sometimes the clusters are few, so only the point dimension is used in the example.

Here are the choices for parallelizing each step in more detail. The centroid of a cluster is the sum of points in it divided by the number of points. Each centroid can be computed separately, and each sum can be computed using parallel reduction. However, if only a few centroids are being computed, computing them independently has several problems:

- The number of clusters might be too few to provide enough parallel slack.
- The partitioning of points into clusters might be grossly imbalanced.
- If the points of a cluster are not kept compact in memory, there may be memory bandwidth issues, because a fetch of a point will bring in its **cache line** with unrelated points.

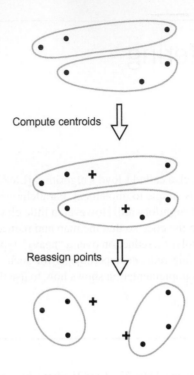

FIGURE 11.1

One iteration of the k-means algorithm with two clusters and six points. Each iteration of the algorithm computes the centroid (+) of each cluster and then reassigns each point to the cluster with the closest centroid.

The example provided here will use only the reduction parallelism approach. Typically, the number of points is much larger than the number of processors and thus provides sufficient parallel slack.

The second step likewise has two possibilities for parallelism. Each point's new cluster can be computed independently, and the distances from it to each centroid can be computed separately. We assume there are enough points to provide parallel slack, and the number of centroids might be small, so the example uses only parallelism across points.

There is another efficiency issue to discuss. The algorithm alternates two patterns over points: reduce to compute centroids and map to reassign points. As discussed in Section 5.2, it is often beneficial to fuse these operations so that only one sweep of memory is required instead of two. Computing a centroid actually involves two steps: computing the sum of its points and then dividing that sum by the size of the cluster. So the iterated steps expand to:

- *Sum*: Compute the sum of the points in each cluster. This is a reduction.
- *Divide*: Divide each cluster sum by the number of points in that cluster.
- *Reassign*: Reassign points to the cluster with the closest centroid. This is a map.

We would like to optimize this using **fusion**. Alas, the reduction and map are in the wrong order to fuse directly, and the divide step separates them. These obstacles are overcome by observing that the k-means algorithm loops over these steps. The first *Sum* step can be peeled from the loop, which permits rotating the loop, so the algorithm looks like:

```
Sum
do {
    Divide
    Reassign
    Sum
} while( any point moved to another cluster );
```

Now the map pattern for step *Reassign* can be fused with the reduction pattern for step *Sum*. The transformed loop executes *Sum* one more time than the original loop executes it, which adds slight overhead. The savings from fusing greatly outweigh this overhead.

11.2 K-MEANS WITH CILK PLUS

Listing 11.1 shows the top-level Cilk Plus code. Take a look at the overall structure. The input is an array `points` of n points and a value k specifying the number of desired clusters. The routine fills array `centroid[0:k]` with the centroids of the clusters, and fills array `cluster_id[0:n]` with the index of each point's centroid in `centroid[0:k]`. The routine assumes that `distance2(p,q)` returns the square of the Euclidean between points p and q.

The `do-while` loop spanning lines 14 to 34 uses the rotated step structure discussed in the previous section to iterate the steps of *Divide*, *Reassign*, and *Sum*. The `cilk_for` on lines 23 to 33 does the fused map/reduce for the *Reassign* and *Sum* steps. The *Reassign* step is expressed using an array notation operation `__sec_reduce_min_index(x)`, which returns the index of the minimum value in array section x. In the code, x is the result of mapping `distance2` over the section `centroid[0:k]` and scalar value `points[i]`. The mapping of the scalar value treats it as a section of k copies of the value. The array notation here is largely for notational convenience, not **vectorization**. The data is in "**array of structures**" form, so it is unlikely to be profitably vectorized unless the hardware has **gather** instructions. See Listing 11.7 (page 287) for equivalent serial code.

The variable `sum` is a **hyperobject**. In a serial version of the code, it would be an array of `sum_and_count` objects. The *j*th object is used to record information about the *j*th cluster, specifically the sum of its points and the number of points. Listing 11.2 shows the definition of `sum_and_count`.

The definition makes fairly minimal assumptions about what a `point` is. All it assumes is the following:

- `point()` constructs an identity element for point addition.
- $q+=p$ sets point q to the sum of points q and p.
- p/n returns a point q such that if n copies of q are added together the sum is p.

The last method, `operator+=`, is not necessary for a sequential k-means algorithm. It is there so the parallel implementation can merge the information in two `sum_and_count` objects.

11.2.1 Hyperobjects

The code uses two hyperobjects:

- `change` counts changes in cluster assignments.
- `sum` accumulates the sum points in each cluster.

```
1  void compute_k_means( size_t n, const point points[], size_t k, cluster_id id[],
       point centroid[] ) {
2
3      // Create initial clusters and compute their sums
4      elementwise_reducer<sum_and_count> sum(k);
5      sum.clear();
6      cilk_for( size_t i=0; i<n; ++i ) {
7          id[i] = i % k;
8          // Peeled "Sum step"
9          sum[id[i]].tally(points[i]);
10     }
11
12     // Loop until clusters do not change
13     cilk::reducer_opadd<size_t> change;
14     do {
15         // Repair any empty clusters
16         repair_empty_clusters( n, points, id, k, centroid, sum );
17
18         // "Divide step": Compute centroids from sums
19         centroid[0:k] = sum.get_array()[0:k].mean();
20
21         sum.clear();
22         change.set_value(0);
23         cilk_for( size_t i=0; i<n; ++i ) {
24             // "Reassign step": Find index of centroid closest to points [i]
25             cluster_id j = __sec_reduce_min_ind(distance2(centroid[0:k],points[i]));
26             if( j!=id[i] ) {
27                 // A different centroid is closer now.
28                 id[i] = j;
29                 ++change;
30             }
31             // "Sum step"
32             sum[j].tally(points[i]);
33         }
34     } while( change.get_value()!=0 );
35 }
```

LISTING 11.1

K-means clustering in Cilk Plus.

Both `change` and `sum` must be hyperobjects because they are updated by concurrent iterations of the `cilk_for` loop. Object `change` is an instance of the Cilk Plus template class `reducer_opadd` defined in `<cilk/reducer_opadd.h>` and performs the obvious addition reduction.

The other hyperobject `sum` requires more work to implement, because it requires a twist slightly beyond the capabilities of the predefined hyperobjects. If *k* were a compile-time constant, then

```
1   struct sum_and_count {
2       sum_and_count() : sum(), count(0) {}
3       point sum;
4       size_t count;
5       void clear() {
6           sum = point();
7           count = 0;
8       }
9       void tally( const point& p ) {
10          sum += p;
11          ++count;
12      }
13      point mean() const {
14          return sum/count;
15      }
16      void operator+=( const sum_and_count& other ) {
17          sum += other.sum;
18          count += other.count;
19      }
20  };
```

LISTING 11.2

Type sum_and_count for computing mean of points in a cluster.

reducer_opadd could be used. We could define a fixed-length vector type, sum_and_count_vec, to hold an array of k sum_and_count objects, and define operator+= on it to do elementwise operator+=. Then variable sum could be declared as a reducer_opdd<sum_and_count_vec> and the program would work.

But k is a runtime value. The construction of the reducer needs to remember k and use it when constructing thread-local views. The solution is to instantiate the predefined template cilk::reducer with a **monoid** that remembers k. Listing 11.3 shows a complete implementation.

There are three parts to the reducer:

- A View that implements a view of the hyperobject
- A Monoid that defines operations views
- An elementwise_reducer wrapper around the mechanics that provides a nice public interface

Class View has an array of k sum_and_count objects. It has responsibility for construction and destruction of the array. Because k is the same for all views, the code makes it part of the Monoid, not the View.

Class Monoid defines operations on views. Its base class defines defaults for the signatures that cilk::reducer expects of a monoid. For example, the Monoid uses the defaults for allocating/deallocating memory for a view and destroying a view. The Monoid overrides the default for constructing

```
1   template<typename T>
2   class elementwise_reducer {
3       struct View {
4           T* array;
5           View( size_t k ) : array( new T[k] ) {}
6           ~View() {delete[] array;}
7       };
8
9       struct Monoid: cilk::monoid_base<View> {
10          const size_t k;
11          void identity(View* p) const {new(p) View(k);}
12          void reduce(View* left, View* right) const {
13              left->array[0:k] += right->array[0:k];
14          }
15          Monoid( size_t k_ ) : k(k_) {}
16      };
17      cilk::reducer<Monoid> impl;
18  public:
19      elementwise_reducer( size_t k ) : impl(Monoid(k), k) {}
20      void clear() {impl.view().array[0:impl.monoid().k].clear();}
21      T* get_array() {return impl.view().array;}
22      operator sum_and_count*() {return get_array();}
23  };
```

LISTING 11.3

Defining a hyperobject for summing an array elementwise in Cilk Plus. The names of each `struct` can be changed. The names of methods `identity` and `reduce` must not be changed, because they are used internally by `cilk::reducer<Monoid>`.

a view initialized to an identity value, because it needs to pass k to the view constructor. The `Monoid` also specifies how to reduce two views. As `cilk::reducer` requires, our method puts the reduction into the left view. Note that k comes from the monoid, not the view. The array notation there provides brevity.

Class `elementwise_reducer` has the actual reducer, as member `elementwise_reducer::impl`. The public methods provide a nice public interface. For example, method `clear`, which applies method `clear()` elementwise to each element in the view, hides the use of the two key methods on `impl`:

- `view()` returns a reference to the current view.
- `monoid()` returns a reference to the monoid.

The constructor for `impl` takes two arguments. The first is the `Monoid`. The second is the argument with which to construct the leftmost view. In the example, this argument is k, so that the reducer will construct the leftmost view as `View(k)`.

11.3 K-MEANS WITH TBB

The k-means algorithm has the same basic structure in TBB as it does in Cilk Plus. The primary differences are:

- The array notation statements are written out as serial loops. Since the array notation was used for brevity, not for vectorization, the loss is only of notational convenience, not performance.
- The hyperobjects are replaced by thread-local storage. Merging of local views into a global view is done with an explicit loop.
- **Tiling** of iterations in the parallel loops is explicit, so that thread-local lookup can be done once per tile.

Listing 11.4 shows the declarations for a type `tls_type` that will hold thread-local views of the `sum_and_count` from Listing 11.2 (page 283). The thread-local storage is implemented using an instance of template `tbb::enumerable_thread_specific`, which implements a collection of thread-local views. The expression `tls.local()` returns the thread-local view for the calling thread. If such a view does not yet exist, the method creates one.

The way a new view is created depends upon how the `enumerable_thread_specific` was constructed. There are three ways, as shown in the following fragment:

```
enumerable_thread_specific<T> a;
enumerable_thread_specific<T> b(x);  // x assumed to have type T
enumerable_thread_specific<T> c(f);  // f assumed to be a functor
```

Local views for `a` will be default-constructed. Local views for `b` will be copy-constructed from exemplar `x`, which must be of type `T`. Local views for `c` will be constructed using `T(f())`.

Our example uses the last way, where `T` is a `view`. The constructor for `view` expects `k` as an argument. In the final code, `k` is a local variable in the surrounding context. So the code will use a lambda expression as `f` when declaring an instance of `tls_type`, like this:

```
tls_type tls([&]{return k;});
```

```
1   class view {
2     view( const view& v );           // Deny copy construction
3     void operator=( const view& v );  // Deny assignment
4   public:
5     sum_and_count* array;
6     size_t change;
7     view( size_t k ) : array(new sum_and_count[k]), change(0) {}
8     ~view() {delete[] array;}
9   };
10
11  typedef tbb::enumerable_thread_specific<view> tls_type;
```

LISTING 11.4

Declaring a type `tls_type` for thread-local views in TBB.

A thread can access all of the views by using STL conventions, because a `enumerable_thread_specific` acts like a STL container of views.

For example, Listing 11.5 accumulates the sum of `change` in all views into a global view and resets the local values. Our k-means example will rely on that code and the similar code in Listing 11.6 that accumulates sums of points. For compilers not supporting C++11 `auto` declarations (Section D.1), replace the `auto` with `tls_type:iterator`.

Using thread local storage for reductions has two limitations compared to the Cilk Plus reducers:

- The reduction operation must be **commutative** as well as **associative**. Reducer hyperobjects merely require associativity.
- Using a serial loop for reducing the local views can become a scalability bottleneck, since its span is inherently $\Omega(P)$.

The latter limitation can be addressed by using TBB's `parallel_reduce` template to reduce the local views if the span becomes an issue. For our example, it is not worth the trouble as long as there are many more points than hardware threads, because then the reduction of local views is a small contributor to the total running time.

```
1  void reduce_local_counts_to_global_count( tls_type& tls, view& global ) {
2      global.change = 0;
3      for( auto i=tls.begin(); i!=tls.end(); ++i ) {
4          view& v = *i;
5          global.change += v.change;
6          v.change = 0;
7      }
8  }
```

LISTING 11.5

Walking local views to detect changes. The variable tls is a `tbb::enumerable_thread_specific<view>`, by way of the `typedef` in Listing 11.4.

```
1  void reduce_local_sums_to_global_sum( size_t k, tls_type& tls, view& global ) {
2      for( auto i=tls.begin(); i!=tls.end(); ++i ) {
3          view& v = *i;
4          for( size_t j=0; j<k; ++j ) {
5              global.array[j] += v.array[j];
6              v.array[j].clear();
7          }
8      }
9  }
```

LISTING 11.6

Walking local views to accumulate a global sum. Each local view is cleared in preparation for the next iteration of the k-means algorithm.

Another feature of TBB used in the example that deserves comment is the explicitly tiled form of `tbb::parallel_for`. The following pattern will be used to iterate over all *n* points in parallel:

```
tbb::parallel_for(
    blocked_range<size_t>(0,n),
    [...]( tbb::blocked_range<size_t> r ) {
        view& v = tls.local();
        for( size_t i=r.begin(); i!=r.end(); ++i ) {
            ...process point i...
        }
    }
);
```

The first argument to `parallel_for` specifies a range over which to iterate. The `parallel_for` splits that range into subranges and applies the functor argument to each subrange. In the pattern, the functor looks up its thread-local view and then processes each point in the subrange. The loop could be written more concisely as:

```
tbb::parallel_for( 0, n,
    [...]( size_t i ) {
        view& v = tls.local();
        ...process point i...
    }
);
```

but at the cost of executing `tls.local()` for each point. The explicitly tiled form of `parallel_for` should be used when there is a profitable opportunity to optimize the inner loop.

TBB does not have reduction operators like `__sec_reduce_min_ind` in Cilk Plus, so the code will use the auxiliary routine `reduce_min_ind` in Listing 11.7. Given that and the previous discussion, the rest of k-means is straightforward to write. Listing 11.8 shows the TBB code.

```
1   int reduce_min_ind( const point centroid[], size_t k, point value ) {
2       int min = −1;
3       float mind = std::numeric_limits<float>::max();
4       for( int j=0; j<k; ++j ) {
5           float d = distance2(centroid[j],value);
6           if( d<mind ) {
7               mind = d;
8               min = j;
9           }
10      }
11      return min;
12  }
```

LISTING 11.7

Routine for finding index of centroid closest to a given point. This routine is a serial equivalent of the `__sec_reduce_min_ind` expression on line 25 in Listing 11.1.

```
1   void compute_k_means( size_t n, const point points[], size_t k, cluster_id id[],
        point centroid[] ) {
2
3       tls_type tls([&]{return k;});
4       view global(k);
5
6       // Create initial clusters and compute their sums
7       tbb::parallel_for(
8           tbb::blocked_range<size_t>(0,n),
9           [=,&tls,&global]( tbb::blocked_range<size_t> r ) {
10              view& v = tls.local();
11              for( size_t i=r.begin(); i!=r.end(); ++i ) {
12                  id[i] = i % k;
13                  // Peeled "Sum step"
14                  v.array[id[i]].tally(points[i]);
15              }
16          }
17      );
18
19      // Loop until ids do not change
20      size_t change;
21      do {
22          // Reduce local sums to global sum
23          reduce_local_sums_to_global_sum( k, tls, global );
24
25          // Repair any empty clusters
26          repair_empty_clusters( n, points, id, k, centroid, global.array );
27
28          // "Divide step": Compute centroids from global sums
29          for( size_t j=0; j<k; ++j ) {
30              centroid[j] = global.array[j].mean();
31              global.array[j].clear();
32          }
33
34          // Compute new clusters and their local sums
35          tbb::parallel_for(
36              tbb::blocked_range<size_t>(0,n),
37              [=,&tls,&global]( tbb::blocked_range<size_t> r ) {
38                  view& v = tls.local();
39                  for( size_t i=r.begin(); i!=r.end(); ++i ) {
40                      // "Reassign step": Find index of centroid closest to points [i]
41                      cluster_id j = reduce_min_ind(centroid, k , points[i]);
42                      if( j!=id[i] ) {
43                          id[i] = j;
44                          ++v.change;
45                      }
46                      // "Sum step"
```

```
47                          v.array[j].tally(points[i]);
48                       }
49                    }
50              );
51
52              // Reduce local counts to global count
53              reduce_local_counts_to_global_count( tls, global );
54         } while( global.change!=0 );
55    }
```

LISTING 11.8

K-Means clustering in TBB.

11.4 SUMMARY

The k-means algorithm is a serial loop that iterates two fundamentally parallel steps: computing centroids and reassigning points, until it converges. By peeling part of the first iteration, the two parallel steps can become a single parallel sweep: map fused with reduction. The reduction type is somewhat heavy in the sense that it is bigger and takes more time to copy than a scalar type. The Cilk Plus implementation shows how to define custom reducer hyperobjects for performing reductions when a suitable built-in reducer is not available. The TBB implementation uses thread-local storage for the reduction, which works when the reduction operation is both commutative and associative.

Bzip2 Data Compression

Bzip2 is a popular file compression program. We show it as a practical application of the **pipeline** pattern. The pattern is more than a classic pipeline because for the sake of scalability some stages process multiple items simultaneously. The TBB implementation shows `parallel_pipeline` in action. The Cilk Plus implementation demonstrates how creative use of **reducers** can go far beyond implementing mathematically pure **reductions**. Another point of the example is that, when designing file formats, you should consider their impact on parallel processing.

12.1 THE BZIP2 ALGORITHM

Bzip2 chops its input stream into blocks, compresses each block separately, and writes the blocks to an output stream. Two features of the output stream affect parallelization considerations:

- Each output block starts on the bit (not byte!) immediately following the previous block.
- A cyclic redundancy check (CRC) code is written after all blocks are written.

The overall steps of the algorithm are:

```
while( not at end of the input stream ) {
    Read a block from the input stream
    Compress the block
    Update CRC
    Realign the block on a bit boundary
    Write the block to the output stream
}
Output final CRC
```

In practice, the realignment and writing can be optimized by fusing them into a single operation that realigns and writes a block, instead of realigning the entire block before writing any of it. Better yet, to reduce the memory footprint of these two fused steps, the block can be treated as a sequence of chunks, and each chunk can be aligned/written separately.

Compression of a block involves the following operations:

1. Run-length encoding, which cheaply compresses long runs of the same character.
2. Burrows–Wheeler transform [BW94], which permutes the block in a way that tends to put similar substrings close to each other. The transform sorts all possible cyclic rotations of the block and, using the sorted order, outputs the *last* letter of each rotation. It also outputs the index of where

the original block occurs in the sorted list of rotations. The original block can be reconstructed from this information [BW94]. For an example of the forward transform, let the block be the string LOGHOG. The result of the sort is:

Index	Rotations	Sorted Rotations
0	LOGHOG	GHOGLO
1	OGHOGL	GLOGHO
2	GHOGLO	HOGLOG
3	HOGLOG	LOGHOG
4	OGLOGH	OGHOGL
5	GLOGHO	OGLOGH

The output of the transform is the last letter of each entry in the sorted list: OOGGLH, and the index 3, which is the index of LOGHOG in the sorted list. In practice, the block can be as long as 900 kilobytes, so the sort can take significant time.

3. Move-to-front coding [BSTW86], which transforms the block so similar substrings that are close to each other produce the same output symbol.
4. Another round of run-length encoding.
5. Huffman coding, which compresses the transformed block, which at this point tends to have high redundancy of some symbols.

In principle, the run-length encoding can be parallelized by parallel **scan**, the Burrows–Wheeler transform can use a parallel sort, and the Huffman transform is a parallelizable **map** pattern. However, the move-to-front transform is serial. Hence, it is more practical to exploit parallelism across blocks, not inside blocks.

Another consideration in favor of parallelizing across blocks is that reading and writing blocks contribute a significant portion of the work. Hence, for good speedup it is critical to do reading, compressing, and writing **concurrently**.

12.2 THREE-STAGE PIPELINE USING TBB

Figure 12.1 sketches a three-stage **pipeline** implementation that can be implemented using tbb:: parallel_pipline. The first and last stages are serial. They each process one block at a time. The tbb::parallel_pipline template guarantees that each serial stage processes items in the same order as the previous serial stage. The middle stage is parallel and does most of the compression work.

However, the initial run-length encoding is done in the serial stage. This is to maintain bitwise compatibility with serial bzip2. In serial bzip2, the blocksize is the maximum size of a block *after* the initial run-length encoding. So block boundaries are determined after run-length encoding. As remarked earlier, parallel scan could be used inside the first stage to parallelize the encoding, though given the low **arithmetic intensity** of run-length encoding it is unlikely to pay off anyway.

Bzip2 is a large application, so only a tiny fraction of the code is shown, specifically the fraction needed to understand how it was parallelized using tbb::parallel_pipeline. In the serial

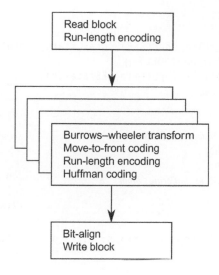

FIGURE 12.1

Three-stage pipeline for bzip2.

version of bzip2, a data structure of type EState describes the current block being compressed. It has many fields. For our purposes here, only the fields related to the initial run-length encoding need to be understood.

```
struct EState {
    ...
    UInt32 state_in_ch;   // Most recently read byte
    Int32  state_in_len;  // Current run-length of state_in_char
    ...
    Int32  nblock;        // Number of input bytes in block
    ...
};
```

In the serial version, there is a single instance of EState. The parallel version needs to be reading the next block, and compressing multiple blocks in parallel, so the parallel version needs one instance of EState per block in flight. However, the two fields shown carry information between blocks. One solution would be to move them to a different structure associated with only the input stage. However, for the sake of minimizing changes to the serial code, a slightly different approach is employed. After the initial pipeline stage reads a block, it remembers the two field values from the current EState, and uses those values to initialize the EState instance for the next block.

Listing 12.1 declares the state for the input stage and the routine that gets a block.

The output stage has some similar information-carrying issues.

- Accumulate the total volume written.
- Create a a CRC that is the combination of the CRC values of each block.
- Concatenate compressed blocks on bit boundaries. When writing a block, any bits beyond the most recent byte written must be included in the first byte written for the subsequence block.

```
1   class InputState {
2   public:
3       InputState() : prev_state_char(256), prev_state_len(0), nbytes_in(0),
            buf_ptr(NULL), buf_end(NULL) {}
4       EState* getOneBlock(FILE* inputFile, EState* s);
5       // Volume of uncompressed data
6       off_t nbytes_in;
7   private:
8       // Values carried between instances of EState
9       UInt32 prev_state_char;
10      Int32 prev_state_len;
11      // Field and routine related to buffering input
12      UChar *buf_ptr;
13      UChar *buf_end;
14      UChar buf[8192];
15      void copy_input_until_stop( EState* s, FILE* infile );
16  };
17
18  void InputState::getOneBlock(FILE* inputFile, EState* s) {
19      // Carry information from previous EState
20      s->state_in_ch = prev_state_char;
21      s->state_in_len = prev_state_len;
22
23      copy_input_until_stop( s, inputFile );
24
25      // Remember information to be carried to next EState
26      prev_state_char = s->state_in_ch;
27      prev_state_len = s->state_in_len;
28
29      // Accumulate total input volume
30      nbytes_in += s->nblock;
31  }
```

LISTING 12.1

Declarations for bzip2 pipeline.

This state is declared in a class `OutputState`. For brevity, a listing is not provided here, but it is analogous to the way `InputState` was done.

The middle compression stage carries no information between blocks, so it needs no corresponding state object. It just calls a function on the the `EState` object passing through the stage.

Now the TBB syntactic mechanics for building and running the pipeline can be detailed. The routine `tbb::parallel_pipeline` takes two parameters:

- A token limit, which is an upper bound on the number of items that are processed simultaneously. Without this limit, a traffic jam behind a serial stage could pile up forever, eventually exhausting memory. Here, a limit equal to the number of hardware threads is reasonable.

- A pipeline constructed by composing `filter_t` objects together with &. Each object is created by function `tbb::make_filter`.

Listing 12.2 shows the key parts of the code. The template arguments to `make_filter` indicate the type of input and output items for the filter. The ordinary arguments specify whether the `filter_t` is parallel or not and specify a functor that maps an input item to an output item. For example, the middle stage is parallel and maps a `EState*` to an `EState*` using `CompressOneBlock`. The last stage has an output type of `void` since it is consuming items, not mapping them.

The functor in the first stage is a special case since it is producing items, not mapping items to items. The argument to it is not an item, but a special object of type `tbb::flow_control` used to

```
1   int BZ2_compressFile(FILE *stream, FILE *zStream, int
        blockSize100k, int verbosity, int workFactor) throw() {
2       ...
3       InputState in_state;
4       OutputState out_state( zStream );
5       tbb::parallel_pipeline(
6           ntoken,
7           tbb::make_filter<void,EState*>( tbb::filter::
                serial_in_order, [&]( tbb::flow_control& fc ) -> EState* {
8               if( !eof(stream) || ferror(stream) ) {
9                   fc.stop();
10                  return NULL;
11              }
12              EState *s = BZ2_bzCompressInit(blockSize100k, verbosity, workFactor);
13              in_state.getOneBlock(stream,s);
14              return s;
15          } ) &
16          tbb::make_filter<EState*,EState*>( tbb::filter::
                parallel, []( EState*s ) -> EState* {
17              if( s->nblock )
18                  CompressOneBlock(s);
19              return s;
20          } ) &
21          tbb::make_filter<EState*,void>( tbb::filter::
                serial_in_order, [&]( EState* s ) {
22              if( s->nblock )
23                  out_state.putOneBlock(s);
24              FreeEState(s);
25          } )
26      );
27      ...
28  }
```

LISTING 12.2

Use of TBB `parallel_pipeline` to coordinate bzip2 actions.

signal the end of input. Invocation of method `stop()` on it tells `parallel_pipeline` that no more items will be produced and that the value returned from the functor should be ignored.

12.3 FOUR-STAGE PIPELINE USING TBB

Breaking the last stage into two stages, one serial and one parallel, can enable more parallelism. At the time of this writing, it is not worth the trouble because the output device is typically a disk that works best when accessed serially; otherwise, time is wasted bouncing the disk head around. However, future storage technologies such as solid-state disk might make the following scheme practical.

The scheme is to separate determining where to write an output block from the actual writing. The "where" part is serial, because it relies on knowing how big the previous blocks are. But the actual writing of an output blocks can be done in parallel, and physically in parallel on some output devices. The scheme replaces the last stage of Figure 12.1 with the two stages shown in Figure 12.2. The top stage is serial and does the operations that involve carrying information between blocks. The bottom stage is parallel and does the realignment and writing.

12.4 THREE-STAGE PIPELINE USING CILK PLUS

As explained in Section 9.4.2, Cilk Plus does not support the general pipeline pattern but can synthesize a serial–parallel–serial pipeline via a **consumer reducer**. Listing 12.3 shows the instance of this approach for bzip2 using the same `InputState` and `OutputState` classes as for the TBB implementation. The organization of routines mimics Listing 9.3 on page 259.

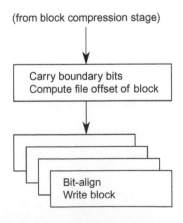

FIGURE 12.2

Possible replacement for last stage of Figure 12.1 that permits parallel writing.

```
1   void SecondStage( EState* s, reducer_consume<OutputState, EState*>& sink ) {
2       if( s->nblock )
3           CompressOneBlock(s);
4       sink.consume( s );
5   }
6
7   void ThirdStage( OutputState* out_state, EState* s ) {
8       if( s->nblock )
9           out_state->putOneBlock(s);
10      FreeEState(s);
11  }
12
13  int BZ2_compressFile(FILE *stream, FILE *zStream, int
        blockSize100k, int verbosity, int workFactor) throw()
        {
14      ...
15      InputState in_state;
16      OutputState out_state( zStream );
17      reducer_consume<OutputState,EState*> sink(&out_state, ThirdStage);
18      while( !feof(stream) && !ferror(stream) ) {
19          EState *s = BZ2_bzCompressInit(blockSize100k, verbosity, workFactor);
20          in_state.getOneBlock(stream,s);
21          cilk_spawn SecondStage(s, sink);
22      };
23      cilk_sync;
24      ...
25  }
```

LISTING 12.3

Sketch of bzip2 pipeline in Cilk Plus using a consumer reducer. The code uses the `reducer_consume` template from Listing 9.4.

12.5 SUMMARY

The bzip2 program partitions a file into blocks and compresses each one separately. Initial and final processing of each block is sequential. Hence, it is well suited to a serial–parallel–serial pipeline structure. The TBB template `parallel_pipeline` directly supports such a pipeline. Cilk Plus has no direct support for pipelines, but the application can be parallelized nonetheless by spawning tasks and assembling the output in order with a consumer reducer.

Merge Sort

In a **divide-and-conquer** algorithm, either the divide or merge step can sometimes become a bottleneck if done serially. Parallel merge sort demonstrates a case where the merge step can be parallelized to avoid a bottleneck by using divide-and-conquer. The net effect is a divide-and-conquer algorithm running inside a divide-and-conquer algorithm. This illustrates the practical importance of having a parallel framework that supports efficient **nested** parallelism.

Serial merge sort has two desirable properties:

- It is stable (that is, the order of equal elements is not changed).
- It has guaranteed asymptotic running time $O(N \lg N)$.

Weighing against these desirable properties is the disadvantage that merge sort is an out-of-place sort, and thus has a bigger memory and cache footprint than in-place sort algorithms. Conversely, Quicksort is an in-place sort, but lacks the other two properties. In particular, though Quicksort's expected time is $O(N \lg N)$, its worst-case time is $O(N^2)$.

Serial merge sort is a divide-and-conquer algorithm where the basic recursive steps are:

1. Divide the sequence into two subsequences.
2. Sort each subsequence.
3. Merge the sorted subsequences.

The merge step has work $\Theta(N)$ to merge N items. If done serially, it can become a bottleneck just as serial partitioning can for Quicksort (Section 8.9.3). Indeed, there is a symmetry to their respective bottlenecks. In Quicksort, a serial divide took time $O(N)$. In merge sort, a serial merge takes time $O(N)$. The effect on the complexity analysis recurrence relations is similar, with similar consequences: The asymptotic speedup for sorting N items is $O(\lg N)$. Though efficient for small core counts and big sequences, it is not **scalable**.

13.1 PARALLEL MERGE

Improving the speedup requires parallelizing the merge step. How to do so is a good lesson in why it is sometimes better to seek a new algorithm than parallelize the obvious serial algorithm. To see this, consider two sorted sequences X and Y that must be merged. The usual serial algorithm inspects the head items of the two sequences and moves the smaller head item to the output sequence. It repeats this incremental inspection until either X or Y becomes empty. Any remaining items are appended to the output. Listing 13.1 shows the code, where X and Y are represented by the half-open intervals [xs,xe) and [ys,ye), respectively.

```
1  void serial_merge( T* xs, T* xe, T* ys, T* ye, T* zs ) {
2     while( xs!=xe && ys!=ye ) {
3        bool which = *ys < *xs;
4        *zs++ = std::move(which ? *ys++ : *xs++);
5     }
6     std::move( xs, xe, zs );
7     std::move( ys, ye, zs );
8  }
```

LISTING 13.1

Serial merge. Appendix D.3 explains the meaning of `std::move`.

A subtle point worth attention is the test in the inner loop. If a key in X and a key in Y are equal, the key in X comes first in the output. This rule for breaking ties ensures that if `serial_merge` is used for a merge sort then the sort is stable.

Trying to parallelize `serial_merge` directly is hopeless. The algorithm is inherently serial, because each iteration of the `while` loop depends upon the previous iteration. However, there is a remarkably simple **divide-and-conquer** alternative to the usual serial algorithm. Without loss of generality, assume that sequence X is at least as long as sequence Y. The sequences can be merged recursively as follows:

1. Split X into two contiguous subsequences X_1 and X_2 of approximately equal length. Let K be the first key of X_2.
2. Use binary search on Y to find the point where K could be inserted into Y. Split Y at that point into two subsequences Y_1 and Y_2.
3. Recursively merge X_1 and Y_1 to form the first part of the output sequence. Recursively merge X_2 and Y_2 to form the second part of the output sequence.

The two sub-merges are independent and thus can be done in parallel. Listing 13.2 shows a Cilk Plus implementation, using the same argument convention as for `serial_merge`. For clarity, the code has been written using full recursion. It is a straightforward exercise to turn it into semi-iterative form as in Quicksort (Listing 8.11 on page 234).

A point sometimes overlooked in implementing parallel merge is retaining the stability condition so that if keys in X and Y are equal then X comes first in the output sequence. Doing so requires a slight asymmetry in the binary search:

- If splitting Y at element $*ym$, then elements of X equal to $*ym$ go in X_1.
- If splitting X at element $*xm$, then elements of Y equal to $*xm$ go in Y_2.

The distinction between `std::upper_bound` and `std::lower_bound` achieves this asymmetry.

Let N be the total length of the two sequences being merged. The recursion depth never exceeds about $2\lg(N/\text{MERGE\_CUT\_OFF})$. The qualification "about" is there because when the sequences do not divide evenly at every level of recursion the depth may be one deeper. The depth limit follows from the observation that each two consecutive levels of recursion cut the problem size about in half or better. Here is a sketch of the proof.

```
1  void parallel_merge( T* xs, T* xe, T* ys, T* ye, T* zs ) {
2      const size_t MERGE_CUT_OFF = 2000;
3      if( xe−xs + ye−ys <= MERGE_CUT_OFF ) {
4          serial_merge(xs,xe,ys,ye,zs);
5      } else {
6          T *xm, *ym;
7          if( xe−xs < ye−ys ) {
8              ym = ys+(ye−ys)/2;
9              xm = std::upper_bound(xs,xe,*ym);
10         } else {
11             xm = xs+(xe−xs)/2;
12             ym = std::lower_bound(ys,ye,*xm);
13         }
14         T* zm = zs + (xm−xs) + (ym−ys);
15         cilk_spawn parallel_merge( xs, xm, ys, ym, zs );
16         /* nospawn */ parallel_merge( xm, xe, ym, ye, zm );
17         // Implicit cilk_sync
18     }
19 }
```

LISTING 13.2

Parallel merge in Cilk Plus.

Let N be the size of the initial problem and N' be the size of the biggest subproblem after two levels of recursion. For simplicity of exposition, only cases where sequences split evenly are considered. The point is to prove $N' \le N/2$.

Let $|X|$ and $|Y|$ denote the length of X and Y, respectively. Without loss of generality, assume $|X| \ge |Y|$. There are two cases:

- The first level of recursion splits X and the second level splits Y. Both sequences have been halved, so $N' = N/2$.
- Both levels split X. This can only happen when $|X| \ge 2|Y|$. Since $|X| + |Y| = N$, we know $|Y| \le N/3$. Therefore, $N' = |X|/4 + |Y| = (N - |Y|)/4 + |Y| = N/4 + (3/4)|Y| \le N/4 + (3/4)(N/3) = N/2$.

13.1.1 TBB Parallel Merge

The parallel merge code can be translated to Intel TBB by implementing the parallel **fork–join** with tbb::parallel_invoke and **lambda expressions** instead of cilk_spawn. Listing 13.3 shows the rewritten lines.

13.1.2 Work and Span of Parallel Merge

The work and span for parallel_merge cannot be found using the recurrence solutions given in Section 8.6, because the recurrences have the wrong form. Instead, other methods have to be used. The

```
1  tbb::parallel_invoke(
2     [=]{parallel_merge( xs, xm, ys, ym, zs );},
3     [=]{parallel_merge( xm, xe, ym, ye, zm );} );
```

LISTING 13.3

Converting parallel merge from Cilk Plus to TBB. The lines shown are the equivalent of the `cilk_spawn`/`cilk_sync` portion of Listing 13.2.

span is analyzed first because it is simpler. In the worst case each two levels of recursion halve the problem size. Each level performs a binary search, so there are two binary searches per halving of the problem size. Hence, the span for `parallel_merge` has the recurrence:

$$T_\infty(N) = 2\Theta(\lg N) + T_\infty(N/2).$$

The 2 before the Θ can be immediately eliminated since it is mathematically swallowed by the Θ. Expanding the remaining recurrence and factoring the Θ yields:

$$T_\infty(N) = \Theta[\lg(N) + \lg(N/2) + \lg(N/4) + \lg(N/3) + \cdots + 1],$$

which is equivalent to:

$$T_\infty(N) = \Theta[(\lg N) + (\lg N) - 1 + (\lg N) - 2 + (\lg N) - 3 + \cdots + 1].$$

The right side is a decreasing arithmetic series starting at $\lg N$ and hence has the quadratic sum $\Theta((\lg N)^2)$.

The recurrence for work is:

$$T_1(N) = \Theta(\lg N) + 2T_1(N/2),$$

which after expanding the recurrence and factoring the Θ becomes:

$$T_1(N) = \Theta[\lg N + 2\lg(N/2) + 4\lg(N/4) + 8\lg(N/8) + \cdots].$$

Substitute $K = \lg N$ to get:

$$T_1(N) = \Theta[K + 2(K - 1) + 4(K - 2) + 8(K - 3) + \cdots + 2^{K-1}(1)].$$

A visual trick to solving this series is to note that the terms are the column sums of the following $K \times K$ triangular matrix:

$$
\begin{matrix}
1 & & & & & \\
1 & 2 & & & & \\
1 & 2 & 4 & & & \\
1 & 2 & 4 & 8 & & \\
\vdots & \vdots & \vdots & \vdots & \ddots & \\
1 & 2 & 4 & 8 & \cdots & 2^{K-1}
\end{matrix}
$$

Each row is a geometric series. The sum of the ith row is $2^i - 1$. Summing all K rows is $2^{K+1} - 2 - k$. Thus $T_1(N) = \Theta(2^K) = \Theta(N)$.

Remarkably, both serial and parallel merging have the same asymptotic work! An intuition for this is that the binary search time $\Theta(\lg N)$ is dominated by the $\Omega(N)$ time required to touch each element in the sub-merges, and hence makes no additional contribution to the asymptotic work. However, the constant factors hiding behind Θ deserve some attention. If base case is as small as possible (that is, MERGE_CUT_OFF$= 1$), then parallel_merge requires about 50% more comparisons than serial_merge. The 50% tax, however, rapidly diminishes if MERGE_CUT_OFF is raised. Raising the latter to 16 reduces the tax to about 6%. In practice, MERGE_CUT_OFF needs to be higher anyway to amortize parallel scheduling overheads, and then the tax practically disappears. Indeed, a more significant concern becomes the less cache-friendly behavior of the search-based merging compared to serial merging, but this too is amortized away by a sufficiently large MERGE_CUT_OFF.

To summarize, the work and span for parallel merge are:

$$T_1(N) = \Theta(N), \tag{13.1}$$

$$T_\infty(N) = \Theta(\lg^2 N), \tag{13.2}$$

which indicates a theoretical speedup of $\Theta\left(\frac{N}{\lg^2 N}\right)$, assuming that memory bandwidth is not a bottleneck.

13.2 PARALLEL MERGE SORT

Turning the sketch (at the chapter opening) of parallel merge sort into code is straightforward. However, merge sort is not an in-place sort because the merge step cannot easily be done in place. Temporary storage is needed. Furthermore, to minimize copying, the merge steps should alternate between merging from the original buffer into the temporary buffer and vice versa. One way to do this is to define parallel merge sort with a flag argument inplace that controls the destination of the sorted sequence:

- If inplace is true, the destination is the original input buffer.
- Otherwise, the destination is the temporary buffer.

In both cases, the non-destination buffer is used as scratch space.

Listing 13.4 shows a Cilk implementation. It sorts a sequence defined by the half-open interval [xs,xe). Argument zs should point to a buffer of length xe−xs.

The parallel base case uses a stable sort in order to preserve stability of the overall sort. The flag inplace flipflops at each recursion level. When sorting in place, the subsorts copy into the temporary buffer, and the parallel_merge operation copies the items back into the original buffer. When not sorting in place, the subsorts are done in place, and the parallel_merge copies the items into the destination buffer.

A TBB implementation is similar, except that the fork–join is implemented with parallel_invoke instead of the Cilk keywords, similar as discussed for the TBB implementation of parallel_merge (Section 13.1).

```
1   void parallel_merge_sort( T* xs, T* xe, T* zs, bool inplace ) {
2       const size_t SORT_CUT_OFF = 500;
3       if( xe-xs<=SORT_CUT_OFF ) {
4           std::stable_sort( xs, xe );
5           if( !inplace )
6               std::move( xs, xe, zs );
7       } else {
8           T* xm = xs + (xe-xs)/2;
9           T* zm = zs + (xm-xs);
10          T* ze = zs + (xe-xs);
11          cilk_spawn parallel_merge_sort( xs, xm, zs, !inplace );
12          /* nospawn */ parallel_merge_sort( xm, xe, zm, !inplace );
13          cilk_sync;
14          if( inplace )
15              parallel_merge( zs, zm, zm, ze, xs );
16          else
17              parallel_merge( xs, xm, xm, xe, zs );
18      }
19  }
```

LISTING 13.4

Parallel merge sort in Cilk Plus.

13.2.1 Work and Span of Merge Sort

Let N be the length of the input sequence. The recurrences for work and span are:

$$T_1(N) = \Theta(N) + 2T_1(N/2),$$
$$T_\infty(N) = \Theta(\lg^2 N) + T_\infty(N/2).$$

The recurrence for T_1 is case 2 of the Master method (see Section 8.6) and has the closed form solution $T_1(N) = \Theta(N \lg N)$. This is the same as for a serial merge sort, which is not surprising since the constituent components of parallel_merge_sort have the same asymptotic work bounds as their counterparts in the serial algorithm. The solution T_∞ can be found by observing that if $K = \lg N$, then the recurrence expands to the series:

$$K^2 + (K-1)^2 + (K-2)^2 + \cdots + 1,$$

which has a cubic sum. Hence, $T_\infty(N) = \Theta(\lg^3 N)$.

Thus, the asymptotic speedup for parallel_merge_sort is $\Theta\left(\frac{N \lg N}{\lg^3 N}\right) = \Theta\left(\frac{N}{\lg^2 N}\right)$. This suggests that, given about a million keys, on the order of a thousand processors might be used profitably if memory bandwidth does not become a constraint.

13.3 SUMMARY

Merge sort is a classic divide-and-conquer algorithm that lends itself to the parallel fork–join pattern and is easily written in Cilk or TBB. However, for good speedup, the merge step must also be parallelized, because otherwise it takes linear time. The merge step can be parallelized by divide-and-conquer, where the divide step generates two submerges that can be run in parallel.

Sample Sort

The sample sort example demonstrates a partitioning-based sort that overcomes the scaling limitation of Quicksort described in Section 8.9.3, which arose because Quicksort's partitioning operation is serial. Sample sort overcomes this deficiency by parallelizing partitioning. The key patterns in the example are **binning** and **packing** of data in parallel. Note that what we have defined as the **partition** pattern just provides a different view of data, whereas what is commonly meant in the description of sorting algorithms by "partitioning" actually reorganizes the data into **bins**. To avoid confusion we call this data reorganization operation "**binning**" in this chapter. This algorithm is also an interesting example of where a *serial* **scan** pays off as part of a practical parallel algorithm.

14.1 OVERALL STRUCTURE

Sample sort divides keys into m bins by building an $m \times m$ matrix of empty buckets and filling the buckets with the keys. Each column corresponds to a bin. Separate rows can be filled concurrently. Figure 14.1 shows the overall phases of the algorithm:

- **Bin:** Split the input into m chunks. Move the contents of each chunk to a separate row of the matrix, dividing it among the buckets in that row.
- **Repack:** Move the contents of each column of buckets back to a contiguous section of the original array.
- **Subsort:** Sort each section.

In the first phase, separate rows are processed in parallel. In the second phase, separate columns are processed in parallel. There is some serial work before or after. The top-level code is shown in Listing 14.1. A production-quality C++ version would be generalized as a template with iterator arguments and a generic comparator and include extra code to ensure exception safety. These generalizations are omitted for the sake of exposition to readers who are not C++ experts.

Furthermore, our analysis will assume that the constructor T() and destructor ~T() are trivial enough to generate no instructions, so that the construction and destruction of array y requires only $O(1)$ work. This is true of C-like types in C++ but generally not true if the constructor or destructor involves user-defined actions. In that case, the code shown has a $\Omega(N)$ bottleneck. Section 14.6 describes how a C++ expert can remove the bottleneck.

When the sequence is no longer than SAMPLE_SORT_CUT_OFF, the code calls Quicksort directly. The best value for SAMPLE_SORT_CUT_OFF will depend on the platform, though it should be at least big enough to subsume all cases where $m = 1$, since binning into a single bin is a waste of time and memory.

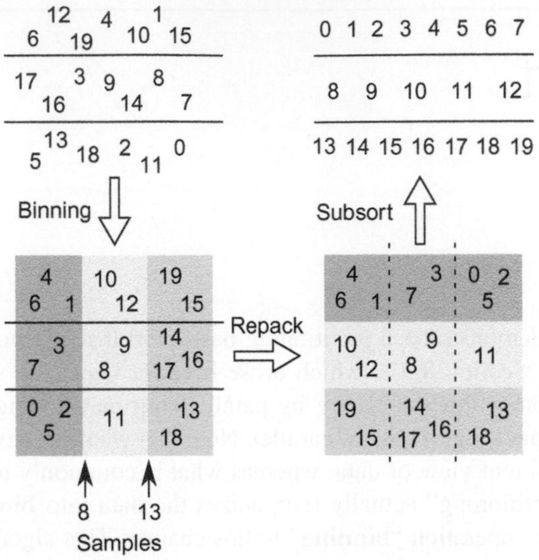

FIGURE 14.1

Sample sort example using a 3 × 3 matrix of buckets, where the samples for binning are 8 and 13. The keys are initially grouped into three rows of a matrix. The binning phase divides each row into buckets, one bucket for each subrange $[-\infty, 8)$, $[8, 13)$, and $[13, \infty)$. The repack phase copies the buckets in a way that transposes the matrix, so that buckets for identical subranges become contiguous in memory. The subsort phase sorts each row.

```
1   const size_t M_MAX = 32;
2
3   void parallel_sample_sort( T* xs, T* xe ) {
4       if( xe−xs<=SAMPLE_SORT_CUT_OFF ) {
5           parallel_quicksort(xs,xe);
6       } else {
7           size_t m = choose_number_of_bins(xe−xs);
8           size_t tally[M_MAX][M_MAX];
9           T* y = new T[xe−xs];
10          bin(xs, xe, m, y, tally);
11          repack_and_subsort(xs, xe, m, y, tally);
12          delete[] y;
13      }
14  }
```

LISTING 14.1

Top-level code for parallel sample sort. This code sequences the parallel phases and is independent of the parallel programming model.

14.2 CHOOSING THE NUMBER OF BINS

If the exact number of available hardware threads (workers) is known, then using one bin per worker is best. However, in work-stealing frameworks like Cilk or TBB, the number of *available* workers is unknown, since the sort might be called from a nested context. Instead, a strategy of **over-decomposition** is used. The number of bins will be chosen so that each bin is large enough to acceptably amortize per-bin overhead. Some of the logic in function bin requires that the number of bins be a power of two. The code is shown below:

```
size_t choose_number_of_bins( size_t n ) {
    const size_t BIN_CUTOFF = 1024;
    return std::min( M_MAX, size_t(1)<<floor_lg2(n/BIN_CUTOFF));
}
```

Function floor_lg2 is presumed to compute the function $k \rightarrow \lfloor \lg k \rfloor$—that is, the position of the most significant 1 in the binary numeral for k.

14.3 BINNING

The binning phase involves several steps:

1. Select sample keys to demarcate the bins.
2. Organize the samples so that a key can be mapped to its bin index quickly.
3. Compute the bin index of each key.
4. Compute the starting address of each bucket.
5. Scatter the keys into the buckets.

A poor choice of demarcation samples can lead to grossly unbalanced bins. Over-sampling improves the odds against bad choices. An over-sampling factor o is chosen and om keys are selected and sorted. Then m evenly spaced samples are extracted from the sorted sequence. A good way to choose o is to make it proportional to the logarithm of the number of keys [BLM+98].

Given a linear array of sorted samples, the bin index of a key can be computed by binary search. The code for the binary search can be tightened into branchless code by rearranging the array to be an implicit binary tree. The root of the tree is stored at index 0. The children of a node with index k are stored at indices $2k + 1$ and $2k + 2$. Listing 14.2 shows the technique.

The code uses an implicit binary tree tree with m-1 nodes to map n keys in x to their respective bin indices. For $i \in [0, n)$, the routine sets *bindex*[i] to the bin index of x[i]. Type bindex_type is an integral type big enough to hold an integer in the range $[0, m)$. The routine also generates a histogram tally of bin indexes, defined as tally[b], of the number of keys with bin index b. The histogram is the sizes of the buckets in a row of our conceptual matrix.

Now the binning routine can be built. The routine divides keys in the interval [xs,xe) among m bins, and copies the keys to buckets in y.

```
1   void map_keys_to_bins( const T x[], size_t n, const T tree[], size_t m,
        bindex_type bindex[], size_t freq[] ) {
2       size_t d = floor_lg2(m);
3       freq[0:m] = 0;
4       for( size_t i=0; i<n; ++i ) {
5           size_t k = 0;
6           for( size_t j=0; j<d; ++j )
7               k = 2*k+2 - (x[i] < tree[k]);
8           ++freq[bindex[i] = k-(m-1)];
9       }
10  }
```

LISTING 14.2

Code for mapping keys to bins.

The conceptual matrix of buckets is represented by y and tally. Each bucket of the matrix is stored in y, ordered left-to-right and top-to-bottom, with the elements within a bucket stored consecutively. Each row of tally is a running sum of bucket sizes; tally[i][j] is the sum of the sizes of buckets $0 \cdots j$ in row i.

This information suffices to reconstitute pointer bounds of a bucket. The beginning of the leftmost bucket for row i is y+i*block_size. The beginning of any other bucket is the end of the previous bucket. The end of bucket (i,j) is y+i*block_size+tally[i][j].

14.3.1 TBB Implementation

Listing 14.3 can be translated to TBB by replacing the cilk_for loop with a tbb::parallel_for and a **lambda expression**, so it looks like this:

```
tbb::parallel_for( size_t(0), m, [=,&tree](size_t i) {
    ...
});
```

The lambda captures all variables **by value**, except for array tree, which is captured **by reference**, to avoid the overhead of copying an array. A subtle C++ technicality is that, although tally is captured by value, its underlying array is *not* copied. This is because in C and C++, a formal parameter declared as an array is treated as a pointer to its zeroth element. Hence, the lambda expression copies only the address of the array, not the array itself.

14.4 REPACKING AND SUBSORTING

The final phase of sample sort has two subphases:

1. Compute where each bin should start in the original array.
2. Move the keys from buckets into their bins, and sort them.

```
1   void bin( T* xs, T* xe, size_t m, T* y, size_t tally[M_MAX]
        [M_MAX] ) {
2       T tree[M_MAX-1];
3       build_sample_tree( xs, xe, tree, m );
4
5       size_t block_size = ((xe-xs)+m-1)/m;
6       bindex_type* bindex = new bindex_type[xe-xs];
7       cilk_for( size_t i=0; i<m; ++i ) {
8           size_t js = i*block_size;
9           size_t je = std::min( js+block_size, size_t(xe-xs) );
10
11          // Map keys to bins
12          size_t freq[M_MAX];
13          map_keys_to_bins( xs+js, je-js, tree, m, bindex+js, freq );
14
15          // Compute where each bucket  starts
16          T* dst[M_MAX];
17          size_t s = 0;
18          for( size_t j=0; j<m; ++j ) {
19              dst[j] = y+js+s;
20              s += freq[j];
21              tally[i][j] – s;
22          }
23
24          // Scatter keys into their respective buckets
25          for( size_t j=js; j<je; ++j )
26              *dst[bindex[j]]++ = std::move(xs[j]);
27      }
28      delete[] bindex;
29  }
```

LISTING 14.3

Parallel binning of keys using Cilk Plus.

The first subphase is merely a matter of summing the columns of `tally`. Each row of `tally` is a running sum of bucket sizes, so the sum of the columns yields a running sum of bin sizes. Since the value of m is typically several orders of magnitude smaller than n, the quadratic time $O(m^2)$ for computing the sums is not a major concern. It is typically too small for effective fork–join parallelism. However, it does lend itself to vector parallelism, and the array notation to do so even simplifies the source code slightly.

The second subphase does most of the work. Each parallel iteration copies a column of buckets into a bin. The bucket boundaries are found via the formulae mentioned in the discussion of method `bin`.

Listing 14.4 shows a Cilk Plus routine implementation of both phases.

A TBB equivalent is a matter of replacing the `cilk_for` statement with `tbb::parallel_for`, similar to the the translation in Section 14.3.1.

```
1   void repack_and_subsort( T* xs, T* xe, size_t m, const T* y, const size_t
        tally[M_MAX][M_MAX] ) {
2       // Compute column sums of tally, forming the running sum of bin sizes
3       size_t col_sum[M_MAX];
4       col_sum[0:m] = 0;
5       for( size_t i=0; i<m; ++i )
6           col_sum[0:m] += tally[i][0:m];
7       assert( col_sum[m-1]==xe-xs );
8
9       // Copy buckets into their bins and do the subsorts
10      size_t block_size = ((xe-xs)+m-1)/m;
11      cilk_for( size_t j=0; j<m; ++j ) {
12          T* x_bin = xs + (j==0 ? 0 : col_sum[j-1]);
13          T* x = x_bin;
14          for( size_t i=0; i<m; ++i ) {
15              const T* src_row = y+i*block_size;
16              x = std::move( src_row+(j==0?0:tally[i][j-1]), src_row+tally[i][j],
                    x );
17          }
18          parallel_quicksort(x_bin,x);
19      }
20  }
```

LISTING 14.4

Repacking and subsorting using Cilk Plus. This is the final phase of sample sort.

14.5 PERFORMANCE ANALYSIS OF SAMPLE SORT

The asymptotic work for sample sort can be summarized as:

- $\Theta(mo \lg mo)$ work to sort the input samples, over-sampled by o, where o is $\Theta(\lg n)$.
- $\Theta(n \lg m)$ work to bin keys into buckets.
- $\Theta(m^2)$ work to compute bin sizes.
- $\Theta(n \lg(n/m))$ work to repack/subsort, assuming a subsort of k keys takes time $O(k \lg k)$.

Keeping m sufficiently small ensures that the work is dominated by the binning and repack/subsort phases, both of which scale linearly if $m = \Theta(p)$ and the $\log p$ startup time of a parallel map is insignificant.

In practice, memory bandwidth is likely to become the bottleneck. The communication between the binning and repack/subsort phases changes ownership of the bucket matrix from columns to rows. Hence, there are inherently $\Omega(n)$ memory transfers required.

There is one other potential hardware-related problem of which to be aware. If m comes close to the number of entries in the translation lookaside buffer, and each bucket is at least a page in size, then the scattering of keys among the m buckets during the binning phase may incur a severe penalty from TLB thrashing (Section 2.4.1, page 44).

```
1  template<typename T>
2  T* destructive_move( T* first, T* last, T* output ) {
3      size_t n = last-first;
4      []( T& in, T& out ){
5          out = std::move(in);
6          in.~T();
7      }( first[0:n], output[0:n] );
8      return output+n;
9  }
```

LISTING 14.5

Using Cilk Plus to move and destroy a sequence, without an explicit loop!

14.6 FOR C++ EXPERTS

As Section 14.1 remarked, our analysis assumes that new T[...] and delete[] take constant time. This is true if the constructor T() and destructor ~T() do nothing, as is the case for C-like types, but not always true for types with non-trivial constructors or destructors. To handle those efficiently requires rethinking the allocation/deallocation of y.

One solution is to construct the array elements in parallel and destroy them likewise. But doing so adds two more parallel phases, adding to synchronization costs and memory traffic. A faster approach is to allocate and deallocate array y as a raw memory buffer. The binning phase can copy–construct the elements into the buffer directly. The repack phase can destroy the copies as it moves them back to the original array.

A combination of array notation (Section B.8) and C++11 lambda expressions enables a concise way to write the routine that destroys the copies after moving them back to the original array, without writing any loop, as shown in Listing 14.5.

The lambda expression creates a functor that moves (Section D.3) the value of out to in, and then explicitly invokes a destructor to revert the location referenced by in to raw memory. The code is unusual in what it does with the functor. Instead of passing it to another routine, it immediately applies the functor to some arguments. The trick here is that those arguments are array sections, so the compiler has license to apply the functor in parallel.

14.7 SUMMARY

The sample sort example showed how to do binning and packing in parallel. The key to efficient binning is over-sampling and *not* trying to do the binning in place as Quicksort does. The packing relied on a serial prefix scan over a histogram to calculate where items should be packed. Most of the work occurs in two parallel map operations, one for binning and one for packing. In both cases, the work is over-decomposed to provide parallel slack (Section 2.5.6).

Cholesky Factorization

Section 8.8 used matrix multiplication to introduce the notion of recursive linear algebra and **cache-oblivious** algorithms, based on the **fork–join** pattern. The Cholesky decomposition example here shows how the pattern applies to parallelizing other operations in dense linear algebra, even when the matrices are triangular. The chapter also gives a brief introduction to the art of using Fortran-oriented **BLAS** routines in C/C++. Though the algorithms apply to large matrices, all you have to know is algebra on 2×2 matrices to understand how they work.

15.1 FORTRAN RULES!

The matrix layout used in the Cholesky routine and subsidiary routines is *column-major*, just like Fortran, not as usual in C/C++, so the layout will be compatible with common implementations of the Basic Linear Algebra Subprograms (BLAS) and Linear Algebra Package (LAPACK). This means each *column* of the matrix is packed consecutively in memory, not each row as is usual in C/C++.

The reason for using a BLAS column-major layout is pragmatic:

- Several recursive routines require serial routines for base cases. Efficient implementations of these serial routines are widely available (such as in Intel MKL) for Fortran array layout.
- Using the same layout enables our routines to be substituted for BLAS routines.

In both cases, the equivalence to BLAS routines may require some thin wrappers that reorder arguments, take addresses of arguments, add implied arguments, or resolve overloading. For example, the following wrapper defines a thin wrapper that implements a triangular solver for leaf cases, using Intel MKL:

```
inline void leaf_trsm(int m, int n, const float b[], int
    ldb, float a[], int lda, char side='L', char transa='N
    ', char diag='N', float alpha=1 ) {
    strsm(&side, "Lower", &transa, &diag, &m, &n, &alpha,
        b, &ldb, a, &lda);
}
```

The wrapper demonstrates the convention for passing arrays. Here a represents a lower-triangular $m \times n$ matrix A. The value lda is the stride in memory between columns, measured in array elements.

The parameter's name is an abbreviation for *leading dimension of A*. So array element $A_{i,j}$ is accessed as a[i+j*lda]. Likewise, there is a rectangular matrix B such that $B_{i,j}$ is accessed as b[i+j*ldb]. Following Fortran conventions in C/C++ is a painful, but practical, concession to the reality that production BLAS libraries cater to Fortran.

Routine leaf_trsm also illustrates the BLAS penchant for using characters where a C/C++ programmer would use an enum. The default values in the wrapper cause it to solve $A \times X = \alpha \cdot B$, and overwrite A with X. Other values change the problem slightly, as follows:

Argument	Mnemonic	Meaning
side	Left	Solve $op(A) \times X = \alpha \cdot B$
	Right	Solve $X \times op(A) = \alpha \cdot B$
transa	Transpose	op is transpose
	Not transpose	op is identity
diag	Unit	Diagonal elements of A are one
	Not unit	Assuming nothing about diagonal elements of A

The argument should be the first letter of the mnemonic, in either lower- or uppercase. For example, passing side='R' and transa='T' to our wrapper asks it to solve $X \times A^T = \alpha \cdot B$. The wrapped BLAS routine expects a *pointer* to the letter. That is why passing a C string for the mnemonic works, too. The second argument to strsm could be "Lollipop" instead of "Lower" to trsm, and it would not make any difference.

The examples also use a matrix multiply routine parallel_gemm, a parallel generic routine similar to the BLAS routine sgemm. It is assumed to be parallelized using the techniques discussed for matrix multiplication in Section 8.8. The usual BLAS version is quite general. It overwrites a matrix C with $\alpha \cdot op(A) \times op(B) + \beta C$, where op is either an identity or transpose operation. Our version has only 12 arguments, since $\beta = 1$ in all our examples. An invocation of our routine looks like:

    parallel_gemm(m, n, k, a, lda, b, ldb, c, ldc, transa, transb, α);

where parameter α is optional and defaults to 1. The rest of the parameters specify the three matrices as follows:

Matrix	Dimensions	Base	Stride	Transpose?
$op(A)$	$m \times k$	a	lda	transa
$op(B)$	$k \times n$	b	ldb	transb
C	$m \times n$	c	ldc	

The transpose arguments follow the conventions described for leaf_trsm.

Our brief introduction to BLAS omitted all possible argument options, such as for upper triangular or complex matrices. Since the BLAS are widespread, searching the Internet for `strsms`, `ssyrk`, and `sgemm` will tell you what you need to know about BLAS routines used in this chapter.

15.2 RECURSIVE CHOLESKY DECOMPOSITION

Our Cholesky decomposition factors a symmetric positive-definite matrix A into a lower triangular matrix L such that $A = LL^T$. The recursion is based on treating A and L as 2×2 matrices of submatrices, like this:

$$A = \begin{bmatrix} A_{00} & A_{10}^T \\ A_{10} & A_{11} \end{bmatrix} \quad L = \begin{bmatrix} L_{00} & 0 \\ L_{10} & L_{11} \end{bmatrix}.$$

The 0 represents a zero submatrix. Submatrices L_{00} and L_{11} are triangular. Submatrices A_{00} and A_{11} are symmetric. Because of the symmetry, submatrix A_{10}^T is redundant. To reduce clutter, it will be omitted from diagrams.

The equation $A = LL^T$ can be rewritten as:

$$\begin{bmatrix} A_{00} & \\ A_{10} & A_{11} \end{bmatrix} = \begin{bmatrix} L_{00} & 0 \\ L_{10} & L_{11} \end{bmatrix} \begin{bmatrix} L_{00}^T & L_{10}^T \\ 0 & L_{11}^T \end{bmatrix},$$

which yields the following equations:

$$A_{00} = L_{00}L_{00}^T, \tag{15.1}$$

$$A_{10} = L_{10}L_{00}^T, \tag{15.2}$$

$$A_{11} = L_{10}L_{10}^T + L_{11}L_{11}^T. \tag{15.3}$$

A **divide-and-conquer** algorithm is a practical corollary of the equations:

1. Solve Equation 15.1 for L_{00}. This step is a Cholesky decomposition of A_{00}, which can be done recursively, because the fact that A is positive semi-definite implies that A_{00} is positive semi-definite.
2. Solve Equation 15.2 for L_{10}. This step is called a *triangular solve*, because L_{00} is triangular.
3. Solve Equation 15.3 for L_{11} as follows:
   a. Let $A_{11}' = A_{11} - L_{10}L_{10}^T$. The computation can overwrite A_{11} with A_{11}'. This step is called *symmetric rank update*.
   b. Solve $A_{11}' = L_{11}L_{11}^T$ for L_{11}. This step is a Cholesky decomposition of A_{11}.

```
1   template<typename T>
2   void parallel_potrf( int n, T a[], int lda ) {
3       if( double(n)*n*n<=CUT ) {
4           // Leaf case – solve with  serial  LAPACK
5           leaf_potf2( n, a, lda );
6       } else {
7           int n2=n/2;
8           // Solve A₀₀ = L₀₀L₀₀ᵀ for L₀₀ and set A₀₀ = L₀₀
9           parallel_potrf( n2, a, lda );
10          // Solve A₁₀ = L₁₀L₀₀ᵀ for L₁₀ and set A₁₀ = L₁₀
11          parallel_trsm( n-n2, n2, a, lda, a+n2, lda );
12          // Set A₁₁ = A₁₁ – L₁₀ × L₁₀ᵀ
13          parallel_syrk( n-n2, n2, a+n2, lda, a+n2+n2*lda, lda );
14          // Solve A₁₁ᵀ = L₁₁L₁₁ᵀ for L₁₁
15          parallel_potrf( n-n2, a+n2+n2*lda, lda );
16      }
17  }
```

LISTING 15.1

Recursive Cholesky decomposition. The inscrutable name `potrf` follows LAPACK conventions [ABB+99].

Listing 15.1 shows code for the algorithm. The algorithm introduces no parallelism. However, it sets up two subproblems where parallelism can be introduced.

15.3 TRIANGULAR SOLVE

The first subproblem that enables parallelism is the triangular solve. It solves for X in the equation $XB^T = A$, where B is a lower triangular matrix. There are two different ways to split the matrices:

1. Split X and A horizontally, so the equation decomposes into:

$$\left[\frac{X_0}{X_1} \right] B^T = \left[\frac{A_0}{A_1} \right],$$

which yields the equations:

$$X_0 B^T = A_0$$
$$X_1 B^T = A_1.$$

An opportunity for parallelism is introduced because X_0 and X_1 can be solved for independently.

2. Split X and A horizontally, and B^T on both axes, so the equation decomposes into:

$$\left[X_0 \mid X_1 \right] \begin{bmatrix} B_{00}^T & B_{10}^T \\ 0 & B_{11}^T \end{bmatrix} = \left[A_0 \mid A_1 \right],$$

which yields the equations:

$$X_0 B_{00}^T = A_0, \tag{15.4}$$

$$X_0 B_{10}^T + X_1 B_{11}^T = A_1. \tag{15.5}$$

No opportunity for parallelism is introduced, because Equation 15.4 must be solved first to find X_0 before Equation 15.5 can be solved to find X_1.

In the latter case, the steps are:

1. Solve the equation $X_0 B_{00}^T = A_0$ for X_0, which is a triangular solve.
2. Set $A_1' = A_1 - X_0 B_{10}^T$. The computation can overwrite A_1' with A'.
3. Solve the equation $X_1 B_{11}^T = A'$ for X_1, which is a triangular solve.

At first, using the second split seems useless. But, if the first split is applied exclusively, then X and A in the leaf cases are long skinny row vectors, and each element of B^T is used exactly once, with no reuse. Consequently, consumption of memory bandwidth will be high. It is better to alternate between splitting vertically and splitting horizontally, so the subproblems remain roughly square and to encourage reuse of elements. Furthermore, the second split is not a complete loss, because the matrix multiplication in step 2 can be parallelized.

Listing 15.2 shows a Cilk Plus incarnation of the algorithm. Translation to TBB is a matter of rewriting the fork–join with `tbb::parallel_invoke`. The number of floating-point arithmetic operations is about `m2`^{2}`n2/6`. The recursion stops when this number is 6· `CUT` or less. The cast to `double` in that calculation ensures that the estimate does not err from overflow.

The recursive decomposition into smaller matrices makes the algorithm into a **cache-oblivious** algorithm (Section 8.8). Like the cache-oblivious matrix multiplication in Section 8.8, one of the recursive splits does not introduce any parallelism. It is beneficial nonetheless because splitting on the longest axis avoids creating long, skinny matrices, which improves cache behavior, as was explained in Section 8.8 for the matrix multiplication example.

15.4 SYMMETRIC RANK UPDATE

The other subproblem with parallelism is the symmetric rank update, which computes $A' = A - CC^T$ and overwrites A with A'. This is similar to routine `MultiplyAdd` in Section 8.8, except that subtraction replaces addition, and only the lower triangular portion needs to be computed, because the result is a symmetric matrix. As with the triangular solve, there are two ways to split the problem, one that enables parallelism and the other that, though serial, helps keep the subproblem roughly "square."

The equations for the two splits are:

1.

$$\begin{bmatrix} A_{00}' & \\ A_{10}' & A_{11}' \end{bmatrix} = \begin{bmatrix} A_{00} & \\ A_{10} & A_{11} \end{bmatrix} - \begin{bmatrix} C_0 \\ C_1 \end{bmatrix} \begin{bmatrix} C_0^T & C_1^T \end{bmatrix}$$

```
1   template<typename T>
2   void parallel_trsm( int m, int n, const T b[], int ldb, T a[], int lda ) {
3       if( double(m)*m*n<=CUT ) {
4           // Leaf case—solve with  serial  BLAS
5           leaf_trsm(m, n, b, ldb, a, lda, 'R', 'T', 'N' );
6       } else {
7           if( m>=n ) {
8               // Partition  A into  ⎡ A₀ ⎤
                                      ⎣ A₁ ⎦
9               int m2=m/2;
10              // Solve X₀ × Bᵀ = A₀, and set A₀ = X₀
11              cilk_spawn parallel_trsm( m2, n, b, ldb, a, lda );
12              // Solve X₁ × Bᵀ = A₁, and set A₁ = X₁
13              parallel_trsm( m−m2, n, b, ldb, a+m2, lda );
14          } else {
15              // Partition  B into  ⎡ B₀₀ᵀ  B₁₀ᵀ ⎤ and A into  ⎡ A₀ │ A₁ ⎤
                                      ⎣  0    B₁₁ᵀ ⎦
16              // where B₀₀ and B₁₁ are lower triangular matrices
17              int n2=n/2;
18              // Solve X₀ × B₀₀ᵀ = A₀, and set A₀ = X₀
19              parallel_trsm( m, n2, b, ldb, a, lda );
20              // Set A₁− = A₀ * B₁₀ᵀ
21              parallel_gemm( m, n−n2, n2,
22                              a, lda, b+n2, ldb, a+n2*lda, lda,
23                              'N', 'T', T(−1), T(1) );
24              // Solve X₁ × B₁₁ᵀ = A₁, and set A₁ = X₁
25              parallel_trsm( m, n−n2, b+n2+n2*ldb, ldb, a+n2*lda, lda );
26          }
27      }
28      // Implicit  cilk_sync
29  }
```

LISTING 15.2

Parallel triangular solve in Cilk Plus.

which yields the equations:

$$A'_{00} = A_{00} - C_0 C_0^T, \tag{15.6}$$

$$A'_{10} = A_{10} - C_1 C_0^T, \tag{15.7}$$

$$A'_{11} = A_{11} - C_1 C_1^T. \tag{15.8}$$

Equation 15.7 is a matrix multiplication, which can be parallelized as discussed in Section 8.8. The other two equations are symmetric rank updates. All three can be computed in parallel.

```
1   void parallel_syrk( int n, int k, const T c[], int ldc, T a[], int lda ) {
2       if( double(n)*n*k<=CUT ) {
3           leaf_syrk( n, k, c, ldc, a, lda );
4       } else if( n>=k ) {
5           int n2=n/2;
6           cilk_spawn parallel_syrk( n2, k, c, ldc, a, lda );
7           cilk_spawn parallel_gemm( n-n2, n2, k,
8                              c+n2, ldc, c, ldc, a+n2, lda,
9                              'N', 'T', T(-1), T(1) );
10          parallel_syrk( n-n2, k, c+n2, ldc, a+n2+n2*lda, lda );
11      } else {
12          int k2=k/2;
13          parallel_syrk( n, k2, c, ldc, a, lda );
14          parallel_syrk( n, k-k2, c+k2*ldc, ldc, a, lda );
15      }
16      // Implicit cilk_sync
17  }
```

LISTING 15.3

Parallel symmetric rank update in Cilk Plus.

2.

$$A' = A - \left[C_0 \mid C_1 \right] \left[\frac{C_0^T}{C_1^T} \right],$$

which yields the equation:

$$A' = A - C_0 C_0^T - C_1 C_1^T.$$

This is essentially two symmetric rank updates, using C_0 and C_1.

The second split enables parallel computation if temporary storage is allocated to compute $C_1 C_1^T$. However, doing so invites the same space and bandwidth problems as doing so for matrix multiplication, as discussed in Section 8.8, so the code will do the two updates serially.

Listing 15.3 shows the Cilk Plus code. Translation to TBB is a matter of using `tbb::parallel_invoke` to express the three-way fork, as shown in Listing 15.4.

15.5 WHERE IS THE TIME SPENT?

The Cholesky decomposition as described involves recursive calls among four algorithms, as shown in Figure 15.1. Each algorithm's base case is a serial version of that algorithm. Since the recursive steps do practically no work, but merely choose submatrices, most of the work is done in the serial leaf code. That leaves a question of how the work is apportioned across the three kinds of leaves. It turns out that the leaf matrix multiplications dominate, because they apply to off-diagonal blocks, whereas

```
1  tbb::parallel_invoke(
2      [=]{parallel_syrk( n2, k, c, ldc, a, lda );},
3      [=]{parallel_gemm( n-n2, n2, k,
4                  c+n2, ldc, c, ldc, a+n2, lda,
5                  'N', 'T', T(-1), T(1) );},
6      [=]{parallel_syrk( n-n2, k, c+n2, ldc, a+n2+n2*lda, lda );});
```

LISTING 15.4

Converting parallel symmetric rank update from Cilk Plus to TBB. The listing shows the TBB replacement for lines 6 to 10 of Listing 15.3.

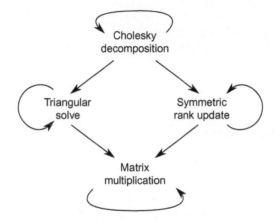

FIGURE 15.1

Cholesky call graph. The call chains eventually reach matrix multiplication, which dominates the running time.

the leaf triangular solve and leaf symmetric rank update apply to diagonal blocks. There are $\Theta(n^2)$ off-diagonal blocks but only $\Theta(n)$ diagonal blocks.

Using fork–join for Cholesky decomposition does have a drawback—it artificially lengthens the span, similar to how recursive decomposition lengthened the span of the binomial lattice problem (Section 8.12.1). A system such as Intel Concurrent Collections avoids lengthening the span by expressing only the dependencies necessary to solve the problem [CKV10]. There is no free lunch, however. That reduction in span discards the simple call-tree reasoning of the Cilk Plus solution and the cache-oblivious benefits, although sufficiently large leaf cases can take care of the memory bandwidth issues. In that case, the concurrent collections approach can deliver superior performance.

15.6 SUMMARY

The Cholesky example demonstrates the power of being able to nest parallelism and think about it locally in each routine. Every routine, though parallel, is called as if it were a serial routine. It also demonstrates how linear algebra can often be done recursively.

Appendices

Appendices

Further Reading

We have carefully avoided diving into topics, no matter how interesting, that were not critical to teaching the keys to structured (parallel) programming. In this appendix, we offer some recommendations on where to learn more about closely associated topics. A deeper understanding of any of these will strengthen your understanding of what is behind good structured programming.

A.1 PARALLEL ALGORITHMS AND PATTERNS

Much has been written on parallel algorithms. We recommend reading a landmark paper focused on classifying algorithms, "The Landscape of Parallel Computing Research: A View from Berkeley" [ABC+06]. This paper used **dwarfs** as the name for common recurring **patterns** found in applications. Later papers switched to calling these **motifs**. This is an excellent starting point, but we also recommend the OUR pattern language [Par11]. This web site contains a set of collaboratively created pattern definitions.

"Introduction to Algorithms" [CLRS09] is a good general introduction to algorithms which also makes some usage of Cilk Plus.

A thorough and scholarly book specifically on parallel patterns is *Patterns for Parallel Programming* [MSM04]. Even though we do not recommend it specifically for parallel programming, we will note that the landmark book to promote patterns for software development is *Design Patterns: Elements of Reusable Object-Oriented Software* [GHJV95]. It is often affectionately called the "gang of four" book.

The key conferences involved in parallel algorithm development would be Symposium on Principles and Practice of Parallel Programming (PPoPP), ACM Symposium on Parallelism in Algorithms and Architectures (SPAA), International Supercomputing in Europe (ISC), and Supercomputing in North America (SC). PPoPP, ISC, and SC are known for notable training opportunities via tutorials held in conjunction with their respective general conferences.

A.2 COMPUTER ARCHITECTURE INCLUDING PARALLEL SYSTEMS

The gold standard for teaching computer architecture is *Computer Architecture: A Quantitative Approach* [HP07] by John L. Hennessy and David A. Patterson. A new book, often described as very approachable and which caters to programmers, is *Computer Systems: A Programmer's*

Perspective [REB11] by Randal Bryant and Dave O'Hallaron. Both of these books explain the fundamental concepts in computer architecture.

For those whose interest runs deep enough to want to engage others with a keen interest in computer architecture, four long-standing conferences are particularly worth investigating: International Symposium on Computer Architecture (ISCA), Architectural Support for Programming Languages and Operating Systems (ASPLOS), International Symposium on High Performance Computer Architecture (HPCA), and International Conference on Parallel Architectures and Compilation Techniques (PACT).

A.3 PARALLEL PROGRAMMING MODELS

Intel Threading Building Blocks [Rei07] is a book that introduces TBB and provides many examples. The book predates **lambda expressions** and a number of additional advanced features of TBB. The documentation that accompanies TBB (http://threadingbuildingblocks.org) is exceptional and a reliable source of current information on all the features of the latest TBB.

The original Cilk home at the Massachusetts Institute of Technology (MIT) continues to maintain useful samples, tutorials, and papers about Cilk. Visiting it at http://supertech .csail.mit.edu/cilk/ is recommended to learn more about Cilk. Intel and the related open source project for Cilk Plus maintain the web site http://cilkplus.org.

Array Building Blocks, likewise, has a set of examples, tutorials, and downloads hosted by Intel at http://intel.com/go/arbb.

The gold standard for learning MPI is *Parallel Programming with MPI* [Pac96]. A good book for learning more about both Open MP and MPI is *Parallel Programming in C with MPI and OpenMP* [Qui03].

If you have an interest in parallel programming for Java, we recommend reading *Java Concurrency in Practice* [PGB+05]. Doug Lea, in particular, has published books on parallel programming for Java that have been exceptionally useful for learning parallel programming concepts regardless of your programming language of choice.

If you want to get a handle on a number of other approaches in programming languages for parallelism, we recommend *Seven Languages in Seven Weeks: A Pragmatic Guide to Learning Programming Languages* [Tat10] by Bruce A. Tate, which examines Clojure, Haskell, Io, Prolog, Scala, Erlang, and Ruby. It is not likely that you will use all seven, but you will gain an appreciation for the many possibilities in designing support for concurrency into programming languages.

Finally, *The Art of Multiprocessor Programming* [HS08] covers a broad set of concerns for parallel programming in an approachable manner with a gentle mix of fables and stories.

The key conferences to consider attending include PPoPP, ISC, and SC, which are spelled out in Section A.1. All three are known for their tutorials, which are usually held just before the general conferences.

We will also recommend Herb Sutter's paper, "The Free Lunch Is Over: A Fundamental Turn Towards Concurrency in Software" [Sut05] which is often cited for how effectively it called attention to the shift to multicore parallelism and the challenge it represents.

Finally, if you have any doubts about the need to abandon **threads** in programming in favor of **tasks**, "The Problem with Threads" [Lee06] is recommended reading. We like to think of it as a modern version of the classic "Go To Statement Considered Harmful" [Dij68], which has come to be so commonly accepted today that it is hard to recall the controversy it raised for more than a decade after its publication. We are confident that programming with threads will go the way of Go To, and these are the two key papers that are heralding the change.

Cilk Plus

This appendix provides a concise introduction to the features of Intel Cilk Plus (Cilk Plus) with an emphasis on portions used within this book. For more complete information, see the Intel Cilk Plus Language Specification and Intel Cilk Plus Application Binary Interface Specification documents, which are available from `http://cilkplus.org`.

Figure B.1 outlines the components of Cilk Plus, as well as the parts of TBB that are recommended for use with it.

B.1 SHARED DESIGN PRINCIPLES WITH TBB

Cilk Plus and TBB purposefully share key attributes as parallel programming models: separation of programmer/tool responsibilities, composability including interoperability with other parallel programming models, support for current programming environments, readability by adhering to serial semantics, and portability of source code.

The key design principle behind effective parallel programming abstractions is that the programmer should identify elements that can be safely executed in parallel. Separately, the runtime environment, particularly the scheduler, should decide during execution how to actually divide the work between processors. This separation of responsibilities allows code to run efficiently on any number of processors, including one processor, without customizing the source code to the number of processors.

B.2 UNIQUE CHARACTERISTICS

Cilk Plus is distinguished by its focus on minimal but sufficient support for parallelism in C and C++. It is easy to learn, able to support sophisticated debugging tools, and provides guarantees that bound memory usage. Cilk Plus does this all while also scaling to high degrees of thread *and* vector parallelism.

Cilk Plus seeks to address shortcomings of a template library approach:

- Usability in C, not just C++
- Support for vector parallelism
- Serial elision, where a Cilk Plus program run with one thread behaves as if the Cilk Plus keywords are replaced with standard C/C++, as will be explained in Section B.4
- Conveying parallel structure to the compiler at a higher level than a template library, which enables more optimization opportunities

329

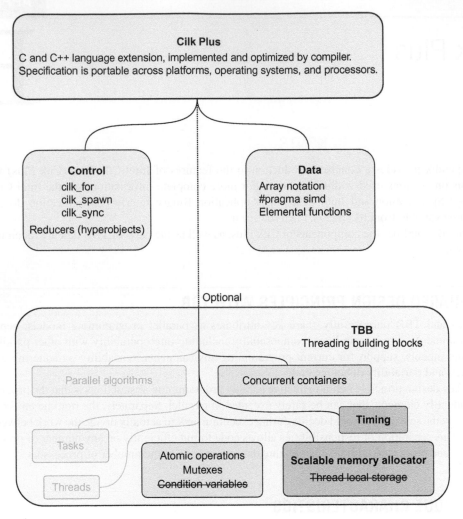

FIGURE B.1

Overview of Cilk Plus. Parts of TBB can be borrowed for foundation functionality. Darkly shaded TBB components are recommended for use with Cilk Plus. Lightly shaded TBB components interoperate with Cilk Plus but may break determinism. Faded components also interoperate but are essentially alternatives to Cilk Plus. Crossed-out portions carry risks. Section B.3 details our recommendations.

These items require compiler support and are therefore beyond the scope of a template library such as TBB.

Because Cilk Plus requires implementation inside a compiler, it is not yet as widely portable as TBB. Thus, to promote adoption of Cilk Plus and make it as widespread as TBB, Intel is making it easy for compiler makers to implement it. Cilk Plus is published as an open language specification *and* an open ABI specification. Furthermore, Intel is working on making all key components open source.

Currently, a portable form of the runtime library is open source, along with a development branch of the GCC compiler that supports `cilk_spawn`, `cilk_sync`, `cilk_for`, reducers, `#pragma simd`, and array notation. The open source version is expected to eventually become a complete Cilk Plus implementation.

B.3 BORROWING COMPONENTS FROM TBB

Cilk Plus does not duplicate functionality that can be borrowed from TBB. Indeed, we encourage Cilk Plus programmers to use components of TBB that are orthogonal to expression of parallelism. These components of TBB are:

- Scalable memory allocator
- `tick_count` timing facility

Some portions of TBB are all right to use but are not the Cilk Plus ideal because they break determinism or greedy scheduling theory:

- Mutexes
- Atomic objects
- Concurrent containers

Consider using alternative solutions based on Cilk Plus **hyperobjects**, if you can, to reap the benefits of determinism.

The parallel algorithms and tasks in TBB can interoperate with Cilk Plus, but using them instead of Cilk Plus forgoes the key value proposition of Cilk Plus.

We discourage combining two of TBB's features with Cilk Plus's control-flow constructs. The feature combinations to avoid are:

- Using condition variables with `cilk_spawn` or `cilk_for`. This is questionable since the purpose of a condition variable is to wait for *another* thread to change state protected by a mutex. Since Cilk Plus task constructs only *permit* thread parallelism, but do not *mandate* it, there might not be another thread. The wait could last forever.
- Mixing thread-local storage with Cilk Plus's `cilk_spawn` or `cilk_for`. This invites trouble. The problem is that Cilk Plus is not about threads. It is about running parallel **strands** of execution, where a strand (Section 8.10) is a segment of control flow with no intervening fork or join point. However, the runtime maps strands to threads in ways that can surprise neophytes. For example, when a worker thread created by the Cilk Plus runtime calls a function, the function can return on a *different* thread.

Hyperobjects are usually an excellent alternative to thread-local storage. The k-means example (Chapter 11) lets you compare these alternatives. The TBB code uses thread-local storage; the Cilk Plus code uses two hyperobjects.

Borrowing can go the other way, too. The Cilk Plus features for vector parallelism (array notation and `#pragma simd`) are an excellent way to exploit vector parallelism in a TBB program, even if the tasking model supported by Cilk Plus is not used. Note that if you express vector parallelism using only **elemental functions** and the #pragma simd, the code will still be portable to other compilers, since ignoring these constructs still gives the expected result.

B.4 KEYWORD SPELLING

This book's spelling of the keywords requires inclusion of the header <cilk/cilk.h>, which has:

```
#define cilk_spawn _Cilk_spawn
#define cilk_sync _Cilk_sync
#define cilk_for _Cilk_for
```

The compiler recognizes only the keywords on the right. The reason is that the introduction of new keywords by a compiler is limited, by convention and standards, to names beginning with an underscore followed by an uppercase letter. Such symbols are reserved to compiler implementers and should never cause a conflict with application code. The header provides more aesthetically pleasing spellings.

Including the <cilk/cilk_stub.h> header file converts a program to its **serial elision** by defining:

```
#define _Cilk_spawn
#define _Cilk_sync
#define _Cilk_for for
```

These substitutions revert the program to a serial program that can be compiled by any C++ compiler. The resulting code will behave just like a Cilk Plus program running on a single thread.

B.5 cilk_for

The syntax for cilk_for is similar to for. It looks like:

cilk_for (*initialization*; *condition*; *increment*) *body*

The *body* can be a single statement or a block of code. Changing a for loop to a cilk_for loop permits the iterations to run in parallel.

A cilk_for loop has the following constraints that do not exist for a for loop:

- Control may not be explicitly transferred out of the body or into it. In particular, return and break are prohibited. A goto must not jump from inside the body to outside of it, or vice versa.
- Control may be implicitly transferred out of the body by an exception. In that case, which other iterations execute depends on the implementation and might not be deterministic. The exception

```
1  cilk_for (int i=ivalue; i<limit; ++i) {
2      a[i] = foo(b[i],c[i]) * 3.0;
3  }
```

LISTING B.1

Simple example use of cilk_for.

thrown from the `cilk_for` is the same as the serial elision would have thrown, even if multiple iterations throw.

- The *initialization* shall declare or initialize a single variable only. This is called the *control variable*. In C, the control variable may be declared outside the `cilk_for` loop. In C++, the initialization must declare the control variable. The variable cannot be declared `const` or `volatile`.
- The control variable may not be modified within the loop body.
- The *increment* must have one of the following forms:

  > *i*++
  > ++*i*
  > *i*−−
  > −−*i*
  > *i*+=*step*
  > *i*−=*step*

  where *i* stands for the control variable, and *step* can be any expression.
- The *condition* must consist of the control variable *i* compared with another expression, which we will call the *limit*. The comparison can be =>, >, <=, <, !=, or ==.
- The *step* (if any) and *limit* expressions must not be affected by the loop body. This is so that the number of iterations can be computed correctly before any iterations commence. For C programs, the value of the control variable, if declared outside the loop, has the same value after a `cilk_for` loop as it would have after a `for` loop.

The language extension specification [Cor11b] explains the details more precisely, with attention to fine points and should be consulted for a complete definition.

B.6 `cilk_spawn` **AND** `cilk_sync`

The `cilk_spawn` keyword specifies that the caller of a function may continue to run without waiting for the called function to return.

```
1   // Simple function call
2   cilk_spawn bar(1);
3   // Lambdas allowed
4   cilk_spawn []{ bar(2); }();
5   // Results allowed
6   result = cilk_spawn bar(4);
7   // Innermost call completes before spawn
8   result = cilk_spawn bar( bar(9) );
9   // Spawn not used, no need, potentially wasteful
10  bar(5);
11  // Wait for all spawns
12  cilk_sync;
```

LISTING B.2

Examples of using `cilk_spawn` and `cilk_sync`.

Execution of a statement with the `cilk_spawn` keyword is called a **spawn**. The function, try block, or `cilk_for` body that contains the spawn is called the **spawning block**. Note that compound statements containing a spawn are *not* spawning blocks unless they fit one of the categories above.

Execution of a `cilk_sync` statement is called a **sync**. A sync waits only for spawns that have occurred in the same spawning block and has no effect on spawns done by other tasks or, done by other threads, nor those done prior to entering the current spawning block. An implicit sync occurs when exiting the enclosing spawning block. Thus, when a spawning block completes, any parallelism that it created is finished. This property simplifies reasoning about program composition and correspondence with its serial elision.

The following snippet illustrates some of these points:

```
void foo() {
   for (int i=0; i<3; ++i) {
      cilk_spawn bar(i);
      if (i%2) cilk_sync;
   }
   // Implicit cilk_sync
```

The snippet has one spawning block: the function body. The body of the `for` loop is *not* a spawning block because it is not the body of a function, try block, or `cilk_for`. The code operates as follows:

1. Spawn `bar(0)` and `bar(1)`.
2. Execute a sync that waits for the spawned calls.
3. Spawn `bar(2)`.
4. Execute the implicit `cilk_sync`.

The scope of the explicit sync is dynamic, not lexical. It applies to all prior spawns by the current invocation of `foo()`, since that is the innermost spawning block.

Jumping into, or out of, a spawning block results in undefined behavior. This includes use of `goto`, `setjmp`, and `longjmp`. "Undefined behavior" is a term of art in language specifications that means *anything* could happen, including crashing your program or turning your computer into a frog. You have been warned.

Behavior is defined if a spawned function throws an exception and does not catch it. The exception is rethrown when execution leaves the corresponding sync. If there are multiple such exceptions for the sync, the sync rethrows the exception that the serial elision would have thrown. The extra exceptions are destroyed without being caught.

B.7 REDUCERS (HYPEROBJECTS)

A hyperobject enables multiple strands of execution to operate in parallel on the same logical object, without locking, yet get the same result as the serial elision would get. Furthermore, a hyperobject avoids contention bottlenecks, because parallel strands get separate local views of the logical object. Section 8.10 discusses the theory of hyperobjects in more detail.

A **reducer** is a hyperobject intended for doing reductions. Cilk Plus reducers work for any operation that can be reassociated. Cilk Plus predefines reducers for common associative operations:

Operation	Header
list accumulation	`<cilk/reducer_list.h>`
min	`<cilk/reducer_min.h>`
max	`<cilk/reducer_max.h>`
addition and subtraction	`<cilk/reducer_opadd.h>`
bitwise AND	`<cilk/reducer_opand.h>`
bitwise OR	`<cilk/reducer_opor.h>`
bitwise EXCLUSIVE OR	`<cilk/reducer_opxor.h>`
string concatenation	`<cilk/reducer_string.h>`
reducer version of `std::ostream`	`<cilk/reducer_ostream.h>`

The last item might seem surprising, since output operations are not normally considered associative. However, a reducer can change operations to reassociate them. For example:

```
(cout << x) << y
```

can be reassociated as:

```
cout << (TOSTRING(x) + TOSTRING(y))
```

where `TOSTRING` denotes conversion to a string and + denotes string concatenation. Section 9.4.2 explains this in more detail. One other reducer mentioned also changes operations: The reducer `reducer_opadd` reassociates subtraction by rewriting $a - b$ as $a + (-b)$.

Another kind of hyperobject is a **holder**. Cilk Plus predefines holders in header `<cilk/holder.h>`. A holder is a kind of reducer where the reduction operation $\otimes$ does one of the following:

Policy	Operation
Keep last	$x \otimes y = y$
Keep indeterminate	$x \otimes y =$ arbitrary choice of x or y

A *keep-last holder* is useful for computing the last value the hyperobject would have after serial execution. It can be thought of as using the C/C++ "comma operator" for reduction. A *keep-indeterminate holder* is useful for holding race-free temporary storage instead of reallocating/freeing it every time a strand needs it. See comments in `<cilk/holder.h>` for more details, options, and examples for holders.

B.7.1 C++ Syntax

Our example uses `reducer_opadd` and is illustrated in Listing B.3. To use a predefined reducer:

1. Include the appropriate reducer header file. Our example uses `#include <cilk/reducer_opadd.h>`.

```
1   #include "cilk/reducer_opadd.h"
2   using namespace std;
3
4   void cpp_serial( int data[], size_t n ) {
5       int result = 47;
6
7       cout << "C++ reduction with for" << endl;
8
9       for (size_t i = 0; i < n; ++i) {
10          result += data[i];
11      }
12
13      cout << "Result is: " << result << endl;
14  }
15
16  void cpp_parallel( int data[], size_t n ) {
17      cilk::reducer_opadd<int> result(47);
18
19      cout << "C++ reduction with cilk_for" << endl;
20
21      cilk_for (size_t i = 0; i < n; ++i) {
22          result += data[i];
23      }
24
25      cout << "Result is: " << result.get_value() << endl;
26  }
```

LISTING B.3

Serial reduction in C++ and equivalent Cilk Plus code. See Listing B.4 for an equivalent example in C.

2. Declare the reduction variable as a reducer_kind<TYPE> rather than as a TYPE. The default value is the identity element of the reduction operation. If you need a different initial value, use a parenthetical expression, not = for the initializer. The = syntax will not work.[1] Our example uses:

```
cilk::reducer_opadd<int> result(47);
```

not this:

```
cilk::reducer_opadd<int> result=47; // WRONG!
```

3. Introduce parallelism, such as changing a for loop to a cilk_for loop. Update the reduction variable (in our example, result) just like before. It is not necessary to worry that the hyperobject now provides a strand-local view of the variable. However, updates are restricted to the reduction

---

[1] Why? Because the C++ standard requires that to use the = syntax the class must have a public copy constructor, even if the compiler optimizes it away. Hyperobjects generally have private copy constructors.

operations supported by the hyperobject. For example, reducer_opadd allows only +=, −=, ++, and −−.

4. Retrieve the reducer's terminal value with method get_value() *after* all strands that update it sync. In our example, this is result.get_value(), and the strands synced when the cilk_for loop finished. Retrieving the reducer's terminal value before all strands sync may return only a partial result.

To illustrate these steps for C++, Listing B.3 shows routines for summing an array of integers. One routine uses for and the other uses cilk_for with a reducer. Otherwise, they are identical C++ code to illustrate equivalence.

The header <cilk/reducer.h> defines a generic reducer that you can use to define your own custom reducer. Section 11.2.1 walks through the mechanics of defining a custom reducer.

B.7.2 C Syntax

Our example uses reducer_opadd and is illustrated in Listing B.4. The steps are:

1. #include the appropriate header for the reducer. Section B.7 lists the types and header files for predefined reducers. Our example uses #include <cilk/reducer_opadd.h>.
2. Declare the reducer object using:

    CILK_C_REDUCER_*type*(*variable_name, variable_type, initial_value*);

    For example, to declare an addition reducer variable result of type int initialized to zero, use:

    CILK_C_REDUCER_OPADD(result, int, 0);

3. After the declaration of the reducer but before the first use, insert:

    CILK_C_REGISTER_REDUCER(*reducer_name*);

    to register the variable with the Cilk Plus runtime. This provides for proper initialization and memory clean-up. It is not strictly needed if the variable *reducer_name* is a global variable.
4. To access the value in a serial region, use the member value of the reducer. In our example, this is result.value. Operations on the member should be restricted to the appropriate operations only, but, unlike in C++, this restriction cannot be enforced by the compiler. Failure to obey this restriction can easily produce invalid results. The Cilk Plus documentation on reduction operations lists the allowed operations. For instance, for OPADD the only allowed operations are +=, −=, ++, and −−.
5. When accessing the value of the reducer from parallel strands, use REDUCER_VIEW(*reducer_name*) to access the value. In our example, this is REDUCER_VIEW(result).
6. When the reducer is no longer needed, insert

    CILK_C_UNREGISTER_REDUCER(*reducer_name*);

    Just like the registration of the variable, this is not strictly needed if the variable is global.

To illustrate these steps for C, Listing B.4 adds an array of numbers together using for and cilk_for with reducers in otherwise identical C code to illustrate equivalence in this C code.

```
1   #include "cilk/reducer_opadd.h"
2
3   void c_serial( int data[], size_t n ) {
4       size_t i;
5       int result = 47;
6
7       printf("C reduction with for\n");
8
9       for (i = 0; i < n; ++i) {
10          result += data[i];
11      }
12      printf("Result is: %d\n", result);
13  }
14
15  void c_parallel( int data[], size_t n ) {
16      size_t i;
17      CILK_C_REDUCER_OPADD(result, int, 47);
18      CILK_C_REGISTER_REDUCER(result);
19
20      printf("C reduction with cilk_for\n");
21
22      cilk_for (i = 0; i < n; ++i) {
23          result.value += data[i];
24      }
25      printf("Result is: %d\n", REDUCER_VIEW(result));
26      CILK_C_UNREGISTER_REDUCER(result);
27  }
```

LISTING B.4

Serial reduction in C and equivalent Cilk Plus code. See Listing B.3 for an equivalent example in C++.

The header `<cilk/reducer.h>` has macros to assist defining your own custom reducer. See that header and the Cilk Plus documentation for details on how to use these macros.

B.8 ARRAY NOTATION

Cilk Plus extends C and C++ with array notation, which lets the programmer specify array sections and operations on array sections. Programming with array notation achieves predictable performance based on mapping parallel constructs to the underlying hardware vector parallelism, and possibly thread parallelism in the future. The notation is explicit and easy to understand and enables compilers to exploit vector and thread parallelism with less reliance on alias and dependence analysis. For example,

```
a[0:n] = b[10:n] * c[20:n];
```

is an unordered equivalent of:

```
for ( int i=0; i<n; ++i )
    a[i] = b[10+i] + c[20+i]
```

Use array notation where your operations on arrays do not require a specific order of operations among elements of the arrays.

B.8.1 Specifying Array Sections

An array section operator is written as one of the following:

[*first* : *length* : *stride*]
[*first* : *length*]
[:]

where:

first is the index of the first element in the section.
length is the number of elements in the section.
stride is the difference between successive indices. The *stride* is optional, and if omitted is implicitly 1. The *stride* can be positive, zero, or negative.

All three of these values must be integers. The *j*th element of an array section $a[i : n : k]$ is $a[i + j \cdot k]$ for $j \in [0,n)$.[2]

The notation *expr*[:] is a shorthand for a whole array dimension if *expr* has array type before decay (conversion to pointer type) and the size of the array is known. If either first or length is specified, then both must be specified. Examples include:

```
float x[10];
x[0:5];      // First five elements of x
x[5:10];     // Last five elements of x
x[1:5:2];    // Elements of x with odd subscripts
x[:];        // All ten elements of x
```

A scalar or array section has a *rank*. A scalar has rank 0. The rank of an array section $a[i : n : k]$ is one more than the rank of *a*. The rank of $a[i]$ is the *sum* of the ranks of *a* and *i*. The rank of *i* must not exceed one. Successive array section operators behave analogously to multiple C/C++ subscripts. The shape of a multidimensional section is a tuple of the section lengths. Examples:

```
int s;
int u[5], v[4];
int a[7][4];
int b[8][7][4];
x;            // rank=0, shape=<>
v[0:4];       // rank=1, shape=<4>
```

---

[2] Note to Fortran 90 programmers: The middle of the triplet is a *length*, not the last index.

```
a[0:7][0:4];        // rank=2, shape=<7,4>
a[0][0:4];          // rank=1, shape=<4>
a[0:7][0];          // rank=1, shape=<7>
b[0:5][0][0:3];     // rank=2, shape=<5,3>
u[v[0:4]];          // rank=1, shape=<4>
```

The last line subscripts array u (rank zero) with an array section (rank one), and the rank of the result is the sum of those ranks.

B.8.2 Operations on Array Sections

Most C and C++ scalar operations act elementwise on array sections and return an elementwise result. For example, the expression a[10:n]−b[20:n] returns an array section of length n where the jth element is a[10+j]−b[20+j]. Each operand must have the same shape, unless it is a scalar operand. Scalar operands are reshaped by replication to match the shape of the non-scalar operands. Function calls are also applied elementwise. Examples include:

```
extern float x[8], y[8], z[8];
extern float a[8][8];
x[0:8] = x[0:8] + y[0:8];        // Vector addition
x[0:8] += y[0:8];                // Another vector addition
x[0:8] = (x[0:8]+y[0:8])/2;      // Vector average
a[3][0:8] = x[0:8];              // Copy x to row 3 of a
a[0:8][3] = x[0:8];              // Copy x to column 3 of a
z[0:8] = pow(x[0:8],3.f);        // Elementwise cubes of x
std::swap(x[0:8],y[0:8]);        // Elementwise swap
x[0:8] = x[0:5];                 // Error – mismatched shape
a[0:5][0:5] = x[0:5];            // Error – mismatched shape
```

The few operators that are not applied elementwise or have peculiar rank rules are:

- **Comma operator:** The rank of x,y is the rank of y.
- **Array section operator:** As described earlier, the rank of $a[i : n : k]$ is one more than the rank of a.
- **Subscript operator:** As described earlier, the rank of the result of $a[i]$ is the sum of the ranks of a and i. The j element of $a[k[0 : n]]$ is $a[k[j]]$. Trickier is the second subscript in $b[0 : m][k[0 : n]]$. Both $b[0 : m]$ and $k[0 : n]$ have rank one, so the result is a rank-two section where the element at subscript i,j is $b[i][k[j]]$.

Note that pointer arithmetic follows the elementwise rule just like other arithmetic. A consequence is that $a[i]$ is not always the same as $*(a + i)$ when array sections are involved. For example, if both a and i have rank one, then $a[i]$ has rank two, but $*(a + i)$ has rank one because it is elementwise unary $*$ applied to the result of elementwise $+$.

Historical note: In the design of array notation, an alternative was explored that preserved the identity $*(a + i) \equiv a[i]$, but it broke the identity $(a + i) + j \equiv a + (i + j)$ when a is a pointer type and made the rank of $a + i$ dependent on the type (not just the rank) of a. It turns out that array notation must break one of the two identities, and breaking associativity was deemed the worse of two evils.

B.8.3 Reductions on Array Sections

There are built-in operations for efficient reductions of array sections. For example, `__sec_reduce_add(a[0:n])` sums the values of array section `a[0:n]`. Here is a summary of the built-in operations. The last column shows the result of reducing a zero-length section.

Operation	Result	If Empty
`__sec_reduce_add`	$\Sigma_i a_i$	0
`__sec_reduce_mul`	$\Pi_i a_i$	1
`__sec_reduce_max`	$\max_i a_i$	"$-\infty$"
`__sec_reduce_min`	$\min_i a_i$	"∞"
`__sec_reduce_max_ind`	j such that $\forall i : a_j \geq a_i$	unspecified
`__sec_reduce_min_ind`	j such that $\forall i : a_j \leq a_i$	unspecified
`__sec_reduce_all_zero`	$\forall i : a_i = 0 \,?\, 1 : 0$	1
`__sec_reduce_all_nonzero`	$\forall i : a_i \neq 0 \,?\, 1 : 0$	1
`__sec_reduce_any_zero`	$\exists i : a_i = 0 \,?\, 1 : 0$	0
`__sec_reduce_any_nonzero`	$\exists i : a_i \neq 0 \,?\, 1 : 0$	0

The "$-\infty$" and "∞" are shorthands for the minimum and maximum representable values of the type.

The result of a reduction is always a scalar. For most of these reduction, the rank of a can be one or greater. The exception is that the rank of a must be one for `__sec_reduce_max_ind` and `__sec_reduce_min_ind`. These return an index of type `ptrdiff_t` that is relative to the section. For example, `__sec_reduce_max_ind(x[40:10])` returns an index in the half-open interval $[0, 10)$, *not* in $[40, 50)$.

Two general reduction operations let you do reduction over a section with type T using your own **combiner** operation. Their signatures are:

```
T __sec_reduce(T initial, T section, T (*f)(T,T));
void __sec_reduce_mutating(T& dest, T section, U (*g)(T*,T));
```

A summary of the arguments follows, with $\otimes$ denoting the combiner operation:

- *initial* is an initial value to use for the reduction.
- *section* is an array section.
- *f(x,y)* returns $x \otimes y$.
- *dest* is a location that contains the initial value for the reduction and is where the result is stored.
- *g(x,y)* sets $*x = *x \otimes y$. The function g can have any return type, because the return value of g is irrelevant.

Listing B.5 shows an example using string concatenation as the reduction operation.

```
1   #include <string>
2   #include <iostream>
3
4   using namespace std;
5
6   string concat( string x, string y ) {
7       return x + " " + y;
8   }
9
10  int main() {
11      string a[] = {"there","was","a","vector."};
12      string b = __sec_reduce( "Once", a[0:4], concat );
13      cout << b << endl;
14      return 0;
15  }
```

LISTING B.5

Example of using `__sec_reduce` to reduce over string concatenation. It prints "Once there was a vector."

B.8.4 Implicit Index

The built-in function `__sec_implicit_index(k)` returns the index of each element along dimension k in an array section implied by context. Examples include:

```
int a[5][8];
// Set a_{i,j} = i-j
a[0:5][0:8] = __sec_implicit_index(0)-__sec_implicit_index(1);
int b[8];
// Set b_{2k} = k
b[0:8:2] = __sec_implicit_index(0);
// Set b_{2k+1} = 10k
b[1:8:2] = 10*__sec_implicit_index(0);
```

The comments for the statements that set b show how the implicit indices are indices into the *section*, not the arrays in the expression.

B.8.5 Avoid Partial Overlap of Array Sections

In C and C++, the effect of a structure assignment *p = *q is undefined if *p and *q point to structures that partially overlap in memory. The assignment is well defined if *p and *q are either completely disjointed or are aliases for exactly the same structure. Cilk Plus extends this rule to array sections. Examples include:

```
extern float a[15];
a[0:4] = a[5:4];        // Okay, disjoint
a[0:5] = a[4:5];        // WRONG! Partial overlap
a[0:5] = a[0:5]+1:      // Okay, exact overlap
```

```
a[0:5:2] = a[1:5:2];     // Okay, disjoint, no locations shared
a[0:5:2] = a[1:5:3];     // WRONG! Partial overlap (both share a[4])
a[0:5] = a[5:5]+a[6:5];  // Okay, reads can partially overlap
```

The last example shows how partial overlap of reads is okay. It is partial overlap of a write with another read or write that is undefined.

Historical note: The original specification of array notation made partial overlap well defined, as in APL and Fortran 90. However, experience showed that doing so required a compiler to often generate temporary arrays, so it could fully evaluate the right side of a statement before doing an assignment. These temporary arrays hurt performance and caused unpredictable space consumption, both at odds with the C++ philosophy of providing abstractions with minimal performance penalty. So the specification was changed to match the rules for structure assignment in C/C++. Perhaps future compilers will offer to insert partial overlap checks into code for debugging.

B.9 #pragma simd

Analogously to how cilk_for gives permission to parallelize a loop, but does not require it, marking a for loop with #pragma simd similarly gives a compiler permission to execute a loop with vectorization. Usually this vectorization will be performed in small chunks whose size will depend on the vector width of the machine. For example, writing:

```
extern float a[];
#pragma simd
for ( int i=0; i<1000; ++i )
    a[i] = 2 * a[i+1];
```

grants the compiler permission to transform the code into something such as:

```
extern float a[];
for ( int i=0; i<1000; i+=4 ) {
    float tmp[4];
    tmp[0:4] = 2 * a[i+1:4];
    a[i:4] = tmp[0:4];
}
```

There is a subtle difference in the parallelization permitted by #pragma simd versus cilk_for. The original loop in our example would *not* be legal to parallelize with cilk_for, because of the dependence between iterations. A #pragma simd is okay in the example because the chunked reads of locations still precede chunked writes of those locations. However, if the orginal loop body reversed the subscripts and assigned a[i+1] = 2 * a[i], then the chunked loop would *not* preserve the original semantics, because each iteration needs the value of the previous iteration. In general, #pragma simd is legal on any loop for which cilk_for is legal, but not vice versa. In cases where only #pragma simd appears to be legal, study dependencies carefully to be sure that it is really legal.

A #pragma simd can be modified by additional clauses, which control chunk size or allow for some C/C++ programmers' fondness for bumping pointers or indices inside the loop. Note that

*#*pragma simd is not restricted to inner loops. For example, the following code grants the compiler permission to vectorize the *outer* loop:

```
#pragma simd
    for ( int i=1; i<1000000; ++i ) {
        while ( a[i]>1 )
            a[i] *= 0.5f;
    }
```

In theory, a compiler can vectorize the outer loop by using masking (Section 2.3) to emulate the control flow of the inner while loop. Whether a compiler actually does so depends on the implementation.

B.10 ELEMENTAL FUNCTIONS

An **elemental function** is a scalar function with markup that tells the compiler to generate extra versions of it optimized to evaluate multiple iterations in parallel. When you call an elemental function from a parallel context, the compiler can call the parallel version instead of the serial version, even if the function is defined in a different source file than the calling context.

The steps for using an elemental function are:

1. Write a function in scalar form using standard C/C++.
2. Add __declspec(vector), and perhaps with optional control clauses, to the function declaration so that the compiler understands the intended parallel context(s) for calling it.[3] Additional clauses let you tell the compiler the expected nature of the parameters:
    uniform(b) indicates that parameter b will be the same for all invocations from a parallel loop. linear(a:k) indicates that parameter a will step by k in each successive invocation from the original serial loop. For example, linear(p:4) says that parameter p steps by 4 on each invocation. Omitting :k is the same as using :1.
3. Invoke the function from a loop marked with *#*pragma simd or with array section arguments.

Listings B.6 and B.7 show definition and use, respectively, of an elemental function. This code will likely perform better than a program where the function is not marked as elemental, particulary when the function is defined in a separate file. Writing in this manner exposes the opportunity explicitly

```
1   __declspec(vector(linear(a),uniform(b)))
2   void bar(float *a, float *b, int c, int d) {
3       if( *a>0 )
4           *a = b[c+d];
5   }
```

LISTING B.6

Defining an elemental function. The declspec tells the compiler to generate, in addition to the usual code, a specialized version for efficiently handling vectorized chunks where a has unit stride and b is invariant.

---

[3] Section B.10.1 describes __attribute__ and C++11 attribute alternatives to __declspec.

```
1  __declspec(vector(linear(a),uniform(b)))
2  void bar(float *a, float *b, int c, int d);
3
4  void foo(float *a, float *b, int* c, int* d, int n) {
5  #pragma simd
6     for( int i=0; i<n; ++i )
7        bar( a+i, b, c[i], d[i] );
8  }
```

LISTING B.7

Calling an elemental function from a vectorizable loop. The `declspec` on the prototype tells the compiler that the specialized version from Listing B.6 exists. As usual in C/C++, a separate prototype is unnecessary if the function is defined first in the same file.

instead of hoping that a super optimizing compiler will discover the opportunity, which is particularly important in examples less trivial than this one.

Alternatively, the caller could call the elemental function from array notation, like this:

```
bar(&a[0:n], b, c[0:n], d[0:n]);
```

B.10.1 Attribute Syntax

If the compiler recognizes GNU-style attributes, you can use `__attribute__((vector))` to mark the function. As of this writing, the Intel compiler recognized both `__declspec` and `__attribute__` forms on Linux and Mac OS, but only the `__declspec` form on Windows.

Here are the first two lines of Listing B.6 written with the GNU-style attribute:

```
__attribute((vector(linear(a),uniform(b))))
void bar(float *a, float *b, int c, int d) {
```

Eventually elemental function markup will be expressible using C++11 attribute syntax.

B.11 NOTE ON C++11

C++11 **lambda expressions** (Section D.2) have a nifty application in Cilk Plus that in effect lets you spawn a statement. Here is an example that spawns the statement `while (foo())bar(baz);`:

```
cilk_spawn [&]{
   while (foo()) bar(baz);
}();
```

The code is really just spawning a functor created by the lambda. Do not forget the trailing parentheses—they are part of the spawned call. See also Section 14.6 for a novel use of a lambda expression with array notation.

B.12 NOTES ON SETUP

Cilk Plus does not require explicit setup in the user code; all capabilities self-initialize as needed. To compile code with Cilk Plus features, the inclusion of a number of Cilk Plus header files may be required. We recommend always using the header `<cilk/cilk.h>`, so you do not have to write "ugly" spellings like `_Cilk_spawn`. Other supplied header files are needed if you are using reducers or the API calls.

The serialization described in Section B.4 can be achieved by including `<cilk/cilk_stub.h>` or using the Intel compiler option `cilk-serialize`.

The Cilk Plus API, defined in `<cilk/cilk_api.h>`, provides some control over the runtime. By default, the number of worker threads is set to the number of cores on the host system. In most cases, the default value works well and should be used. However, you can increase or decrease the number of workers under program control using the following API call:

```
__cilkrts_set_param("nworkers",n)
```

or via the environment variable `CILK_NWORKERS`. You may want to use fewer workers than the number of processor cores available in order to run tests or to reserve resources for other programs. In some cases, you may want to oversubscribe by creating more workers than the number of available processor cores. This may be useful if you have workers waiting on locks, or if you want to test a parallel program on a single-core computer.

There are additional detailed "under the hood" controls and information exposed in the Cilk Plus API—for example:

```
__cilkrts_get_worker_number()  Gets worker number.
__cilkrts_get_total_workers()  Gets total number of workers.
```

Consult the Cilk Plus documentation for more information. We stress that using the two queries as part of an algorithm is usually a sign of bad style in Cilk Plus. The whole point of Cilk Plus is to abstract away the number of workers.

B.13 HISTORY

The Cilk language has been developed since 1994 at the MIT Laboratory for Computer Science. It is based on ANSI C, with the addition of just a handful of Cilk-specific keywords.

Cilk is a faithful extension of C and the serial elision (Section B.4) of any well-defined Cilk program is always a valid serial implementation in C that matches the semantics of the parallel Cilk program. Despite several similarities, Cilk is not directly related to AT&T Bell Labs' Concurrent C.

In the original MIT Cilk implementation, the first Cilk keyword was `cilk`, which identified a function as written in Cilk. This keyword was needed to distinguish Cilk code from C code, because in the original implementation Cilk procedures could call C procedures directly, but C procedures could not directly call or spawn Cilk procedures.

A commercial version of Cilk, called Cilk++, that supported C++ and was compatible with both GCC and Microsoft C++ compilers was developed by Cilk Arts, Inc. The `cilk` keyword morphed into `extern "cilk"`. Cilk++ introduced the notion of hyperobjects [FHLLB09], which elegantly eliminated the need for several keywords in the original Cilk pertaining to reductions.

In July 2009, Intel Corporation acquired, from Cilk Arts, the Cilk++ technology and the Cilk trademark. In 2010, Intel released a commercial implementation in its compilers combined with some data parallel constructs, under the name Intel Cilk Plus. Intel has also released specifications, libraries, code, and the ability to use the "Cilk Plus" name (trademark) with other compilers.

Intel Cilk Plus extends Cilk and Cilk++ by adding array extensions, being incorporated in a commercial compiler (from Intel), and having compatibility with existing debuggers. Intel Cilk Plus adopted a significant simplication proposed by Cilk++ team: Eliminate the need to distingush Cilk linkage from C/C++ linkage. This was a major improvement in usability, particularly for highly templated libraries, where linkage specifications can become confusing or impossible. Furthermore, erasing the distinction between Cilk and C/C++ functions enabled C/C++ functions to be spawned directly.

Intel has published both a language specification and an ABI specification to enable other compilers to implement Cilk Plus in a compatible way and to optionally utilize the Intel runtime. The Cilk Plus extensions to C and C++ have also been implemented in a development branch version of the GCC compiler.

Intel has stated its desire to refine Cilk Plus and to enable it to be implemented by other compilers to gain industry-wide adoption.

B.14 SUMMARY

Cilk Plus is a language specification that provides for both thread and vector parallelism in C and C++ via keywords, syntax for array operations, elemental functions, and pragmas. Much more information is available at `http://cilkplus.org`.

TBB

C

This appendix provides a concise introduction to Intel Threading Building Blocks (Intel TBB). It covers the subset used by this book. A good introduction is available in the O'Reilly Nutshell Book on TBB, which covers the essentials of TBB [Rei07]. The book was published in 2007 when TBB version 2.0 appeared, so some newer features are not covered. It is nevertheless a solid introduction to TBB. For a more complete guide, see the TBB Reference, Tutorial, and Design Patterns documents, which can be downloaded from `http://threadingbuildingblocks.org/`.

TBB is a collection of components that outfits C++ for parallel programming. Figure C.1 illustrates these components. At the heart of TBB is a task scheduler, which is most often used indirectly via the parallel algorithms in TBB, such as `tbb::parallel_for`. The rest of TBB provides thread-aware memory allocation, portable synchronization primitives, scalable containers, and a variety of useful utilities. Each part is important for parallelism. Indeed the non-tasking features are intended for use with other parallelism frameworks such as Cilk Plus, ArBB, and OpenMP, so that those frameworks do not have to duplicate key functionality.

C.1 UNIQUE CHARACTERISTICS

TBB shares many of the key attributes of Cilk Plus as enumerated in Section B.1, but it differs form Cilk Plus on several points:

- TBB is designed to work without any compiler changes, and thus be quickly portable to new platforms. As a result, TBB has been ported to a multitude of key operating systems and processors, and code written with TBB can likewise be easily ported.
- As a consequence of avoiding any need for compiler support, TBB does not have direct support for vector parallelism. However, TBB combined with array notation or `#pragma simd` from Cilk Plus or auto-vectorization can be an effective tool for exploiting both thread and vector parallelism.
- TBB is designed to provide comprehensive support for C++ developers in one package. It supports multiple paradigms of parallel programming. It goes beyond the strict fork–join model of Cilk Plus by supporting pipelines, dataflow, and unstructured task graphs. The additional power that these features bring is sometimes worth the additional complexity they bring to a program.
- TBB is intended to provide low-level services such as memory allocation and atomic operations that can be used by programs using other frameworks, including Cilk Plus.

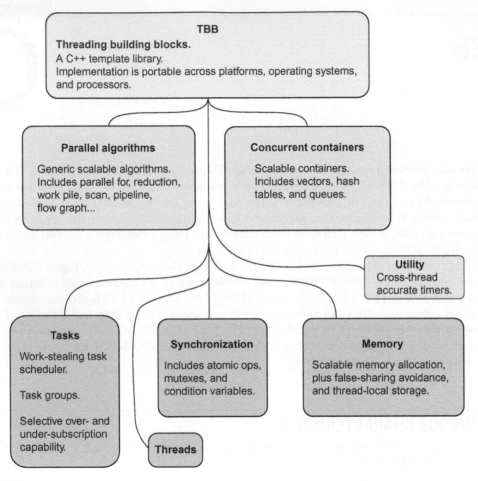

FIGURE C.1

Overview of Threading Building Blocks.

TBB is an active open source project. It is widely adopted and often cited in articles about parallelism in C++. It continues to grow as the parallel ecosystem evolves.

C.2 USING TBB

Include the header <tbb/tbb.h> to use TBB in a source file. All public identifiers are in namespace tbb or tbb::flow. In the following descriptions, the phrase "in parallel" indicates that parallelism is permitted if resources allow, but is not mandated. As with Cilk Plus, the license to ignore unnecessary parallelism allows the TBB task scheduler to use parallelism efficiently.

C.3 `parallel_for`

The function template `parallel_for` maps a functor across range of values. The template takes several forms. The simplest is:

```
tbb::parallel_for(first,last,f)
```

where f is a functor. It evaluates the expression $f(i)$ in parallel for all i in the half-open interval [$first,last$), Both $first$ and $last$ must be of the same integral type. It is a parallel equivalent of:

```
for (auto i=first; i<last; ++i) f(i);
```

A slight variation specifies a stride:

```
tbb::parallel_for(first,last,stride,f)
```

It is like the previous version, except that the possible values of i step by $stride$, starting with $first$. This form is a parallel equivalent of:

```
for (auto i=first; i<last; i+=stride ) f(i);
```

Another form of `parallel_for` takes two arguments:

```
tbb::parallel_for(range,f)
```

It decomposes $range$ into subranges and applies f to each subrange, in parallel. Hence, the programmer has the opportunity to optimize f to operate on an entire subrange instead of a single index. This version in effect exposes the tiled implementation of the map pattern used by TBB.

This form of parallel for also generalizes the parallel map pattern beyond one-dimensional ranges. The argument $range$ can be any *recursively splittable range* type. A type R is such a type if it has the following methods:

`R::R(const R&)`	Copy constructor.
`R:: R()`	Destructor.
`bool R::is_divisible() const`	True if splitting constructor can be called, false otherwise.
`bool R::empty() const`	True if range is empty, false otherwise.
`R::R(R& r, split)`	Splitting constructor. It splits range `r` into two subranges. One of the subranges is the newly constructed range. The other subrange is overwritten onto `r`.

The implementation of `parallel_for` uses these methods to implement a generic recursive map in the spirit of Listing 8.1.

C.3.1 `blocked_range`

The most commonly used recursive range is `tbb::blocked_range`. It is typically used with integral types or random-access iterator types. For example, `blocked_range<int>(0,8)` represents the index range $\{0,1,2,3,4,5,6,7\}$. An optional third argument called the *grainsize* specifies the maximum size for splitting. It defaults to 1. For example, the following snippet splits a range of size 30 with grainsize 20 into two indivisible subranges of size 15:

```
// Construct half-open interval [0,30) with grainsize of 20
blocked_range<int> r(0,30,20);
assert(r.is_divisible());
// Call splitting constructor
blocked_range<int> s(r);
// Now r=[0,15) and s=[15,30) and both have a grainsize 20
// Inherited from the original value of r
assert(!r.is_divisible());
assert(!s.is_divisible());
```

Listing 4.2 on page 126 shows an example that uses blocked_range with parallel_for.

A two-dimensional variant is called tbb::blocked_range2d. It permits using a single parallel_for to iterate over two dimensions at once, which sometimes yields better cache behavior than nesting two one-dimensional instances of parallel_for.

C.3.2 Partitioners

The range form of parallel_for takes an optional *partitioner* argument, which lets the programmer specify performance-related tactics [RVK08]. The argument can have one of three types:

- auto_partitioner: The runtime will try to subdivide the range sufficiently to balance load, but no further. This behavior is the same as when no partitioner is specified.
- simple_partitioner: The runtime must subdivide the range into subranges as finely as possible; that is, method is_divisible will be false for the final subranges.
- affinity_partitioner: Request that the assignment of subranges to underlying threads be similar to a previous invocation of parallel_for or parallel_reduce with the same affinity_partitioner object.

These partitioners also work with parallel_reduce.

An invocation of parallel_for with a simple_partitioner looks like:

```
parallel_for(r,f,simple_partitioner());
```

This partitioner is useful in two scenarios:

- The functor *f* uses a fixed amount of memory for temporary storage, and hence cannot deal with subranges of arbitrary size. For example, if *r* is a blocked_range, the partitioner guarantees that *f* is invoked on subranges not exceeding the grainsize of *r*.
- The work for *f*(*r*) is highly unbalanced in a way that fools the auto_partitioner heuristic into not dividing work finely enough to balance load.

An affinity_partitioner can be used for **cache fusion** (Section 4.4). Unlike the other two partitioners, it carries state. The state holds information for replaying the assignment of subranges to threads. Listing C.1 shows an example of its use in a common pattern: serially iterating a map. In the listing, variable ap enables cache fusion of each map to the next map. Because it is carrying information between serial iterations, it must be declared outside the serial loop.

```
1   void relax(
2       double* a, // Pointer to array of data
3       double* b, // Pointer to temporary storage
4       size_t n,   // Number of data elements
5       int iterations // Number of serial iterations
6   ) {
7       assert(iterations%2==0);
8       // Partitioner should be declared outside the loop
9       tbb::affinity_partitioner ap;
10      // Serial loop around a parallel loop
11      for( size_t t=0; t<iterations; ++t ) {
12          tbb::parallel_for(
13              tbb::blocked_range<size_t>(1,n-1),
14              [=]( tbb::blocked_range<size_t> r ) {
15                  size_t e = r.end();
16  #pragma simd
17                  for( size_t i=r.begin(); i<e; ++i )
18                      b[i] = (a[i-1]+a[i]+a[i+1])*(1/3.0);
19              },
20              ap);
21          std::swap(a,b);
22      }
23  }
```

LISTING C.1

Example of `affinity_partitioner`. TBB uses the variable `ap` to remember which threads ran which subranges of the previous invocation of `parallel_for` and biases execution toward replaying that assignment. The `pragma simd` is for showmanship. It makes the impact of the partitioner more dramatic by raising arithmetic performance so that memory bandwidth becomes the limiting resource.

C.4 `parallel_reduce`

Function template `parallel_reduce` performs a reduction over a recursive range. It has several forms. The form used in this book is:

```
T result = tbb::parallel_reduce(
    range,
    identity,
    subrange_reduction,
    combine);
```

where:

- `range` is a recursive range as for `parallel_for`, such as `blocked_range`.
- `identity` is the identity element of type T. The type of this argument determines the type used to accumulate the reduction value, so be careful about what type it has.

- `subrange_reduction` is a functor such that *subrange_reduction(subrange,init)* returns a reduction value over *init* and *subrange*. The type of *subrange* is the type of the *range* argument to `parallel_reduce`. The type of *init* is *T*, and the returned reduction value must be convertible to type *T*. Do not forget to include the contribution of *init* to the reduction value.
- `combine` is a functor such that *combine(x,y)* takes two arguments of type *T* and returns a reduction value for them. This function must be associative but does not need to be commutative.

Listings 5.5 and 5.6 in Section 5.3.4 show example invocations. The latter listing demonstrates how to do accumulation at higher precision than the values being reduced.

An alternative way to do reduction is via class `tbb::enumerable_thread_specific`, as demonstrated in Section 11.3. General advice on which to use:

- If type *T* takes little space and is cheap to copy, or the combiner operation is non-commutative, use `parallel_reduce`.
- If type *T* is large and expensive to copy *and* the combiner operation is commutative, use `enumerable_thread_specific`.

C.5 parallel_deterministic_reduce

Template function `parallel_deterministic_reduce` is a variant of `parallel_reduce` that is **deterministic** even when the combiner operation is non-associative. The result is *not* necessarily the same as left-to-right serial reduction, even when executed with a single worker, because the template uses a fixed tree-like reduction order for a given input.

As of this writing, `parallel_deterministic_reduce` is a "preview feature" that must be enabled by setting the preprocessory symbol TBB_PREVIEW_DETERMINISTIC_REDUCE=1 either on the compiler command line or *before* including TBB headers in a source file.

C.6 parallel_pipeline

Template function `parallel_pipeline` is used for building a **pipeline** of serial and parallel stages. See Section 9.4.1 for details and Listing 12.2 for an example.

C.7 parallel_invoke

Template function `parallel_invoke` evaluates a fixed set of functors in parallel. For example,

```
tbb::parallel_invoke(f,g,h);
```

evaluates the expressions `f()`, `g()`, and `h()` in parallel and waits until they all complete. Anywhere from 2 to 10 functors are currently supported. Listing 13.3 (page 302) and Listing 15.4 (page 322) show uses of `parallel_invoke`. Both listings cross-reference similar code in Cilk Plus, so you can compare the syntactic difference.

C.8 task_group

Class task_group runs an arbitrary number of functors in parallel. Listing C.2 shows an example.

In general, a single task_group should not be used to run a large number of tasks, because it can become a sequential bottleneck. Consider using parallel_for for a large number of tasks.

If one of the functors throws an exception, the task group is cancelled. This means that any tasks in the group that have not yet started will not start at all, but all currently running tasks will keep going. After all running tasks in the group complete, one of the exceptions thrown by the tasks will be thrown to the caller of wait. Hence, if nested parallelism is created by nesting task_group, the exception propagates up the task tree until it is caught.

Listing 8.12 on page 235 shows a use of task_group.

C.9 task

Class tbb::task is the lowest-level representation of a task in TBB. It is designed primarily for efficient execution, not convenience, because it serves as a foundation, and thus should impose minimal performance penalty. Higher level templates such as parallel_for and task_group provide

```
1   // Item in a linked  list
2   class morsel {
3   public:
4       void munch();
5       morsel* next;
6   };
7
8   // Apply method munch to each item in a linked
9   // list  rooted at p
10  void munch_list( morsel* p ) {
11      tbb::task_group g;
12      while( p ) {
13          // Call munch on an item
14          g.run( [=]{p->munch();} );
15          // Advance to the  next  item
16          p = p->next;
17      }
18      // Wait for all  tasks  to complete
19      g.wait();
20  }
```

LISTING C.2

Using task_group.

convenient interfaces. Tasks can be spawned explicitly, or implicitly when all of their predecessor tasks complete. See the discussion of Listing 8.13 on pages 236–237 for how to use it.

C.9.1 empty_task

A tbb::empty_task is a task that does nothing. It is sometimes used for synchronization purposes, as in Listing 8.13 on pages 236–237.

C.10 atomic

Atomic objects have update operations that appear to happen instantaneously, as a single indivisible task. They are often used for lock-free synchronization. Atomic objects can be declared as instances of the class template tbb::atomic<T>, where T is an integral, enum, or pointer type. Listing C.3 shows an example use case.

```
1  float array[N];
2  tbb::atomic<int> count;
3
4  void append( float value ) {
5      array[count++] = value;
6  }
```

LISTING C.3

Example of using atomic<int> as a counter.

If m threads execute count++ at the same time, and its initial value is k, each thread will get a distinct result value drawn from the set $k, k+1, \ldots, k+m-1$, and afterward count will have value $k+m$. This, is true even if the threads do this simultaneously. Thus, despite the lack of mutexes, the code correctly appends items to the array.

In the example it is critical to use the value returned by count++ and not reread count, because another thread might intervene and cause the reread value to be different than the result of count++.

Here is a description of the atomic operations supported by a variable x declared as a tbb::atomic <X>:

- *read, write*: Reads and writes on x are atomic. This property is not always true of non-atomic types. For example, on hardware with a natural word size of 32 bits, often reads and writes of 64-bit values are not atomic, even if executed by a single instruction.
- *fetch-and-add*: The operations x+=k, x−=k, ++x, x++, −−x, and x−− have the usual meaning, but atomically update x. The expression x.fetch_and_add(k) is equivalent to (x+=k)−k.
- *exchange*: The operation x.fetch_and_store(y) atomically performs x=y and returns the previous value of x.

```
1   // Node in a linked list
2   struct node {
3      float data;
4      node* next;
5   };
6
7   // Root of a linked list
8   tbb::atomic<node*> root;
9
10  // Atomically prepend node a to the list
11  void add_to_list( node* a ) {
12     for(;;) {
13        // Take snapshot of root
14        node* b = root;
15        // Use the snapshot as link for a
16        a->next = b;
17        // Update root with a if root is still equal to b
18        if( root.compare_and_swap(a,b)==b ) break;
19        // Otherwise start over and try again
20     }
21  }
22
23  // Atomically grab pointer to the entire list and reset root to NULL
24  node* grab_list() {
25     return root.fetch_and_store((node*)NULL);
26  }
```

LISTING C.4

Using atomic operations on a list.

- *compare-and-swap*: The operation `x.compare_and_swap(y,z)` atomically performs `if(x==z) x=y`, and returns the original value of `x`. The operation is said to succeed if the assignment happens. Code can check for success by testing whether the return value equals `z`.

Listing C.4 shows uses of compare-and-swap and exchange to manipulate a linked list.

Doing more complicated list operations atomically is beyond the scope of this appendix.

In particular, implementing *pop* with a compare-and-swap loop scheme similar to the one in `add_to_list` requires special care to avoid a hazard called the *ABA problem* [Mic04]. The code shown has a benign form of the ABA problem, which happens when:

1. A thread executes `node* b=a`, and a was NULL.
2. Another threads executes `add_to_list` and `grab_list`.
3. The thread in step 1 executes `root.compare_and_swap(a,b)`. The compare-and-swap sees that *a == NULL* and succeeds, just as if no other thread intervened.

The point is that a successful compare-and-swap does *not* mean that no thread intervened. Here, there is no harm done because as long as `root==a->next` when the compare-and-swap succeeds, the resulting list is correct. But, in other operations on linked structures, the effects can corrupt the structure or even cause invalid memory operations on freed memory.

Compare-and-swap loops also require care if there might be heavy contention. If P threads execute a compare-and-swap loop to update a location, $P-1$ threads will fail and have to try again. Then $P-2$ threads will fail, and so forth. The net burden is $\Theta(P^2)$ attempts and corresponding memory traffic, which can saturate the memory interconnect. One way to avoid the problem is *exponential backoff*—wait after each compare-and-swap fails, and double the wait after each subsequent failure.

C.11 enumerable_thread_specific

An object e of type enumerable_thread_specific<T> has a separate instance (or "local view") of T for each thread that accesses it. The expression e.local() returns a reference to the local view for the calling thread. Thus, multiple threads can operate on a enumerable_thread_specific without locking. The expression e.combine(*combine*) returns a reduction over the local view. See Section 11.3 for more details on how to use enumerable_thread_specific.

C.12 NOTES ON C++11

Though TBB works fine with C++98, it is simpler to use with C++11. In particular, C++11 introduces **lambda expressions** (Section D.2) and auto declarations (Section D.1) that simplify use of TBB and other template libraries. Lambda expressions are already implemented in the latest versions of major C++ compilers. We strongly recommend using them to teach, learn, and use TBB, because once you get past the novelty, they make TBB code easier to write and easier to read.

Additionally, TBB implements most of some C++11 features related to threading, thus providing an immediate migration path for taking advantage of these features even before they are implemented by C++ compilers. This path is further simplified by the way that TBB's injection of these features into namespace std is optional.

These features are:

- std::mutex: A mutex with a superset of the C++11 interface. The superset includes TBB's interface for mutexes.
- std::lock_guard: C++11 support for exception-safe scoped locking.
- std::thread: A way to create a thread and wait for it to complete. Sometimes threads really are a better solution than tasks, particularly if the "work" must be preemptively scheduled or mostly involves waiting for something to happen. Also, note that threads provide mandatory parallelism, which may be important when interacting with the outside world or in a user interface. Tasks provide optional parallelism, which is better for efficient computation.
- std::condition_variable: A way to wait until the state protected by a mutex meets a condition.

The parts of the C++11 interface not implemented in TBB are those that involve time intervals, since those would have involved implementing the C++11 time facilities. However, TBB does have equivalents to this functionality, based on TBB's existing `tick_count` interface for time.

A condition variable solves the problem of letting a thread wait until a state protected by a mutex meets a condition. It is used when threads need to wait for some other thread to update some state protected by a mutex. The waiting thread(s) acquire the mutex, check the state, and decide whether to wait. They wait on an associated condition variable. The `wait` member function atomically releases the mutex and starts the wait. Another thread acquires mutex associated with the condition, modifies the state protected by the mutex, and then signals one or all of the waiter(s) when it is done. Once the mutex is released, the waiters reacquire the mutex and can recheck the state to see if they can proceed or need to continue waiting.

Condition variables should be the method of choice to have a thread wait until a condition changes. TBB makes this method of choice portable to more operating systems.

C.13 HISTORY

The development of TBB was done at Intel and with the involvement of one of the authors of this book, Arch Robison. We can therefore recount the history of TBB from a personal perspective.

TBB was first available as a commercial library from Intel in the summer of 2006, not long after Intel shipped its first dual-core processors. It provided a much needed comprehensive answer to the question, "What must be fixed or added to C++ for parallel programming?" TBB's key programming abstractions for parallelism focused on logical specification of parallelism via algorithm templates. By also including a task-stealing scheduler, a thread-aware memory allocator, portable mutexes, global timestamps, and concurrent containers, TBB provided what was needed to program for parallelism in C++. The first release was primarily focused on strict **fork–join** or loop-type **data parallelism**.

The success of Intel TBB would, however, have been limited if it had remained a proprietary solution. Even during the release of version 1.0, Intel was in discussions with early customers on the future direction of TBB in both features and licensing.

Watching and listening to early adopters, such as Autodesk Maya, highlighted that much of the value of TBB was not only for data parallelism but also for more general parallelism using tasks, pipelines, scalable memory allocation, and lower-level constructs like synchronization primitives. Intel also received encouragement to make TBB portable by creating and supporting it via an open source project.

This customer feedback and encouragement led, only a year later, to version 2.0, which included a GPL v2 with the runtime exception version of both the source and binaries, as well as maintaining the availability of non-GPL binaries. Intel's customers had said that this would maximize adoption, and the results have definitely shown they were right.

Intel increased the staffing on TBB, worked proactively to build a community to support the project, and continued to innovate with new usage models and features over the next few years. We have been amazed and humbled by the response of such users as Adobe Systems, Avid, Epic Games, Dream-Works, and many others, along with that of other community members. TBB now has a very large user community and has had contributions that have led to Intel TBB being ported to many operating systems, platforms, and processors. We appreciate Intel's willingness to let us prove that an open source project initiated by Intel, yet supporting non-x86 processors, not only made sense—but would be very popular with developers. We've definitely proven that!

Through the involvement of customers and community, TBB has grown to be the most feature-rich and comprehensive solution for parallel application development available today. It has also become the most popular!

The TBB project was grown by a steady addition of ports to a wide variety of machines and operating systems and the addition of numerous new features that have added to the applicability and power of TBB.

TBB was one of the inspirations for Microsoft's Task Parallel Library (TPL) for .NET and Microsoft's Parallel Patterns Library (PPL) for C++. Intel and Microsoft have worked jointly to specify and implement a common subset of functionality shared by TBB and Microsoft's Parallel Patterns Library (PPL). In some cases, Intel and Microsoft have exchanged implementations and tests to ensure compatibility. An appendix of *The TBB Reference Manual* summarizes the common subset.

The most recent version of TBB, version 4.0, adds a powerful capability for expressing parallelism as data flowing through a graph. Use of TBB continues to grow, and the open source project enjoys serious support from Intel and others.

The Intel Cilk Plus project complements TBB by supplying C interfaces, simpler syntax, better opportunity for compiler optimization, and data parallel operations that lead to effective vectorization. None of these would be possible without direct compiler support. Intel briefly considered calling Cilk Plus simply "compiled TBB." While this conveyed the desire to extend TBB for the objectives mentioned, it proved complicated to explain the name so the name Cilk Plus was introduced. The full interoperability between TBB and Cilk Plus increases the number of options for software developers without adding complications. Like TBB, Intel has open sourced Cilk Plus to help encourage adoption and contribution to the project. TBB and Cilk Plus are sister projects at Intel.

C.14 SUMMARY

Intel Threading Building Blocks is a widely used and highly portable template library that provides a comprehensive set of solutions to programs using tasks in C++. It also provides a set of supporting functionality that can be used with or without the tasking infrastructure, such as concurrency-safe STL-compatible data structures, memory allocation, and portable atomics. Although we focus on tasks in this book due to their increased machine independence, safety, and scalability over threads, TBB also implements a significant subset of the C++11 standard's thread support, including platform-independent mutexes and condition variables. Much more information is available at http://threadingbuildingblocks.org.

C++11

D

This appendix explains new features in the C++ 2011 standard, informally called C++11, that are used in this book. These features are available in several widely used C++ compilers. This is not intended to be a full tutorial on these features, but should provide enough information to enable understanding of the examples. It also explains suitable substitutes for use with C++ 1998 compilers.

D.1 DECLARING WITH auto

C++11 permits the auto keyword to be used in place of a type in some contexts where the type can be deduced by the compiler. Here is an example:

```
std::vector<double> v;
...
for (auto i = v.begin(); i != v.end(); ++i) {
   auto& x = *i;
   ...
}
```

The C++98 equivalent would be:

```
std::vector<double> v;
...
for (std::vector<double>::iterator i = v.begin(); i != v.end(); ++i) {
   double& x = *i;
   ...
}
```

C++11 introduces a range-based for statement that can make this example even shorter, but it was not widely available at the time of this writing.

D.2 LAMBDA EXPRESSIONS

Lambda expressions are a C++11 feature already supported by several compilers, such as Intel C++ 12.0, GCC 4.5, and Microsoft Visual Studio 2010. Lambda expressions are important because they greatly simplify using templates to implement control structures, including parallel ones. A key point

```
1   #include <algorithm>
2
3   class comparator {
4       const float key;
5   public:
6       comparator( float key_ ) : key(key_) { }
7       bool operator()( const float& x ) const {
8           return (x < key);
9       }
10  };
11
12  // Return number of keys in [ first , last ) that are less than given key
13  size_t count_less_than_key(
14      float* first,
15      float* last,
16      float key
17  ) {
18      return std::count_if(first, last, comparator(key));
19  }
```

LISTING D.1

Using a manually written functor comparator.

to understand is there is nothing magic about lambda expressions. A lambda expression is simply a concise way to create a function object that could otherwise be written manually.

For example, consider the standard library template std::count(*first,last,pred*). It counts the number of elements in the half-open interval [*first,last*) for which predicate *pred* holds. Listing D.1 shows an example that counts how many elements are less than a key of type float.

Class comparator is called a *function object*, or **functor**. It has three parts:

- A field for storing the key
- A constructor that captures the key
- A definition of what to do when the class is applied like a function

For example, the following fragment constructs a comparator that compares against 0 and applies it as a function to −1.

```
comparator c(0);              // Calls constructor for comparator
bool is_negative = c(-1);  // Calls comparator::operator()
```

As the counting example shows, writing functor objects can be a lot of work. Lambda expressions make the compiler do this work for you. Listing D.2 shows the counting example rewritten with a lambda expression.

The explicit class definition has completely disappeared. The lambda expression builds the equivalent for you.

```
1   // Return number of keys in [ first , last ) that are less than given key
2   size_t count_less_than_key(
3       float* first,
4       float* last,
5       float key
6   ) {
7       return std::count_if(first, last,
8           [=]( const float& x ) {
9               return x < key;
10          }
11      );
12  }
```

LISTING D.2

Using a lambda expression lets Listing D.1 be rewritten more concisely.

The lambda expression here has three parts:

- A part [=] that describes how to capture local variables outside the lambda
- A parameter list (const float& x), which can be omitted if there are no parameters
- A definition {return key;}

For the sake of exposition, these parts will be discussed in reverse order, from simplest to most subtle.

The definition is a compound statement that becomes the body of the operator() that the compiler will generate. The argument list for a lambda expression becomes the argument list of the operator(). A lambda expression can optionally specify a return type after the argument list. The notation is ->return-type. Here is the lambda expression from the example, rewritten with an explicit return type:

```
[=]( const float& x )->bool {return x < key;}
```

Often the return type does not need to be specified, because if omitted it is inferred by the following rules:

- If the definition is a single statement return *expr*, the return type is the type of *expr*.
- Otherwise, the return type is void.

The capture part describes how to capture local variables. Global variables are never captured since they can be globally referenced. A local variable can be captured **by value** or **by reference**. Capture by value copies the variable into the function object. Capture by reference creates a reference in the function object back to the local variable; the corresponding field in the function object becomes a reference. A lambda expression can specify the kind of capture or none at all:

```
[=]     capture by value
[&]     capture by reference
[]      capture nothing
```

```
1   class assign {
2      float &x, &y;
3      float a, b;
4   public:
5      assign( float& x_, float& y_, float a_, float b_ ) :
6         x(x_), y(y_), a(a_), b(b_) {}
7      void operator()() {x=a; y=b;}
8   };
9
10  float foo( float& x, float b ) {
11     float a=2;
12     float y;
13     auto op = assign(x,y,a,b);
14     op();
15     return y;
16  }
```

LISTING D.3

Mixed capture with handwritten functor. The code is equivalent to Listing D.4.

```
1   float foo( float& x, float b ) {
2      float a=2;
3      float y;
4      auto op = [=,&x,&y] {x = a; y = b;};
5      op();
6      return y;
7   }
```

LISTING D.4

Mixed capture modes. The lambda expression captures x and y by reference and a and b by value.

The same lambda can capture different variables differently. The initial = or & specifies a default, which can be overridden for specific variables. Here are some examples:

[=,&x,&y]   capture by value, except that x and y are captured by reference

[&,x,y]   capture by reference, except that x and y are captured by value

Listing D.4 shows mixed capture modes. The auto in the listing is more than a convenience—lambda expressions have anonymous type and hence it is impossible to name that type in the declaration. Listing D.4 shows that an equivalent functor can be written by hand.

For parallel programming, choosing the proper capture mode can be critical. Capture by value incurs the cost of making a private copy of the captured object. Capture by reference incurs the cost of an extra level of indirection when the object is accessed. In general, use capture by value if the object is small and quick to copy and does not need to be modified. Doing so avoids the extra level of indirection incurred for capture by reference and avoids potential for races. In particular, pointers are small objects. They should be captured by value if they are not going to be modified, even if they point to objects that are going to be modified. Otherwise, use capture by reference, and think carefully about whether there could be races on the local variable being referenced. And, remember, a lambda expression is just a convenience. The object it generates can be reasoned about like a handcrafted function object.

D.3 `std::move`

The C++11 notation $y = $ `std::move`(x) is similar to $y = x$, except that it gives license to change the value of x. For example, if x is an instance of `std::vector`, the move may set x to empty. The advantage is that the license permits significant optimizations in some cases. For example, suppose y is an empty vector and x is a vector with N elements. Assignment takes $\Theta(N)$ time, because each element must be copied. Moving can be done in $\Theta(1)$ time, because it only needs to move internal pointers and size information from x to y, and not copy the vector's contents. In other words, moving is allowed to transfer resources from x to y.

C++11 also adds a "move" counterpart of `std::copy`. Given iterators `first`, `last`, and `result`, a call

```
std::move(first,last,result)
```

moves items in the range `[first,last)` to `[result,result+(last-first))`. Afterward, items in the range `[first,last)` have unspecified values.

For old compilers that do not support `std::move`, you can use one of two replacements for `y = std::move(x)`:

- **assignment**: The assignment $y = x$ is a valid replacement and, for C-like types, has performance similar to that of `y=std::move(x)`. However, for more complicated types, assignment may introduce additional copying overhead that moving can avoid. For example, if y and x are instances of `std::vector`, assignment copies the vector elements, whereas moving does not.
- **swap**: The expression `swap(y,x)` is a valid replacement and, for some object types such as STL containers, may be faster than `y=x`. The reason is that STL containers often implement `swap` in a way that swaps a few internal pointers instead of copying full state. However, `swap` introduces an unnecessary update of x and thus may be slower for C-like types.

You can replace `std::move(first,last,result)` with `std::copy(first,last,result)`, possibly adding additional copying overhead that moving avoids.

The `std::move` feature is based on a language feature called *rvalue references* [HSK08].

Glossary

E

The specialized vocabulary used in this book is defined here. In some cases, where existing terminology is ambiguous, we have given all meanings but note which meaning we primarily use in this book.

absolute speedup: Speedup in which the best parallel solution to a problem is compared to the best serial solution to the same problem, even if they use different algorithms. See *relative speedup*.

access controls: Any mechanism to regulate access to something, but for parallel programs this term generally applies to shared memory. The term is sometimes extended to I/O devices as well. For parallel programming, the objective is generally to provide deterministic results by preventing an object from being modified by multiple tasks simultaneously. Most often this is referred to as *mutual exclusion*, which includes locks, mutexes, atomic operations, and *transactional memory* models. This may also require some control on reading access to prevent viewing of an object in a partially modified state.

actual parallelism: The number of physical *workers* available to execute a parallel program.

algorithmic skeleton: Synonym for *pattern*, specifically the subclass of patterns having to do with algorithms.

algorithm strategy pattern: A class of patterns that emphasize the parallelization of the internal workings of algorithms.

aliasing: Refers to when two distinct program identifiers or expressions refer to overlapping memory locations. For example, if two pointers p and q point to the same location, then p[0] and q[0] are said to alias each other. The potential for aliasing can severely restrict a compiler's ability to optimize a program, even when there is no actual aliasing.

Amdahl's Law: Speedup is limited by the non-*parallelizable* serial portion of the work. Compare with other attempts to characterize the bounds of parallelism: *span complexity* and *Gustafson–Barsis' Law*. See Section 2.5.4.

application binary interface (ABI): A set of binary entry points corresponding to an *application programming interface*. Fixed ABIs are useful to allow relinking to different implementations of a library module.

application programming interface (API): An interface (set of function calls, operators, variables, and/or classes) by which an application developer uses a module. The implementation details of a module are ideally hidden from the application developer and the functionality is only defined through the API.

arithmetic intensity: The ratio of computational (typically arithmetic) operations to communication, where communication includes memory operations. Comparing this ratio for an algorithm with the hardware's ratio gives a hint of whether computation or communication will be the limiting resource. See Section 10.3.

array operations: See *vector operations*.

array processors: See *vector processor*.

array-of-structures (AoS): A data layout for collections of heterogeneous data where all the data for each element is stored in adjacent physical locations, even if the data are of different types. Compare with *structure-of-arrays*.

associative cache: A cache organization where copies of data in main memory can be stored anywhere in the cache.

associative operation: An operation $\otimes$ is associative if $(a \otimes b) \otimes c = a \otimes (b \otimes c)$. Modular integer arithmetic is associative. Real addition is associative, but floating-point addition is not. However, sometimes the roundoff differences from reassociating floating-point addition are small enough to be ignored, in which case floating-point operations can be considered approximately associative.

asymptotic complexity: Algebraic limit on behavior, including time and space but also ratios such as *speedup and efficiency*. See *big O notation, big Omega notation*, and *big Theta notation*.

asymptotic efficiency: An *asymptotic complexity* measure for *efficiency*.

asymptotic speedup: An *asymptotic complexity* measure for *speedup*.

atomic operation: An operation guaranteed to appear as if it occurred indivisibly without interference from other threads. For example, a processor might provide a memory increment operation. This operation needs to read a value from memory, increment it, and write it back to memory. An atomic increment guarantees that the final memory value is the same as would have occurred if no other operations on that memory location were allowed to happen between the read and the write. See Section C.10, and *lock* and *mutual exclusion*.

atomic scatter pattern: A *non-deterministic* data pattern in which multiple writers to a single storage location result in exactly one value being written and all others being discarded. The value written is chosen non-deterministically from the multiple sources. The only guarantee is that the resulting value in the target memory locations will be one of the values being written by at least one of the writers. See Section 6.2.

attached co-processor: A separate processor, often on an add-in card (such as a PCIe card), usually with its own physical memory, which may or may not be in a separate address space from the host processor. Often also known as an accelerator (although it may only accelerate specific workloads).

auto-vectorization: Automatically generating *vectorized* code from programs expressed using serial programming languages.

autotuning: The process of automatically adjusting parameters in parameterized code in order to achieve optimal performance.

available parallelism: See *potential parallelism*.

bandwidth: The rate at which information is transferred, either from memory or over a communications channel. This term is used when the process being measured can be given a frequency-domain interpretation. When applied to computation, it can be seen as being equivalent to *throughput*.

barrier: When a computation is broken into phases, it is often necessary to ensure that all threads complete all the work in one phase before any thread moves onto another phase. A barrier is a form of *synchronization* that ensures this. Threads arriving at a barrier wait there until the last thread arrives, then all threads continue. A barrier can be implemented using an *atomic operation*. For example, all threads might try to increment a shared variable, then *block* if the value of that variable does not equal the number of threads that need to synchronize at the barrier. The last thread to arrive can then reset the barrier to zero and release all the blocked threads.

big O notation: Complexity notation that denotes an upper bound; written as $O(f(n))$. Big O notation is useful for classification of algorithm efficiency. In particular, big O notation is used to classify algorithms based on how they respond to changes in their input set in terms of processing time or other characteristics of interest.

 For instance, a bubble sort routine may be described as taking $O(n^2)$ time because the time to run a bubble sort routine is proportional to the square of the size of the data set to sort. Since big O notation is about asymptotic growth, it may neglect significant constant factors. A pair of algorithms with running times of $n^2 + 100n + 10^{19}$ and $5n^2 + n + 2$, respectively, are both generally described as $O(n^2)$, despite significant differences in performance for most values of n.

 For characterizing the suitability of an algorithm for parallel execution, *big O* analysis applies to both the *work complexity* and the *span complexity*, but typically *big Theta notation* is preferred. See Section 2.5.7.

big Omega notation: Complexity notation that denotes a lower bound; written as $\Omega(f(N))$. See Section 2.5.7.

big Theta notation: Complexity notation that denotes an upper and a lower bound; written as $\Theta(f(N))$. See Section 2.5.7.

binning: The process of subdividing labeled data in a collection into separate sub-collections, each with a unique label. See *bin pattern*.

bin pattern: A generalized version of the *split pattern*, which is in turn a generalization of the *pack pattern*, the bin pattern takes as input a collection of data and a collection of labels to go with every element of that collection, and reorganizes the data into a category (a bin) for every unique label in the input. The determinisitic version of this pattern is stable, in that it preserves the original order of the input collection. One major application of this pattern is in radix sort. It can also be used to implement the *category reduction pattern*. See Section 6.4.

BLAS: The Basic Linear Algebra Subprograms are routines that provide standard building blocks for basic vector and matrix operations. The Level 1 BLAS perform scalar, vector, and vector–vector operations; the Level 2 BLAS perform matrix–vector operations; and the Level 3 BLAS perform matrix–matrix operations. Because the BLAS are efficient, portable, and widely available, they are commonly used in the development of high-quality linear algebra software (LAPACK, for example). A sophisticated and generic implementation of BLAS has been maintained for decades at `http://netlib.org/blas`. Vendor-specific implementations of BLAS are common, including the Intel Math Kernel Library (MKL), which is a highly efficient version of BLAS and other standard routines for Intel architecture.

block: Block can be used in two senses: (1) a state in which a thread is unable to proceed while it waits for some synchronization event, or (2) a region of memory. The second meaning is also used in the sense of dividing a loop into a set of parallel tasks of a suitable *granularity*. To avoid confusion in this book, the term *tile* is generally used for the second meaning, and likewise the term *tiling* is preferred over "blocking."

branch and bound pattern: A *non-deterministic* pattern designated to find one satisfactory answer when many may be possible. Branch refers to using concurrency, and bound refers to limiting the computation in some manner—for example, by using an upper bound (perhaps the best result found so far). This pattern is often used to implement search, where it is highly effective. See Section 3.7.1.

burdened span: The *span* augmented with overhead costs.

by reference: A parameter to a function that acts exactly as if it were the original location passed to the function.

by value: A parameter to a function that is a copy of the original value passed to the function.

cache: A part of memory system that stores copies of data temporarily in a fast memory so that future uses for that data can be handled more quickly than if the request had to be fetched again from a more distant storage. Caches are generally automatic and are designed to enhance programs with *temporal locality* and/or *spatial locality*. Caching systems in modern computers are usually multileveled.

cache coherence: A mechanism for keeping multiple copies of the same data in different caches consistent.

cache conflict: When multiple locations in memory are mapped to the same location in a cache only a subset of them can be kept in cache.

cache fusion: An optimization for a sequence of *vector operations* where the vector operations are broken into *tiles* and the entire sequence executed on each tile, so that the intermediate values can be kept in cache.

cache line: The units in which data retrieved and held by a *cache*; in order to exploit spatial locality, they are generally larger than a word. The general trend is for increasing cache line sizes, which are generally large enough to hold at least two double-precision floating-point numbers, but unlikely to hold more than eight on any current design. Larger cache lines allow for more efficient bulk transfers from main memory but worsen certain issues, including *false sharing* which generally degrades performance.

cache-oblivious programming: Refers to designing an algorithm to have good cache behavior without knowing the size or design of the cache system in advance. This is usually accomplished by using recursive patterns of data locality so that locality is present at all scales. See Section 8.8, as well as [ABF05] and [Vit08].

cancellation: The ability to stop a running (or ready to run) task from another task. Used in the speculative selection pattern discussed in Section 3.6.3.

category reduction pattern: A combination of search and segmented reduction, this is the form of reduction used in the map–reduce programming model. Each input has a label, and reduction occurs only between elements with the same label. The output is a set of reduction results for each unique label. See Section 3.6.8.

circuit complexity: See *span complexity*.

closures: Objects that consist of a function definition and a copy of the environment (that is, the values of all variables referenced by the function) in effect at the time and visible from the scope in which the function was defined. See *lambda function* and Section 3.4.4.

cloud: A set of computers, typically maintained in a data center, that can be allocated dynamically and accessed remotely. Unlike a *cluster*, cloud computers are typically managed by a third party and may host multiple applications from different, unrelated users.

cluster: A set of computers with distributed memory communicating over a high-speed interconnect. The individual computers are often called *nodes*.

codec: An abbreviation for coder–decoder, a module that implements a data compression and decompression algorithm in order to reduce memory storage or communication bandwidth. For example, codecs that compress to/from MPEG4 are common for video.

code fusion: An optimization for a sequence of *vector operations* that combines the operations into a single *elemental function*.

coherent masks: When the SPMD programming model is emulated on SIMD machines using *masking*, the situation where the masks contain all 0's or all 1's.

collective operation: An operation, such as a *reduction* or a *scan*, that acts on a collection of data as a whole. See Chapter 5.

collision: In the *scatter pattern*, or when using random writes from parallel tasks, a collision occurs when two items try to write to the same location. The result is typically *non-deterministic* since it depends on the timing of the writes. In the worst case, a collision results in garbage being written to the location if the writes are not *atomic* and are not protected with *locks*. See Sections 3.5.5 and 6.2.

combiner operation: The (ideally) associative and (possibly) commutative operation used in the definition of *collective operations* such as *reduction* and *scan*. See Chapter 5.

communication: Any exchange of data or *synchronization* between software tasks or threads. Understanding that communication costs are often a limiting factor in scaling is a critical concept for parallel programming.

communication avoiding algorithm: An algorithm that avoids communication, even if it results in additional or redundant computation.

commutative operation: A commutative operation $\oplus$ satisfies the equation $a \oplus b = b \oplus a$ for all a and b in its domain. Some techniques for vectorizing reductions require commutativity.

composability: The ability to use two components with each other. Can refer to system features, programming models, or software components. See Section 1.5.4.

concurrent: Logically happening simultaneously. Two tasks that are both logically active at some point in time are considered to be concurrent. Contrast with *parallel*.

continuation: The state necessary to continue a program from a certain logical location in that program. A well-known example is the statement following a subroutine call, which will be where a program continues after a subroutine finishes (returns). The continuation is more than just the location; it also includes the state of data, variable declarations, and so forth at that point.

continuation passing style: A style of programming in which the *continuations* of operations are explicitly created and managed.

control dependency: A *dependency* between two tasks where whether or not a task executes depends on the result computed by another task.

convergent memory access: When memory accesses in adjacent *SIMD lanes* access adjacent memory locations.

cooperative scheduling: A thread scheduling system that allows thread to switch tasks only at predictable switch points.

core: A separate subprocessor on a multicore processor. A core should be able to support (at least one) separate and divergent flow of control from other cores on the same processor. Note that there is some inconsistency in the use of this term. For example, some graphic processor vendors use the term as well for SIMD *lanes* supporting *fibers*. However, the separate flows of control in fibers are simulated with masking on these devices, so there is a performance penalty for divergence. We will restrict the use of the term *core* to the case where control flow divergence can be done without penalty.

critical path: The longest chain of *tasks* ordered by *dependencies* in a program.

DAG: See *directed acyclic graph*.

data dependency: A *dependency* between two tasks where one task requires as input data the output of another task.

data locality: See *locality*.

data parallelism: An attempt to an approach to parallelism that is more oriented around data rather than tasks. However, in reality, successful strategies in parallel algorithm development tend to focus on exploiting the parallelism in data, because data decomposition (generating tasks for different units of data) scales, but functional decomposition (generation of hetereogeneous tasks for different functions) does not. See *Amdahl's Law*, *Gustafson–Barsis' Law*, and Section 2.2.

deadlock: A programming error that occurs when at least two tasks wait for each other and each will not resume until the other task proceeds. This happens easily when code requires locking multiple mutexes; for example, each task can be holding a mutex required by the other task. See Section 2.6.3.

dependencies: A relationship among tasks that results in an ordering constraint. See *data dependency* and *control dependency*.

depth: See *span complexity*.

deque: A double-ended queue.

design pattern: A general term for *pattern* that includes not only *algorithmic strategy patterns* but also patterns related to overall code organization.

deterministic: A deterministic algorithm is an algorithm that behaves predictably. Given a particular input, a deterministic algorithm will always produce the same output. The definition of what is the "same" may be important due to limited precision in mathematical operations and the likelihood that optimizations including *parallelization* will rearrange the order of operations. These are often referred to as "rounding" differences, which result when the order of mathematical operations to compute answers differs between the original program and the final concurrent program. Concurrency is not the only factor that can lead to *non-deterministic* algorithms but in practice it is often the cause. Use of programming models with sequential semantics and eliminating data races with proper access controls will generally eliminate non-determinism other than the "rounding" differences.

directed acyclic graph: A graph that defines a partial order so that nodes can be sorted into a linear sequence with references only going in one direction. A directed acyclic graph has, as its name suggests, directed edges and no cycles.

direct memory access (DMA): The ability of one processing unit to access another processing unit's memory without the involvement of the other processing unit.

direct-mapped cache: A cache in which every location in memory can be stored in only one location in the cache, typically using a modular function of the address.

distributed memory: Memory which is located in multiple physical locations. Accessing data from more remote locations typically has higher *latency* and possibly lower *bandwidth* than accessing local memory.

distributed memory: Memory that is physically located in separate computers. An indirect interface, such as message passing, is required to access memory on remote computers, while local memory can be accessed directly. Distributed memory is typically supported by *clusters*, which, for purposes of this definition, we are considering to be a collection of computers. Since the memory on *attached co-processors* also cannot typically be addressed directly from the host, it can be considered, for functional purposes, to be a form of distributed memory.

divergent memory access: When memory accesses in adjacent SIMD lanes access non-adjacent memory locations. See *convergent memory access*.

divide-and-conquer pattern: Recursive decomposition of a problem. Can often be parallelized with the *fork–join* parallel pattern. See Section 8.1.

domain-specific language (DSL): A language with specialized features suitable for a specific application domain, along with (typically) some restrictions to make optimization for that domain easier. For instance, an image processing language might support direct specification of the *stencil pattern* but restrict the use of general pointers. Domain-specific languages are often *embedded languages*, in which case they are called *embedded domain-specific languages*, or EDSLs.

dwarf: A workload is which typical of some class of workloads. Sometimes used as a synonym for *pattern*.

efficiency: Efficiency measures the return on investment in using additional hardware to operate in parallel. See Section 2.5.2.

elemental function: A function used in a *map pattern*. An elemental function syntactically is defined as acting on single item inputs, but in fact is applied in parallel to all the elements of a collection. An elemental function can be vectorized by replicating the computation it specifies across multiple *SIMD* lanes. See Sections 4.1 and B.10.

embarrassing parallelism: Refers to an algorithm that can be decomposed into a large number of independent tasks with little or no synchronization or communication required. See *map pattern*.

embedded language: A programming system whose syntax is supported using another language; for example, ArBB supports an embedded interface in C++. The computations specified using this interface are not, however, performed by C++. Instead, ArBB supports a set of types and operations in C++. Sequences of these operations can be recorded by ArBB and are then dynamically recompiled to machine language. See Section B.10.

expand pattern: A pattern in which each element of a *map pattern* can output zero or more data elements, which are then assembled into a single (possibly segmented) array. Related to the *pack pattern*. See Sections 3.6.7 and 6.4.

false sharing: Two separate tasks in two separate cores may write to separate locations in memory, but if those memory locations happened to be allocated in the same cache line, the cache coherence hardware will attempt to keep the cache lines coherent, resulting in extra interprocessor communication and reduced performance, even though the tasks are not actually sharing data. See Section 2.4.2.

fiber: A very lightweight unit of parallelism that (conceptually) has its own flow of control but is mapped onto a single lane of a SIMD processor. Divergent control flow between fibers on a single SIMD processor is simulated by masking updates to registers and memory. See Section 2.3. A masked implementation has implications for performance. In particular, divergent control flow reduces lane utilization. There may also be limitations on control flow; for example, GOTO may not be supported, only nested control flow. Note that the term fiber is not universally accepted. In particular, on GPUs, fibers are often called *threads* and what we call threads are called *work groups* in OpenCL.

Fibonacci numbers: The Fibonacci numbers are defined by linear recurrence relationship and suffer from overuse in computer science as examples of recursion as a result. Fibonacci numbers are defined as $F(0) = 0$ and $F(1) = 1$ plus the relationship defined by $F(N) = F(N-1) + F(N-2)$.

fine-grain locking: Locks that are used to protect parts of a larger data structure from race conditions. Such locks avoid locking the entirety of a large data structure during parallel accesses.

fine scale: A level of parallelism with very small units of parallel work. Reduction of overhead is very important for fine-scale parallelism to be effective, since otherwise the overhead will dominate the computation.

Flynn's characterization: A classic categorization of parallel processors by Flynn [Fly72] based on whether they have multiple flows of control or multiple streams of data. See Section 2.4.3.

fold: A collective operation in which every output is a function of all previous outputs and all inputs up to the current output point. A fold is based on a *successor function* that computes a new output value and a new state for the fold for each new input value. A *scan* is a special, parallelizable case of a fold where the successor function is associative.

fork: The creation of a new thread or task. The original thread or task continues in parallel with the forked thread or task. See *spawn*.

fork–join pattern: A pattern of computation in which new (potential) parallel flows of control are created/split with *forks* and terminated/merged with *joins*. See Sections 3.3.1 and 8.1.

fork point: A point in the code where a *fork* takes place.

fully associative cache: See *associative cache*.

functional decomposition: An approach to parallelization of existing serial code where modules are run on different threads. This approach does not give more than a constant factor of speedup at best since the number of modules in a program is fixed.

functional unit: A hardware processing element that can do a simple operation, such as a single arithmetic operation.

functor: A class which supports a function-call interface. Unlike functions in C and C++ however, functors can also hold state and can support additional interfaces to modify that state. See *lambda functions*.

fusion: An optimization in which two or more things with similar forms are combined. See *loop fusion, cache fusion*, and *code fusion*.

future: An approach to asynchronous computing in which a computation is specified but does not necessarily begin immediately. Instead, construction of a future returns an object which can be used to query the status of the computation or wait for its completion.

future-proofed: A computer program written in a manner so it will survive future computer architecture changes without significant changes to the program itself being necessary. Generally, the more abstract a programming method is, the more future-proof that program is. Lower-level programming methods that in some way mirror computer architectural details will be less able to survive the future without change. Writing in an abstract, more future-proof fashion may involve tradeoffs in efficiency, however.

gather pattern: A set of parallel random reads from memory. A gather takes a collection of addresses and an input collection and returns a collection of data drawn from the input collection at the given locations. Gathers are equivalent to random reads inside a *map pattern*. See Sections 3.5.4 and 6.1.

geometric decomposition pattern: A pattern that decomposes the computational domain for an algorithm into a set of possibly overlapping subdomains. A special case is the *partition pattern*, which is when the subdomains do not overlap. See Sections 3.5.3 and 6.6.

GPU: A graphics processing unit is an attached graphics processor originally specialized for graphics computations. GPUs are able to support arbitrary computation, but they are specialized for massively parallel, fine-grained computations. They typically use multithreading, multiple threads per core, and *fibers* and make extensive use of *latency hiding*. They are typically able to maintain the state for many more threads in memory than CPUs, but each thread can have less total state.

grain: A unit of work to be run serially. See *granularity*.

grain size: The amount of work in a *grain*.

granularity: The amount of decomposition applied to the *parallelization* of an algorithm, and the **grain size** of that decomposition. If the granularity is too coarse, there are not enough parallel tasks to effectively make use of all parallel hardware units and hide latency. If the granularity is too fine, there are too many parallel tasks and overhead may dominate the computation.

graphics accelerators: A processor specialized for graphics workloads, usually in support of real-time graphics APIs such as Direct3D and OpenGL. See *GPU*.

graph rewriting: A computational pattern where nodes of a graph are matched against templates and substitutions made with other subgraphs. When applied to directed acyclic graphs (trees with sharing), this is known as *term graph rewriting* and is equivalent to the lambda calculus, except that it also explicitly represents sharing of memory. See Section 3.6.9.

greedy scheduling: A scheduling strategy in which no worker idles if there is work to be done.

grid: A distributed set of computers that can be allocated dynamically and accessed remotely. A grid is distinguished from a cloud in that a grid may be supported by multiple organizations and is usually more heterogeneous and physically distributed.

Gustafson–Barsis' Law: A different view on Amdahl's Law that factors in the fact that as problem sizes grow the serial portion of computations tend to shrink as a percentage of the total work to be done. Compare with other attempts to characterize the bounds of parallelism, such as *Amdahl's Law* and *span complexity*. See Section 2.5.5.

halo: In the implementation of the *stencil pattern* on *distributed memory* a set of elements surrounding a *partition* that are replicated on different workers to allow each portion of the partition to be computed in parallel.

hardware thread: A hardware implementation of a task with a separate flow of control. Multiple hardware threads can be implemented using multiple cores, or they can run concurrently or simultaneously on one core in order to hide latency using methods such as *hyperthreading* of a processor core. See Sections 1.2 and 2.5.9.

heap allocation: An allocation mechanism that supports unstructured memory allocations of different sizes and at arbitrary times in the execution of a program. Compare with *stack allocation*.

heterogeneous computer: A computer which supports multiple processors each with specialized capabilities or performance characteristics.

holders: A form of *hyperobject* useful for managing temporary task-local storage.

host processor: The main control processor in a system, as opposed to any graphics processors or co-processors. The host processor is responsible for booting and running the operating system.

hyperobjects: A mechanism in Cilk Plus to support operations such as reduction that combine multiple objects. See Section B.7. For examples using hyperobjects, see Sections 5.3.5, 8.10, and 11.2.1.

hyperthreading: Multithreading on a single processor core. With hyperthreading, also called simultaneous multithreading, multiple *hardware threads* may run on one core and share resources, but some benefit is still obtained from parallelism or concurrency. For example, the processor may draw instructions from multiple hyperthreads to fill superscalar instruction slots, or the processor may switch between multiple hyperthreads in order to hide memory access latency. Typically each hyperthread has, at least, its own register file and program counter, so that switching between hyperthreads is relatively lightweight.

implementation pattern: A pattern that is specific to efficient implementation (usually of some other pattern) using specific hardware mechanisms.

instance: In a *map pattern* one invocation of an elemental function on one element of the map.

instruction-level parallelism (ILP) wall: The limits to automatic parallelism given by the amount of parallelism naturally available at the instruction level in serial programs.

intrinsics: Intrinsics appear to be functions in a language but are supported by the compiler directly. In the case of SSE or vector intrinsics, the intrinsic function may map directly to a small number, often one, of machine instructions which the compiler inserts without the overhead of a real function call. For a discussion of SSE intrinsics, see Section 5.3.3.

irregular parallelism: parallelism with dissimilar tasks with unpredictable dependencies.

iteration pattern: A serial pattern in which the same sequence of instructions is executed repeatedly and in sequence.

join: When multiple flows of control meet and a single flow continues onwards. Not to be confused with a *barrier*, in which all the incoming flows continue onwards.

join point: A point in the code where a *join* takes place.

kernel: A general term for a small section of code that (1) executes a large amount of computation relative to other parts of the program (also known as a hotspot), and/or (2) is the key code sequence for an algorithm.

lambda expression: an expression that returns a *lambda function*.

lambda function: A lambda function, for programmers, is an anonymous function. Long a staple of languages such as LISP, it was only recently supported for C++ per the C++11 standard. A lambda function enables a fragment of code to be passed to another function without having to write a separate named function or functor. This ability is particularly handy for using TBB. See Section D.2.

lane: An element of a SIMD register file and associated functional unit, considered as a unit of hardware for performing parallel computation. SIMD instructions execute computations across multiple lanes.

latency: The time it takes to complete a task—that is, the time between when the task begins and when it ends. Latency has units of time. The scale can be anywhere from nanoseconds to days. Lower latency is better in general. See Section 2.5.1.

latency hiding: Schedules computations on a processing element while other tasks using that core are waiting for long-latency operations to complete, such as memory or disk transfers. The latency is not actually hidden, since each task still takes the same time to complete, but more tasks can be completed in a given time since resources are shared more efficiently, so throughput is improved. See Section 2.5.9.

latent parallelism: See *potential parallelism*.

linear speedup: Speedup in which the performance improves directly proportional to the physical processing resources available. Considered to be optimal.

Little's formula: A formula relating parallelism, concurrency, and latency.

livelock: A situation in which multiple workers are active, but are not doing useful work and are not making forward progress. See *deadlock*.

load balancing: Distributing work across resources so that no resource idles while there is work to be done.

load imbalance: A situation where uneven sizes of tasks assigned to workers results in some workers finishing early and then idling while waiting for other workers to complete larger tasks. See *load balancing*.

locality: Refers to either *spatial locality* or *temporal locality*. Maintaining a high degree of locality of reference is a key to scaling. See Section 2.6.5.

lock: A mechanism for implementing *mutual exclusion*. Before entering a mutual exclusion region, a thread must first try to acquire a lock on that region. If the lock has already been acquired by another thread, the current thread must *block*, which it may do by either suspending operation or spinning. When the lock is released, then the current thread is free to acquire it. Locks can be implemented using *atomic operations*, which are themselves a form of mutual exclusion on basic operations, implemented in hardware. See Section 2.6.2.

loop-carried dependencies: A dependency that exists between multiple iterations of an *iteration pattern*.

loop fusion: An optimization where two loops with the compatible indexing executed in sequence can be combined into a single loop.

mandatory concurrency: See *mandatory parallelism*.

mandatory parallelism: Parallelism that is semantically required for program correctness. See Section 9.6.

many-core processor: A *multicore* processor with so many cores that in practice we do not enumerate them; there are just "lots." The term has been generally used with processors with 32 or more cores, but there is no precise definition.

map pattern: Replicates a function that is applied to all elements of a collection, producing a new collection with the same shape as the input. The function being replicated is called an *elemental function* since it applies to the elements of an actual collection of input data. See Sections 3.3.2 and Chapter 4.

masking: A technique for emulating *SPMD* control flow on *SIMD* machines in which elements that are not active are prohibited from updating externally visible state.

megahertz era: A historical period of time during which processors doubled clock rates at a rate similar to the doubling of transistors in a design, roughly every 2 years. Such rapid rise in processor clock speeds ceased at just under 4 GHz (4,000 megahertz) in 2004. Designs shifted toward adding more cores, marking the shift to the *multicore era*.

member function: A function associated with an object and which can access instance-specific object state.

memory fences: A synchronization mechanism which can ensure that memory operations before the fence are completed and are visible before memory operations after the fence.

memory hierarchy: See *memory subsystem*.

memory subsystem: The portion of a computer system responsible for moving code and data between the main system memory and the computational units. The memory subsystem may include additional connections to I/O devices including graphics cards, disk drives, and network interfaces. A modern memory subsystem will generally have many levels, including some levels of caching both on and off the processor die. Coherent memory subsystems, which are used in most computers, provide for a single view of the contents of the main system memory despite temporary copies in caches and concurrency in the system. See Section 2.4.1.

memory wall: A limit to parallel scalability given by the fact that memory (and more generally, communication) *bandwidth* and in particular *latency* are not scaling at the same rate as computation.

merge scatter pattern: In a merge scatter, results that collide while implementing a *scatter pattern* are combined with an associative operator. The operator needs to be associative so the answer is the same regardless of the order in which elements are combined. We might also want to use this operator to combine scattered values with the previous contents of the target array. The merge scatter pattern can be used to implement histograms, for example. See Section 6.2.

metaprogramming: The use of one program to generate or manipulate another, or itself. See also *template metaprogramming*.

method: See *member function*.

MIC: The Intel Many Integrated Core architecture is designed for highly parallel workloads. The architecture emphasizes higher core counts on a single die, and simpler more efficient cores, than on a traditional CPU. A prototype with up to 32 cores and based on 45-nm process technology, known as Knight Ferry, was made available, but not sold, by Intel in 2010 and 2011. A product built on 22-nm process technology with more than 50 cores is expected in late 2012 or sometime in 2013.

MIMD: Multiple Instruction, Multiple Data, one of Flynn's classes of computer that supports multiple threads of control, each with its own data access. See *SIMD* and Section 2.4.3.

monoid: An *associative operation* that has an identity.

Moore's Law: Describes a long-term trend that the number of transistors that can be incorporated inexpensively on an integrated circuit chip doubles approximately every 2 years. It is named for Intel co-founder Gordon Moore, who described the trend in his 1965 paper in *Electronics Magazine*. This forecast of the pace of silicon technology has essentially described the basic business model for the semiconductor industry as well as being a driving force of technological and social change since the late 20th century.

motif: Sometimes used as a synonym for *pattern*.

multicore: A processor with multiple subprocessors, each subprocessor (known as a *core*) supporting at least one hardware thread.

multicore era: Time after which processor designs shifted away from rapidly rising clock rates and shifted toward adding more cores. This era began roughly in 2005.

multiple-processor systems: A system with two or more processors implemented on separate physical dies.

mutex: Short for *mutual exclusion*, and also used as a synonym for *lock*.

mutual exclusion: A mechanism for protecting a set of data values so that while they are manipulated by one parallel thread they cannot be manipulated by another. See *lock* and *transactional memory*.

nesting pattern: Refers to the ability to hierarchically compose other patterns. The nesting pattern simply means that all "tasks" in the pattern diagrams within this book are actually locations within which general code can be inserted. This code can in turn be composed of other patterns.

Network interface controller (NIC): A specialized communication processor.

node (in a cluster): A shared memory computer, often on a single board with multiple processors, that is connected with other nodes to form a *cluster* computer or supercomputer.

non-deterministic: Exhibiting a lack of deterministic behavior, so results can vary from run to run of an algorithm. See more in the definition for *deterministic*.

non-uniform memory access (NUMA): A memory system in which certain banks of memory take longer to access than others, even though all the memory uses a single address space. See also *distributed memory*.

objects: Objects are a language construct that associate data with the code to act on and manage that data. Multiple functions may be associated with an object and these functions are called the *methods* or *member functions* of that object. Objects are considered to be members of a class of objects, and classes can be arranged in a hierarchy in which subclasses inherit and extend the features of superclasses. The state of an object may or may not be directly accessible; in many cases, access to an object's state may only be permitted through its methods. See Section 3.4.5.

offload: Placing part of a computation on an *attached device* such as a GPU or co-processor.

online: An algorithm which can begin execution before all input data is read.

OpenCL: Open Computing Language, initiated by Apple Corporation, is now a standard defined by the Khronos group for graphics processors and *attached co-processors*. However, OpenCL can also be used to specify parallel and vectorized computations on multicore host processors.

optional parallelism: Parallelism that is specified by a programming model but is not semantically necessary. Antonym is *mandatory parallelism*.

over-decomposition: A parallel programming style where many more tasks are specified than there are physical workers for executing it. This can be beneficial for *load balancing* particularly in systems that support *optional parallelism*.

over-subscription: More threads run on a system than it has physical workers, resulting in excessive overhead for switching between multiple threads or exceeding the number of threads that can be supported by the operating system. This can be avoided by using a programming model with *optional parallelism*.

pack pattern: A data management pattern where certain elements of a collection are discarded and the remaining elements are placed in a contiguous sequence, maintaining the order of the original input. Related to the *expand pattern*.

page: The granularity at which virtual to physical address mapping is done. Within a page, the mapping of virtual to physical memory addresses is continuous. See Section 2.4.1.

parallel: Physically happening simultaneously. Two tasks that are both actually doing work at some point in time are considered to be operating in parallel. When a distinction is made between *concurrent* and *parallel*, the key is whether work can ever be done simultaneously. Multiplexing of a single processor core, by multitasking operating systems, has allowed concurrency for decades even when simultaneous execution was impossible because there was only one processing core.

parallel pattern: *Patterns* arising specifically in the specification of parallel applications. Examples of parallel patterns include the *map pattern*, the *reduction pattern*, the *fork–join pattern*, and the *partition pattern*.

parallel slack: The amount of "extra" parallelism available above the minimum necessary to use the parallel hardware resources. See Sections 2.4.2 and 2.5.6.

parallelism: Doing more than one thing at a time. Attempts to classify types of parallelism are numerous; read more about classifications of parallelism in Sections 2.2 and 2.3.

parallelization: The act of transforming code to enable simultaneous activities. The parallelization of a program allows at least parts of it to execute in parallel.

partition pattern: A pattern that decomposes the computational domain for an algorithm into a set of non-overlapping subdomains called *tiles* or *blocks* (although *tile* is the term preferred in this book). See the *geometric decomposition pattern*, which is similar but allows overlap between subdomains. The partition pattern is a special case of the geometric decomposition pattern that does not allow overlap. See Section 6.6.

pattern: A recurring combination of data and task management, separate from any specific algorithm. Patterns are universal in that they apply to and can be used in any programming system. Patterns have also been called *dwarfs*, *motifs*, and algorithmic skeletons. Patterns are not necessarily tied to any particular hardware architecture or programming language or system. Examples of patterns include the *sequence pattern* and the *object pattern*. See *parallel pattern* and Chapter 3.

PCIe bus: A peripheral bus supporting relatively high bandwidth and DMA, often used for attaching specialized co-processors such as *GPUs* and *NICs*.

permutation scatter pattern: A form of the *scatter pattern* in which multiple writes to a single storage location are illegal. This form of scatter is deterministic, but can only be considered safe if collisions are checked for. See Section 6.2.

pipeline pattern: A set of data processing elements connected in series, generally so that the output of one element is the input of the next one. The elements of a pipeline are often executed concurrently. Describing many algorithms, including many signal processing problems, as pipelines is generally quite natural and lends itself to parallel execution. However, in order to scale beyond the number of pipeline stages, it is necessary to exploit parallelism within a single pipeline stage. See Sections 3.5.2, 9.2, 12.2, and C.6.

potential parallelism: At a given point of time, the number of parallel tasks that could be used by a parallel implementation of an algorithm, given sufficient hardware resources. Additional hardware resources above the potential parallelism in an algorithm are not usable. If the potential parallelism is larger than the physical parallelism, then the tasks will need to share physical resources by *serialization*. Also known as *latent parallelism* and *available parallelism*.

power wall: A limit to the practical clock rate of serial processors given by thermal dissipation and the non-linear relationship between power and switching speed.

pragma: A form of program markup used to give a hint to a compiler but not change the semantics of a program. Also called a "compiler directive."

precision: The detail in which a quantity is expressed. Lack of precision is the source of rounding errors in computation. The finite number of bits used to store a number requires some approximation of the true value. Errors accumulate when multiple computations are made to the data in operations such as reductions. Precision is measured in terms of the number of digits that contain meaningful data, known as significant digits. Since precision is most often considered in reference to floating-point numbers, significant digits in computer science have often been measured in bits (binary digits) because most floating-point arithmetic is done in radix-2. With the advent of IEEE-754-2008, radix-10 arithmetic is once again popular and precision of such data would be expressed in terms of decimal digits. See Section 5.1.4.

preemptive scheduling: A scheduling system that allows a thread to switch tasks at any time.

priority scatter pattern: A deterministic form of the *scatter pattern* in which an attempt to write multiple values in parallel to a single storage location results in one value (and only one) value being stored based on a priority function, while all other values are discarded. The unique priority given to each parallel write in a priority scatter can be assigned in such a way that the result is deterministic and equivalent to a serial implementation. See Section 6.2.

process: A application-level unit of parallel work. A process has its own thread of control and is managed by the operating system. Usually, unless special provisions are made for *shared memory*, a process cannot access the memory of another process.

producer–consumer: A relationship in which the producer creates data that is passed to the consumer to utilize or further process. If data is not consumed exactly when it is produced, it must be buffered. Buffering introduces challenges of stalling the producer when the buffer is full, and stalling the consumer when the buffer is empty.

pure function: A function whose output depends only on its input, and that does not modify any other system state.

race condition: Non-deterministic behavior in a parallel program that is generally a programming error. A race condition occurs when concurrent tasks perform operations on the same memory location without proper synchronization and one of the memory operations is a write. Code with a race may operate correctly sometimes and fail other times. See Section 2.6.1.

recurrence pattern: A sequence defined by a recursive equation. In a recursive equation, one or more initial terms are given and each further term of the sequence is defined as a function of the preceding terms. Implementing recurrences with recursion is often inefficient since it tends to recompute elements of the recurrence unnecessarily. Recurrences also occur in loops with dependencies between iterations. In the case of a single loop, if the dependence is associative, it can be *parallelized* with the *scan pattern*. If the dependence is inside a multidimensional loop nest, the entire nest can always be parallelized over $n - 1$ dimensions using a hyperplane sweep, and it can also often be parallelized with the fork–join pattern. See Sections 3.3.6, 7.5, and 8.12.

recursion: The act of a function being re-entered while an instance of the function is still active in the same thread of execution. In the simplest and most common case, a function directly calls itself, although recursion can also occur between multiple functions. Recursion is supported by storing the state for the continuations of partially completed functions in dynamically allocated memory, such as on a stack, although if higher-order functions are supported a more complex memory allocation scheme may be required. Bounding the depth of recursion can be important to prevent excessive use of memory.

reduce: Apply operation to merge a collection of values to a single value. An example is summing a sequence of values. See *reduction pattern*.

reducers: Hyperobjects that can implement *reduce* operations.

reduction pattern: The most basic *collective* pattern, a reduction combines all the elements in a collection into a single element using pairwise applications of a *combiner operation*. In order to allow *parallelization*, the combiner operation should be associative. In order to allow for efficient *vectorization*, it is useful if the combiner operation is also commutative. Many useful reduction operations, such as maximum and (modular integer) addition, are both associative and commutative. Unfortunately, floating-point addition and multiplication are not, which can lead to potential *non-determinism*. See Section 5.1.

reduction variable: A variable that appears in a loop for combining the results of many different loop iterations.

refactoring: Reorganizing code to make it better suited for some purpose, such as parallelization.

registers: Very fast but usually very limited on-core storage for intermediate results.

regular parallelism: A class of algorithms in which the tasks and data dependencies are arranged in a regular and predictable pattern.

relative speedup: Speedup in which a parallel solution to a problem is compared to a serialization of the same solution, that is, using the same algorithm. See *absolute speedup*.

relaxed sequential semantics: See *sequential semantics* for an explanation.

response time: The time between when a request is made and when a response is received.

rotate pattern: A special case of the *shift pattern* that handles boundary conditions by moving data from the other side of the collection. See Section 6.1.2.

safety: A system property that automatically guards against certain classes of programmer errors, such as race conditions.

saturation: Saturation arithmetic has maximum and minimum values that are utilized when computation would logically arrive at higher or lower values if unbounded numerical representations were utilized. Saturation arithmetic is needed only because numerical representations on computer systems are almost always limited in precision and range. In floating-point arithmetic, the concept of positive and negative infinity as uniquely represented numbers in the floating-point format is utilized and is the default in instances of saturation. In integer arithmetic, wrap-around arithmetic is generally the default. Special instructions for saturation arithmetic are available in modern instruction sets (such as MMX), often originally motivated by graphics where the desire to make a graphical pixel brighter and brighter by increasing the value of a pixel was frustrated by a sudden dimming of the pixel due to wrap-around arithmetic. In an 8-bit unsigned number format, the addition of 254 with 9 will result in an answer of 7 in wrap-around or 255 in saturation arithmetic. Likewise, the subtraction of 11 from 7 would result in 252 in wrap-around vs. 0 in saturation arithmetic. Note, however, that saturation arithmetic for signed numbers is not associative.

scalability: A measure of the increase in performance as a function of the availability of more hardware to use in parallel. See Section 2.5.2.

scalable: An application is *scalable* if its performance increases when additional parallel hardware resources are added. See *scalability*.

scalar promotion: When a scalar and a vector are combined using a vector operation, the scalar is automatically treated as a vector with all elements set to the same value.

scan pattern: Pattern arising from a one-dimensional recurrence relationship in the definition of a computation. This often arises as a loop-carried dependency where the computation of one iteration is dependent on the results of a prior iteration. Such loops are, surprisingly, still parallelizable if the dependency can be expressed as an associative operation. See Section 5.4.

scatter pattern: A set of input data and a set of indices is given, and each element of the input is written at the given location. Scatter can be considered the inverse of the *gather pattern*. A collision in output occurs if the set of indices maps multiple input data to the same location. There are at least four ways to resolve such collisions: *permutation scatter*, *atomic scatter*, *priority scatter*, and *merge scatter*. See Section 3.5.5.

search pattern: A pattern that finds data that meets some criteria within a collection of data. See Section 3.6.5.

segmentation: A representation of a collection divided into non-uniform non-overlapping subdomains. Operations such as reduction and scan can be generalized to operate over the segments of a collection independently while still being perfectly load balanced. See Section 3.6.6.

selection pattern: A serial pattern in which one of two flows of control are chosen based on a Boolean control expression.

semantics: What a programming language construct does, as opposed to how it does it (pragmatics) or how it is expressed (syntax).

separating hyperplane: A plane that can be used to determine the sweep order for executing a multidimensional *recurrence* in parallel.

sequence pattern: The most fundamental serial pattern in which tasks are executed one after the other, with each task completing before the next one starts. See Section 3.2.1.

sequential bottlenecks: See *serial bottlenecks*.

sequential consistency: Sequential consistency is a memory consistency model where every task in a concurrent system sees all memory writes (updates) happen in the exact same order, and a task's own writes occur in the order that the task specified. See Section 2.6.1.

sequential semantics: Refers to when a (parallel) program can be executed using a single thread of control as an ordinary sequential program without changing the semantics of the program. Parallel programming with sequential semantics has many advantages over programming in a manner that precludes serial execution and is therefore strongly encouraged. Such programs are considered easier to understand, easier to debug, more efficient on sequential machines, and better at supporting nested parallelism. Sequential semantics casts parallelism as an accelerator and not as mandatory for correctness. This means that one does not need a conceptual parallel model to understand or execute a program with sequential semantics. Examples of *mandatory parallelism* include producer–consumer relationships with bounded buffers (hence, the producer cannot necessarily be completely executed before the consumer because the producer can become blocked) and message passing (e.g., MPI) programs with cyclic message passing. Due to timing, precision, and other sources of inexactness, the results of a sequential execution may differ from the concurrent invocation of the same program. Sequential semantics solely means that any such variation is not due to the semantics of the program. The term "relaxed sequential semantics" is sometimes used to explicitly acknowledge the variations possible due to non-semantic differences in serial vs. concurrent executions. See Section 1.1 See *serial semantics.*

serial: Neither concurrent nor parallel.

serial bottlenecks: A region of an otherwise parallel program that runs serially.

serial consistency: A parallel program that produces the same result as a specific serial ordering of its tasks.

serial elision: The serial elision of a Cilk Plus program is generated by erasing occurrences of the `cilk_spawn` and `cilk_sync` keywords and replacing `cilk_for` with `for`. Cilk Plus is a faithful extension of C/C++ in the sense that the serial elision of any Cilk Plus program is both a serial C/C++ program *and* a semantically valid implementation of the Cilk Plus program. The term *elision* arose from earlier versions of Cilk that lacked `cilk_for`, so eliding (omitting) the two other keywords sufficed. The term "C elision" is sometimes used, too, harking back to when Cilk was an extension of C but not C++. See Section B.4.

serial illusion: The apparent serial execution order of machine language instructions in a computer. In fact, hardware is naturally parallel, and many low-level optimizations and high-performance implementation techniques can reorder operations.

serial semantics: Same as *sequential semantics*.

serial traps: A serial trap is a programming construct that semantically requires serial execution for proper results in general even though common cases may be overconstrained with regard to concurrency by such semantics. The term "trap" acknowledges how such constructs can easily escape attention as barriers to parallelism, in part because they are so common and were not intentionally designed to preclude parallelism. For instance, `for`, in the C language, has semantics that dictate the order of iterations by allowing an iteration to assume that all prior iterations have been executed. Many loops do not rely upon side-effects of prior iterations and would be natural candidates for parallel execution, but they require analysis in order for a system to determine that parallel execution would not violate the program semantics. Use of `cilk_for`, for instance, has no such serial semantics and therefore is not a serial trap. See examples in Section 1.3.3.

serialization: Refers to when the tasks in a potentially parallel algorithm are executed in a specific serial order, typically due to resource constraints. The opposite of *parallelization.*

set associative cache: A cache architecture in which a particular location in main memory can be stored in a (small) number of different locations in cache.

shared address space: Even if units of parallel work do not share a physical memory, they may agree on conventions that allow a single unified set of addresses to be used. For example, one range of addresses could refer to memory on the host, while another range could refer to memory on a specific co-processor. The use of unified addresses simplifies memory management.

shared memory: Refers to when two units of parallel work can access data in the same location. Normally doing this safely requires *synchronization*. The units of parallel work—*processes*, *threads*, *tasks*, and *fibers*—can all share data this way, if the physical memory system allows it. However, processes do not share memory by default and special calls to the operating system are required to set it up.

shift pattern: A special case of the *gather pattern* that translates (that is, offsets the location of) data in a collection. There are a few variants based on how boundary conditions are handled. The basic pattern fills in a default value at boundaries, while the *rotate pattern* moves data from the other side of the collection. See Section 6.1.2.

SIMD: Single Instruction, Multiple Data, one of Flynn's classes of computer that supports a single operation over multiple data elements. See *MIMD* and Section 2.4.3.

simultaneous multithreading: A technique that supports the execution of multiple threads on a single core by drawing instructions from multiple threads and scheduling them in each superscalar instruction slot.

SIMT: Single Instruction, Multiple Threads, a variation on Flynn's characterizations that is really a collection of multiple SIMD processors, with control flow emulated on SIMD machines using a mechanism such as masking. See Section 2.4.3.

software thread: A software thread is a virtual hardware thread—in other words, a single flow of execution in software intended to map one for one to a hardware thread. An operating system typically enables many more software threads to exist than there are actual hardware threads by mapping software threads to hardware threads as necessary. See Section 2.3.

space complexity: A complexity measure for the amount of memory used by an algorithm as a function of problem size.

span: How long a program would take to execute on an idealized machine with an infinite number of processors. The *span* of an algorithm can also be seen as the critical path in its task dependency graph. See *span complexity*.

span complexity: Span complexity is an asymptotic measure of complexity based on the *span*. In the analysis of parallel algorithms and in particular in order to predict their *scalability*, this measure is as important as *work complexity*. Other synonyms for *span complexity* in the literature are *step complexity*, *depth*, or *circuit complexity*. Compare with other attempts to characterize the bounds of parallelism: *Amdahl's Law* and *Gustafson-Barsis' Law*. See Section 2.5.6.

spatial locality: Nearby when measured in terms of distance (in memory address). Compare with *temporal locality*. Spatial locality refers to a program behavior where the use of one data element indicates that data nearby, often the next data element, will probably be used soon. Algorithms exhibiting good spatial locality in data usage can benefit from cache line structures and prefetching hardware, both common components in modern computers.

spawn: Generically, the creation of a new *task*. In terms of Cilk Plus, `cilk_spawn` creates a spawn, but the new task created is actually the *continuation* and not the call that is the target of the spawn keyword. See *fork*.

spawning block: The function, try block, or `cilk_for` body that contains the spawn. A sync (`cilk_sync`) waits only for spawns that have occurred in the same spawning block and have no effect on spawns done by other tasks or threads, nor those done prior to entering the current spawning block. A sync is always done, if there have been spawns, when exiting the enclosing spawning block.

speedup: Speedup is the ratio between the latency for solving a problem with one processing unit versus the latency for solving the same problem with multiple processing units in parallel. See Section 2.5.2.

split pattern: A generalized version of the *pack pattern* that takes an input collection and a set of Boolean labels to go with every element of that collection. It reorganizes the data so all the elements marked with `false` are at one end of the output collection (rather than discarding them as with the pack pattern), and all the elements marked with `true` are at the other end of the collection. The determinisitic version of this pattern is stable, in that it preserves the original order of the input collection in each output partition. One major application of this pattern is in base-2 radix sort. The *bin pattern* is a generalization to more than two categories. See Section 6.4.

SPMD (Single Program, Multiple Data): A programming system that runs a single function on multiple programming elements, but allows each instance of the function to follow different control flow paths. See also *SIMD, MIMD,* and *SIMT*.

stencil pattern: A regular input data access pattern based on a set of fixed offsets relative to an output position. The stencil is repeated for every output position in a grid. This pattern combines the *map pattern* with a local *gather* over a fixed set of relative offsets and can optionally be implemented using the *shift pattern*. Stencil operations are common in algorithms that deal with regular grids of data, such as image processing. For example, convolution is an image processing operation where the inputs from a stencil are combined linearly using a weighted sum. See Chapter 7.

step complexity: See *span complexity*.

strand: In Cilk Plus, a serially executed sequence of instructions that does not contain a spawn or sync point. In the directed acyclic graph model of Section 2.5.2, a strand is a vertex with at most one outgoing and at most one incoming edge. A `cilk_spawn` ends the current strand and starts two new strands, one for the callee and one for the continuation of the caller. A `cilk_sync` ends one or more strands and starts a new strand for the continuation after the join.

strangled scaling: A programming error in which the performance of parallel code is poor due to high contention or overhead, so much so that it may underperform the non-parallel (serial) code. See Section 2.6.4.

strip-mining: When implementing a stencil or map, an optimization that groups instances in a way that avoids unnecessary and redundant memory accesses and aligns memory accesses with vector lanes.

strong scalability: A form of scalability that measures how performance increases when using additional workers but with a fixed problem size. See *Amdahl's Law* and *weak scalability*.

structure-of-arrays (SoA): A data layout for collections of heterogeneous data where all the data for each component of each element of the collection is stored in adjacent physical locations, so that data of the same type is stored together. Compare with *array-of-structures*.

successor function: In a *fold*, the function that computes a new state given the old state and a new input item.

superlinear speedup: Speedup where performance grows at a rate greater than the rate at which new workers are added. Since linear scalability is technical optimal, superlinear speedup is typically the result of cache effects, changes in the algorithm behavior, or speculative execution.

superscalar processor: A processor that can execute multiple instructions in a single clock cycle.

superscalar sequence pattern: A sequence of tasks ordered by data dependencies rather than being ordered by a single sequential ordering. This allows parallel (superscalar) execution of tasks that have no relative ordering relative to each other. See Sections 3.6.1.

switch-on-event multithreading: A technique that supports the execution of multiple threads on a single core by switching to another thread on a long-latency event, such as a cache miss.

sync: In terms of Cilk Plus, `cilk_sync` creates a sync point. Control flow pauses at a sync point until completion of all spawns issued by the spawning block that contains the sync point. A sync is not affected by spawns done by other tasks or threads, nor those done prior to entering the current spawning block. An sync is always done when exiting a spawning block that contained any spawns. This is required for program *composability*.

synchronization: The coordination, of tasks or threads, in order to obtain the desired runtime order. Commonly used to avoid undesired *race conditions*.

tail recursion: A form of recursion where a result of the recursive call is returned immediately without modification to the parent function. Such uses of recursion can be converted to *iteration*.

target processor: A (typically specialized) processor to which work can be *offloaded*. See *host processor*.

task: A lightweight unit of potential parallelism with its own control flow. Unlike threads, tasks usually do not imply mandatory parallelism. Threads are a mechanism for executing tasks in parallel, whereas tasks are units of work that merely provide the *opportunity* for parallel execution; tasks are not themselves a mechanism of parallel execution.

task parallelism: An attempt to classify parallelism as more oriented around tasks than data. We deliberately avoid use of this term because its meaning varies. In particular, elsewhere "task parallelism" can refer to tasks generated by functional decomposition *or* to irregular tasks still generated by data decomposition. In this book, any parallelism generated by data decomposition, regular or irregular, is considered data parallelism. See Section 2.2.

template metaprogramming: The use of generic programming techniques to manipulate and optimize source code before it is compiled. Specifically, the template rewriting rules in C++ can be interpreted as a functional language for manipulating C++ source code. Some high-performance libraries make use of this fact to automatically perform optimizations of C++ code by, for example, fusing operations together. See the more general term *metaprogramming*.

temporal locality: Nearby when measured in terms of time; compare with *spatial locality*. Temporal locality refers to a program behavior in which data is likely to be reused relatively soon. Algorithms exhibiting good temporal locality in data usage can benefit from the data caching common in modern computers. It is not unusual to be able to achieve both temporal and spatial locality in data usage. Computer systems are generally more able to achieve optimal performance when both are achieved, hence the interest in algorithm design to do so.

thread: In general, a *software thread* is any software unit of parallel work with an independent flow of control, and a *hardware thread* is any hardware unit capable of executing a single flow of control (in particular, a hardware unit that maintains a single program counter). Threads are a mechanism for implementing tasks. A multitasking or multithreading operating system will multiplex multiple software threads onto a single hardware thread by interleaving execution via software-created time-slices. A multicore or many-core processor consists of multiple cores to execute at least one independent software thread per core through duplication of hardware. A multithreaded or hyper-threaded processor core will multiplex a single core to execute multiple software threads through interleaving of software threads via hardware mechanisms.

thread parallelism: A mechanism for implementing parallelism in hardware using a separate flow of control for each task. See Section 2.3.

throughput: Given a set of tasks to be performed, the rate at which those tasks are completed. Throughput measures the rate of computation, and it is given in units of tasks per unit time. See *bandwidth* and *latency* and Section 2.5.1.

tile: A region of memory, typically a section of a larger collection, such as might result from the application of the *partition pattern*. See *granularity*, *block*, and *tiling*.

tiled decomposition: See *tiling.*

tiled SIMD: Execution of an *SPMD* program using an array of *SIMD* processors, each such processor with a separate thread of control.

tiling: Dividing a loop into a set of parallel tasks of a suitable *granularity*. In general, tiling consists of applying multiple steps on a smaller part of a problem instead of running each step on the whole problem one after the other. The purpose of tiling is to increase the reuse of data in caches. Tiling can lead to dramatic performance increases when a whole problem does not fit in cache. We prefer the term "tiling" to "blocking" and "tile" rather than "block." Tiling and tile have become the more common term in recent times. Sections 5.1.3 and 7.3 for more discussion.

time complexity: A complexity measure for the amount of time used by an algorithm as a function of problem size.

TLB: A Translation Lookaside Buffer is a specialized cache used to hold translations of virtual to physical page addresses. The number of elements in the TLB determines how many pages of memory can be accessed simultaneously with good efficiency. Accessing a page not in the TLB will cause a TLB miss. A TLB miss typically causes a trap to the operating system so that the page table can be referenced and the TLB updated. See Section 2.4.1.

TLB miss: Occurs when a virtual memory access is made for which the page translation is not available in the *TLB*.

TLB thrashing: The overhead caused by the high *TLB miss* rate that results when a program frequently accesses more pages than can be covered by a *TLB*.

transaction: An atomic update to data, meaning that the results of the update either are not seen or are seen in their entirety. Transactions satisfy the need for atomic data updates to a central repository without requiring an ordering on the updates. Transactions are motivated by the need to have updates be observed in an "all or nothing" fashion. Consider an update to a hotel reservation in an online system, from an "economy room for $75/night" to a "penthouse suite for $9800/night." We do not want a separate task to see a partial update and bill us for $9800/night for an economy room. In general, transaction operations will be non-associative and the outcome will not be deterministic if the order in which the individual operations are performed is non-deterministic. The *merge* *scatter pattern* with a non-associative operator can result in simple forms of the transaction pattern. See Sections 3.7.2 and 6.2.

transactional memory: A way of accessing memory so that a collection of memory updates, called a *transaction*, will be visible to other tasks or threads all at once. Additionally, for a transaction to succeed, any data read during the transaction must not be modified during the transaction by other tasks or threads. Transactions that fail are generally retried until they succeed. Transactional memory offers an alternative method of mutual exclusion from traditional locking that may enhance the scalability of an algorithm in certain cases. Intel Transactional Support Extensions (TSX) support is an example of hardware support for transactional memory.

Translation Lookaside Buffer: See *TLB*.

uniform parameter: A parameter that is broadcast to all the elements of a map and therefore is the same for each instance of the map's *elemental function*. See *varying parameter*.

unpack pattern: The inverse of the *pack pattern*, this operation scatters data back into its original locations. It may optionally fill in a default value for missing data.

unsplit pattern: The inverse of the *split pattern*, this operation scatters data back into its original locations. Unlike the case with the *unpack pattern*, there is no missing data to worry about.

unzip pattern: The inverse of the *zip pattern*, this operation deinterleaves data and can be used to convert from array-of-structures to structure-of-arrays.

varying parameter: A parameter to a *map pattern* that delivers a different element to each instance of the map's *elemental function*. See *uniform parameter*.

vector intrinsics: An *instrinsic* used to specify a *vector operation*.

vector operation: A low-level operation that can act on multiple data elements at once in *SIMD* fashion.

vector parallelism: A mechanism for implementing parallelism in hardware using the same flow of control on multiple data elements. See Section 2.3.

vector processor: A form of SIMD processor in which large amounts of data are streamed to and from external memory. True vector processors are rare today, so this term now is also used for processors with SIMD instructions that can act on short, fixed-length vectors held in registers.

vectorization: The act of transforming code to enable simultaneous computations using vector hardware. Instructions such as MMX, SSE, and AVX instructions utilize vector hardware. The vectorization of code tends to enhance performance because more data is processed per instruction than would be done otherwise. Vectorization is a specialized form of parallelism. See also *vectorize*.

vectorize: Converting a program from a scalar implementation to a vectorized implementation to utilize vector hardware such as SIMD instructions (MMX, SSE, AVX, etc.).

vector units: *functional units* that can issue multiple operations of the same type in a single clock cycle in *SIMD* fashion.

virtual memory: Virtual memory decouples the address used by software from the physical addresses of real memory. The translation from virtual addresses to physical addresses is done in hardware which is initialized and controlled by the operating system. See Section 2.4.1.

VLIW (Very Large Instruction Word): An processor architecture which supports instructions which can explicitly issue multiple operations in a single clock cycle. See *superscalar processor*.

weak scalability: A form of scalability that measures how performance increases when using additional workers with a problem size that grows at the same rate. See *Gustafson-Barsis's Law* and *strong scalability*.

work: The computational part of a program, as contrasted with communication or coordination. An abstract unit of such computation.

work complexity: The asymptotic number of operations required by an algorithm to run on a single thread. Work complexity is essentially the traditional asymptotic complexity for sequential running time, although frequently, so speedup ratios can be computed, it is better to use *big Theta notation* rather than *big O notation*. Related terms include *span complexity*.

worker: An abstract unit of actual parallelism, for example, a *core* or a *SIMD lane*.

working set: For an algorithm, the set of data that should be maintained in cache for good performance.

work-span: A model for parallel computation that can be used to compute both upper and lower bounds on speedup. See Section 2.5.6. Related terms include *span complexity* and *work complexity*.

workpile pattern: An extension of the *map pattern* that allows new work items to be added during execution from inside the elemental function. If the map pattern can be thought of as a *parallelization* of a `for` loop, the workpile pattern can be thought of as a generalization of a `while` loop. See Section 3.6.4.

work-stealing: A *load balancing* technique where *workers* that become idle search for and "steal" pending work from other, busy workers.

zip pattern: A special case of the *gather pattern* that interleaves elements from collections, converting from structure-of-arrays to array-of-structures. See Section 6.1.3.

Bibliography

[AB98]   M. Akra and L. Bazzi. On the solution of linear recurrence equations. *Computational Optimization and Applications*, 10(2):195–210, 1998.

[ABB+99] E. Anderson, Z. Bai, C. Bischof, S. Blackford, J. Demmel, J. Dongarra, J. Du Croz, A. Greenbaum, S. Hammarling, A. McKenney, and D. Sorensen. *LAPACK User's Guide*, 3rd ed. SIAM, Philadelpha, PA, 1999 (http://www.netlib.org/lapack/lug).

[ABC+06] K. Asanovic, R. Bodik, B. C. Catanzaro, J. J. Gebis, P. Husbands, K. Keutzer, D. A. Patterson, W. L. Plishker, J. Shalf, S. W. Williams, and K. A. Yelick. *The Landscape of Parallel Computing Research: A View from Berkeley*, Technical Report EECS-2006-183. EECS Department, University of California, Berkeley, 2006.

[ABF05]   L. Arge, G. S. Brodal, and R. Fagerberg. Cache-oblivious data structures. In D. Mehta and S. Sahni, Eds., *Handbook of Data Structures and Applications*. CRC Press, Boca Raton, FL, 2005, Chapter 34, p. 27.

[AD07]   M. Aldinucci and M. Danelutto. Skeleton-based parallel programming: functional and parallel semantics in a single shot. *Computer Languages, Systems, and Structures*, 33(3–4):179–192, 2007.

[Adv10]   S. Adve. Data races are evil with no exceptions: technical perspective. *Communications of the ACM*, 53(11):84, 2010.

[AF11]   A. Aviram and B. Ford. Deterministic OpenMP for race-free parallelism. In *Proceedings of 3rd USENIX Workshop on Hot Topics in Parallelism* (HotPar '11). USENIX Association, Berkeley, CA, 2011.

[Ale77]   C. Alexander. *A Pattern Language: Towns, Buildings, Construction*. Oxford University Press, Oxford, UK, 1977.

[ALKK90] A. Agarwal, B.-H. Lim, D. Kranz, and J. Kubiatowicz. APRIL: a processor architecture for multiprocessing. In *Proceedings of 17th Annual International Symposium on Computer Architecture*, IEEE Press, Piscataway, NJ, 1990, pp. 104–114.

[Amd67]   G. M. Amdahl. Validity of the single-processor approach to achieving large scale computing capabilities. In *Proceedings of the American Federation of Information Processing Societies Spring Joint Computer Conference*. AFIPS Press, Montvale, NJ, 1967, pp. 483–485.

[AMSS10] J. Alglave, L. Maranget, S. Sarkar, and P. Sewell. Fences in weak memory models. In T. Touili, B. Cook, and P. Jackson, Eds., *Computer Aided Verification*, Lecture Notes in Computer Science, Vol. 6174. Springer, Berlin, 2010, pp. 258–272.

[BHC+93] G. E. Blelloch, J. C. Hardwick, S. Chatterjee, J. Sipelstein, and M. Zagha. Implementation of a portable nested data-parallel language. In *PPOPP '93: Proceedings of the Fourth ACM SIGPLAN Symposium on Principles and Practice of Parallel Programming*. ACM Press, New York, 1993, pp. 102–111.

[Ble90]   G. E. Blelloch. *Vector Models for Data-Parallel Computing*. MIT Press, Cambridge, MA, 1990.

[Ble93]   G. E. Blelloch. Prefix sums and their applications. In J. H. Reif, Ed., *Synthesis of Parallel Algorithms*. Morgan Kaufmann, San Francisco, CA, 1993.

[Ble96]   G. E. Blelloch. Programming parallel algorithms. *Communications of the ACM*, 39(3):85–97, 1996.

[BLM+98] G. E. Blelloch, C. E. Leiserson, B. M. Maggs, C. G. Plaxton, S. J. Smith, and M. Zagha. An experimental analysis of parallel sorting algorithms. *Theory of Computing Systems*, 31:135–167, 1998.

[BM93]   J. L. Bentley and M. D. McIlroy. Engineering a sort function. *Software: Practice and Experience*, 23:1249–1265, 1993.

[BMR+96]   F. Buschmann, R. Meunier, H. Rohnert, P. Sommerlad, and M. Stal. *Pattern-Oriented Software Architecture: A System of Patterns*. Wiley, New York, 1996.

[BOA09]   M. Billeter, O. Olsson, and U. Assarson. Efficient stream compaction on wide SIMD many-core architectures. *High-Performance Graphics*, August 2009, pp. 159–166.

[Boa11]   OpenMP Architecture Review Board. *OpenMP Application Program Interface: Version 3.1*. July 2011.

[Boe11]   H.-J. Boehm. How to miscompile programs with "benign" data races. In *Proceedings of 3rd USENIX Workshop on Hot Topics in Parallelism* (HotPar '11). USENIX Association, Berkeley, CA, 2011.

[Bor09]   U. Bordoloi. *Image Convolution Using OpenCL^{TM}—A Step-by-Step Tutorial*. AMD Developer Central, October 2009 (http://developer.amd.com/sdks/amdappsdk/documentation/imageconvolutionopencl/pages/ImageConvolutionUsingOpenCL_3.aspx).

[Bre74]   R. P. Brent. The parallel evaluation of general arithmetic expressions. *Journal of the Association for Computing Machinery*, 21(2):201–206, 1974.

[BSTW86]   J. L. Bentley, D. D. Sleator, R. E. Tarjan, and V. K. Wei. A locally adaptive data compression scheme. *Communications of the ACM*, 29:320–330, 1986.

[BW94]   M. Burrows and D. J. Wheeler. *A Block-Sorting Lossless Data Compression Algorithm*, Technical Report 124. Digital Systems Research Center, Palo Alto, CA, 1994.

[BYP+91]   M. Butler, T.-Y. Yeh, Y. Patt, M. Alsup, H. Scales, and M. Shebanow. Single instruction stream parallelism is greater than two. In *Proceedings of the 18th Annual International Symposium on Computer Architecture* (ISCA '91). ACM Press, New York, 1991, pp. 276–286.

[Cat10]   B. Catanzaro. *OpenCL^{TM} Optimization Case Study: Simple Reductions*. AMD Developer Central, August 2010 (http://developer.amd.com/documentation/articles/Pages/OpenCL-Optimization-Case-Study-Simple-Reductions.aspx).

[CKP+96]   D. E. Culler, R. M. Karp, D. Patterson, A. Sahay, E. E. Santos, K. E. Schauser, R. Subramonian, and T. von Eicken. LogP: a practical model of parallel computation. *Communications of the ACM*, 39:78–85, 1996.

[CKV10]   A. Chandramowlishwaran, K. Knobe, and R. W. Vuduci. Performance evaluation of concurrent collections on high-performance multicore computing systems. In *Proceedings of the IEEE International Parallel & Distributed Processing Symposium* (IPDPS). IEEE Press, Piscataway, NJ, 2010, pp. 1–12.

[CLRS09]   T. H. Cormen, C. E. Leiserson, R. L. Rivest, and C. Stein. *Introduction to Algorithms*, 3rd ed. MIT Press, Cambridge, MA, 2009.

[Coh96]   J. Cohen. *A History of ALGOL 68*. ACM Press, New York, 1996, pp. 27–96.

[Col89]   M. Cole. *Algorithmic Skeletons: Structured Management of Parallel Computation*. Pitman/MIT Press, Cambridge, MA, 1989.

[Cor11a]   Intel. *Intel® 64 and IA-32 Architectures Software Developer's Manual*. Intel Corporation, Santa Clara, CA, 2011.

[Cor11b]   Intel. *Intel® Cilk Plus Language Extension Specification, Version 1.1*. Intel Corporation, Santa Clara, CA, 2011.

[Cor11c]   Intel. *Intel® Core^{TM} i5 Desktop Processor Turbo Boost Frequency Table*. Intel Corporation, Santa Clara, CA, 2011 (http://www.intel.com/support/processors/corei5/sb/CS-032278.htm).

[Cro84]   F. C. Crow. Summed-area tables for texture mapping. In *SIGGRAPH '84: Proceedings of the 11th Annual Conference on Computer Graphics and Interactive Techniques*. ACM Press, New York, 1984, pp. 207–212.

[DF90]   P. K. Dubey and Michael J. Flynn. Optimal pipelining. *Journal of Parallel and Distributed Computing*, 8:10–19, 1990.

[DG04]   J. Dean and S. Ghemawat. MapReduce: simplified data processing on large clusters. In *Proceedings of the 6th Symposium on Operating Systems Design and Implementation*. USENIX Association, Berkeley, CA, 2004.

[DHKC09]   S. Dawson-Haggerty, A. Krioukov, and D. E. Culler. *Power Optimization—A Reality Check*, Technical Report UCB/EECS-2009-140. EECS Department, University of California, Berkeley, 2009.

[Dij68]   E. Dijkstra. Go To statement considered harmful. *Communications of the ACM*, 11(3):147–148, 1968.

[ERB+10]   Y. Etsion, A. Ramirez, R. M. Badia, E. Ayguade, J. Labarta, and M. Valero. Task superscalar: using processors as functional units. In *Proceedings of 3rd USENIX Workshop on Hot Topics in Parallelism* (HotPar '11). USENIX Association, Berkeley, CA, 2011.

[FG94]   A. L. Fisher and A. M. Ghuloum. Parallelizing complex scans and reductions. In *Proceedings of ACM SIGPLAN Conference on Programming Language Design and Implementation*. ACM Press, New York, 1994, pp. 135–146.

[FHLLB09]   M. Frigo, P. Halpern, C. E. Leiserson, and S. Lewin-Berlin. Reducers and other Cilk++ hyperobjects. In *Proceedings of the 21st ACM Symposium on Parallelism in Algorithms and Architectures* (SPAA '09). ACM Press, New York, 2009, pp. 79–90.

[Fly72]   M. J. Flynn. Some computer organizations and their effectiveness. *IEEE Transactions on Computers*, C-21(9):948–960, 1972.

[GC94]   B. Gendron and T. G. Crainic. Parallel branch-and-bound algorithms: survey and synthesis. *Operations Research*, 42(6):1042–1066, 1994.

[GDX08]   L. Grigori, J. W. Demmel, and H. Xiang. Communication avoiding Gaussian elimination. In *Proceedings of the 2008 ACM/IEEE Conference on Supercomputing*. IEEE Press, Piscataway, NJ, 2008, pp. 29:1–29:12.

[GHJV95]   E. Gamma, R. Helm, R. Johnson, and J. Vlissides. *Design Patterns: Elements of Reusable Object-Oriented Software*. Addison-Wesley, Boston, MA, 1995.

[GPM11]   K. Garanzha, J. Pantaleoni, and D. McAllister. Simpler and faster HLBVH with work queues. *High Performance Graphics*, August 2011, pp. 59–64.

[Gus88]   J. L. Gustafson. Reevaluating Amdahl's law. *Communications of the ACM*, 31:532–533, 1988.

[HF99]   P. Hung and M. J. Flynn. *Optimum Instruction-Level Parallelism (ILP) for Superscalar and VLIW Processors*, Technical Report CSL-TR-99-783. Stanford University, Stanford, CA, 1999.

[HLJH09]   J. Hoberock, V. Lu, Y. Jia, and J. C. Hart. Stream compaction for deferred shading. In *Proceedings of the Conference on High Performance Graphics 2009*. ACM Press, New York, 2009, pp. 173–180.

[HLL10]   Y. He, C. E. Leiserson, and W. M. Leiserson. The Cilkview scalability analyzer. In *Proceedings of the 22nd ACM Symposium on Parallelism in Algorithms and Architectures* (SPAA '10). ACM Press, New York, 2010, pp. 145–156.

[HP07]   J. L. Hennessy and D. A. Patterson. *Computer Architecture: A Quantitative Approach*. Morgan Kaufmann, San Francisco, CA, 2007.

[HS08]   M. Herlihy and N. Shavit. *The Art of Multiprocessor Programming*. Morgan Kaufmann, San Francisco, CA, 2008.

[HSJ86]   W. D. Hillis and G. L. Steele, Jr. Data parallel algorithms. *Communications of the ACM*, 29:1170–1183, 1986.

[HSK08]   H. E. Hinnant, B. Stroustrup, and B. Kozicki. *A Brief Introduction to rvalue References*. Artima Developer, Walnut Creek, CA, 2008.

[HW04]   E. R. Hansen and G. W. Walster, Eds. *Global Optimization Using Interval Analysis*. CRC Press, Boca Raton, FL, 2004.

[Inc09a]   Apple. *OpenCL Parallel Prefix Sum (aka Scan) Example*. Mac OS X Developer Library, Apple, Inc., Cupertino, CA, 2009.

[Inc09b]   Apple. *OpenCL Parallel Reduction Example*. Mac OS X Developer Library, Apple, Inc., Cupertino, CA, 2009.

[JW89]   N. P. Jouppi and D. W. Wall. Available instruction-level parallelism for superscalar and super-pipelined machines. In *International Conference on Architectural Support for Programming Languages and Operating Systems* (ASPLOS '89). ACM Press, New York, 1989, pp. 290–302.

[Kam05]   T. Kamiya. *Japanese Sentence Patterns for Effective Communication*. Kodansha USA, New York, 2005.

[Kay96]   A. Kay. *The Early History of Smalltalk*. ACM Press, New York, 1996, pp. 511–598.

[KLDB10]   J. Kurzak, H. Ltaief, J. Dongarra, and R. M. Badia. Scheduling linear algebra operations on multicore processors. *Concurrency and Computation: Practice and Experience*, 22(1):15–44, 2010.

[KM03]   D. Koufaty and D. T. Marr. Hyperthreading technology in the netburst microarchitecture. *IEEE Micro*, 23(2):56–65, 2003.

[Knu76]   D. E. Knuth. Big omicron and big omega and big theta. *SIGACT News*, 8:18–24, 1976.

[Kon11]   S. V. Konstantin. Apache Hadoop: The scalability update. *;login:, The USENIX Magazine,* 36(3): 7–13, 2011.

[KS10]   F. B. Kjolstad and M. Snir. Ghost cell pattern. In *Proceedings of the 2010 Workshop on Parallel Programming Patterns* (ParaPLoP '10). ACM Press, New York, 2010, pp. 4:1–4:9.

[KTB11]   D. P. Kroese, T. Taimre, and Z. I. Botev. *Handbook of Monte Carlo Methods*. John Wiley & Sons, New York, 2011.

[Lam74]   L. Lamport. The parallel execution of DO loops. *Communications of the ACM*, 17(2):83–93, 1974.

[Lee06]   E. A. Lee. *The Problem with Threads*, Technical Report UCB/EECS-2006-1. EECS Department, University of California, Berkeley, 2006 (a published version of this paper is in *IEEE Computer*, 39(5):33–42, 2006).

[LLM08]   G. Lashari, O. Lhoták, and M. McCool. Control flow emulation on tiled SIMD architectures. In L. J. Hendren, Ed., *Compiler Construction, 17th International Conference*, Lecture Notes in Computer Science, Vol. 4959. Springer, Berlin, 2008, pp. 100–115.

[Llo82]   S. P. Lloyd. Least squares quantization in PCM. *IEEE Transactions on Information Theory*, 28(2):129–137, 1982.

[MAB+02]   S. MacDonald, J. Anvik, S. Bromling, D. Szafron, J. Schaeffer, and K. Tan. From patterns to frameworks to parallel programs. *Parallel Computing*, 28(12):1663–1683, 2002.

[Mac67]   J. MacQueen. Some methods for classification and analysis of multivariate observations. In *Proceedings of the Berkeley Symposium on Mathematical Statistics and Probability*. University of California Press, Berkeley, 1967, pp. 281–297.

[Mic04]   M. M. Michael. Hazard pointers: safe memory reclamation for lock-free objects. *IEEE Transactions on Parallel and Distributed Systems*, 15:491–504, 2004.

[MMS05]   B. L. Massingill, T. G. Mattson, and B. A. Sanders. Reengineering for parallelism: an entry point for PLPP (Pattern Language for Parallel Programming) for legacy applications. In *Proceedings of the Twelfth Pattern Languages of Programs Workshop*, 2005.

[MSM04]   T. G. Mattson, B. A. Sanders, and B. L. Massingill. *Patterns for Parallel Programming*. Addison Wesley, Reading, MA, 2004.

[MSS04]   S. MacDonald, D. Szfron, and J. Schaeffer. Rethinking the pipeline as object-oriented states with transformations. In *Proceedings of the Ninth International Workshop on High-Level Parallel Programming Models and Supportive Environments*. IEEE Press, Piscataway, NJ, 2004, pp. 12–21.

[Nau81]   P. Naur. *The European Side of the Development of ALGOL*. ACM Press, New York, 1981, pp. 92–139.

[Pac96]   P. S. Pacheco. *Parallel Programming with MPI*. Morgan Kaufmann, San Francisco, CA, 1996.

[Par11]   Berkeley ParLab. *A Pattern Language for Parallel Programming, Version 2.0*. EECS Department, University of California, Berkeley (http://parlab.eecs.berkeley.edu/wiki/patterns/patterns).

[Per81]   A. J. Perlis. *The American Side of the Development of ALGOL*. ACM Press, New York, 1981, pp. 75–91.

[PGB+05]   T. Peierls, B. Goetz, J. Bloch, J. Bowbeer, D. Lea, and D. Holmes. *Java Concurrency in Practice*. Addison-Wesley, Boston, MA, 2005.

[PvE93]   M. J. Plasmeijer and M. C. J. D. van Eekelen. *Functional Programming and Parallel Graph Rewriting*. Addison-Wesley, Boston, MA, 1993.

[PvE99]   M. J. Plasmeijer and M. C. J. D. van Eekelen. Keep it CLEAN: a unique approach to functional programming. *SIGPLAN Notices*, 34(6):23–31, 1999.

[Qui03]   M. J. Quinn. *Parallel Programming in C with MPI and OpenMP*. McGraw-Hill, New York, 2003.

[RDN93]   L. Rauchwerger, P. K. Dubey, and R. Nair. Measuring limits of parallelism and characterizing its vulnerability to resource constraints. In *Proceedings of the 26th Annual International Symposium on Microarchitecture*. IEEE Computer Society Press, Los Alamitos, CA, 1993, pp. 105–117.

[REB11]   D. R. O'Hallaron and R. E. Bryant. *Computer Systems: A Programmer's Perspective*. Prentice Hall, Upper Saddle River, NJ, 2011.

[Rei07]   J. Reinders. *Intel Threading Building Blocks*. O'Reilly & Associates, Inc., Sebastopol, CA, 2007.

[RJ10]   A. D. Robison and R. E. Johnson. Three layer cake for shared-memory programming. In *Proceedings of the 2010 Workshop on Parallel Programming Patterns* (ParaPLoP '10), ACM Press, New York, 2010, pp. 5:1–5:8.

[RVK08]   A. Robison, M. Voss, and A. Kukanov. Optimization via reflection on work stealing in TBB. In *IEEE International Symposium on Parallel and Distributed Processing*. IEEE Press, Piscataway, NJ, 2008, pp. 1–8.

[SCB+98]   A. Snavely, L. Carter, J. Boisseau, A. Majumdar, K. S. Gatlin, N. Mitchell, J. Feo, and B. Koblenz. Multi-processor performance on the Tera MTA. In *Supercomputer '98: Proceedings of the 1998 ACM/IEEE Conference on Supercomputing* (CDROM). IEEE Computer Society, Washington, DC, 1998, pp. 1–8.

[Shi07]   J. Shin. Introducing control flow into vectorized code. In *PACT '07: Proceedings of the 16th International Conference on Parallel Architecture and Compilation Techniques*. IEEE Computer Society, Washington, DC, 2007, pp. 280–291.

[SMDS11]   J. K. Salmon, M. A. Moraes, R. O. Dror, and D. E. Shaw. Parallel random numbers: as easy as 1, 2, 3. In *Proceedings of 2011 International Conference for High Performance Computing, Networking, Storage and Analysis*. ACM Press, New York, 2011, pp. 16:1–16:12.

[SSRB00]   D. Schmidt, M. Stal, H. Rohnert, and F. Buschmann. *Pattern-Oriented Software Architecture: Patterns for Concurrent and Networked Objects*, Vol. 2. Wiley & Sons, New York, 2000.

[Str69]   V. Strassen. Gaussian elimination is not optimal. *Numerische Mathematik*, 14:354–356, 1969.

[Sub06]   SPEC CPU Subcommittee. SPEC CPU2006 benchmark descriptions. *Computer Architecture News*, 34(4):1–17, 2006 (http://www.spec.org/cpu2006/publications/CPU2006benchmarks.pdf).

[Sut05]   H. Sutter. The free lunch is over: a fundamental turn towards concurrency in software. *Dr. Dobbs Journal*, 30(3), 2005.

[SW81]   T. F. Smith and M. S. Waterman. Identification of common molecular subsequences. *Journal of Molecular Biology*, 147:195–197, 1981.

[Tat10]   B. A. Tate. *Seven Languages in Seven Weeks: A Pragmatic Guide to Learning Programming Languages*. Pragmatic Bookshelf, Flower Mound, TX, 2010.

[TBRG10]   E. Tejedor, R. M. Badia, R. Royo, and J. L. Gelpi. Enabling HMMER for the grid with COMP superscalar. In *Procedia Computer Science*, 1(1):2629–2638, 2010.

[TCK+11]   Y. Tang, R. A. Chowdhury, B. C. Kuszmaul, C.-K. Luk, and C. E. Leiserson. The Pochoir stencil compiler. In *Proceedings of the 23rd ACM Symposium on Parallelism in Algorithms and Architectures* (SPAA '11). ACM Press, New York, 2011, pp. 117–128.

[TEL95]   D. M. Tullsen, S. J. Eggers, and H. M. Levy. Simultaneous multithreading: maximizing on-chip parallelism. *SIGARCH Computer Architecture News*, 23:392–403, 1995.

[TM98]   C. Tomasi and R. Manduchi. Bilateral filtering for gray and color images. In *Proceedings of the Sixth International Conference on Computer Vision*. IEEE Press, New York, 1998, pp. 839–846.

[TvPG06]   O. Trachsel, C. von Praun, and T. R. Gross. On the effectiveness of speculative and selective memory fences. In *Proceedings of the 20th IEEE International Parallel and Distributed Processing Symposium* (IPDPS '06). IEEE Press, New York, 2006.

[Val90]   L. G. Valiant. A bridging model for parallel computation. *Communications of the ACM*, 33:103–111, 1990.

[VBC06]   N. Vasilache, C. Bastoul, and A. Cohen. *Polyhedral Code Generation in the Real World*, Lecture Notes in Computer Science, Vol. 3923. Springer, Berlin, 2006, pp. 185–201.

[VF05]   V. Venkatachalam and M. Franz. Power reduction techniques for microprocessor systems. *ACM Computing Surveys*, 37:195–237, 2005.

[Vis10]   U. Vishkin. *Thinking in Parallel: Some Basic Data-Parallel Algorithms and Techniques*. University of Maryland, College Park, 2010 (http://www.umiacs.umd.edu/users/vishkin/PUBLICATIONS/classnotes.pdf).

[Vis11]   U. Vishkin. Using simple abstraction to reinvent computing for parallelism. *Communications of the ACM*, 54:75–85, 2011.

[Vit08]   J. S. Vitter. *Algorithms and Data Structures for External Memory*, Foundations and Trends in Theoretical Computer Science. Now Publishers, Boston, MA, 2008.

[Wal11]   I. Wald. Active thread compaction for GPU path tracing. In *Proceedings of the ACM SIGGRAPH Symposium on High Performance Graphics* (HPG '11). ACM Press, New York, 2011.

[WJNB95]   P. R. Wilson, M. S. Johnstone, M. Neely, and D. Boles. Dynamic storage allocation: a survey and critical review. In *Proceedings of the 1995 International Workshop on Memory Management* (IWMM '95). Springer-Verlag, London, 1995, pp. 1–116.

Index

Page numbers followed by "*f*" indicates figures and "*t*" indicates tables.

Printed and bound by CPI Group (UK) Ltd, Croydon, CR0 4YY

03/10/2024

01040327-0007